2

Tim Richards

Exploring Jazz Piano

Harmony / Technique / Improvisation

Acknowledgments

This book is dedicated with love to my mother, Wendy, who bought me my first piano.

Thanks are due to my piano teachers, Carola Grindea and Mantle Childe, and to the many jazz musicians who have imparted knowledge or helped me along the way – John Burch, Hal Galper, David Baker, Richie Bierach, Dave Liebman, Jamey Aebersold, John Taylor, Gordon Beck, Geoff Castle, Alan Skidmore, Eddie Harvey and John Crawford.

For encouragement and advice during the early stages of preparing the manuscript, I'd like to warmly thank Luke Davidson, Charles Alexander, John Kember and Ruth Herbert.

For their help with discographical details, I am indebted to Dave Blackmore, Dominic Howles, Matt Home and all the musicians in 'Great Spirit' who took the trouble to list their favourite albums. Dominic and Matt also deserve a big thank you for their excellent contributions to the CD accompanying this book.

Finally, thanks to Wendy Lampa and the production team at Schott for their unfailing commitment to this project.

The publishers would like to thank the following for use of their material in this publication:

Jowcol Music; Universal/Island Music Limited; Robins J.J. Sons Inc; Redwood Music Limited; International Music Publications Limited; Music Sales Corporation; Orpheus Music Co, Prestige Music Ltd; Octave Music Publishing Inc; Warner Bros. Publications Inc; George Gershwin Music, Du Bose and Dorothy Heyward Memorial Fund; Warner/Chappell Music Ltd; EMI Mills Music, Inc; Famous Music Corporation; Boosey & Hawkes Music Publishers Ltd; Jazz Horn Music Corporation; Sony/ATV Music Publishing (UK) Limited; Prestige Music Co, Prestige Music Ltd; EMI Feist Catalogue Inc and EMI United Partnership Ltd; Bambalina Music Publishing Co; Harms Ins; Williamson Music, Redwood Music Ltd; Red Start Songs Inc; Sam Fox Music Publishing Co; Universal-Polygram International Publishing, inc and Bourne Co. for their copyright music.

William Ellis, Christian Him (Jazz Index); Redferns Music Picture Library; Lee Tanner (Jazz Image), for their photographs.

ED 12829

British Library Cataloguing-in-Publication Data. A catalogue record for this book is available from the British Library.

ISBN 1-902455-25-8
ISMN M-2201-2328-3

Copy-editing by Helen Peres da Costa
Designed and typeset by www.adamhaystudio.com
Music setting by Bill Holab
Front and back cover photograph (Tim Richards) © William Ellis, www.william-ellis.com
Printed in Germany • S&Co.7986

2

Piano

Tim Richards

Exploring Jazz Piano

Harmony / Technique / Improvisation

www.schott-music.com

Mainz · London · Madrid · New York · Paris · Prague · Tokyo · Toronto

Photographs

About the Author

Tim Richards has been active on the jazz scene since the early 1980s and is best known for his leadership of the modern jazz group 'Spirit Level', formed in Bristol in 1979, which toured in almost every European country, playing original material in jazz clubs and at festivals opposite such names as Joe Zawinul, McCoy Tyner, Joe Henderson, Horace Silver, Miles Davis and Jan Garbarek.

In recent years he has won acclaim as a composer and arranger, in 1999 expanding 'Spirit Level' to a nine-piece band and renaming it 'Great Spirit'. This band has toured the UK several times with a line-up featuring some of London's best jazz musicians, many of whom are band leaders in their own right.

Tim also enjoys playing in the more traditional setting of the piano trio, with bass and drums, and has released two acclaimed CDs of standards, blues and originals on the 33 Records label (see below). The trio has delighted audiences from Istanbul to Inverness and continues to perform frequently.

Tim currently teaches jazz piano classes at London's Morley and Goldsmiths Colleges. He has pieces in the Associated Board's jazz piano syllabus and also works for the AB as a jazz examiner.

www.timrichards.ndo.co.uk

Selected Discography

Great Spirit 'Epistrophy'
33Jazz120 (2005)
Nine-piece band featuring Jason Yarde, Ed Jones, Tony Kofi, Dick Pearce, Roger Beaujolais, Leon Stenning, Tom Herbert, Seb Rochford.

Tim Richards Trio 'Twelve by Three'
33Jazz72 (2003)
With Dominic Howles (bass) and Matt Home (drums) – the rhythm section on the CD for this book. Includes *Twelve by Three.*

Great Spirit/Best of Spirit Level 1979–1990 (2 CDs)
33Jazz051 (1999)
Nine-piece band featuring Gilad Atzmon, Denys Baptiste, Tony Kofi, Dick Pearce, Roger Beaujolais, Dave Colton, Davide Mantovani, Dave Ohm. Includes *The Lost Valley.*
Spirit Level quintet/quartet tracks feature Paul Dunmall or Jerry Underwood (sax), Dave Holdsworth or Jack Walrath (trumpet). Includes *Dustbiter, Orinoco.*

Tim Richards' & Sigi Finkel's Soundscape 'Shibop'
FMR CD61-0499 (1999)
Quartet with Vienna-based saxophonist (Austrian 'Jazz Musician of the Year' 2000), Phil Scragg (bass), Marc Parnell (drums).

Tim Richards Trio 'The Other Side'
33Jazz037 (1998)
With Kubryk Townsend (bass) and Kenrick Rowe or Andrea Trillo (drums). Includes *Beautiful Love, Caravan, Coincidence Calypso.*

Sigi Finkel & Tim Richards 'Dervish Dances'
ORF CD155 - Edition Jazz Austria (1997)
Saxophone and piano duets. Includes *Seventh Heaven.*

Spirit Level 'On The Level'
33Jazz021 (1994)
Quartet with saxophonist Jerry Underwood. Includes *Y Todavia la Quiero, Seventh Heaven.*

Contents

** All pieces are by Tim Richards unless otherwise indicated.*

Chapter 8:

Diminished chords and scales

Introduction

This is the third of a series of publications by Schott, following on from *Exploring Jazz Piano 1* and *Improvising Blues Piano* (IBP). Having covered most of the basic jazz chords in Vol. 1, including major, dominant and minor ninths, this book ventures into slightly more exotic territory.

Beginning with modal jazz and quartal harmony, we'll be expanding our harmonic vocabulary to include sus 4, sharp eleventh, thirteenth, diminished and altered chords, and to widen our range of improvisational techniques. For an overview of the harmonic material covered, see the 'Chord Voicings Chart', Appendix VI, p. 280.

As in Vol.1 and IBP, easier pieces are found at the start of every chapter. However, the technical progression is not always predictable. If you get bogged down with a piece, skip it and try the next one. Or go to the start of the next chapter, returning to the harder piece(s) later.

The ability to play jazz and improvise convincingly does not come without dedication and application. Appendix VII (p. 282) contains some useful practice routines drawing on material from both volumes.

Don't get discouraged if the way sometimes seems thorny. Although learning theory may seem like an intellectual process, jazz is above all about personal expression, so the feelings you convey in your improvisations are ultimately more important than the notes you play. Cast aside any inhibitions and let the muse take over...

I hope you get as much out of this journey as I have in writing this book.

Tim Richards
London 2005

The CD

Every piece in the book can be heard on the CD. Get into the habit of listening to it as well as reading the music – learning pieces by ear is a viable alternative.

Tracks played on piano alone are recorded in stereo, just like an ordinary audio CD. However, some of the other tracks may sound a little strange as the instruments have been panned left and right for educational purposes.

If you've just picked up this book, and would like to get a taste of the pieces it contains, programme your CD player to play the following tracks:

1 – 5 – 6 – 7 – 9 – 20 – 24 – 27 –
32 – 33 – 36 – 37 – 40 – 43 – 46

Select the 'mono' setting on your amplifier, if it has one, to eliminate the panning.

● **Drums** Tracks with drums accompaniment have been recorded with stereo separation. Although drums and piano were recorded at the same time, they have been panned left and right in the recording studio. If you wish to eliminate the piano from the recording, you can play along with the drums alone by silencing the right-hand channel. There are two ways of achieving this:

- Turn the balance knob on your amplifier to the left, so that no sound comes out the right-hand speaker.
- If you have no balance control, use headphones, but only listen to the left can. The other one can be positioned behind your ear so that you don't hear it.

For the pieces with drums, the piano generally plays a bass line in the left hand, which is why the bass is not necessary.

● **Bass and drums** The trio tracks have the piano on the right, bass on the left, with the drums split between both channels. By silencing the piano as described above, you can play along with bass and drums, as if you were the pianist in my trio!

● **Playing along** All the tracks can be used for this purpose, without using the stereo separation. Initially, practise each hand separately, at the same time as the piano on the recording. If you can't keep up, practise at a slower tempo, away from the CD, and try again when you've had a chance to get up to speed. When the left- and right-hand parts are both known, try them together. At this point, you should silence the piano and play along with just the drums (or bass and drums) to guide you.

● **Improvisation** *Reflections* (track 1), *Eleventh Hour* (track 2), *The Message* (track 9), *Blue in Green* (track 32) and *Seventh Heaven* (track 37) are 'mini performances', complete with improvised solos that demonstrate the topic under discussion.

I improvise for a single chorus only on *Summertime* (track 24), *Softly as in a Morning Sunrise* (track 41) and *Twelve by Three* (track 46), switching to chords (comping) for the remaining chorus(es), before recapping the head. I hope these solos will start you off in the right direction, so that you'll fill the 'blank' sections yourself. Try these sections without the piano too, focussing on the bass in the left-hand channel as a guide.

If you'd like to hear solos that stretch out a little more, please listen to my commercially available recordings, many of which include pieces from this book (see p. 4).

● **Comping** This term is short for 'accompanying' and refers to the playing of chords behind your own or someone else's solo. Examples can be heard in the solo sections of the following tunes:

10 *Thirteenth Groove*
13 *Ladybird*
22 *Crossing the Tracks*
23 *Don't Stop the Carnival*
29 33 *Tension & Release Blues #1 & #2*
34 *Tune Up*
39 *Blue Bossa*
44 *Beautiful Love*

Try out your own solos here when playing along with the CD. If you want to provide your own left-hand accompaniment, silence the piano as described above. Practise the comping too – not only the chord shapes but also their rhythm and articulation. Studies in comping include:

4 *Hot and Cold – Montuno*
6 *Quartal Comping*
12 *II – V Comping*
14 15 *Swinging Comping #1 & #2*
17 *Bossa Nova Comping #2*
19 *Bebop Bridge*
30 *Bird Blues Comping*
35 36 *Rhythm Changes Comping #1 & #2*
42 *Minor Turnaround Workout – Comping*
45 *Blues in Fourths*

No melody or improvisation is played on these tracks. You can however use them as play-along tracks for practising improvisation, with or without the piano chords on the right channel.

● **The workouts** These tracks alternate two- or four-bar phrases with gaps, during which you should repeat what you've just heard or improvise a response to it. In *Short II – V Workout* (track 11), the gaps are four bars long. In the following pieces, the gaps are two bars long:

21 26 *Turnaround Workout #1 & #2*
28 *Diminished Scale Workout*
31 *Blues Turnaround Workout* (from 1:08)
43 *Minor Turnaround Workout – Improvisation*

● **Walking bass lines** Playing bass lines in the left hand and chords in the right is a useful accompaniment style for any situation without a bassist. Walking bass lines are used in the left hand of:

14 15 *Swinging Comping #1 & #2*
16 *Dominant Seventh Workout #2*
42 *Minor Turnaround Workout – Comping*

The following tracks also begin with a walking bass, but the left hand switches to chords when the bassist enters for the head or improvisation:

10 *Thirteenth Groove*
24 *Summertime*
31 *Blues Turnaround Workout*
33 *Tension & Release Blues #2*

● **Latin bass lines** These are featured in the following tracks:

4 *Hot and Cold – Montuno*
17 *Bossa Nova Comping #2*
23 *Don't Stop the Carnival*
27 *Caravan*
38 *On Green Dolphin Street*
39 *Blue Bossa*

Before you start

No book on playing jazz piano can claim to cover comprehensively the vast range of styles that have come into existence since the beginnings of the music over 100 years ago. Jazz has become so diverse that it is in danger of becoming a meaningless word.

● **Listening** Faced with this bewildering variety, the jazz pianist has a lot of choices to make. The most important thing is to keep an open mind, and to listen to other musicians as much as possible, on records, on the radio, and at live gigs. At the end of Vol. 1 (p. 228) you'll find a 'Suggested Listening' discography outlining some of the most important pianists to be aware of, and their best recordings. Check out as many as possible of these and immerse yourself in the music. It's also essential to listen to other instruments too – see Appendix V in this volume (p. 278) for more recommended albums.

● **Learning the language** Learning to play jazz (or any other musical idiom) is very similar to learning a language. In order to sound like a native speaker you have to constantly listen and copy. All the great innovators in jazz have had a sound knowledge and experience of earlier styles.

Improvising can be compared to having a conversation. When speaking amongst friends we don't plan in advance what to say – we use our knowledge of sentence construction, grammar and vocabulary to express ourselves spontaneously. Playing jazz is no different. Scales, arpeggios and patterns are just the basic elements we need to communicate our ideas.

● **The improvisation boxes** These contain suggested notes that fit the given chords for your solo, often a scale, arpeggio or pentatonic scale. You are not obliged to use all the notes, nor do you have to play them in the order given. You can change the register of the notes too, and play them in your own rhythm. Remember that they're just a suggestion – other notes may sound good too, or you can just do your own thing!

● **Pre-hearing ideas** Most improvising musicians pre-hear phrases a split-second before playing them. Imagine the contour or rhythm of a phrase and let your fingers try to find the notes as best they can. Perfecting this connection between what you hear and what you play is vital if you want to play jazz. If you don't hear anything in your head, there's a danger you'll be just moving your fingers and playing notes at random – not very inspiring for the listener!

● **Singing** Even if you're not proud of your voice or confident at singing, incorporate it into your practice. Everytime you learn a new scale or pattern, sing it as well as playing it. Then sing a variation on it and try to play that. This is particularly beneficial with arpeggios, pentatonic scales and blues scales, since they contain only a few notes and their sound is easy to retain in your head. Many musicians sing along in unison with their improvised lines, the ultimate proof that they're playing what they hear. Transcribing solos, or just playing along with records and copying what you hear, is the logical extension of this process. If you can't play something, sing it first.

● **Articulation** The piano is a percussion instrument. Classical piano technique does not always bring this element to the fore, whereas many jazz pianists embrace it. A pianist's touch is an important aspect of his/her style, which is one reason why classical players don't always sound convincing when interpreting jazz material. Feel free to personalise individual notes or chords by accenting them.

● **Pulse** Jazz usually needs a constant, metronomic pulse in order to sound authentic. The concept of a 'groove' is not so prevalent in classical music, which often calls for a more flexible rhythmic approach, especially at the transitions between sections. Always tap your foot, feel the music in your body, and play with a steady beat. The metronome is your friend!

Checklist: Topics covered in Vol. 1

The technical and theoretical level of this book is a little higher than its predecessor. Familiarity with most of the following is assumed:

Chords

- Triads: major, minor, augmented and diminished
- Seventh chords: major, dominant, minor, half-diminished and diminished
- Ninth chords: major, dominant and minor
- Sixth and 6/9 chords: major and minor
- Inversions, arpeggios and broken chords of the above

The five basic chord-types and their chord symbols are shown in Fig 8.1, p. 121. See also 'Symbols used in this book' (p. 284) and the 'Chord voicings chart' (p. 280).

Voicings

- Open triads: **R53**, **3R5** or **53R**
- Shells: **R7** or **R3**
- Tritones: **37** or **73** (dominant chords)
- Three-note rootless voicings: **735** or **379**
- Four-note rootless voicings: **3579** or **7935**
- Two-handed voicings: **R7/35**, **R5/37** or **R3/79**
- Five-note voicings: **R7/359** or **R3/795**
- Quartal voicings: **369** (perfect fourths for major chords)
- Shearing block chords and 'drop two' voicings

Scales

- Major scales in all keys (and their fingering)
- Scale patterns (three- and four-note groups, thirds, etc)
- Major and minor pentatonic scales and patterns
- The blues scale, ♭3 pentatonic scale and top harmony
- Harmonic, melodic and natural minor scales
- Mixolydian, Dorian, Aeolian and Phrygian modes
- Whole-tone scales

Theory

- Roman numerals
- Long and short **II** – **V** sequences
- **II** – **V** – **I** and **III** – **VI** – **II** – **V**
- The cycle of fifths and diatonic cycle
- Secondary dominants
- Tritone substitution
- Walking bass lines, run-ups and run-downs
- Horizontal and vertical improvisation
- Target notes and pick-ups
- Twelve-bar blues

If many of these topics are unfamiliar, you are strongly advised to spend some time with Vol. 1, which deals with them all from first principles. If you are new to improvising, I suggest starting with the previous volume, *Improvising Blues Piano*. Because blues generally uses only one chord-type (the dominant seventh) and has an easily grasped twelve-bar structure, it's the ideal place to begin developing your improvisational ability.

Chapter Six
Elevenths, fourths & quartal harmony

We now continue to add notes to the basic four-note seventh chords, as begun in Vol. 1. Having dealt with ninths in Chapter 5, the next extension is the eleventh, the same note as the fourth of the scale. As well as exploring eleventh chords, this chapter will also show you how to voice any chord in fourth intervals, by using quartal harmony.

Adding the fourth to a major seventh chord produces a clash between it and the major third, which is only a semitone away. This clash is still heard if the fourth is an octave higher than the third, as in Fig 6.1(a) below:

Fig 6.1: Major eleventh chords

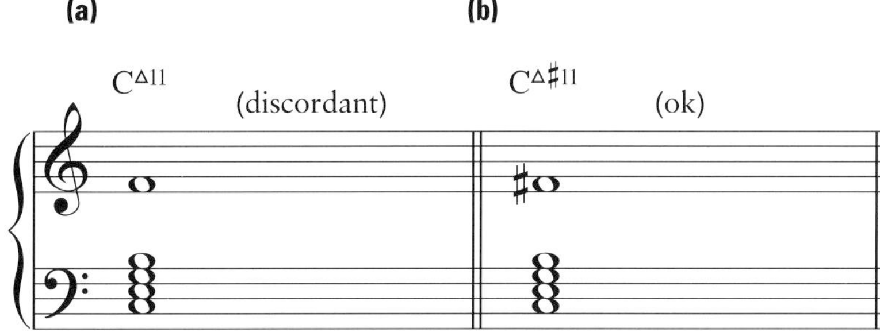

To avoid the clash, the fourth is usually raised by a semitone, as in Fig 6.1(b). The resulting chord is given the symbol CΔ♯4 or CΔ♯11, pronounced 'C major seven sharp four', or 'C major seven sharp eleven'. The meaning of these two symbols is the same.

Dominant seventh chords can also have fourths added:

Fig 6.2: Dominant eleventh chords

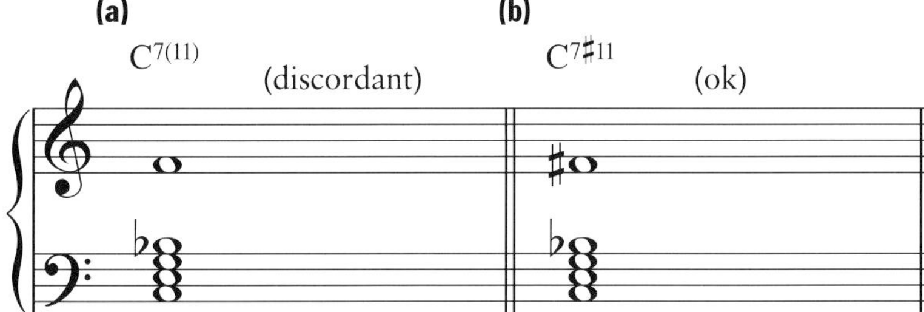

In Fig 6.2(a) the same clash can be heard between the fourth and the major third as in Fig 6.1.Very often, this clash is avoided by leaving out the third of the chord, given rise to the term 'sus 4', short for 'suspended fourth' (see overleaf).

Another solution is shown at Fig 6.2(b) – raising the fourth. This chord symbol is pronounced 'C seven sharp 11'. In a chord symbol, remember that **7** without a Δ, 'maj' or ♮ in front of it always indicates a ♭**7**.

Minor seventh and half-diminished chords both sound fine with an added fourth:

Fig 6.3: Minor and half-diminished eleventh chords

In this case, there is no need to raise the fourth of either chord to produce a more concordant sound. Indeed, the half-diminished chord already contains the ♭**5**, which is the same note as ♯**4** anyway.

Suspended fourth chords

In a **II** – **V** – **I**, the seventh of the minor (**II**) chord drops a semitone, becoming the third of the dominant (**V**) chord:

Fig 6.4: 7 falls to 3 in a II – V – I

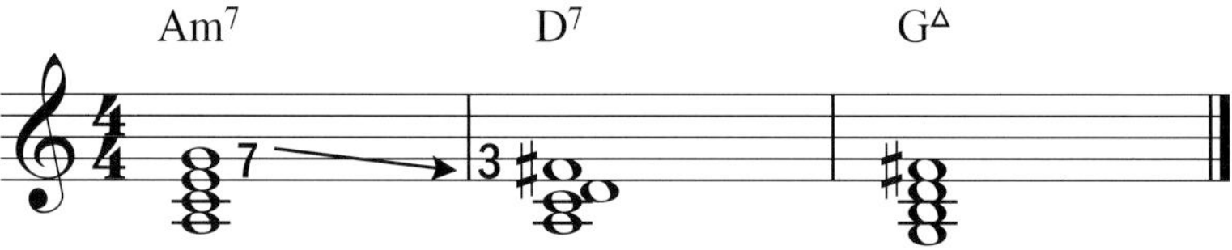

When the seventh (G in the above example) is retained in the bar belonging to the **V** chord, rather than falling to **3**, it is said to be 'suspended'. As the G becomes the fourth of D7, the resulting chord is named D7sus4:

Fig 6.5: II – V – I with sus 4 chord

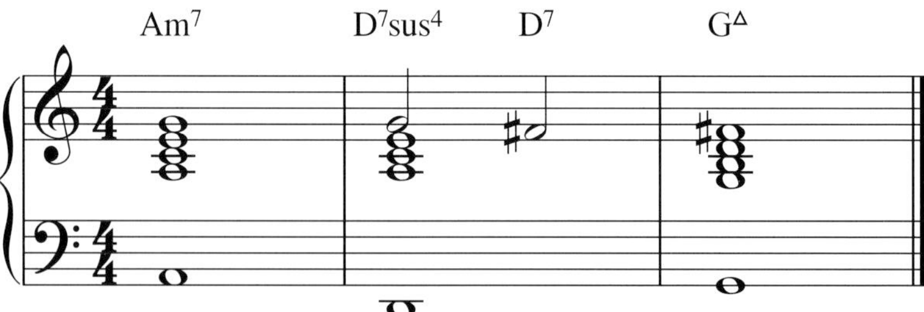

The D7sus4 voicing used above can be thought of as Am7 with a D bass, or Am7/D. Because the ninth (E) is also present, the chord symbol could also be D9sus4. Memorise how to find this two-handed voicing in any key:

Fig 6.6: Play a minor seventh chord based on 5 of the sus 4 chord

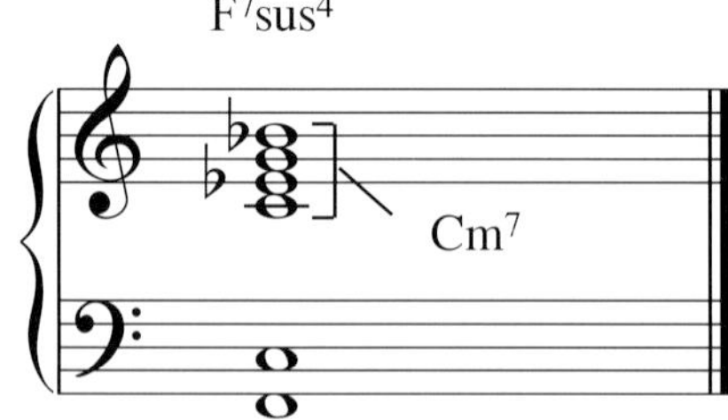

Here's a simple way of playing a sus 4 chord in one hand only: take a root position dominant seventh chord and move **3** up a semitone to become **4**.

Fig 6.7: V – I with sus 4 chord

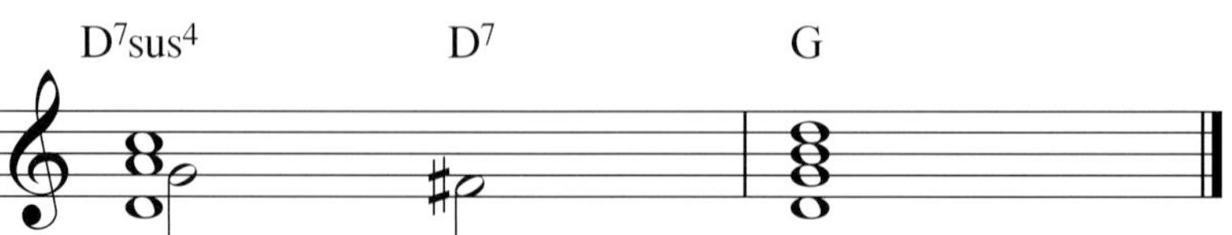

Postbop harmony

The title track on Herbie Hancock's great 1965 album 'Maiden Voyage' is a classic example of 'postbop' harmony, and contains three sus 4 chords, lasting four bars each, in a 32-bar AABA structure.

Fig 6.8: (a) *Maiden Voyage* voicings (play 4 bars on each chord)

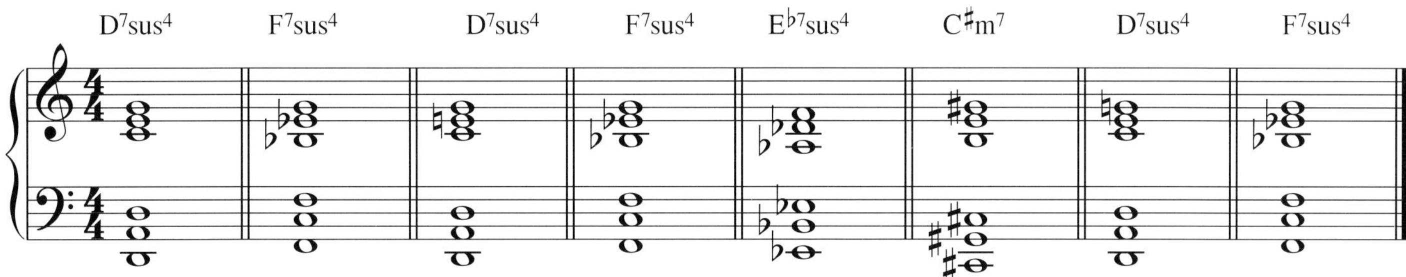

The sus 4 chords are used as a sound in their own right, without resolving them as described on the previous page. Because of this, the piece has a floating, impressionistic sound and an ambiguous sense of key that perfectly expresses the lyrical mood. This type of harmony became fashionable in jazz in the 1960s, influenced by C20th classical composers like Ravel and Debussy. It is also called 'non-functional' harmony, as the chords do not follow traditional rules like **II – V – I**.

The right-hand notes for the D7sus4 voicing above are a C major triad, formed from **7**, **9** and **11** of the chord. To find these right-hand notes for any sus 4 chord, think 'play a major triad based on ♭**7**'.

Instead of counting up to the seventh, you'll arrive at the same note if you think down a tone from the root instead. Thus, in slash chord notation:

$$\text{D9sus4} = \frac{\text{C triad}}{\text{D}}$$

Here are the other two sus 4 chords from *Maiden Voyage* expressed the same way:

$$\text{F9sus4} = \frac{\text{E}\flat\text{ triad}}{\text{F}} \qquad \text{E}\flat\text{9sus4} = \frac{\text{D}\flat\text{ triad}}{\text{E}\flat}$$

The right hand can play the triad in any inversion, giving a choice of three different top notes. The fifth can be added above the root in the left hand if you wish:

Fig 6.8: (b) For sus 4 chords play a major triad a tone down from the root

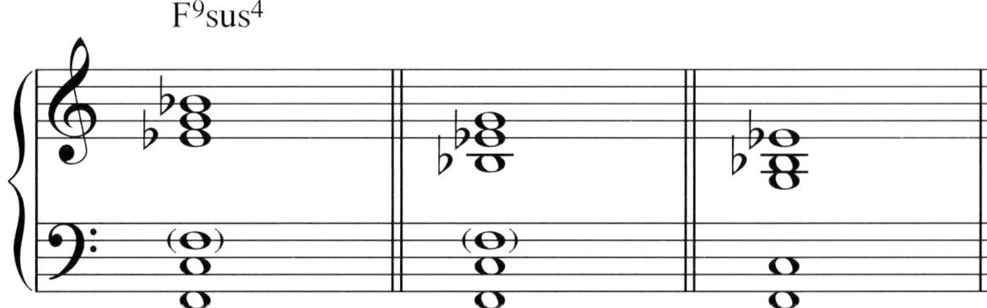

Reflections overleaf follows the same chord sequence as Fig 6.8(a), and shows how you might improvise over sus 4 chords lasting four bars each. See also p. 18.

1 **with bass & drums**

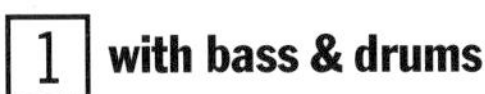

Reflections

♩ = 120
(straight 8s)

This improvisation follows the chord sequence of Herbie Hancock's *Maiden Voyage*.
Use sustain pedal to get a floating feel, but keep a strong sense of pulse throughout.

Tim Richards

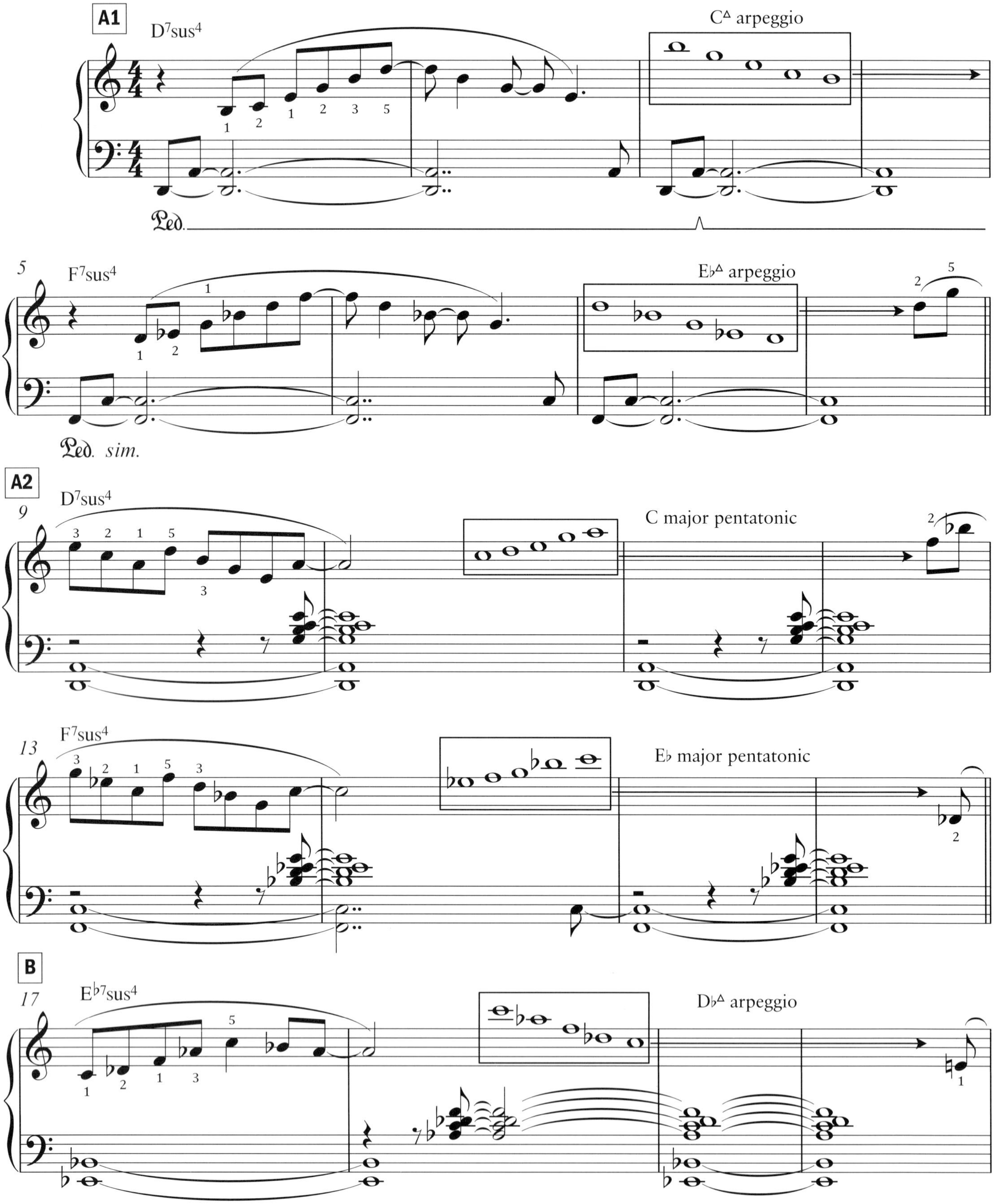

A1
D7sus4
C△ arpeggio
Ped.
5
F7sus4
E♭△ arpeggio
Ped. sim.
A2
9
D7sus4
C major pentatonic
13
F7sus4
E♭ major pentatonic
B
17
E♭7sus4
D♭△ arpeggio

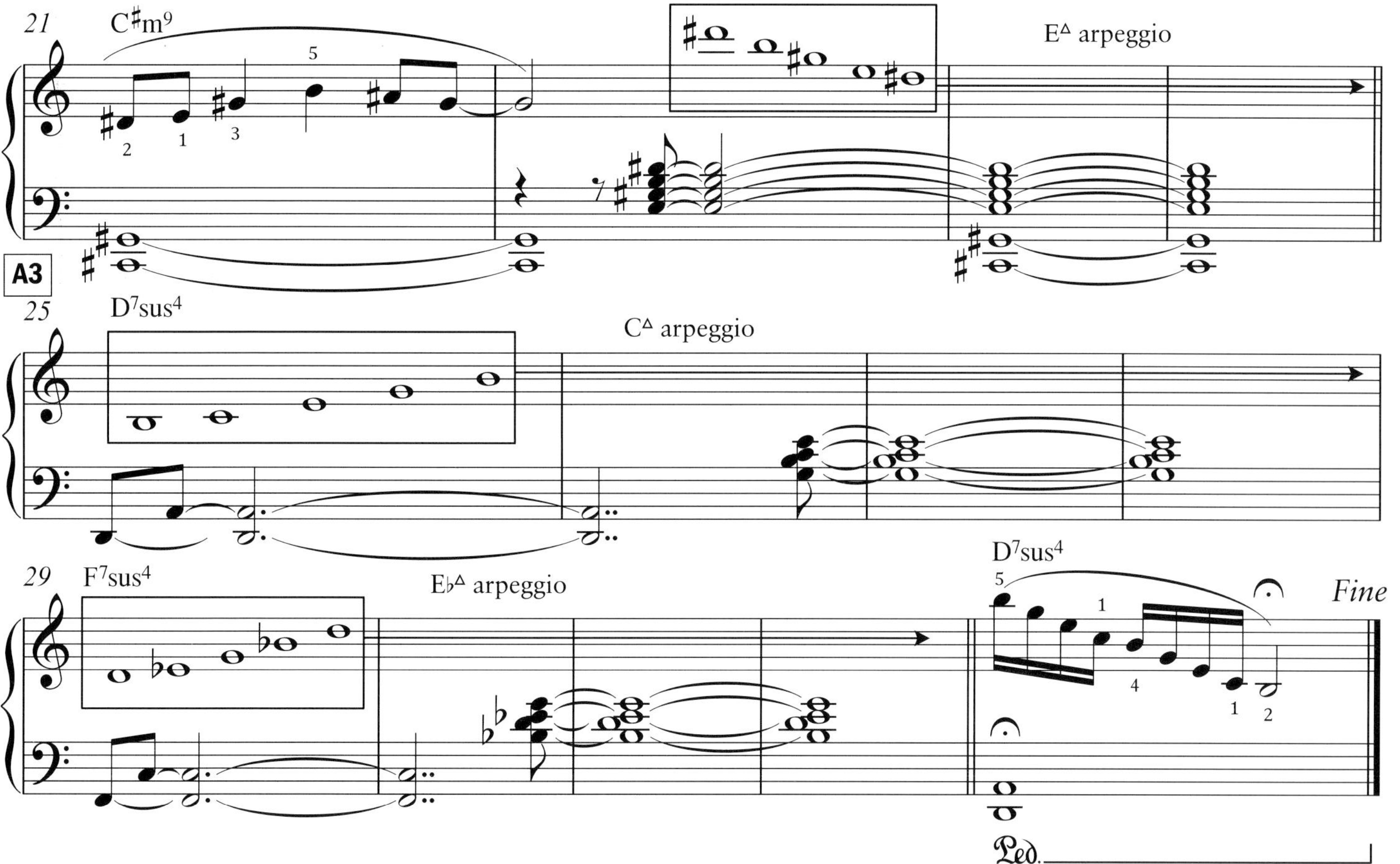

Checkpoint: Reflections

● **Left hand** For the first eight bars, just **R** and **5** are played to underpin the right-hand arpeggios, repeating every two bars. From 'A2' onwards, the left hand also plays a chord in the centre of the keyboard:

Fig 6.9: D7sus4

Compare this chord to the two-handed D7sus4 voicing in Fig 6.8(a) – rather than just playing a C triad in the right hand, we now have a C∆ shape, in second inversion. You'll also recognise it as a rootless Am9 shape, tying in with the 'minor seventh chord on **5**' principle, as shown in Fig 6.6.

● **Sustain pedal** Use this to connect the deep **R** and **5** with the central chord so that they both sound together. To avoid muddying the sound, change the pedal every two or four bars, depending on how busy the right hand is.

● **Foot-tap** Avoid tapping with the right foot when using the sustain pedal – a very bad habit! Keep time with the left foot instead, tapping four times in every bar.

● **C#m9 chord** Many people mistakenly play bars 21–24 as C#7sus4, like the other chords, but it should in fact be minor. The chord shape given here for the left hand is a **3579** rootless voicing. The same shape is suggested as an E∆ arpeggio for the right-hand improvisation. Alternatively, you could use the Dorian mode on C#.

● **Right hand** The arpeggios and pentatonic scales suggested for the sus 4 chords are all a tone down from the roots of the chords (see overleaf). Practise both of these so you can use them interchangeably over all three sus 4 chords.

Modal improvisation over sus 4 chords

In conventional harmony a sus 4 chord takes exactly the same scale as an ordinary dominant seventh – the Mixolydian mode – although the third of the scale is avoided until the resolution. In a modal situation, with the chords lasting several bars, different strategies are necessary to bring out the character of the sus 4 chord.

We have seen how it can be voiced by playing either a minor seventh chord on **5**, Am7/D, or a major triad on **7**, C/D. In fact, this amounts to much the same thing, because Am is the relative minor of C major, and has similar notes (Am7 = C6).

For D7sus4, improvising scales or arpeggios based on Am or C will give you a much better result than thinking from a D root, as the tendency to stress **3** (F♯) is removed.

The easiest way to achieve this is to think down a tone (rather than counting up to the seventh), as shown in *Reflections*. Here are some options, therefore, for D7sus4:

Fig 6.10: Base your sus 4 improvisation a tone down from the root

(a) C major triad

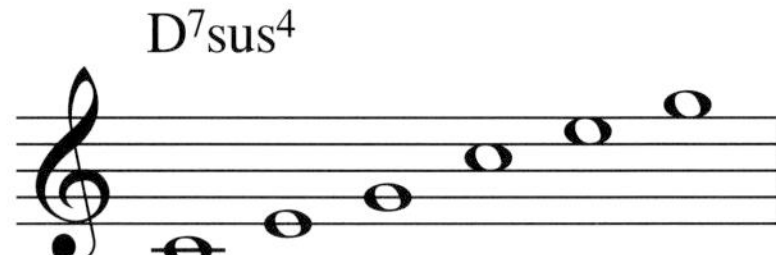

(b) C6 arpeggio (equivalent to the Am7 in Fig 6.5)

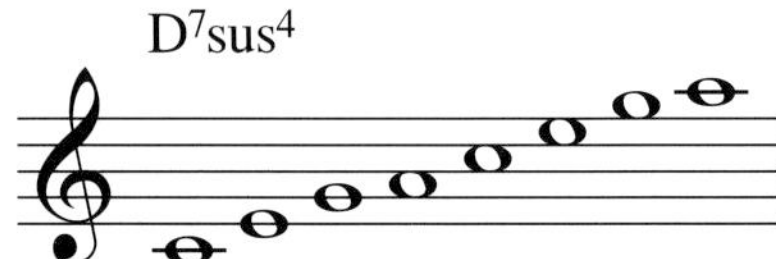

(c) C∆ arpeggio (equivalent to Am9)

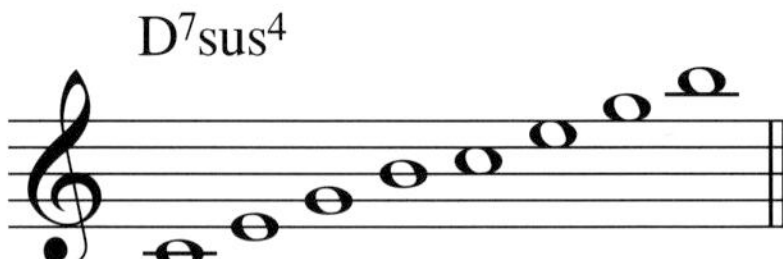

(d) C major pentatonic scale (equivalent to A minor pentatonic)

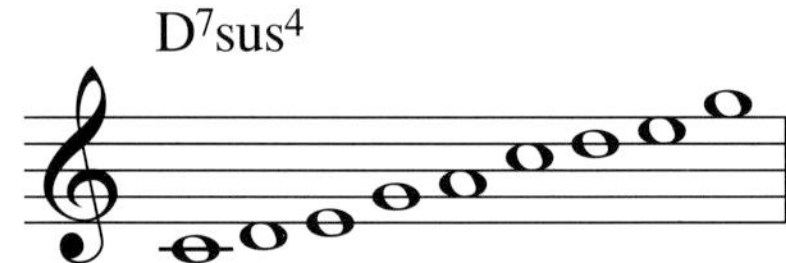

All of these successfully avoid the third of the chord and will give excellent results.

Assignments: Reflections

❶ **Listen to *Maiden Voyage*** Check out Herbie Hancock's 1965 recording to hear examples of improvisation over sus 4 chords, not only during the piano solo, but also the trumpet and tenor sax solos by Freddie Hubbard and George Coleman. Try to work out some of their phrases on the piano.

❷ **Arpeggios** Practise the 'tone down' arpeggios for all three sus 4 chords, playing them in different inversions, up and down over several octaves. Also explore broken chord patterns using the same notes.

❸ **Pentatonic scales** Memorise these for all three sus 4 chords, exploring patterns such as those in Vol. 1, pp. 182–183 and *Dream Improvisation*, p. 185.

❹ **Improvise** Introduce some of the ideas from steps 2–3 into the two-bar gaps present in every line of *Reflections,* practising with the CD (track 1). When you're comfortable with this, silence the piano on the recording using the balance control and improvise freely, playing along with bass and drums only. See also Assignments, p. 37.

Sharp eleven chords

A sharpened eleventh is the same as a raised fourth, and can be found in both major and dominant chords, as shown in Figs 6.1 and 6.2. Raising the fourth by a semitone gives the chords a very bright sound, and can be indicated in a chord symbol by **♯4** or **♯11**.

Sharp eleven chords are often played as two-handed voicings with triads in the right hand, a tone up from the root of the chord, enabling the fifth to be retained in the left hand:

Fig 6.11: Polychords with major triads a tone up

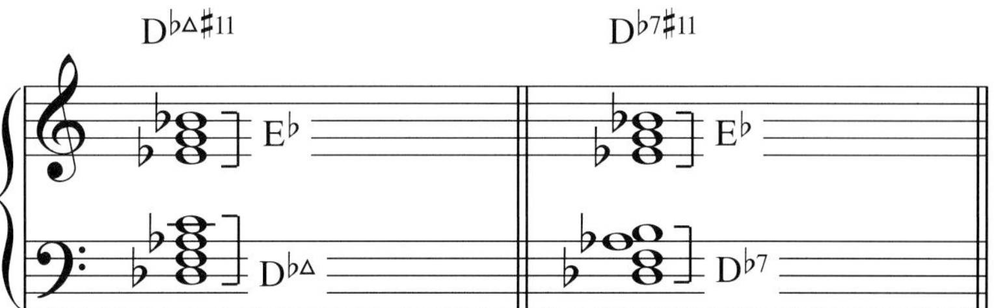

This type of voicing, known as a 'polychord', is used for the sharp eleven chords in *Eleventh Hour* overleaf. Polychords are dealt with more fully in Chapter 9.

You played a **♯11** in *White Russian* (Vol. 1, p. 214), in bar 3, where G appears as the melody note against a D♭Δ left hand. Because the fourth note of a regular D♭ major scale is G♭, G is the **♯4**. The D♭Δ left-hand chord given in the solo sequence included this G in preference to **5**, as in (b) below:

Fig 6.12: (a) Major seventh chord **(b) with ♯4 in place of 5**

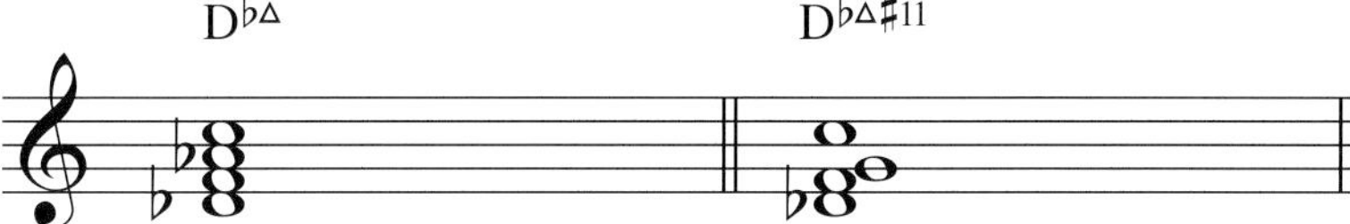

In *White Russian*, notice that the G (the **♯4**) is also present in the F harmonic minor scale suggested for improvisation over D♭Δ and C7. This scale works well when improvising horizontally over these two chords, but a sharp eleven chord by itself would normally imply a 'Lydian' scale.

The Lydian mode

Lydian scales always have raised fourths. In a D♭ major scale, raising G♭ to G (from **4** to **♯4**) gives rise to the Lydian mode:

Fig 6.13: Lydian mode on D♭

This scale has the same notes as A♭ major (four flats) – it is the fourth mode of A♭, starting on D♭.

You have already played the Lydian mode in several pieces, when using the same major scale to improvise over both **I** and **IV** major seventh chords, eg:

- *Major Seventh Workout* (Vol. 1, p. 97): over the second chord of each pair
- *Open Up!* (Vol. 1, p. 138): over B♭Δ in the key of F (see Fig 4.8)
- *Autumn Leaves* (Vol. 1, p. 150): over E♭Δ in the key of B♭ (see Fig 4.31)

For dominant chords with raised fourths, simply flatten the seventh of the Lydian scale shown above. This is known as a 'Lydian dominant' scale.
The next piece, *Eleventh Hour,* combines sharp eleven and sus 4 chords.

2 with bass & drums

♩ = 160
(swing 8s)

Eleventh Hour

Tim Richards

This piece features postbop style harmony, the chords moving in parallel fashion to give a deliberately vague sense of key. Note the progression up in minor thirds in the 'B' section.

A Solo (Use the left-hand shapes in brackets the second time around.)

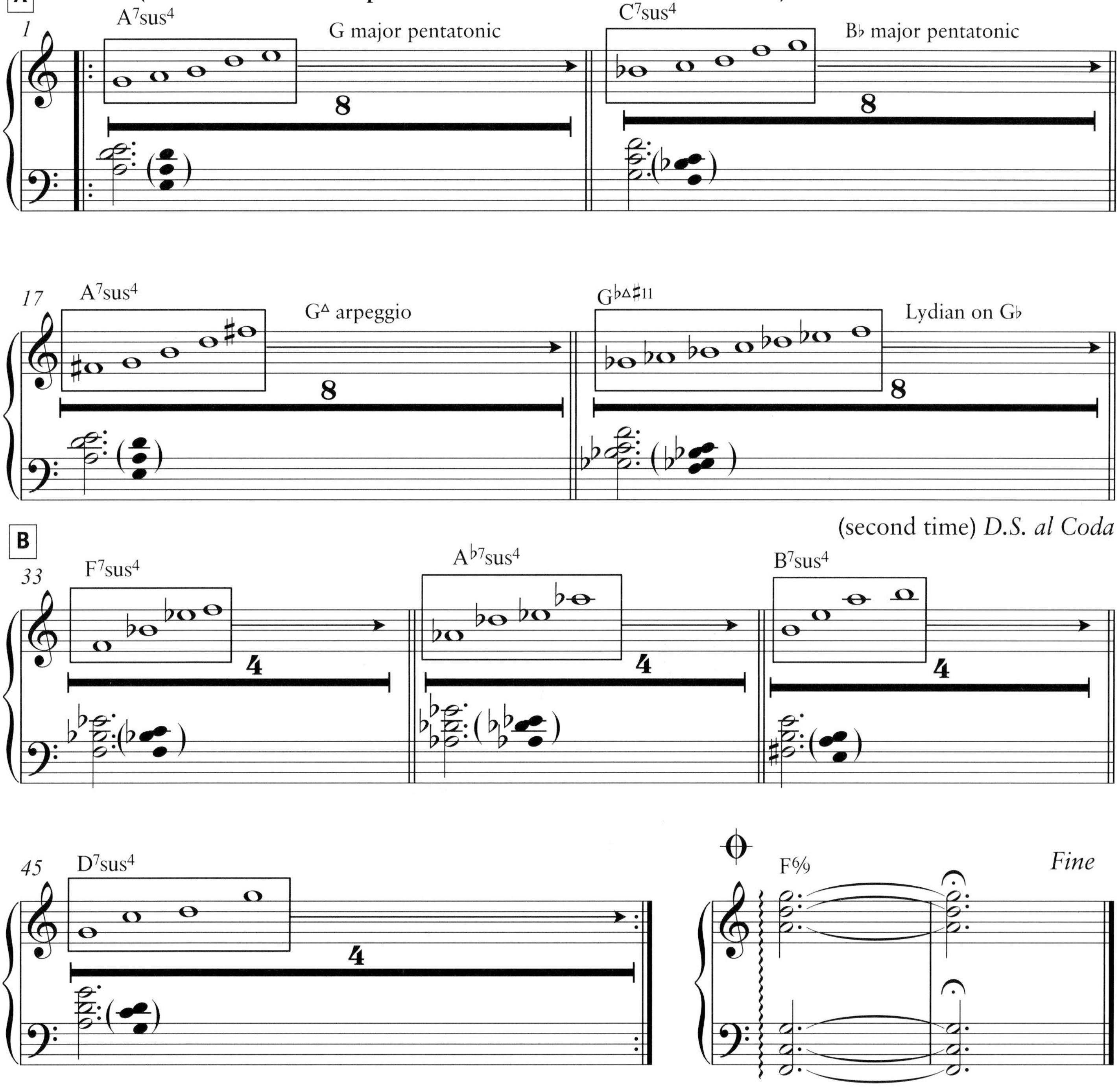

1 A7sus4 — G major pentatonic — 8 | C7sus4 — B♭ major pentatonic — 8

17 A7sus4 — G△ arpeggio — 8 | G♭△♯11 — Lydian on G♭ — 8

B (second time) *D.S. al Coda*

33 F7sus4 — 4 | A♭7sus4 — 4 | B7sus4 — 4

45 D7sus4 — 4

F6/9 *Fine*

Checkpoint: Eleventh Hour

● **ABA form** The melody has an ABA form, totalling 40 bars (16 – 8 – 16). For the solo the form is just AB, with some of the chords omitted to give a simpler sequence to improvise over. Also, each section is extended, giving twice as many bars on each chord.

● **Solo section – quartal sus 4 voicings** There are two possible perfect fourth shapes that are compatible with sus 4 chords:

Fig 6.14

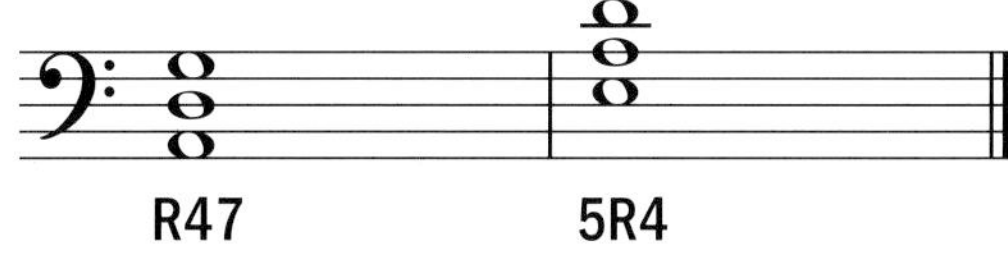

The left hand of the solo section uses both these voicings (sometimes inverted) keeping all the chords in the same register – near middle C.

John Taylor, probably the most influential and in-demand British pianist on the scene today. After playing with saxophonists John Surman and Alan Skidmore in the 1960s, he forged an international career working with Jan Garbarek, Peter Erskine and others, recording for the German ECM label and forming his own group 'Azimuth', featuring trumpeter Kenny Wheeler and vocalist Norma Winstone. An exceptional improviser, his hallmarks are an incredibly fluid right hand, cutting-edge harmonies, and an impressive sense of timing.

● **Bridge (section 'B')** Because the roots go up in minor thirds, playing the **R47** left-hand voicing from Fig 6.14 for all four chords takes you too high up the keyboard. Using the second voicing (**5R4**) for B7sus4 and D7sus4 brings the shapes just a semitone higher than F7sus4 and A♭7sus4:

Fig 6.15: Combining the two shapes

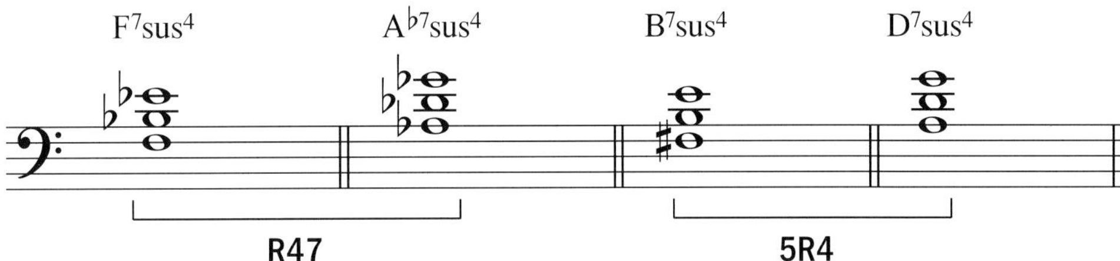

● **Inverted quartal shapes** As we saw in Vol. 1, Fig 5.14, perfect fourth shapes can be inverted, giving six possible quartal shapes for each sus 4 chord:

Fig 6.16: C7sus4 quartal shapes with inversions

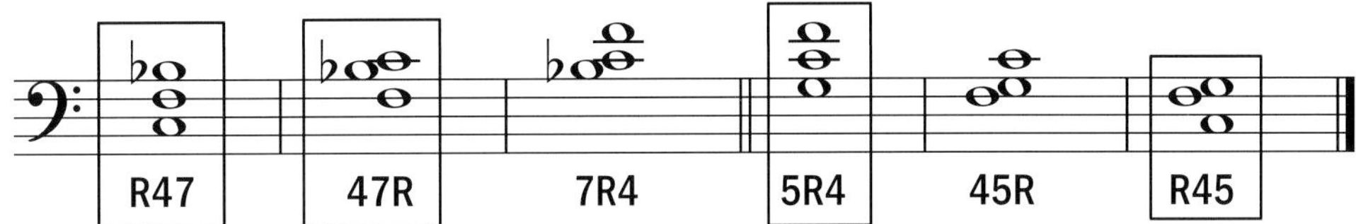

The boxed shapes are the ones used as left-hand chords in the solo section.

● **Sharp eleven chords** These occur in bar 12 and 13 of the melody. In both cases the right hand plays a triad a tone up from the root of the chord (see Fig 6.11).

The 'tone up' principle can also be used when improvising over Δ7♯11 chords, as an alternative to using the Lydian scale. Over G♭Δ♯11 the right hand can therefore play an A♭ triad arpeggio or A♭ major pentatonic. Finger the A♭ pentatonic with the thumb on F and C, like F minor pentatonic (which has the same notes).

● **Improvising in fourths** The right-hand suggestions for the solo include many of the arpeggio and pentatonic scale ideas we looked at in *Reflections* (Fig 6.10).

However, in the bridge, the right-hand suggestions are taken from the two perfect fourth chord shapes based on **R47** or **5R4** (Fig 6.14). Practise the following useful hand positions for all four chords of the bridge:

Fig 6.17: Four-note quartal hand positions for F7sus4

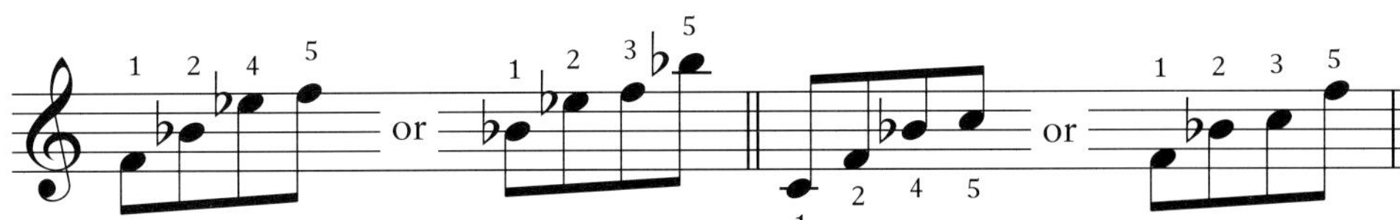

Here's an example of a phrase that combines some of these hand positions:

Fig 6.18: Sample improvisation over the first four bars of the bridge

● **3/4 time signature** On the next few pages you'll find some tips on playing and improvising in 3/4. For Assignments, see p. 28.

Playing in 3/4 time

Although not as common as 4/4, the 3/4 time signature has been used in jazz since the days of Fats Waller, who wrote *The Jitterbug Waltz* in 1942. Experiments in the 1950s and 60s by drummer Max Roach (the album 'Jazz in 3/4 Time') and pianist Dave Brubeck further popularised the meter.

Today the ability to swing and improvise in 3/4 are essential skills for the jazz musician. Here's a selection of tunes written in 3/4 or 6/8 time, listed by composer, together with the some of the albums they appear on:

Dave Brubeck:	*It's a Raggy Waltz* – 'Time Further Out'
	Three to Get Ready – 'Time Out'
Mongo Santamaria:	*Afro Blue* – John Coltrane: 'Live at Birdland' (McCoy Tyner on piano)
Rodgers/Hammerstein:	*My Favourite Things* – Coltrane: 'My Favourite Things' (Tyner on piano)
Frank Loesse:	*Inchworm* – Coltrane: 'Coltrane' (Tyner on piano)
McCoy Tyner:	*Groove Waltz* – 'Nights of Ballads & Blues'
	Contemplation – 'The Real McCoy'
Bill Evans:	*Waltz for Debby* – 'At the Village Vanguard'
	B Minor Waltz – 'You Must Believe in Spring'
	34 Skiddoo – 'How My Heart Sings' and 'Re: Person I Knew'
Fain/Hilliard:	*Alice in Wonderland* – Bill Evans: 'Sunday at the Village Vanguard'
Frank Churchill:	*Someday my Prince will Come* – Bill Evans: 'Portrait in Jazz', and Miles Davis: 'Someday my Prince will Come' (Wynton Kelly on piano)
Freddie Hubbard:	*Up Jumped Spring* – 'Backlash'
Chick Corea	*Windows* – 'Inner Space' and Stan Getz: 'Sweet Rain'
Toots Thielemanns:	*Bluesette* – features similar changes to 'Bird Blues' (see p. 161)
Wes Montgomery:	*West Coast Blues* – 'Incredible Jazz Guitar' (Tommy Flanagan on piano)
Miles Davis:	*All Blues* – 'Kind of Blue' (Bill Evans on piano)
Wayne Shorter:	*Footprints* – 'Adam's Apple' (minor blues, Herbie Hancock on piano)

A few well-known standards were actually written in 3/4 (*Tenderly, Fly Me to the Moon*, etc), but are more often performed in 4/4.

Here are some of the rhythms you might use in a bass line or when comping:

Fig 6.19: Various ways of breaking up a bar of 3/4

The last two bars imply a 6/8 feel, a time signature that is often combined with 3/4 to get away from the 'oom-pah-pah' feel of a straight waltz. 6/8 is a 'compound' time signature, meaning that each beat consists of a dotted quarter-note, giving only two beats per bar. In *Eleventh Hour* (p. 20) the right-hand melody is clearly in 3/4 throughout, but the left-hand bass line is in 6/8 underneath, as shown by the division of most bars into two dotted quarter-notes.

Play the following two-handed accompaniment exercise with a strong foot-tap as marked:

Fig 6.20: Alternating bars of 6/8 and 3/4

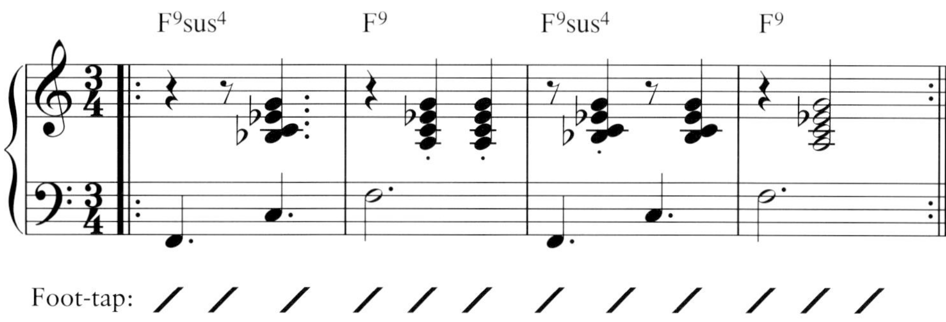

In the first and third bars see how the second bass note is on the 'two and', creating the 6/8 feel. Before playing Fig 6.20 in its entirety, clap each bar over and over, combining the rhythm of chords and bass line against your 3/4 foot-tap.

When using these rhythms for comping purposes, create variety by mixing them up, so you don't always use them in the same order. You can also refer to them in your right-hand improvisations.

Polyrhythms

Creating a 6/8 or 'two feel' in 3/4 time is an example of a 'polyrhythm' – two or more rhythms existing simultaneously. The most important polyrhythms are 'two against three' and 'three against two'. Tap these on your left and right knees, synchronising your counting alternately with the right hand and left hand as marked:

Fig 6.21

(a) Two against three

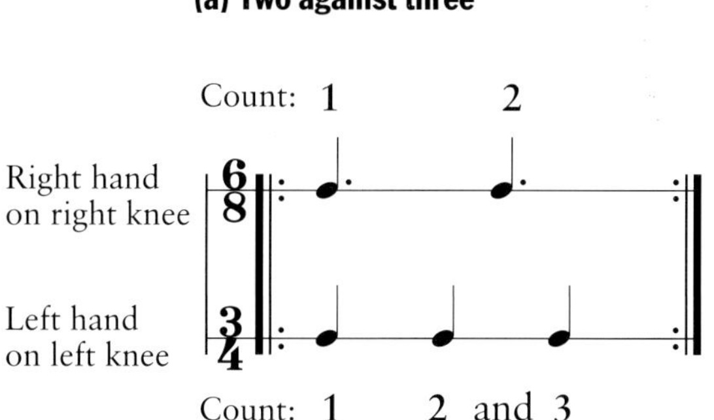

(b) Three against two

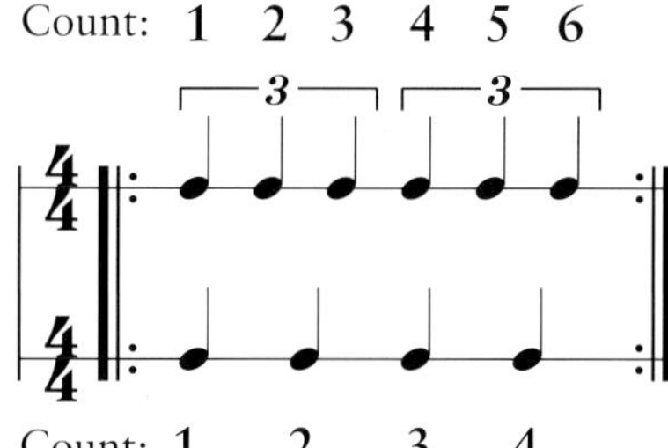

Practise these until both hands are tapping even streams of notes and you can switch the count from one hand to the other without interrupting the timing. Using a metronome will help. When you've mastered this, transfer it to the piano, playing single notes in the right hand, bass line or chords in the left.

Because 6/8 has two beats per bar, prolonged use of the 6/8 feel can disguise the 3/4 nature of a piece. Two bars of 6/8 contain four beats, which could then be interpreted as one bar of 4/4. That's why a blues in 3/4 (such as *Footprints* or *Bluesette*) usually lasts twenty four bars rather than twelve. See also *Blues in Three* (IBP, p. 220).

To hear how the three time signatures are linked, play the exercise overleaf which is based on C minor (Dorian):

Fig 6.22: The same phrase in 3/4, 6/8 and 4/4, with typical bass lines

To check you are playing this exercise correctly, note the following:

- The right hand should sound exactly the same in all three examples
- The changes in feel are indicated by the bass line only
- In the 6/8 example, the second bass note of each bar is between the second and third foot-taps
- For the third example, adjust the foot-tap to equal the dotted quarter-note in 6/8

Experienced jazz musicians are very alert to polyrhythmic possibilities, and like to exploit them in their improvisations. This kind of thing is often sparked off by interaction with the other musicians in a jazz group, especially the drummer.

Here's another way to demonstrate the connection between 4/4 and 6/8:

Fig 6.23: Alternating bars of 4/4 and 6/8 (play with unchanging foot-tap)

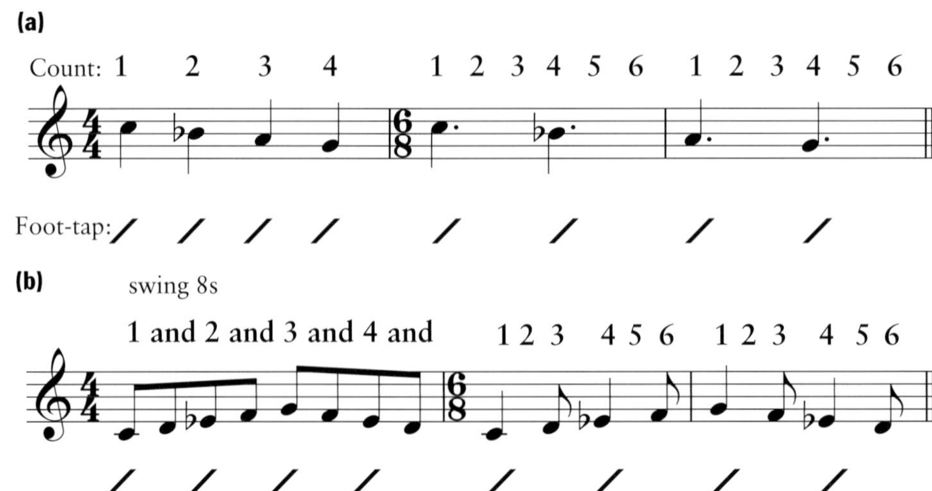

The 4/4 and 6/8 bars should sound the same as there is no bass line, only the count is different. Two bars of 6/8 take up the same time as one bar of 4/4.

Example (b) also shows the strong connection between swing eighth-notes and triplets – the quarter-note/eighth-note pairs in the 6/8 bars can be thought of as the first and third notes of a triplet in 4/4.

Sus 4 chords and II – Vs

In *Eleventh Hour*, the melody in the bridge (bars 17–24) implies a resolution for each sus 4 chord:

Fig 6.24

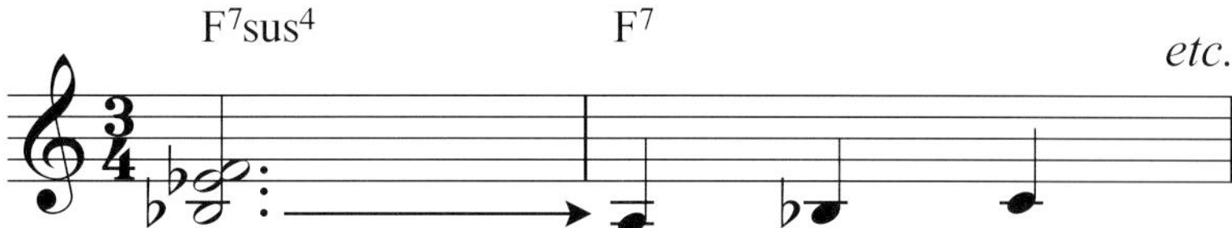

The chords could therefore be thought of as four **II** – **V**s, like this:

‖ Cm^{7}/F | F^{7} | E♭m^{7}/A♭ | A♭^{7} | F♯m^{7}/B | B^{7} | Am^{7}/D | D^{7} ‖

When improvising over the bridge you have the freedom to revert to more of a functional harmony sound by treating each sus 4 chord as a **II** – **V**. Because the bar-lines in the solo structure are doubled, you'll have to play each **II** – **V** twice:

Fig 6.25: II – V patterns for bridge of *Eleventh Hour*

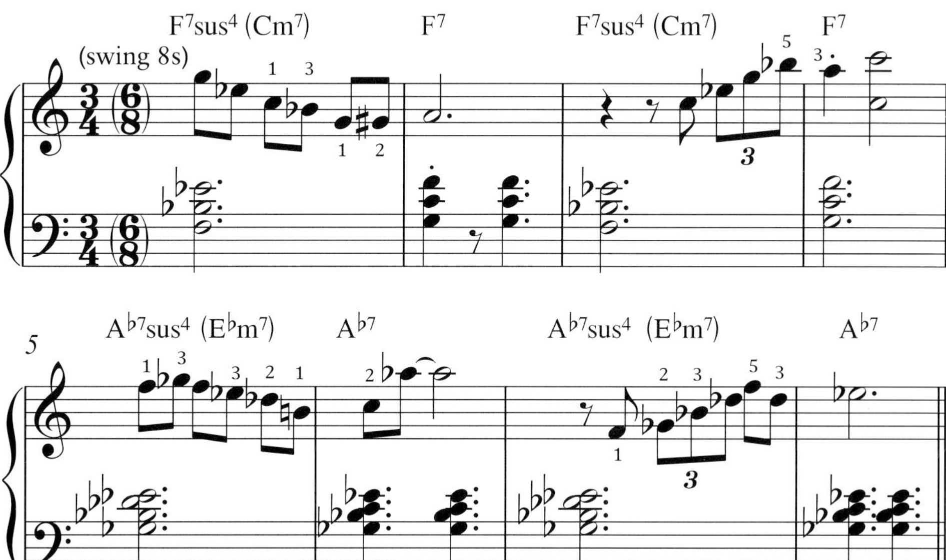

The right-hand lines now resolve onto the third of the chord in every second bar (or the fifth of the chord in bar 8). The left hand must be compatible with this resolution. Note the new perfect fourth shape in bars 2 and 4 (**25R**).

Instead of resolving the sus 4 chords in every other bar, you could make the change just once every four bars. The chords would then be:

etc.

‖ 3/4 (6/8) Cm^{7} | ⁒ | F^{7} | ⁒ | E♭m^{7} | ⁒ | A♭^{7} | ⁒ ‖

Assignments and Improvisation Tips: Eleventh Hour

❶ **Melody** Memorise the melody and chord voicings, noting the structure of the two polychords used:

- Sus 4 chords – right-hand triads tone down from the root
- Sharp 11 chords – right-hand triads tone up from the root

❷ **Improvise in eighth-notes** Using the pentatonic scales or major seventh arpeggios suggested, play right-hand lines over some of the left-hand chordal rhythms given in Fig 6.19. Keep tapping your foot in three, even when implying a 6/8 feel:

Fig 6.26: G major pentatonic phrase over 6/8 chords

Also play this example with the left-hand rhythm reversed (ie: two chords in bars 2 and 4, one chord in bars 1 and 3). Aim to become completely at home improvising eighth-note lines over both the 3/4 and 6/8 left hand.

Play two- and four-bar phrases to help you count the eight-bar sections for the four chords in section 'A'. Take care to change chord and scale without any hesitations.

❸ **Improvise in triplets** Whether you're in 3/4 or 6/8, triplets will sound great. Here's a G major pentatonic exercise over A7sus4, with a 6/8 left hand:

Fig 6.27: Three-note groups (descending), four-note groups (ascending)

Work out similar patterns for the other chords until your fingers can find the notes confidently, playing in triplets over 3/4 and 6/8 left-hand chords.

❹ **Bridge – fourths** The suggested notes in section 'B' are all perfect fourth patterns. Familiarise yourself with these for all four chords by playing the configurations given in Figs 6.17 and 6.18 over F7sus4, A♭7sus4, B7sus4 and D7sus4. Don't forget to try quartal lines in triplets as well:

Fig 6.28: R47 triplet arpeggio

❺ **Bridge – other techniques** Explore pentatonic scales and major seventh arpeggios, as for the 'A' section. Also try out some of the **II – V** ideas given on the previous page. Try them all with both 6/8 and 3/4 left-hand chords.

Kenny Barron, whose influences range from Art Tatum and Ellington to Monk and Bud Powell, has recorded with Dizzy Gillespie, Stan Getz, Freddie Hubbard and many others. Versatility, coupled with cutting-edge contemporary stylings, have made him one of the most popular sidemen of recent years. In the 1980s he co-led the group 'Sphere', and is also a very fine composer.

Minor eleventh chords

Minor seventh chords containing the fourth can be played in two hands, which allows the ninth to be included too.

Fig 6.29: Minor eleventh chord (two-handed voicing)

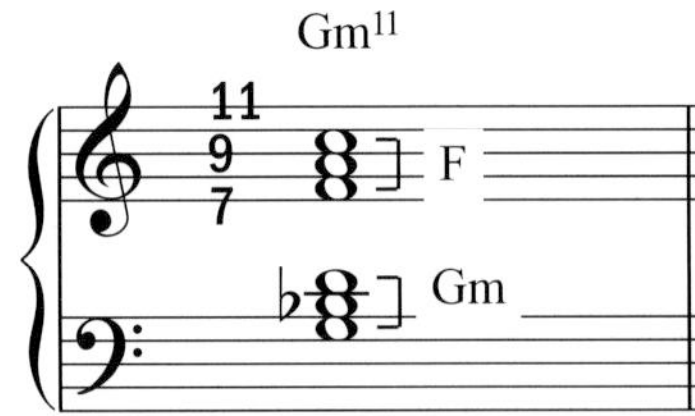

Notice that **7**, **9** and **11** form a major triad in the right hand. As with sus 4 chords, this triad is a tone down from the root – the difference is the presence of the minor third in the left hand. The above voicing is useful when the melody note is the fourth of the minor chord, as in *Tune Up* (p. 183) and *In a Sentimental Mood* (Vol. 1, p. 220, bar 9).

One of the best ways of playing a minor eleventh in one hand is as a 'stretch' voicing, which spans an interval of a ninth (an octave plus a tone):

Fig 6.30

(a) Stretch voicing for Gm11

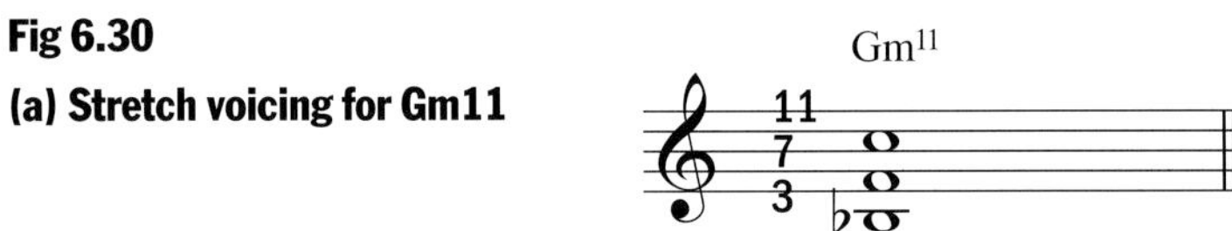

(b) II – Vs played as stretch voicings

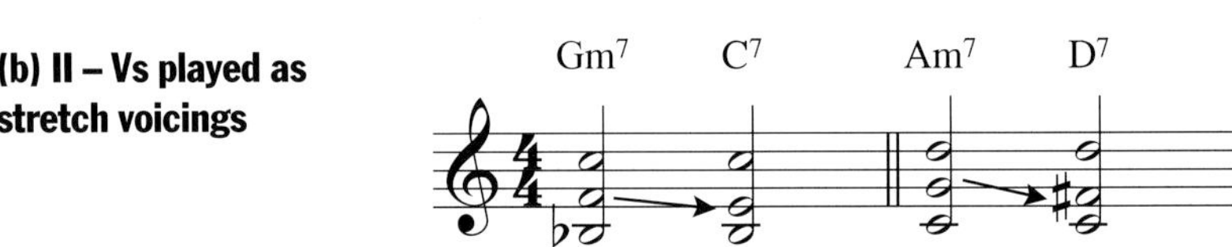

To find a stretch voicing for a minor seventh chord, place the right thumb on **3** and build notes up in perfect fifths.

Quintal harmony

Because the minor eleventh stretch voicing contains two perfect fifth intervals, it could be called a 'quintal' voicing. These voicings are closely related to quartal voicings, since a fifth interval can be obtained by inverting a perfect fourth. Here is an example of a six-note quintal voicing for F∆:

Fig 6.31: Two-handed voicing containing only perfect fifths

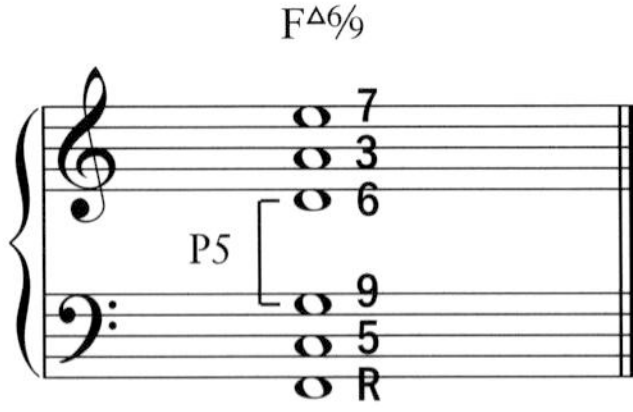

As well as both hands containing perfect fifths, the interval between the hands in Fig 6.31 is also a perfect fifth. This is not always the case – perhaps the most commonly used quintal voicing has only a semitone between the two hands:

Fig 6.32: Two-handed quintal voicing for Gm11

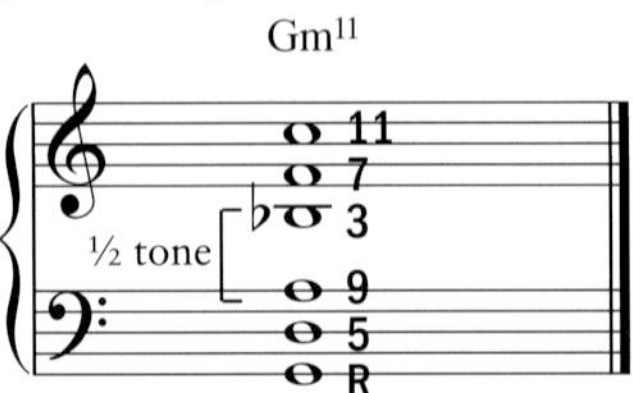

This voicing for a minor eleventh chord is sometimes referred to as the 'Kenny Barron voicing'. Most of the voicings above appear in the next piece, *Hot and Cold*.

3

♩ = 80
(straight 8s)

Hot and Cold

Play the introduction *rubato*, extending the fills between the two-handed arpeggios for as long as you wish. In contrast, the montuno section must be played in strict tempo.

Tim Richards

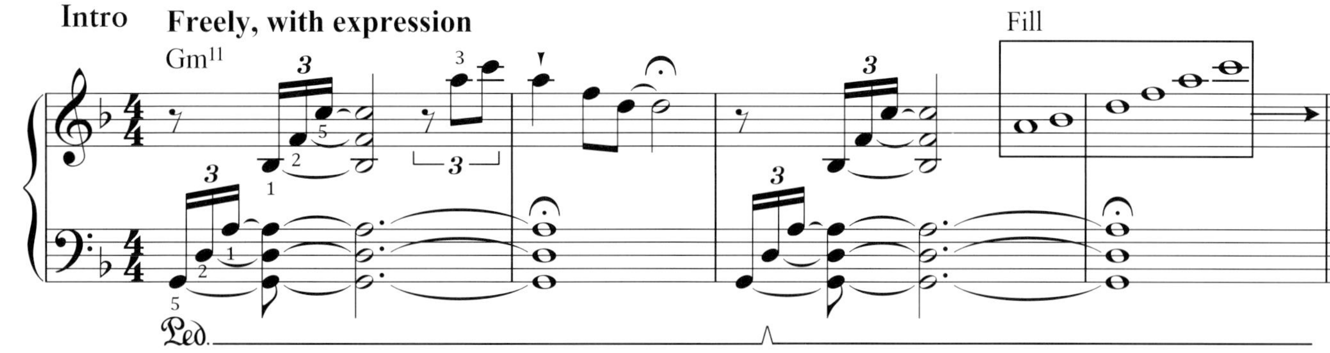

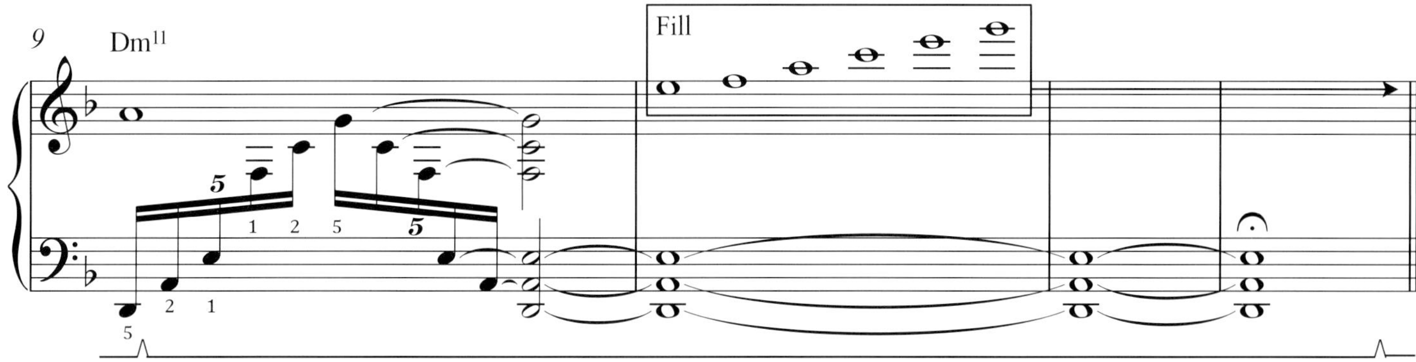

4 with drums

♩ = 120 (a tempo)
(straight 8s)

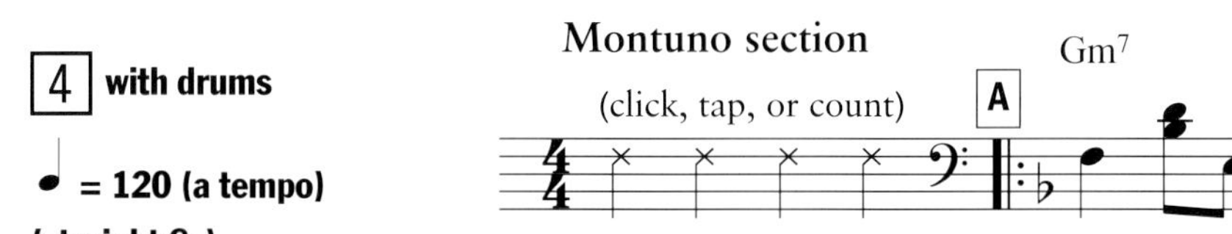

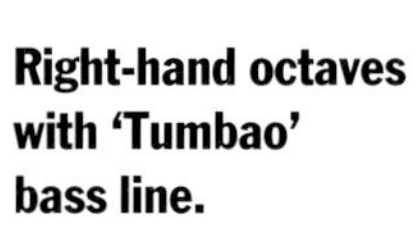

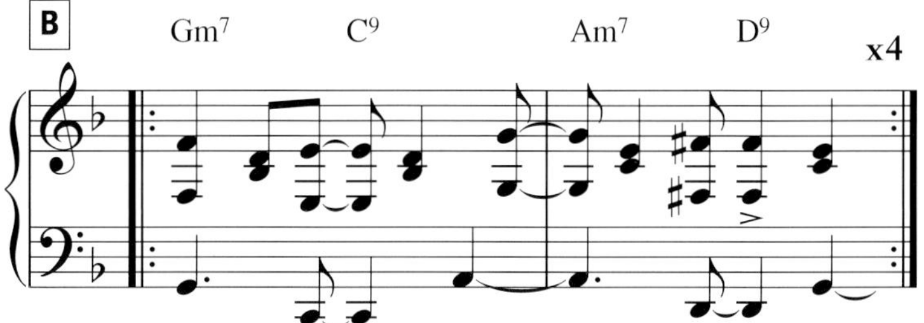

Stretch voicings with simple bass line.

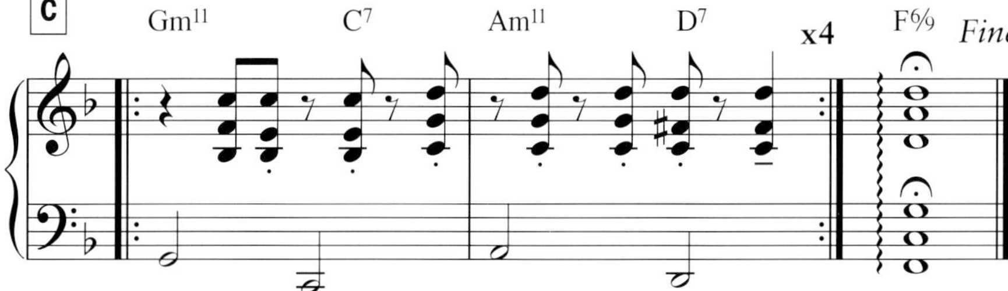

Checkpoint: Hot and Cold

● **Quintal voicings** The Gm11 and Dm11 two-handed arpeggios in the introduction are both the 'Kenny Barron' voicing from Fig 6.32. A similar shape is used for E♭7♯11, with the hands a tone apart instead of a semitone:

Fig 6.33: Sharp eleven quintal voicing

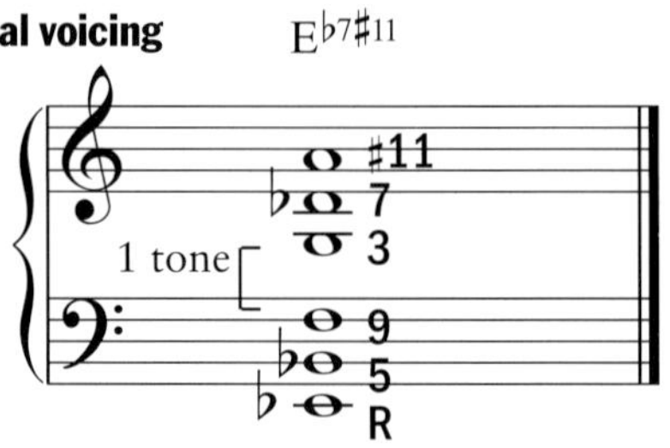

E♭7♯11

1 tone

♯11
7
3
9
5
R

For all these voicings, the left hand plays **R59**, as in *Eleventh Hour.* The right-hand part of Fig 6.33 can be used by itself as a stretch voicing in either hand, for E♭7♯11 (**37 ♯11**) and also for A7 (**73R**). For more on stretch voicings, see *Got my Mojo Workin'* and *St Louis Blues*, IBP, pp. 122–123 and 200.

● **Montuno section** After the last chord of the introduction has died away, count in the montuno section at the faster tempo and play any of the montunos given. The right-hand rhythm in 'A' and 'B' is exactly the same. Clap and memorise it before attempting the notes:

Fig 6.34: Montuno rhythm

Compare this to the similar rhythm in *Montuno for Monty*, Vol. 1, pp. 73–75.

● **II – Vs** The second bar of the montuno section (Am7 – D7) is a tone up from the first bar (Gm7 – C7), and leads back to it, since D7 is the dominant of G minor. Note how the bottom note of the voicings in section 'A' descend in semitones:

Fig 6.35: Rootless voicings – moving notes

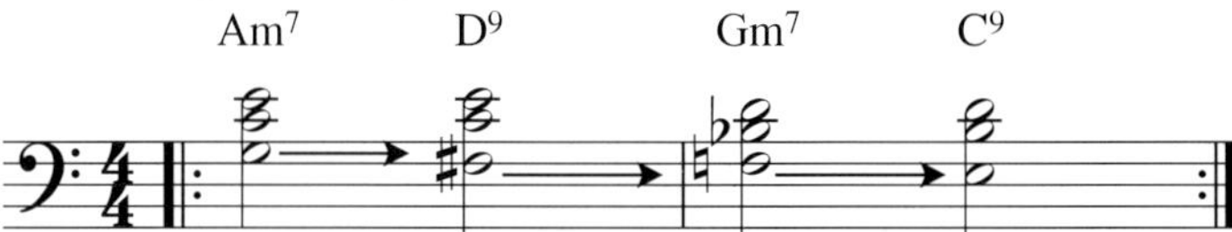

Section 'B', features the same montuno with the moving note doubled in octaves. This is a more professional way of playing a montuno and projects much better because of the double notes.

● **Simple bass line** Many pianists play montunos with both hands, leaving the bass line to the bass player. When first learning the montunos, however, use the simple bass line given for the left hand at 'C' as a reference point – half-notes only. Play with a metronome, tapping your foot on 'one' and 'three', together with the left-hand bass notes.

● **Tumbao bass line** When you've mastered the right-hand montuno at 'A' or 'B', try the more authentic 'Tumbao' bass given for 'B', in which the roots of the first chord of each bar are played a whole beat early, on the 'four' of the previous bar (see Vol. 1, Fig 2.30). This takes practice to co-ordinate; memorise the bass line first without the right hand, playing it over and over with foot-tap and metronome.

Fig 6.36: Tumbao

Apart from the first, none of the bass notes coincide with the foot-tap.

Two-handed II – V voicings

If playing with a bassist, you could play the **II** – **V** chords in the montuno section of *Hot and Cold* as two-handed voicings, alternating **R7** and **R3** shells in the left hand:

Fig 6.37

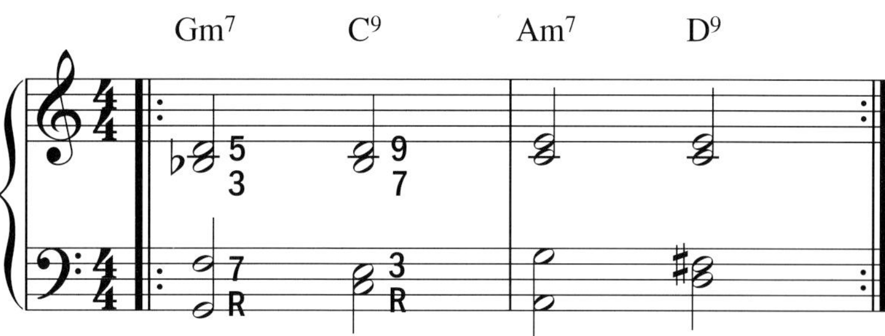

NB: The right hand stays the same during the change from **II** to **V** – the fifth of the **II** chord (top note) becomes the ninth of the **V** chord.

We'll be using this type of voicing later on in tunes such as *II – V Comping* (p. 74), *Ladybird* (p. 78), and *Bird Blues Comping* (p. 161).

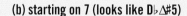

Assignments and Improvisation Tips: Hot and Cold

❶ **Intro** This should be played with a flexible pulse, pausing at the *fermata* signs to let the music breathe. Explore different ideas for your fills over Gm11 and Dm11, using the arpeggios suggested, or major pentatonic scales a tone down (same as for sus 4 chords). The Dorian scale on each is also a good choice for these chords.

Although only played once on the CD, you could repeat the intro before moving on to the Montuno section. Try including some improvisation over E♭7♯11 too – perhaps using the Lydian dominant scale (see Fig 9.21), or one of the following arpeggios:

Fig 6.38: Arpeggios for E♭7♯11

(a) starting on 5 (looks like B♭m∆)

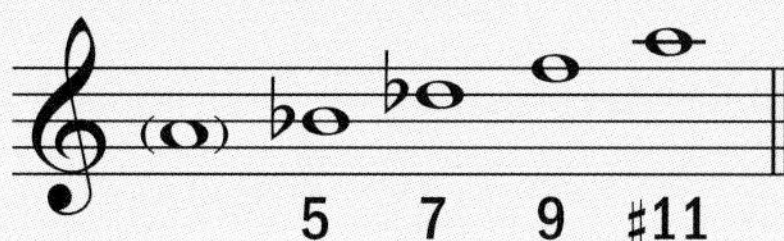

(b) starting on 7 (looks like D♭∆♯5)

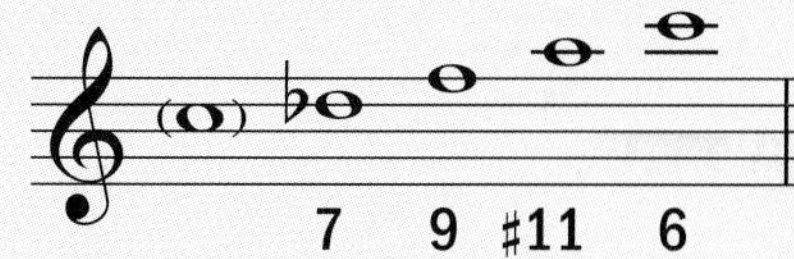

❷ **Montunos** Spend time practising these with and without a bass line, as described in the checkpoint. 'A' and 'B' are interchangeable – if you have mastered them both you may go straight from one to the other without changing the bass line.

❸ **Invite a friend** These montunos are ideal backing figures for another soloist – invite a friend to improvise a solo on another instrument, or the top part of the piano, whilst you accompany them with the montuno underneath.

❹ **Improvise** When it's your turn to solo, play the rootless chords shown in Fig 6.35 in the left hand. The right hand could use the G blues scale (see Vol. 1, p. 155) or the **♭3** pentatonic on G (Vol. 1, p. 190). Try this with the CD.

❺ **Two-handed voicings** With the CD, try comping by playing the voicings shown in Fig 6.37 in the rhythm of the montuno at 'C'.

❻ ***Funky Two-Five*** Review this piece from Vol. 1, p. 188. During the intro, try the stretch voicings for Gm11 – C7 in the right hand (Fig 6.30(b)), playing them in the same rhythm as the written chord shapes.

Major scales and quartal harmony

Bill Evans was one of the first to explore the potential of the fourth in his right-hand lines. In his solo in *Night and Day* from the 1958 album 'Everybody Digs Bill Evans', he rearranges the notes of an E♭ major scale to give the following pattern:

Fig 6.39: E♭ major scale in groups of descending fourths

Later in the solo he phrases in triplets, making the fourths less obvious:

Fig 6.40: Bill Evans' triplet phrasing

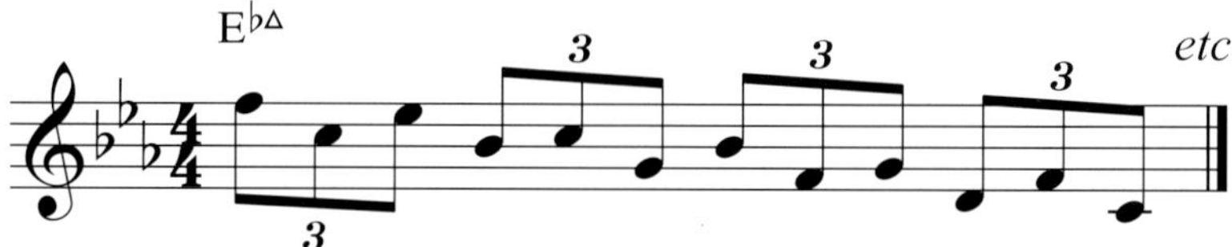

If you start on the seventh of any major scale and go up in perfect fourths, you'll pass through all the notes of the scale in turn, in the order shown below:

Fig 6.41: F major scale played as ascending fourths

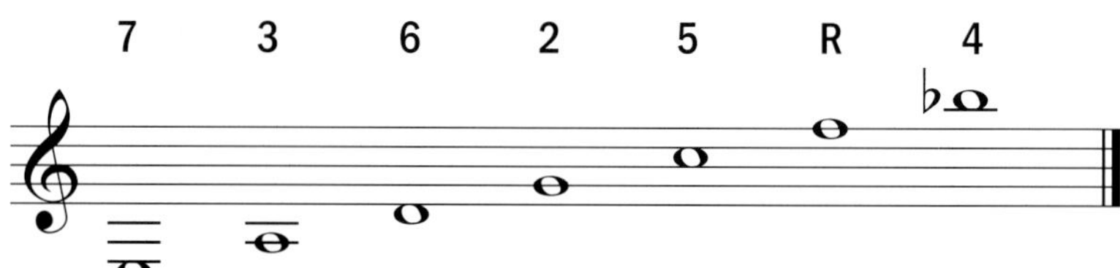

Taking any three adjacent notes of this series will give five possible three-note quartal chord shapes using only perfect fourths:

Fig 6.42: Quartal chord shapes derived from F major scale

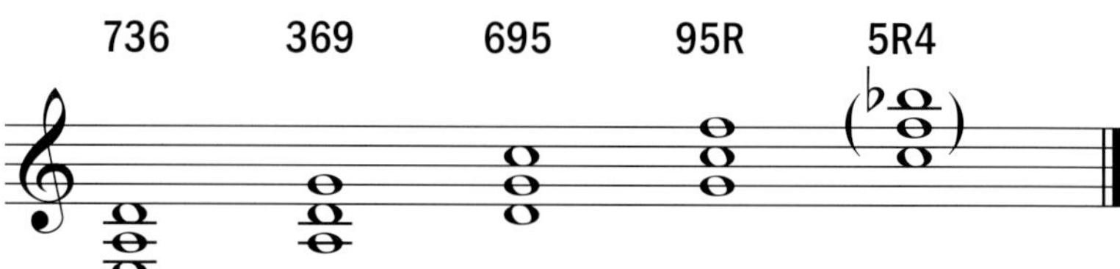

The first four of these are possible shapes for FΔ or F6/9. The last shape (in brackets) is not acceptable as it contains the fourth, B♭, which is incompatible with a major chord.

Changing the register of the first four chords (as in Fig 6.43) allows them to be played more practically as two pairs a tone apart. Memorise the formula so you can find these quartal pairs for any major (Δ) or 6/9 chord:

Fig 6.43: For major chords build perfect fourths on 2, 3, 6 or 7 of the major scale

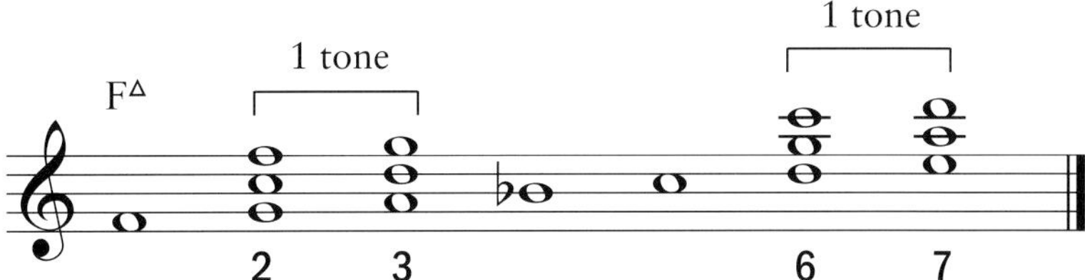

We used the second shape, **369**, for the major chords in *Dream Improvisation* (Vol. 1, p. 185), but the other three are new possibilities. Try using all four shapes to generate single-note improvised lines in the right hand, as in this example from *Orinoco* (Vol. 1, p. 211):

Fig 6.44: *Orinoco*, bars 17–20 – sample improvisation using quartal shapes

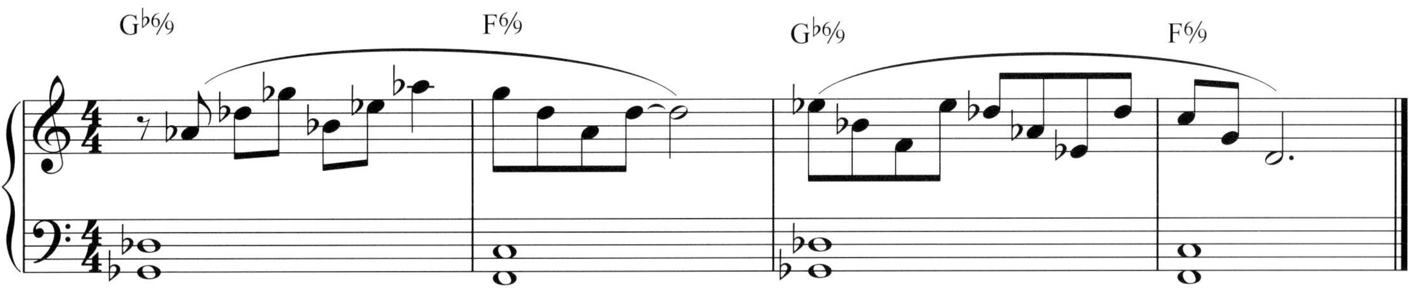

Quartal minor seventh chords

As we saw in Fig 6.42, it is not possible to play a perfect fourth voicing on the root of a major chord. With minor chords, however, as with sus 4 chords, a **R47** voicing sounds fine. Compare the following tertiary and quartal voicings for Cm:

Fig 6.45: Cm11 (a) voiced in thirds (b) voiced in fourths

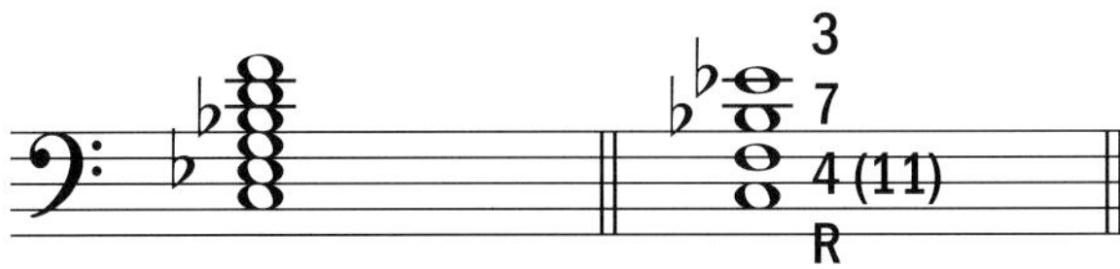

The quartal version (b) has a more open sound as the notes are more widely spaced. Three-note shapes can be derived from it by omitting the top or bottom note:

Fig 6.46: Perfect fourth shapes for Cm7

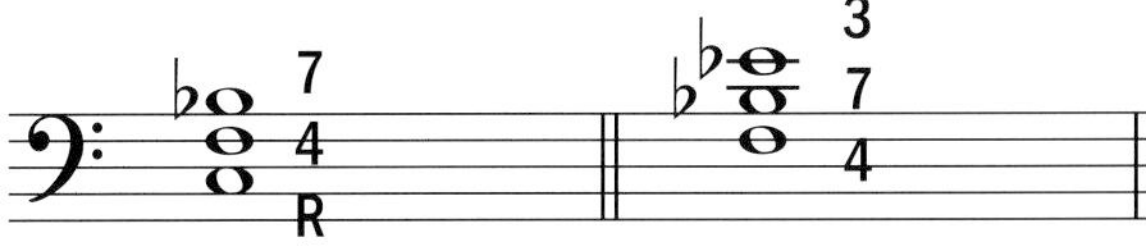

The 'So What' voicing

The first shape in Fig 6.46 is like a **R7** shell with an added fourth (F). Let's try adding this fourth to the left-hand shell of the **R7/35** minor seventh voicing from Fig 6.37:

Fig 6.47: Two-handed quartal voicing – R47/35

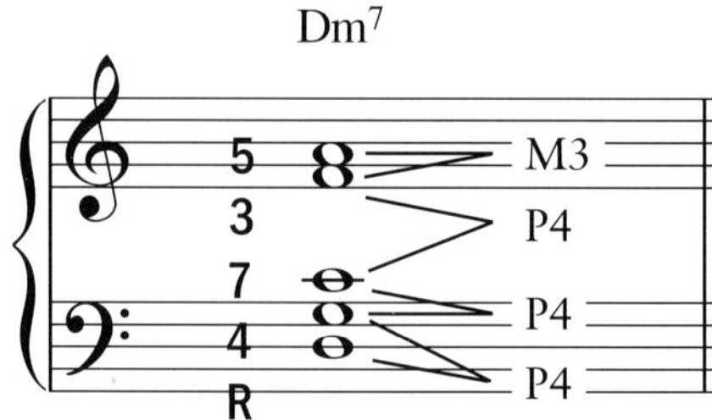

The fourth makes the voicing sound much more contemporary, and has been added by pianists since the innovations of Bill Evans, McCoy Tyner and Chick Corea in the 1960s. The **R47/35** voicing has come to be known as the 'So What' voicing, after it's use in the Miles Davis composition *So What* from his famous 1959 album 'Kind of Blue'. Notice how the two top notes are a major third apart, brightening up the sound of the fourths below.

Along with *Milestones* and *Maiden Voyage*, *So What* was one of the first modal tunes. It has only two chords, Dm7 and E♭m7, in AABA form:

The tune is based on a repeated 'call and response' motif between bass and piano, which plays the following chords every two bars in answer to the bass melody:

Fig 6.48: 'So What' chords – R47/35

You can think of these chords as Em7 and Dm7, both in **R47/35** format. Both are played during the Dm sections of the melody, since they both come from the Dorian mode on D (cf: *Drifting*, Vol. 1, p. 130, and Fig 3.68).

Assignments: So What

❶ **Transpose the 'So What' voicings** Move Fig 6.48 up a semitone to E♭m for the 'B' section. As before, you need to play the voicing on **R** and **2**, a tone apart – like E♭m7 and Fm7. Memorise the two shapes in both keys.

❷ **Play along** Get hold of a copy of 'Kind of Blue' and play along with Bill Evans' chords in the melody of *So What*, as in Fig 6.48. This rhythmic figure will also work fine as comping behind any of the solos. (Remember to come in on the third beat of every other bar.) Follow the AABA form throughout.

NB: The original release of 'Kind of Blue' plays about a quarter tone sharp due to a technical fault in the recording. To avoid intonation problems, try to obtain the more recent reissue (CK64935) in which this problem has been corrected.

'So What' voicings for other chords

One of the reasons the 'So What' voicing is so popular with today's pianists is its versatility. Not only can you play it for minor seventh or m11 chords, it can also stand in for many other chord types. Try playing the Dm voicing from Fig 6.47, holding it with the sustain pedal, and adding either a low B♭, an F, or an E♭ with the left hand:

Fig 6.49: The 'So What' voicing for major chords

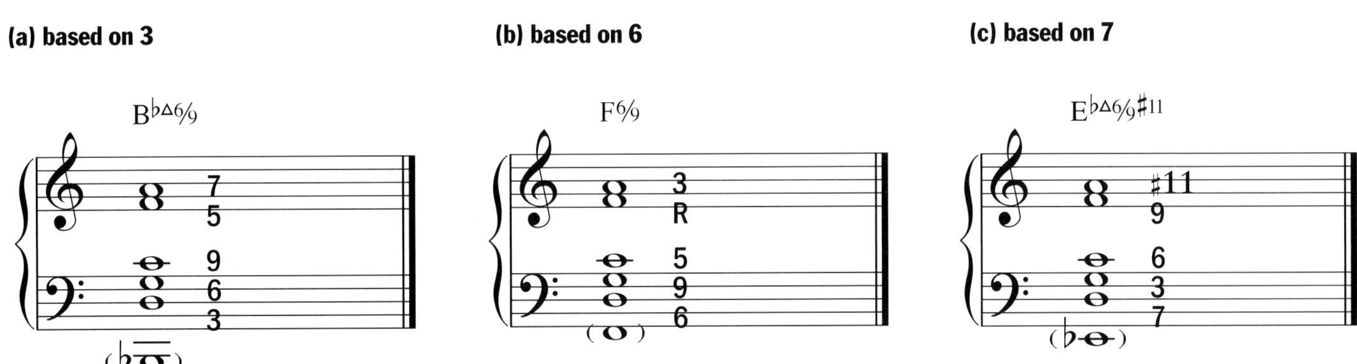

In Fig 6.49(a) you are hearing a B♭Δ chord with added **6** and **9**. In this context the 'So What' voicing is rootless (**369/57**). At (b) you're also hearing a 6/9 chord, but without the major seventh (**695/R3**). Voicing (c) should only be used if a major ♯**11** chord is indicated.

Finally, with G in the bass, you'll hear G9sus4, the voicing being **5R4/79**. To find this voicing for other sus 4 chords, just remember to base it on **5**. This is shown below, along with the voicing for C♯m7, following the chord sequence of *Reflections* and/or *Maiden Voyage:*

Fig 6.50: 'So What' voicings for sus 4 chords

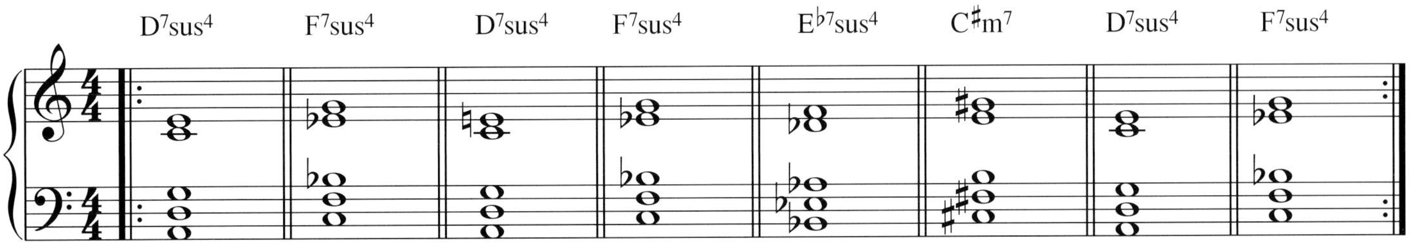

D7sus4 F7sus4 D7sus4 F7sus4 E♭7sus4 C♯m7 D7sus4 F7sus4

Assignments: 'So What' voicings

❶ ***Reflections/Maiden Voyage*** Memorise the voicings in Fig 6.50 and use them to comp with the CD behind *Reflections* (track 1). You could also get hold of the Herbie Hancock record and play along behind the melody of *Maiden Voyage.*

❷ **Develop your fluency** Practise the 'So What' voicing up and down in tones and semitones so your fingers get used to finding it in any key. Some people prefer to play two notes in the left hand instead of three – played like this, the right hand will feature a major triad in second inversion.

Create interest when comping in *Maiden Voyage* or *Reflections* by moving the basic voicings in Fig 6.50 briefly up a tone and back. You could also move each one up or down a semitone and back, taking them briefly outside the key.

5 **with bass & drums**

♩ = 200
(swing 8s)

Impressions

John Coltrane
arr. Tim Richards

The left-hand chord shapes here are typical of the quartal voicings pioneered by pianist McCoy Tyner whilst a member of the ground-breaking Coltrane quartet *c.*1960–65.

21

A3

25 Dm7

Ped.

29

to *Quartal Comping* (p. 45)

Checkpoint: Impressions

● **Chord sequence** The chords of this tune are exactly the same as for Miles Davis' *So What*. Head and solos both have a 32-bar AABA form, in which the bridge is a semitone higher (section 'B').

● **Left hand fifths** Every four or eight bars, **R5** of the chord is played deep down and held with the sustain pedal while the left hand travels up to explore various other shapes in the centre of the keyboard. Once you have played the first central chord, release the sustain pedal. This typical McCoy Tyner device anchors the piece harmonically as the central shapes are often rootless and might otherwise be ambiguous. See also *Drifting* (Vol. 1, p. 130).

● **Quartal voicings** The central voicings comprise perfect fourth chords in pairs, a tone apart. For the first eight bars, the fourths are based on **R** and **2** of the Dorian scale (bottom notes are D and E), like the left hand of the 'So What' voicing (Fig 6.48).

For the second eight bars, another pair of perfect fourth chords is used, based on **4** and **5** of the Dorian scale (bottom notes are G and A). These four Dm voicings are easy because they contain only white notes. They are shown below in the treble clef:

Fig 6.51: Perfect fourths based on R, 2, 4 and 5 of Dorian scale on D

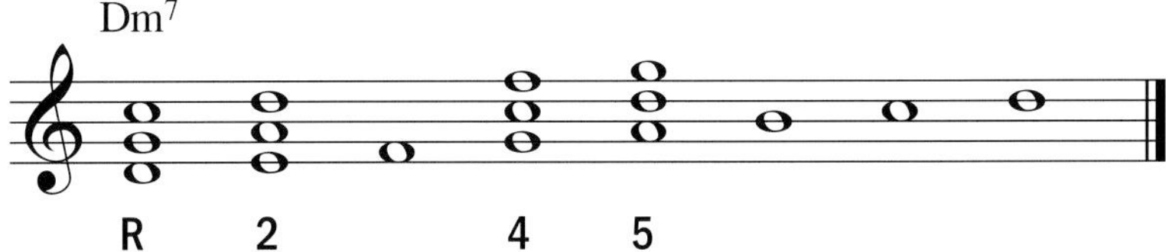

For the bridge, the chords must contain only notes of the Dorian scale on E♭. The same pairs of chords are used, based on **R** and **2**, and **4** and **5** of the scale:

McCoy Tyner, pianist with the legendary John Coltrane quartet from 1960 – 65, and one of the most influential stylists in jazz. His period with Coltrane saw him redefine the parameters of jazz piano, developing his own sound based on fourths, clusters and pentatonic runs, all played with great rhythmic drive. His style changed again in the 1970s, becoming relentlessly percussive. He remains an unmistakable voice.

Fig 6.52: Perfect fourths following Dorian scale on E♭

● **Right-hand melody** Coltrane recorded this tune several times with many variations. The basic melody is given in the first eight bars, but this is often varied and embellished, as in bar 9 onwards. Don't take the notation too literally – listen to the original recordings to get the feel.

For Assignments, see p. 46.

Pentatonic scales and fourths

When we played the major pentatonic scale in 'thirds' (Vol. 1, Figs 5.10 and 5.11), we discovered that this pattern produces four intervals of a perfect fourth, and only one other interval – a major third. Here is the same pattern played in double notes:

Fig 6.53: F major pentatonic played in double notes

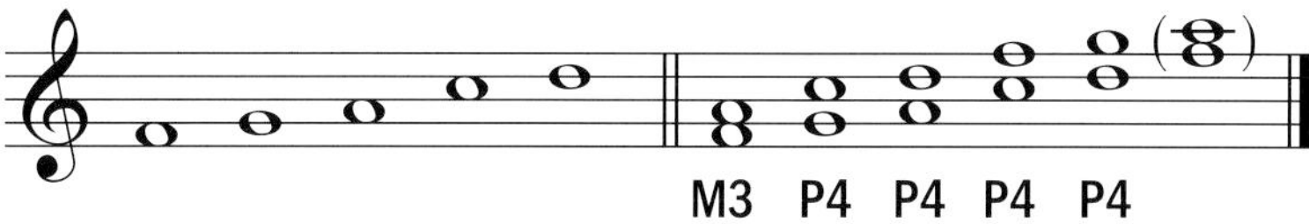

Another way to reveal the strong connection between the major pentatonic scale and the interval of a fourth is to rearrange the order of the notes. Try starting on the third (A) and playing alternate notes:

Fig 6.54: F major pentatonic played as ascending perfect fourths

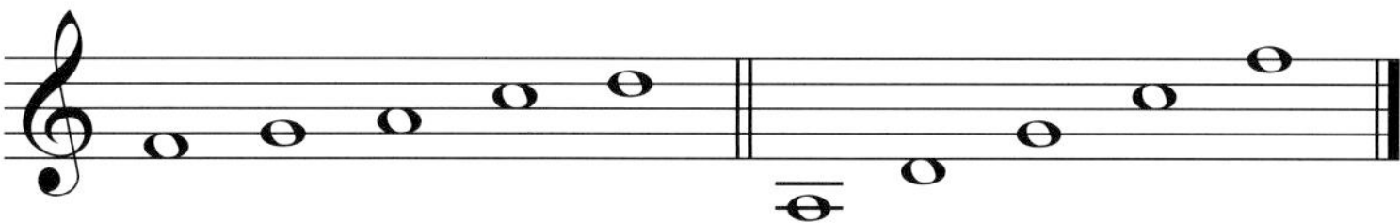

This is the central part of the ascending fourths series we derived by starting on the seventh note of the F major scale on p. 34 (Fig 6.41).

Octave displacement

Whether playing fourth lines derived from pentatonic or major scales, octave displacement is often useful to prevent them from ascending the keyboard too quickly. An ascending fourths series can be rearranged several ways to make it more convenient to play, without disturbing the order of the notes:

Fig 6.55

(a) Two-note groups down in tones

(b) Three-note groups up in minor thirds

For any given chord, you must start an ascending fourths series on the correct note of the scale, or it will go outside the scale. For major chords, start on **7** (as above). For minor chords, you could start on **2** or **6**:

Fig 6.56: Ascending fourth patterns for Fm7

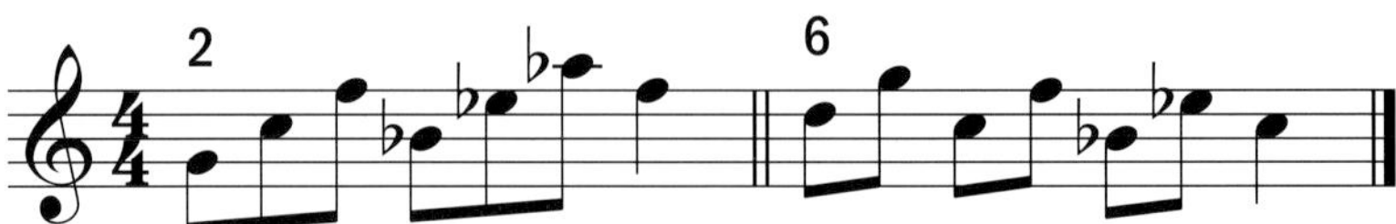

Advanced players deliberately use ascending fourth patterns to go outside the normal harmony, resolving back to notes of the scale at the end of the phrase:

Fig 6.57: Using fourths to go 'outside'

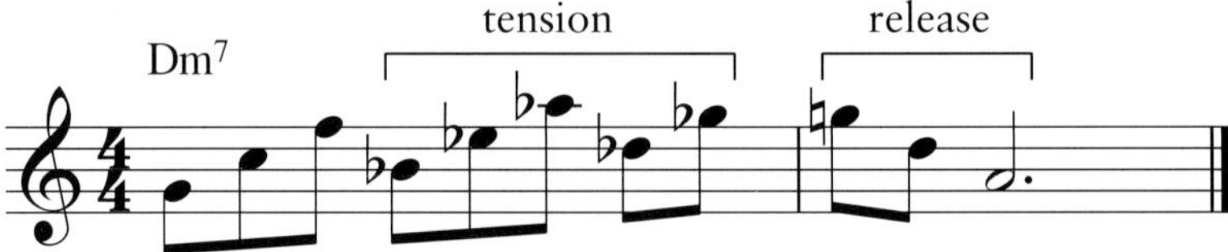

Walking bass lines for modal tunes

When playing a modal tune such as *Impressions* in the absence of a bass player, the ability to play a walking bass in the left hand is a very useful alternative to the chords given on the previous page. Because each chord lasts so long, you can't just keep repeating the same two- or four-bar bass line as it will be too monotonous.

Good bass players are able to keep walking on any chord for as long as necessary without seeming to repeat themselves. It may seem that the bass line is improvised, and it often is, but there are certain general guidelines which should be followed:

- Play quarter-notes only. Don't be tempted to play triplets, eighth-notes, or to syncopate. The interest in a walking bass line is as much in the choice of notes as the rhythm, which should be steady and even.
- Play *legato*. Work on your fingering if you have difficulty with this.
- Play descending lines as well as ascending ones. This will help to keep the bass line low down on the keyboard. If you find yourself playing in the octave below middle C, that's too high!
- Play lines based on scales (eg: **R232**) as well as chords (eg: **R353**).
- Always play the root of a chord on the first beat of the bar in which it first occurs.
- When the chord stays the same for several bars, repeat the root at least every two bars, on the first beat.
- Never play the root of a chord on the second or fourth beat of the bar in 4/4 time. This will make it sound like you have dropped a beat.
- Add chromatic notes (outside the scale) if necessary to ensure the roots occur where you want them to. These notes are boxed in Fig 6.58.
- Avoid big jumps, connecting chords smoothly. Approaching the root of a new chord from a semitone above or below is always effective.

Here are some two-bar bass lines for Dm7 that fulfill the above conditions:

Fig 6.58

(a) Notes of scale only (Dorian)

(b) Ascending scale with chromatic note

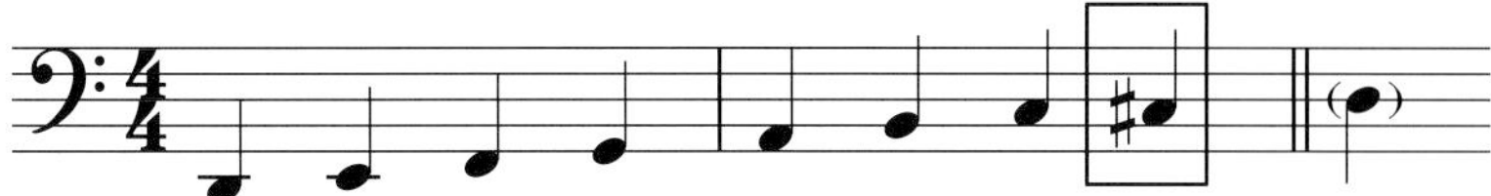

(c) Descending scale with chromatic note

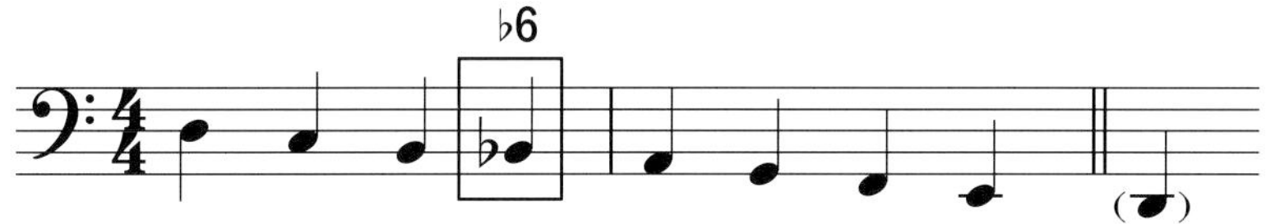

(d) Ascending triad with chromatic run-up from 6 (B)

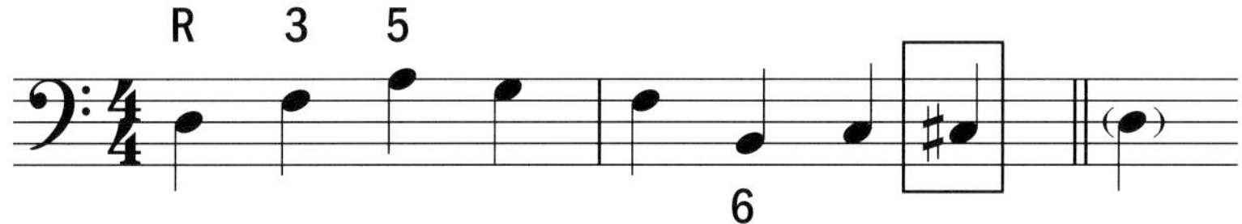

(e) Descending triad with extra note (E)

Memorise the above bass lines and use them to accompany the melody of *Impressions*, as an alternative to the left-hand chords. You could also try a simple improvisation in the right hand, as described in Assignment 5, p. 46.

Walking bass lines are an important left-hand style for any solo pianist, or for accompanying others when no bassist is present (with chords in the right hand). Other tunes in this book that feature walking bass lines in a non-modal context include:

Thirteenth Groove (p. 62), *Swinging Comping #1* and #2 (pp. 81 and 85), *Dominant Seventh Workout #2* (p. 94), *Bebop Bridge* (Fig. 7.71), *Caravan* (bridge, p. 145), *Blues Turnaround Workout* (p. 164), *Tension and Release Blues* #2 (p. 180) and *Minor Turnaround Workout – Comping* (p. 252).

See also Vol. 1, *Take the 'A' Train* (Figs 2.24–2.27), *Dominant Seventh Workout #1* (Fig 3.43) and *The Theme* (bridge, p. 122, and Fig 3.54).

Playing chords on every note of the Dorian mode

In *Impressions* we saw how it is possible for the left hand to play four different shapes as an expression of one chord symbol, by using the related scale of the chord as a source of notes for quartal voicings.

This innovation is often credited to Miles Davis who started to think in terms of scales as a means of generating chords. The resulting modal style of jazz was typified by long periods (4–16 bars) on the same chord, and by tunes with far fewer chords than the usual jazz or bebop standards prevalent at that time.

With so long on one chord, the musicians' inventiveness is stretched to the limit. This applies not only to the soloist, but also to the accompanist, who must provide an interesting chordal backing without seeming to repeat the same voicings over and over.

The solution is to experiment with as many shapes as possible for the chord in question. Pianists like Bill Evans and McCoy Tyner started to play quartal shapes in the left hand on *every* note of the Dorian mode:

Fig 6.59: Quartal shapes on every note of the Dorian scale on D

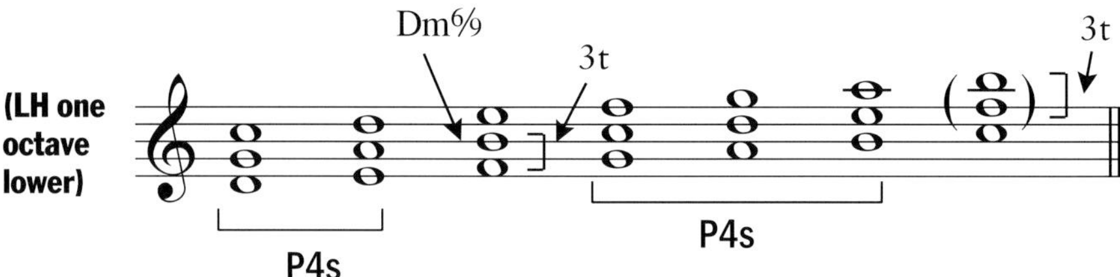

In order not to go outside the mode, the third shape above is different from the others: it has an augmented fourth (tritone) as the bottom interval (F – B) rather than a perfect fourth like the others. You may recognise this **369** shape as a rootless Dm 6/9 chord (see Vol. 1, Fig 5.44).

The last voicing (in brackets) has an augmented fourth on top, and is used less often as it sounds quite discordant.

When comping (accompanying a soloist), it is useful to be able to play two-handed voicings, especially when playing with a bass player. The right hand can add two notes to create five-note voicings over the whole scale, using only notes from the Dorian mode. The added notes can be either a third or a perfect fourth apart – experiment to find out which sound best. Here are some possibilities:

Fig 6.60: Two-handed chords following the Dorian scale on D

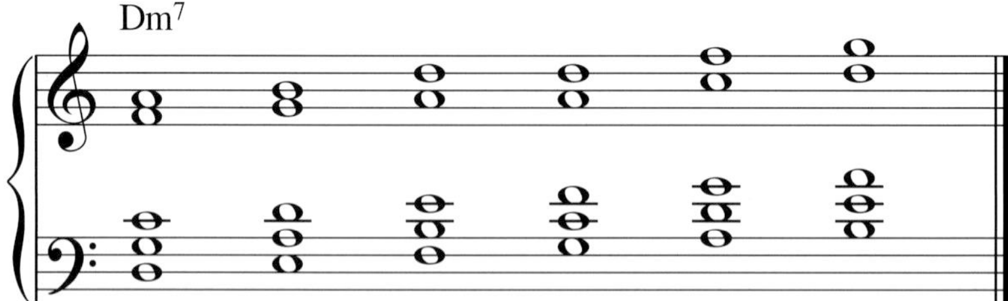

The first two shapes are the 'So What' voicings, which we have now extended over the whole scale. Any of these shapes can be considered as Dm7!

Quartal Comping opposite explores these two-handed shapes for Dm7 and E♭m7 over the same 32-bar chord sequence as *Impressions/So What*, and follows on from the *Impressions* melody on the CD. We'll also see how another important way to create interest is to take things briefly outside the harmony and back again.

6 with bass & drums

♩ = 200

(swing 8s)

Quartal Comping

Tim Richards

These two-handed chords are played on the CD after the *Impressions* melody (track 5), without a break, and follow the same AABA structure and chord sequence. You could use them behind someone else's improvised solo.

to *First Impression* (p. 50)

Checkpoint: Quartal Comping

● **Dorian modes** All the voicings use notes taken from the Dorian mode on D (or E♭ in the bridge). The only exceptions are the chords in boxes (see below). Refresh your memory of the two Dorian modes before attempting the piece:

Fig 6.61: Dorian scales

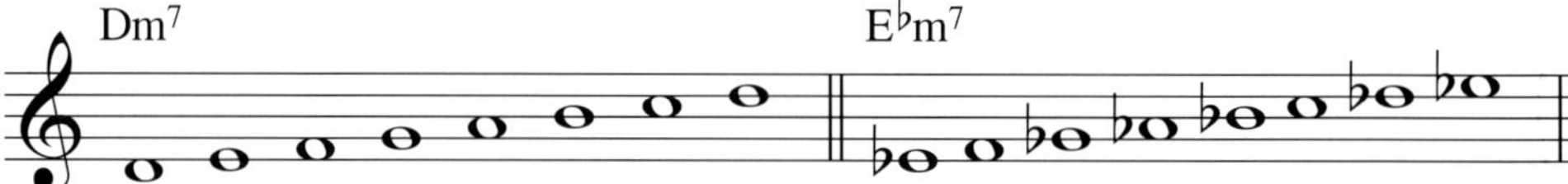

● **Taking it out** The chords in the boxes marked 'outside' are formed by moving the previous voicings up a semitone (ie: going outside the mode). This technique is common in modal playing, and creates interest in passages of static harmony – as long as you resolve back again. The 'outside' chords clash with the bass line, creating tension, which is then released when you go back to the mode.

In bars 3 and 22, the chord moves up a semitone for just half a bar before returning. Here is the left-hand part by itself with all the chords on the beat:

Fig 6.62: Bars 3–4

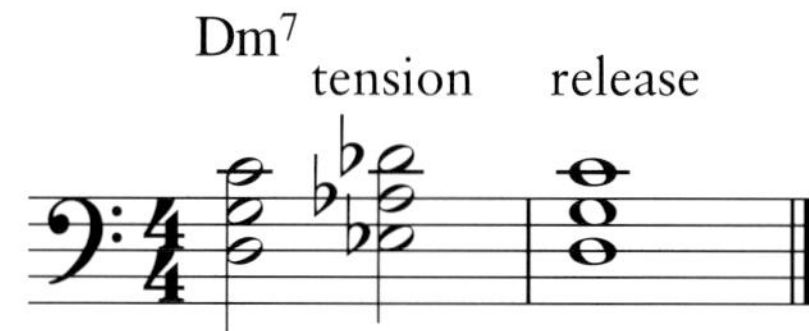

In 'A3', this concept is taken a stage further, with two chords outside the mode for a whole bar before returning. Here is the left-hand part with all the chords on the beat:

Fig 6.63: Bars 25–27

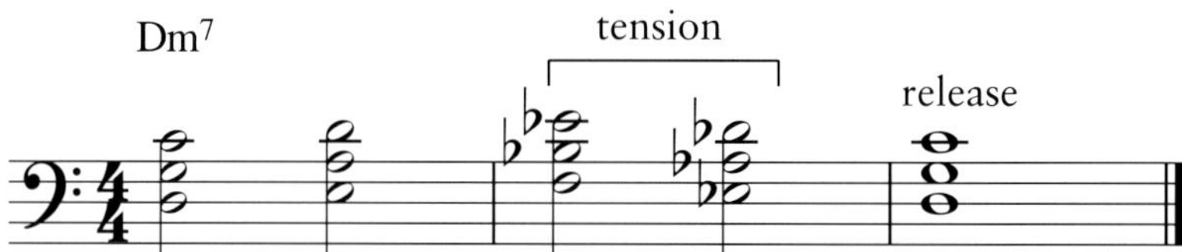

In practice, any of these chords can be 'pushed' (played on '2 and' or '4 and').

Assignments and Improvisation Tips: Impressions

❶ **Play along** Memorise the first eight bars of the right-hand melody (p. 38) and play it with the CD (track 5), transposing it up a semitone for the bridge. Then memorise the left-hand chords and practise them in the same way. Finally try the hands together, playing along with bass and drums only (left channel), and exploring the melodic variations given. Listen to the Coltrane version for inspiration!

❷ **Right-hand improvisation** Base this on the Dorian scales (Fig 6.61), exploring scale patterns (Vol. 1, pp. 98–99), with track 5 as a backing again – no left hand yet. With modal tunes, it is a challenge keeping to the form without getting lost, especially when your solo stretches over several 32-bar choruses. Try to phrase in two- and four-bar chunks to help you keep track, so that you know when to go to the bridge. Don't overplay, but leave gaps during which you can listen to the bass line to check where you are (the bass generally plays the root every two bars).

❸ **Add left-hand chords** Repeat your improvisation with the left-hand chords given on p. 38. See pp. 47–9 for more improvisation ideas, and *First Impression* (p. 50) for an example.

❹ ***Quartal Comping*** Play these two-handed voicings over the backing (track 6, bass and drums only). You can practise them over three choruses if you start with track 5, which also gives you a count-in. Memorise the voicings, and vary their order, rhythm and articulation when you repeat the sequence. Invite a friend to play a solo on top!

❺ **Walking bass** Listen to the bass line on the left channel of the CD (tracks 5–6–7), and note how it features some of the two-bar patterns suggested on p. 43. Memorise these and practise accompanying a friend by playing a bass line under his/her solo. When you feel fluent with the bass line, try adding a solo of your own in the right hand, keeping it very simple at first so as not to disrupt the left-hand flow.

Modal improvisation

Minor seventh chords are especially suitable for modal treatment, because any note of the Dorian scale sounds ok in the right hand over a left-hand chord. This is not true of major or dominant chords, where the fourth has to be treated with care and is sometimes referred to as an 'avoid' note.

The least successful melody note for Dm7 is the sixth (B). However in a modal situation this note can still work if you choose your left-hand chord shape wisely:

Fig 6.64: Emphasising the sixth with quartal left-hand shapes

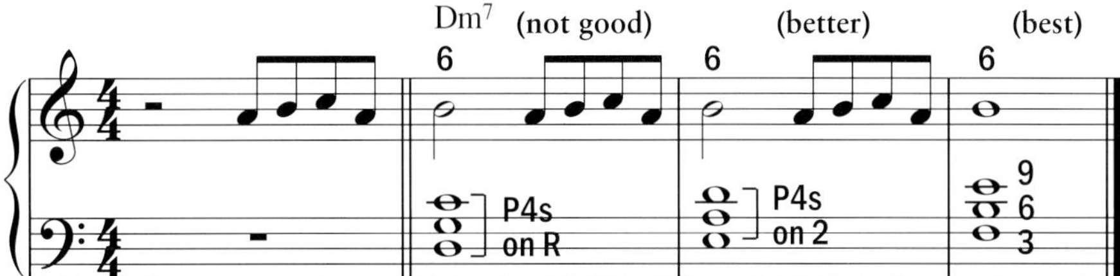

When improvising over long stretches on the same chord, the left hand will rarely stay on just one shape. Try alternating two shapes while the right hand plays a scale or scale pattern (see Assignment 3 opposite):

Fig 6.65: Scale pattern with quartal left hand built on 4 and 5

Retaining the two-bar rhythm in the left hand will help you keep track of the bars and make you less likely to lose the form. Here is another suggestion that includes the shape based on the third of the chord:

Fig 6.66: Using a 369 shape in the left hand

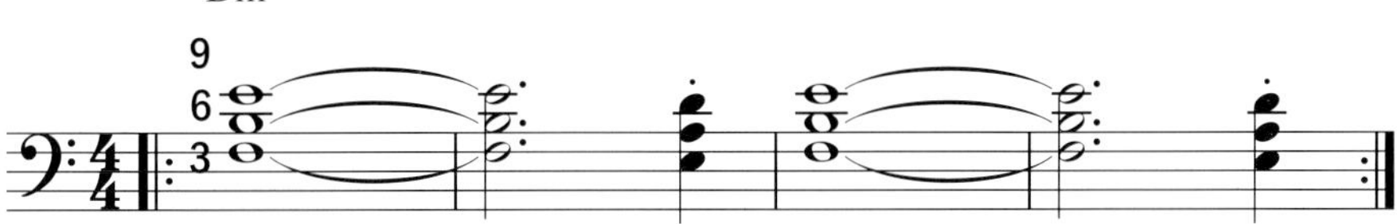

Both the above examples illustrate the importance of varying the left-hand articulation. Here they tend to alternate short (*staccato*) and long (held) chords.

As well as Dorian scales, the right hand could also use:

- The minor pentatonic scale (miss out **2** and **6** from the Dorian mode)
- The flat 3 pentatonic scale (miss out **4** and **7** from the Dorian mode)

You could also play any arpeggio or broken chord formed of notes from the mode. The most successful ones are based on **R**, **3**, **5** or **7**:

- Dm7 – try arpeggios of Dm7, FΔ, Am7 or CΔ
- E♭m7 – try arpeggios of E♭m7, G♭Δ, B♭m7, D♭Δ

Don't restrict yourself to playing these in root position, experiment with other inversions. The third inversion is particularly effective:

Fig 6.67: CΔ and FΔ arpeggios over Dm7

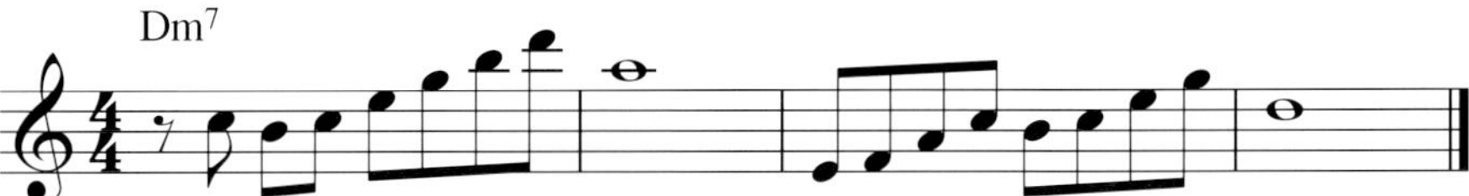

Going outside

In *Quartal Comping* we created tension and release by moving the chords temporarily out of the key and back again. This is also an important technique when improvising a solo, and is demonstrated overleaf by *First Impression*. 'Outside' passages can occur in either hand, in several ways:

- Both hands move out of the key together (as in *Quartal Comping*)
- Left hand moves out, right hand stays in the key
- Right hand moves out, left hand stays in the key

Try playing patterns using the Dorian mode or minor pentatonic scale, over a left-hand chord that goes up a semitone and back:

Fig 6.68: Taking it out in the left hand only

An easy way to take a right-hand line outside is to move a group of two or four notes up or down by a semitone. This is known as 'side-slipping':

Fig 6.69

(a) Side-slipping with two notes

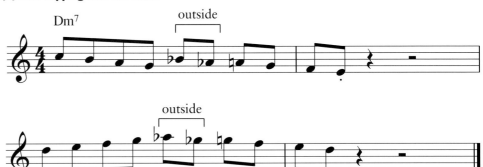

(b) Side-slipping with four notes

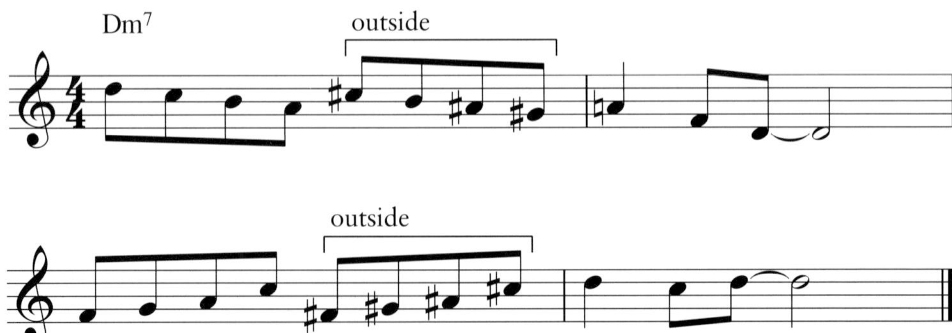

The notes that are moved can be part of a scale, arpeggio, pentatonic, or just a motif that you have previously established in the key. Advanced players sometimes move a motif up or down in minor thirds, another effective way of going outside, but this requires practise as it takes longer for the line to resolve back:

Fig 6.70

(a) Moving a four-note motif up in minor thirds

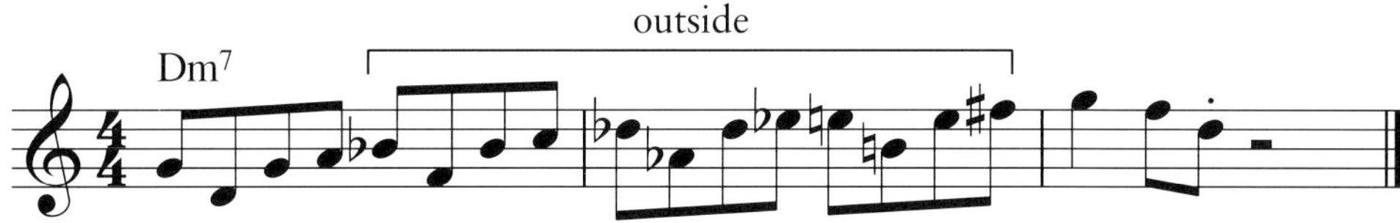

(b) Moving a four-note motif down in minor thirds

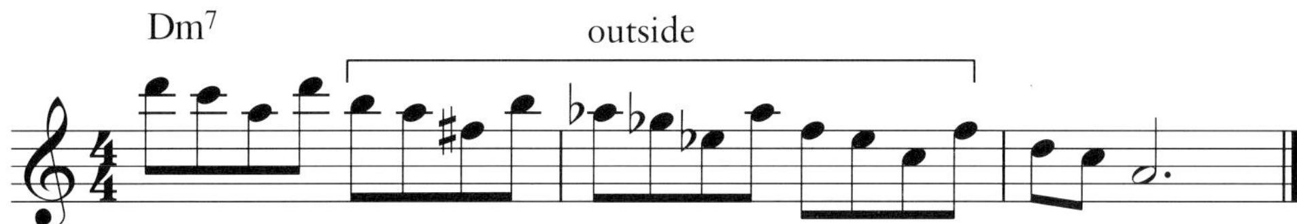

You can also move motifs up or down in tones, major thirds, flattened fifths, etc, all of which will eventually come back to the original key. With four-note groups, strive to make your line resolve back to the key on the first beat of the bar, as in the examples above. Practise the fingering to make these ideas flow convincingly.

7 with bass & drums

♩ = 200

(swing 8s)

First Impression

Tim Richards

This solo follows *Quartal Comping* without a break on the CD and is over the same chords as *Impressions*. All the notes are from the Dorian scale on D or E♭, apart from the 'outside' notes or chords in boxes.

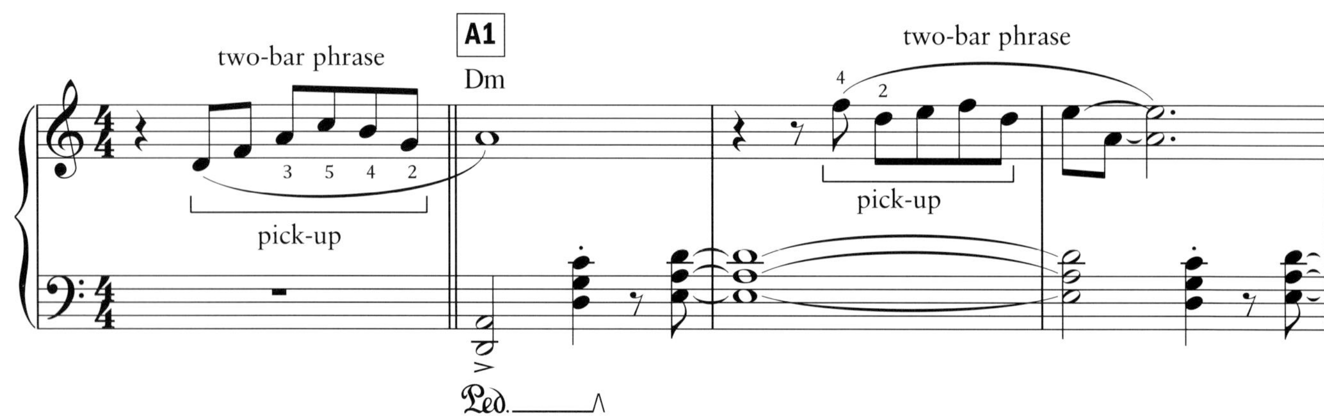

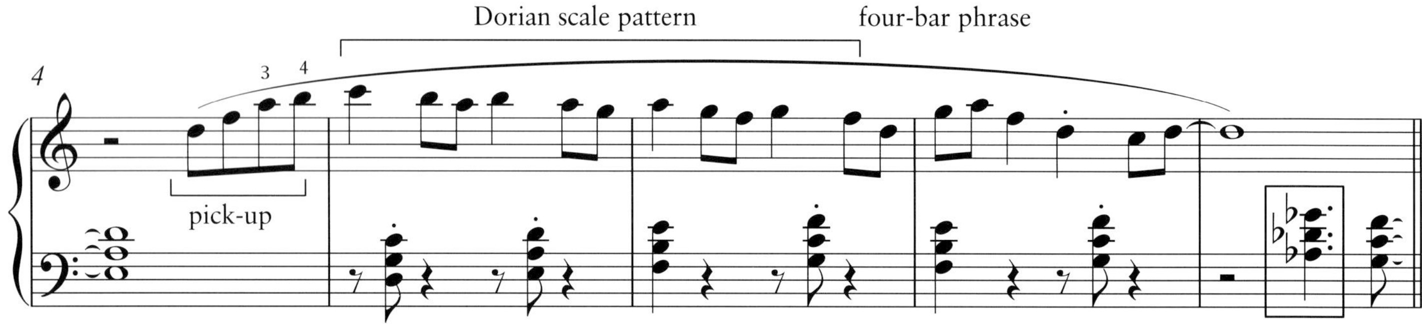

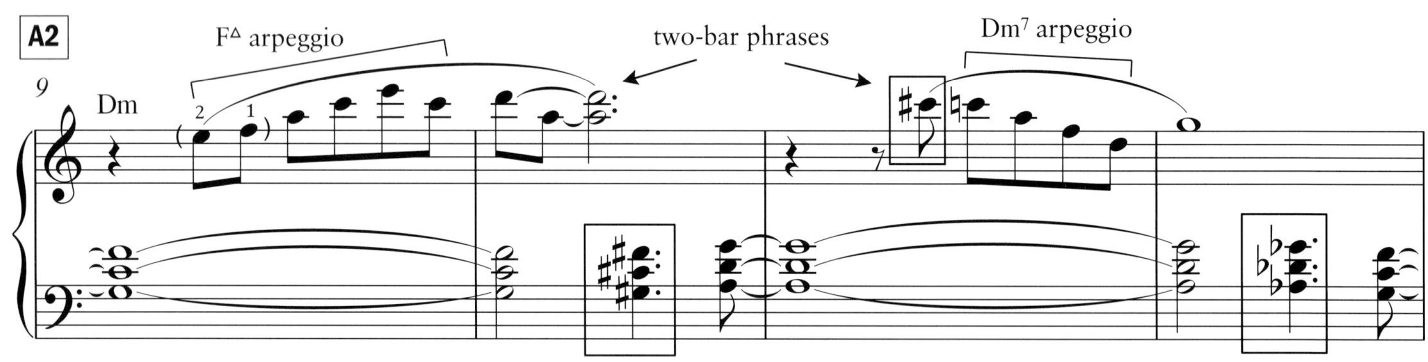

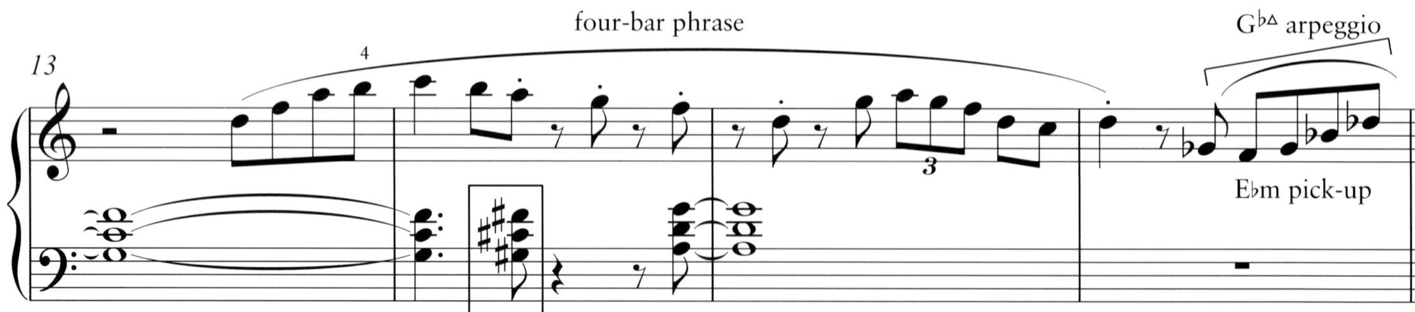

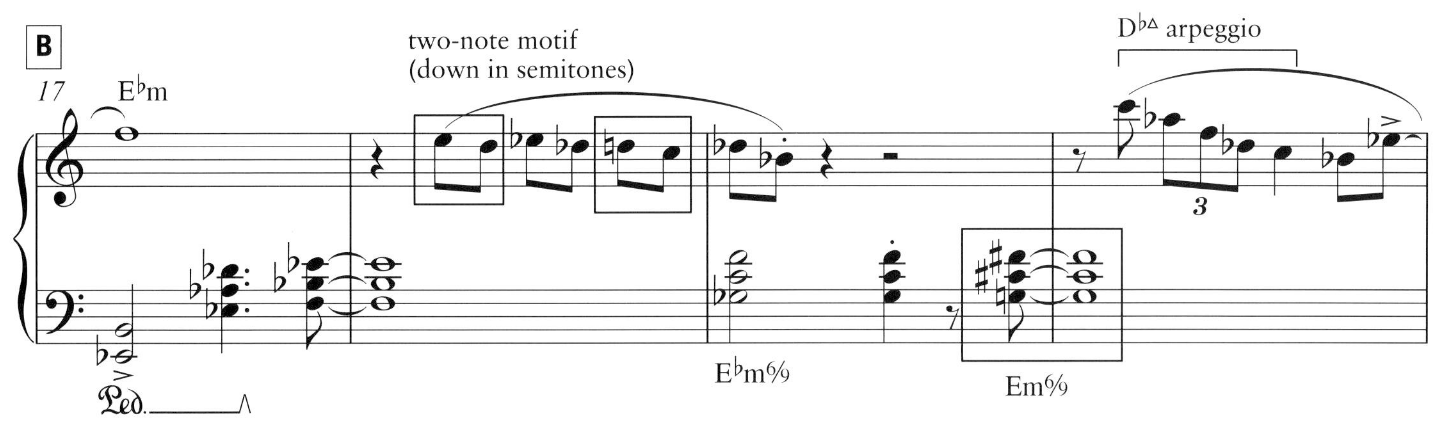

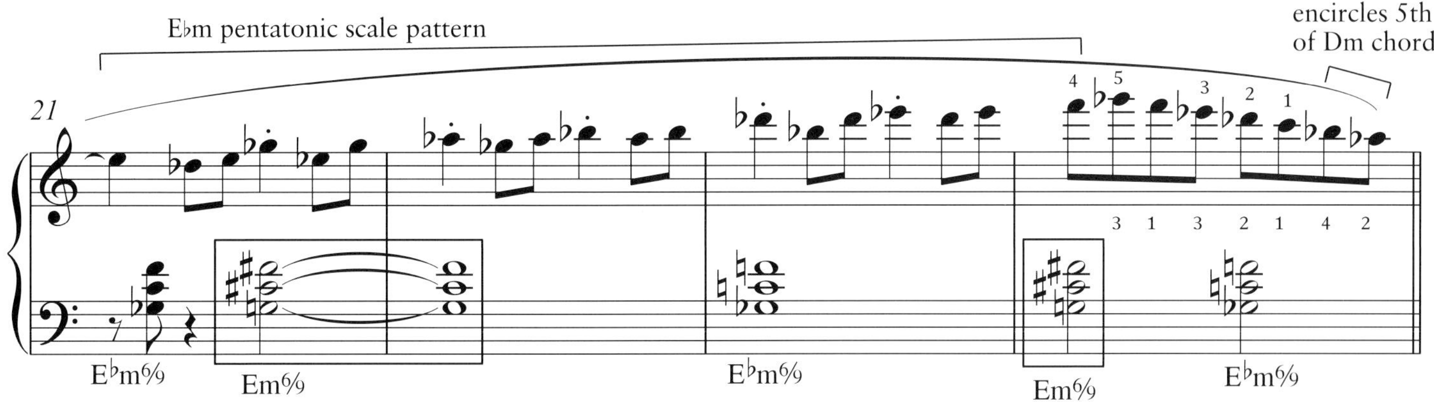

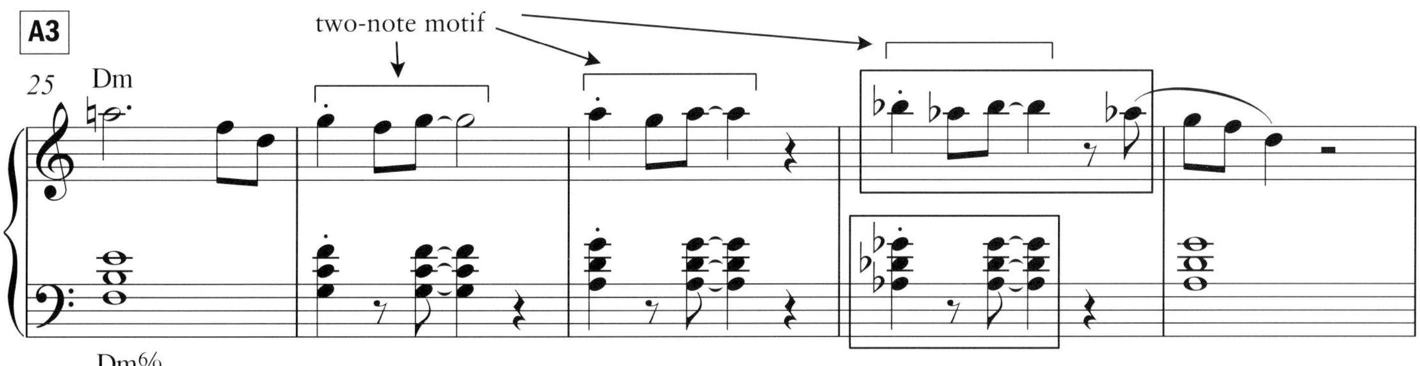

Repeat ad lib.
or play melody
(p. 38)

8 **with bass & drums**

Dustbiter

Tim Richards

♩ = 160
(swing 8s)

Quartal voicings are used throughout this tune, which combines a minor blues tonality with some post-bop harmonies implying distant keys. A version can be heard on the 'Best of Spirit Level' CD (33Jazz051).

D.C. to Intro to finish

Checkpoint: Dustbiter

● **Two-handed fourths** The intro sets up a C minor groove using a new technique – two pairs of notes, a fourth in each hand. Take care to use the fingering suggested which permits rapid movement between adjacent shapes without jumping. Here's an overview of the different configurations used:

Fig 6.71: Quartal shapes with two notes in each hand

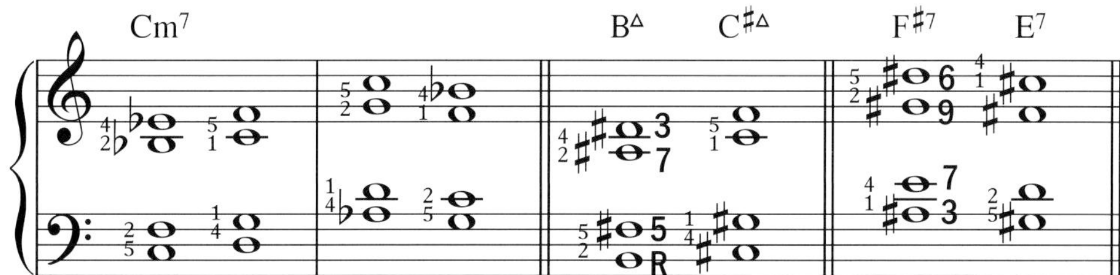

The rootless voicings for F♯7 and E7 have **3** and **7** in the left hand (tritones).

We'll be revisiting this important comping style more comprehensively in *Tune Up* (see Figs 9.16–9.18), *Rhythm Changes Comping #1* and *#2* (pp. 192 and 196) and *Blues in Fourths* (p. 266).

● **Blues form** The 24-bar form is like a long meter 12-bar blues (eight bars on the **I** chord instead of four). Instead of the expected chords in the last eight bars, however, there is a complete departure from the key of C minor (bar 19 onwards).

● **Minor chords up and down in tones** Bars 17–18 feature minor sevenths moving down in tones: Cm7 – B♭m7 – A♭m7, finishing with a semitone down to Gm7. This is not so surprising, but four bars later they are echoed by minor chords moving up in tones: Em7 – F♯m7 – A♭m7 – B♭m7. These chords have a definite postbop flavour implying two unrelated keys: Em7 – F♯m are **II** and **III** in the key of D major, A♭m7 – B♭m7 are **II** and **III** in the key of G♭major.

● **Postbop harmonies** Following on from these parallel minor chords, two sets of chords a tone apart provide another contrast with the established key – BΔ/C♯Δ and F♯7/E7. These chords are about as far as you can get from C minor!

The function of all these 'foreign' chords is to introduce an element of surprise into the last eight bars of the tune, contrasting with the rather static and predictable harmonies that precede them. Taking a wider view, they are just another manifestation of tension and release, on the largest time scale we've seen so far.

Assignments and Improvisation Tips: Dustbiter

❶ **Two notes in each hand** Practise the chord pairs in Fig 6.71 with the fingering shown in the melody, until you can alternate between chords quickly and cleanly without using the same finger on adjacent notes.

❷ **Quartal left hand** Practise the left-hand accompaniment in bars 1–4 (Cm7) and 9–12 (Fm7) by itself, working on your sustain pedal technique until there are no gaps between the low **R5** and the higher quartal chords. Memorise the shapes.

❸ **Head** Work on the head in both hands, four or eight bars at a time until you have no problems with any of the co-ordination. Bars 17–24 will probably require some extra attention.

❹ **Postbop improvisation** Try soloing round the form of the tune, playing over a similar left-hand accompaniment to the written one. In the right hand, try Dorian or minor pentatonic scales in the Cm and Fm sections, but during the last eight bars play arpeggio or broken chord patterns following the chords in Fig 6.72 – you cannot play a single scale across these changes! I would recommend simplifying the last eight bars as follows:

Fig 6.72: Left hand for bars 17–24

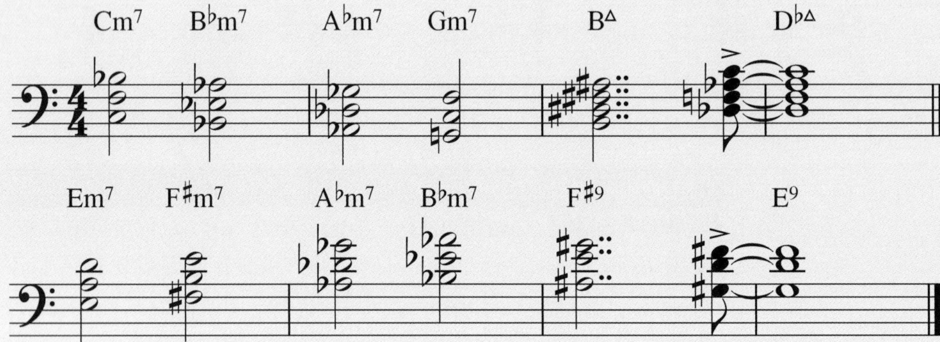

❺ **Play along** Although there is only one chorus on track 8 (the head), use it to practise the melody and/or solo, with bass and drums only.

❻ **Blues improvisation** For an easier solo, drop the chords in the last eight bars and substitute regular Cm blues changes instead – but don't expect to use track 8 as a backing! The 24-bar solo sequence would be:

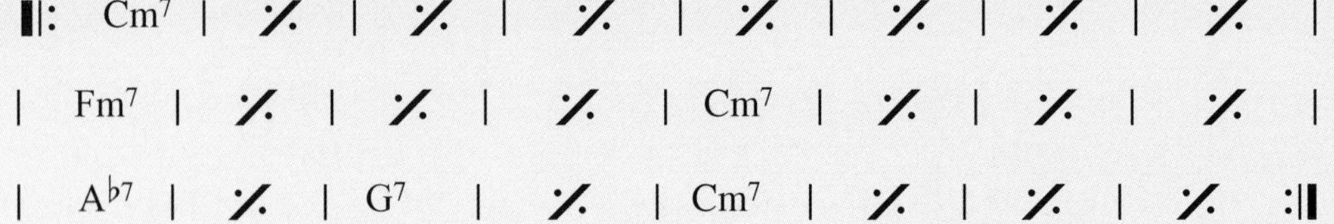

After your solo, return to the head to finish (play the intro first as a 'tag' if you wish). Combining a simple solo sequence with a more complex head is known as a 'head arrangement'.

For more on blues, see , pp. 264–72, 'Minor Blues', *Blues in Fourths*, and *Twelve by Three,* and IBP (pp. 214–16) *Four Finger Blues* and *C Jam Blues.*

Quartal II – V – I

Some players like to apply quartal voicings to 'normal' harmonic situations like **II – V – I**, introducing a contemporary slant to familiar chordal material. If attempting this it will help to remember the following:

Fig 6.73

(a) For minor sevenths build perfect fourths on R, 4 or 5

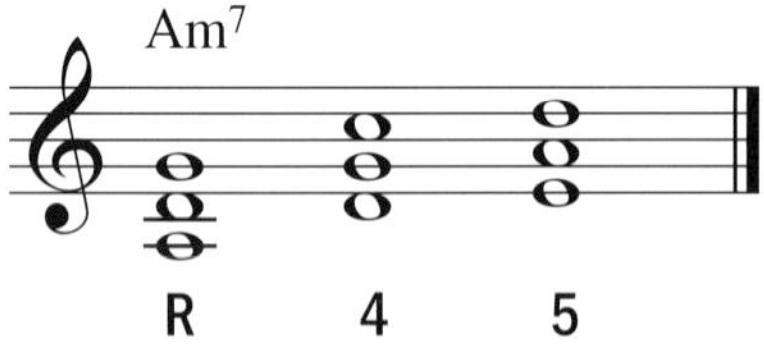

(b) For major sevenths or 6/9 chords build perfect fourths on 3, 6 or 7

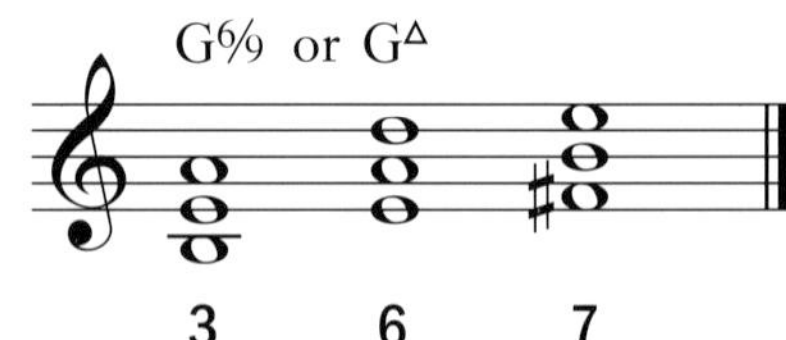

Dominant seventh chords cannot easily be voiced using perfect fourths, since they always contain a tritone interval (augmented fourth) between **3** and **7**. Nevertheless it is possible to play postbop-style **II – V – I**s using only perfect fourths by choosing shapes that go up in semitones, as in the following examples:

Fig 6.74: Quartal II – V – I (shapes go up in semitones)

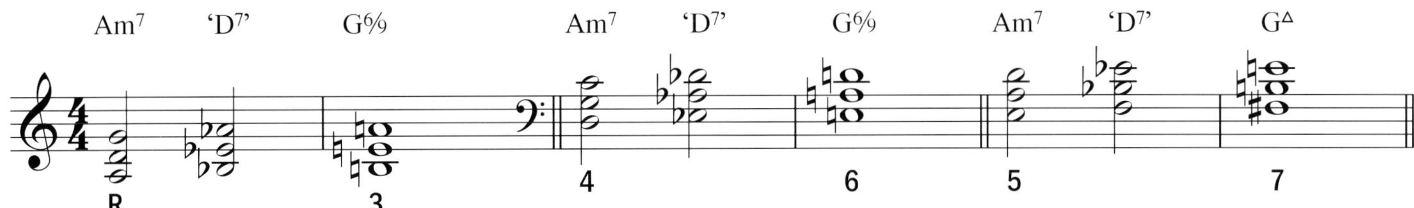

The middle shapes are not strictly D7 at all – they are just shapes that conveniently connect Am7 with GΔ. Any notes outside of D7 introduce tension which is released when you go to the 'correct' shape for the **I** chord. Don't use voicings like this in a traditional or mainstream situation, or when accompanying singers!

● **Quartal dominant chords** Including the augmented fourth alongside the perfect fourth in our three-note voicings gives us two other options for quartal dominant shapes:

Fig 6.75: Quartal shapes containing a tritone (#4)

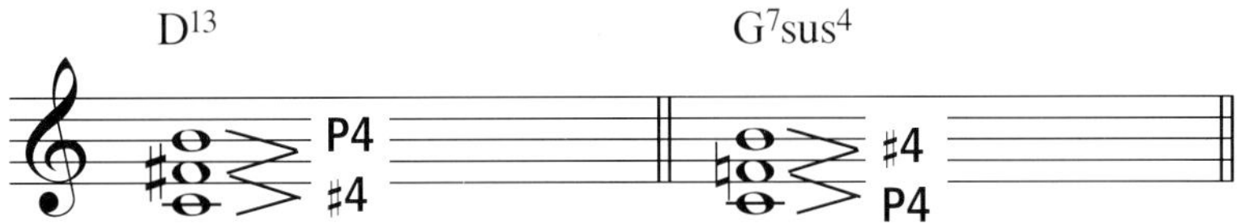

The first of these is by far the most commonly used, and can be interpreted as **736** of D7 – try playing a D root low down in the left hand. Including **6** in a dominant chord turns it into a 'thirteenth' – the subject of the next chapter.

The second shape can be interpreted as **473** of G7sus4. Normally one wouldn't include the third in a sus 4 chord, but this is one way it can be done – as far away from the fourth as possible, usually at the top of the voicing.

Assignments: Quartal II – V – I

❶ **Quartal II – V – I chords** Play the different versions in Fig 6.74 in the right hand, with low roots in the left hand to hear the true sound of the chords.

❷ **Add an improvisation** Now play the shapes in the left hand and add a right-hand improvisation. Starting a line on Am7 and finishing in the GΔ bar, try to match the left-hand chord when playing over the 'D7' part. That way both hands will go outside together and give a convincing impression of tension and resolution. If you wish, try this over a long **II – V – I** instead, giving you a whole bar on each chord.

❸ **Pick a tune** Incorporate some of these techniques into a tune which contains some **II – V – I**s, replacing the given left hand with the quartal shapes above. This is more likely to work in the improvisation than during the melody, which may clash during the **V** chord. Depending on the key, some of the shapes in Fig 6.74 may be too high up the keyboard – remember you can invert them as follows:

Fig 6.76: Inverted perfect fourth shapes (up in semitones)

The best tunes to choose are those which can be adapted effectively to a postbop flavour, eg: *Tune Up* (p. 183), *On Green Dolphin Street* (p. 206) or *Softly as in a Morning Sunrise* (p. 236), rather than ballads like *Misty* or *In a Sentimental Mood*.

Chapter Six: Final Checkpoint

In this chapter you have learnt several new types of chord: elevenths, sharp elevenths and suspended fourths. We've also spent quite a bit of time looking at a new way of voicing chords using perfect fourths, and the implications of this on the right-hand line.

● **Quartal harmony** As we've seen, minor chords lend themselves particularly well to voicing in fourths, but you should be able to find a set of fourths that works for most other types of chord too – it's a question of starting in the right place. Here are some possibilities:

Fig 6.77: Starting points for building perfect fourths

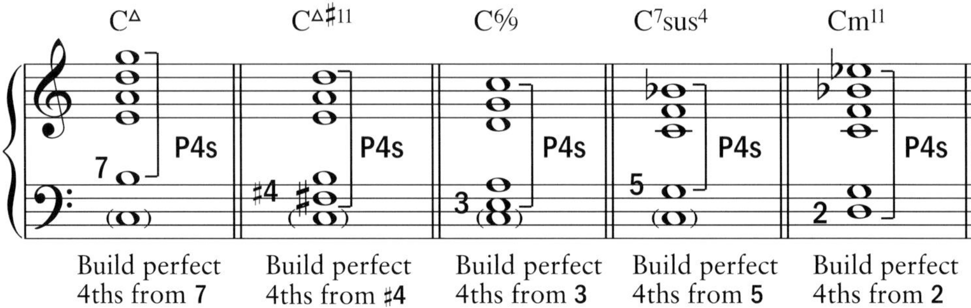

If we include a tritone (augmented fourth) as the bottom interval, building perfect fourths above that, even more chords can be included:

Fig 6.78: Perfect fourths with tritones (3t) on the bottom

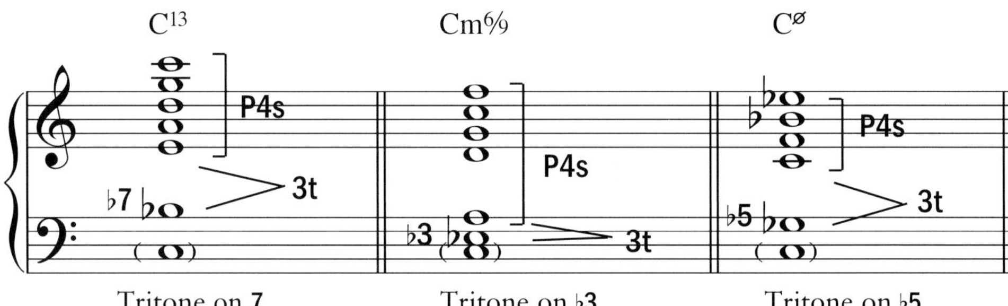

Use these sets of fourths to derive two-handed voicings, playing two or three notes in each hand. To help you remember them, think of the scale of each chord. Also pick out three-note quartal shapes to use as left-hand voicings – as we saw in *Impressions* (p. 38) these shapes often work well in pairs, a tone apart:

Fig 6.79: Quartal shapes following the scale of each chord

As well as playing these shapes when comping, arpeggiating them to create patterns in the right hand when improvising will bring a postbop flavour to your solos.

Chapter Seven
Thirteenth chords

The thirteenth is an extension generally added to dominant seventh chords, which will greatly enrich your sound when playing in a blues tonality or over II – V sequences.

The thirteenth is the same note as the sixth of the major scale (see Vol. 1, Fig 5.1).

9 – same note as **2**   **11** – same note as **4**   **13** – same note as **6**

The term 'thirteenth' is usually reserved for a dominant chord with an added sixth. When sixths are added to major or minor ninth chords the resulting chords are called 6/9 and m6/9, as we saw in Vol. 1, Figs 5.12 and 5.44.

A full thirteenth chord can also include **9** and **11** and could be played thus:

Fig 7.1: Dominant thirteenths

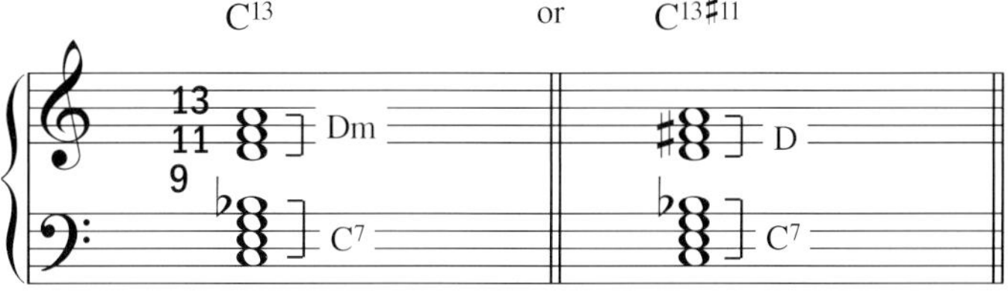

The symbol C13 (pronounced 'C thirteen') really means 'C7 with an added sixth', and always implies a ♭**7**, which must not be omitted (**9** and **11** are optional). The eleventh, when present, is often raised as in the second example above, to avoid clashing with the third of the chord. Note how **9**, **11** and **13** form a minor or major triad based on the second note of the scale.

An ordinary dominant seventh chord can be converted to a thirteenth by moving the fifth of the voicing up a tone, turning it into a sixth:

Fig 7.2: Replacing 5 with 6

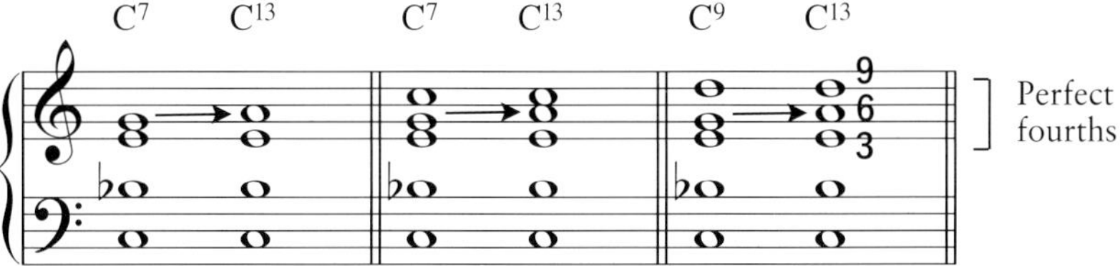

The voicings above, with **R7** shells in the left hand, are more practical than the rather dense seven-note voicings shown in Fig 7.1. The lack of a fifth in the chords is not a problem – in fact, jazz musicians often omit it in a dominant chord, playing the sixth in preference because of the way it colours the sound.

In preparation for *The Message* overleaf, transpose the second and third C13 voicings in Fig 7.2 to the following keys, and memorise them:

A♭13 – A13 – B♭13 – B13 – D♭13 – E♭13 – F13 – G♭13 – G13

9 with bass & drums

♩ = 184 (swing 8s)

The Message

Tim Richards

Two-handed thirteenth chords are used here in 'call and response' with the right-hand melody, recalling gospel-influenced numbers like Bobby Timmons' *Moanin'* or Horace Silver's *Filthy McNasty*.

Checkpoint: The Message

● **AAB form** The two 'A' sections add up to 16 bars. This is the same length as the 'B' section, which includes a truncated version of the opening melody in the last four bars.

● **Two-handed shapes** Two thirteenth voicings are used (see Fig 7.2):

'A' section and coda – **R7/36R**

'B' section (from bar 16) – **R7/369**

The second voicing has perfect fourths in the right hand, based on the third of each chord – **369**.

● **Solo section** This has a similar form and chords to the melody, although it is 4 bars shorter, and some of the passing chords have been omitted. The left-hand chords suggested are three-note rootless thirteenth shapes – see Fig 7.3 overleaf for their formation. Notice that interest is created by moving the C13 shape down a semitone (to B13) and back every two bars. The F13 shape goes up a semitone (to G♭13) and back.

Gene Harris recorded prolifically for the Blue Note label in the 1950s and 60s with his popular trio 'The Three Sounds'. After his comeback in the mid-80s he continued to perform his own brand of dynamic, hard-swinging jazz, combining a strong blues and funk influence with mainstream and bebop stylings.

● **Pentatonic scales** The three scales suggested for the 'A' sections of the solo are interchangeable. All three crop up in the first eight bars of the melody – see if you can pinpoint them. The minor third in the first two scales adds colour to the C13, establishing a bluesy tonality which is often appropriate when a dominant seventh chord is found as the tonic.

● **Breaks** The solo begins in bar 32 of the head when the bass and drums drop out for you to play the blues scale pick-up. Only one chorus solo is played on the CD, but in real life you'd play a similar pick-up in bar 28 of the solo to launch you into another chorus. Although the chord here is D♭13, a C blues scale phrase will sound best, anticipating the chord that follows (C13).

Assignments and Improvisation Tips: The Message

❶ **Thirteenth voicings** You'll need to practise the two-handed shapes until you can find them quickly enough. To start with, get used to playing left-hand **R7** shells up and down in semitones, without the right-hand part. Try this without looking!

Then practise right-hand perfect fourth shapes (eg: ADG) in the same way, without the left-hand shells, before putting the hands together and playing the complete **R7/369** voicings up and down in semitones.

❷ **Duet** Ask a friend to play the melody on another instrument (or on your piano, an octave higher than written), whilst you play the two-handed chords only. Make sure you both tap your feet to the same pulse throughout.

❸ **Improvise** Play along in the right hand with the CD (track 9, bass and drums only) using the scales suggested. Although the 28-bar solo sequence only occurs once on the CD, you'd normally repeat the AAB form as many times as you wish.

❹ **Add left-hand chords** Under your right-hand improvisation play the rootless thirteenth shapes suggested, in various rhythms. See below for their formation.

Playing thirteenth chords in one hand

Instead of playing thirteenths as two-handed voicings, jazz pianists often omit some of the notes (eg: **R** and **5**), creating rootless voicings. Here is an easy way to form a classic three-note thirteenth shape from a root position triad:

- Move the root down to become ♭**7**
- Move the fifth up to become **6**

Fig 7.3: Formation of 736 thirteenth voicing from major triad

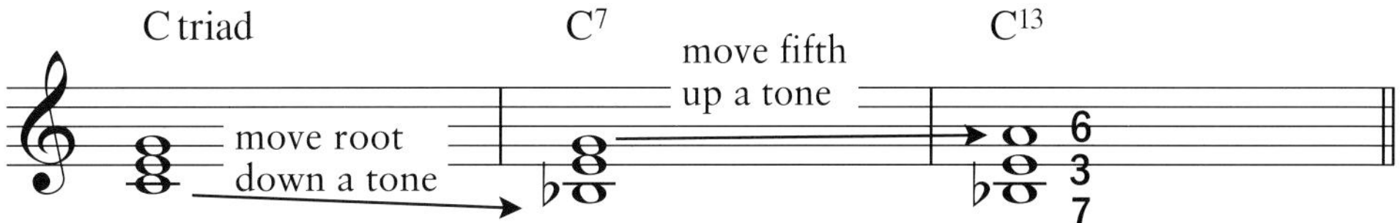

Note the interval structure of this **736** thirteenth shape – augmented fourth on the bottom, perfect fourth above. This shape can often be played in place of a regular dominant seventh or ninth. Jazz musicians do not wait to be told to play thirteenths – they play them because they like the sound of them!

In readiness for the next piece, *Thirteenth Groove,* practise the following **736** shapes in the right hand, in the centre of the piano, with low roots in the left hand:

D7 – D♭7 – C7 – B7 – B♭7 – A7 – A♭7 – G7 – G♭7

Just as you practised perfect fourth shapes up and down in semitones for Assignment 1 above, do this with the new shape. Eventually you should be able to find the chords without looking at the keyboard, in either hand.

In a **II** – **V** or a **II** – **V** – **I** sequence, you can often play a thirteenth on the **V** chord, even if not specified by the chord symbols. This is easy if you play the minor chord as **379** – you just need to drop the middle note by a semitone:

Fig 7.4: Rootless three-note shapes for II – V

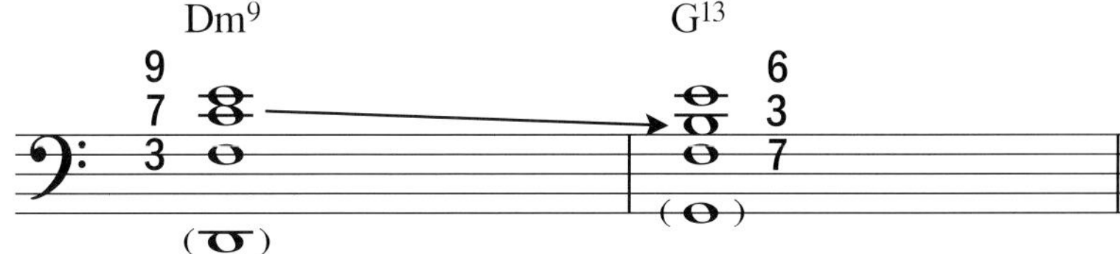

For *Thirteenth Groove* overleaf, practise Fig 7.4 for the following chords:

Am7 – D7 A♭m7 – D♭7 Gm7 – C7 F♯m7 – B7

For more on thirteenth shapes, see *Comping Blues* and *The Other Side*, IBP, pp. 160 and 172.

10 with drums
Bass enters for Head and Solos

♩ = 112 (swing 8s)

Thirteenth Groove

Tim Richards

The first page is an exercise in right-hand chordal 'chops' against a steady walking bass line – an important accompaniment style. Make sure your right-hand eighth-note feel really swings!

Head and Solos

Checkpoint: Thirteenth Groove

● **Blues tonality** This piece is in the key of B♭ major. Because most of the chords are dominant sevenths, including the **I** chord B♭13, it sounds bluesy. As in *The Message*, the melody (p. 58) features both the major and minor third of the key (D and D♭/C♯). Much of it is based on the B♭ minor pentatonic, with a ♭**3** pentatonic implied in bar 3 (see Fig 7.8).

● **Moving up a semitone** Although the bass line remains on B♭ for all of section 'A' (8 bars), in bar 4 the right hand moves temporarily up to B13 which is played as a long (held) chord on the '3 and'. Give this chord a heavy accent to contrast with the lighter, *staccato* chords that precede it. By including this variation we have also turned the two-bar rhythm pattern into a four-bar one.

On the second page notice how this B13 is played by the left hand in the second half of *every* bar of the 'A' section. Moving temporarily up a semitone in passages of static harmony is an effective device for creating tension and release.

● **Section 'B'** The bass line here uses mainly **R** and **5** with some connecting notes. The more complex variations in the second half (from bar 15) are optional.

● **II – V chords** In section 'C' four **II** – **V**s descend in semitones. These are derived from the chords of the introduction (D13, D♭13, C13, B13) by adding a minor chord in front of each one, a fourth below, so that D13 becomes Am9 – D13, and so on.

Playing rhythms in triplet feel

Because swing eighth-notes are indicated for *Thirteenth Groove*, the right-hand chordal stabs on p. 62 must be interpreted with a triplet feel. To help you phrase correctly, the main chordal rhythms are shown below against a stream of triplets dividing each beat into three. Clap the rhythms whilst tapping your foot on the downbeats, not too fast, about 88 bpm, imagining the triplets underneath.

Fig 7.5: Bars 1–2

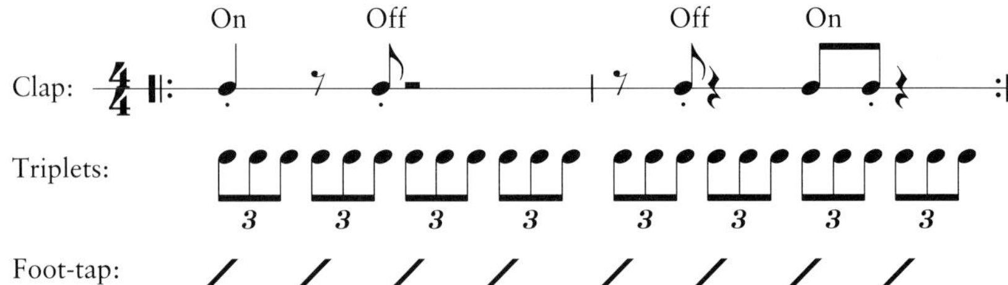

The 'off' chords, notated on the second half of the beat, should actually coincide with the third note of the triplet. After clapping the rhythm, transfer it to the piano, playing the chords as crisply as possible, *staccato* against the *legato* bass line.

Pay special attention to the pair of eighth-notes in the second bar – these should be played with a long-short articulation with only the second chord *staccato*. Overall this accompaniment should have a rather lazy feel – remember to relax!

In section 'B' a new two-bar rhythm pattern is used for the A♭13 and G♭13 chords in which the G♭ chord is 'pushed' (anticipated), coming in on '4 and':

Fig 7.6: Bars 9–16

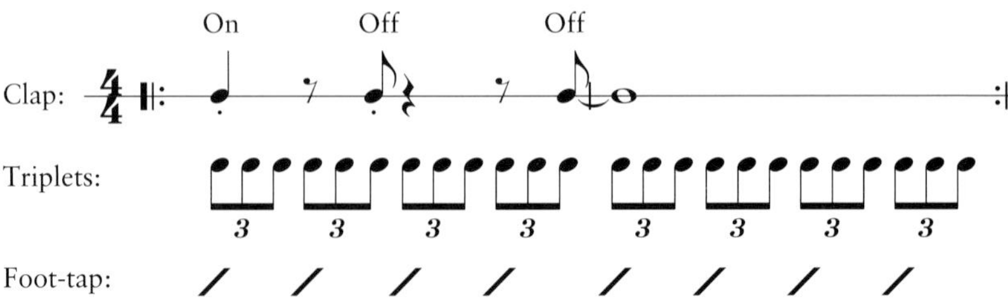

In section 'C' a less pushy rhythm is used, the first chord of each pair being delayed in every bar so that it enters on '1 and':

Fig 7.7: Bars 17–20

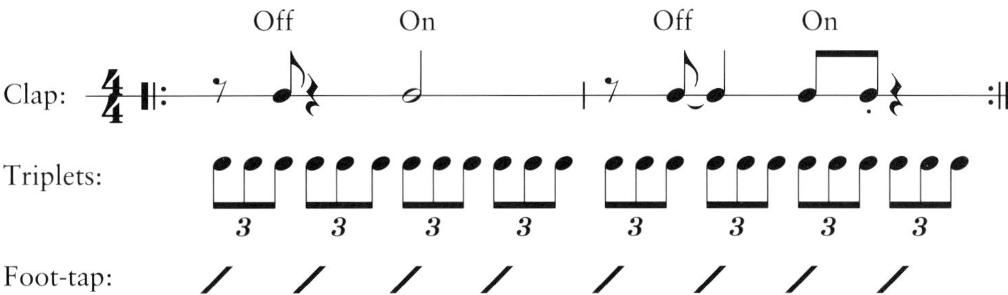

Thirteenth chords

Assignments and Improvisation Tips: Thirteenth Groove

❶ **Bass and chords** Work out on the three sections on the first page in turn, repeating each one over and over. Before moving to the next section, you should have memorised the bass line and feel so comfortable with the right-hand chordal rhythm that you no longer need to read it. When you have mastered the co-ordination of the 'on' and 'off' chords in each section, check you are playing them with the correct swing feel (see Figs 7.5–7.7).

❷ **Accompaniment** Team up with another musician and ask them to play the melody (beginning in bar 24) whilst you play the accompaniment as on the first page. Try to do this from memory so that they can read from the book themselves. When you reach bar 24, repeat from section 'A' while they take an improvised solo. If you wish, try out some different right-hand chordal rhythms, keeping the bass line the same.

❸ **Melody (second page)** First play the left hand by itself using the bass line on the CD as a backing (from 0:51, left-channel only). Repeat until you have memorised the chord shapes and rhythms. Next spend some time working on the melody in the same way, before trying the hands together. Away from the CD, you could also play the melody with the bass line from p. 62 in the left hand, instead of the chords.

❹ **Solo** Try improvising in the right hand alone over the left-hand chords in the solo section of the CD (1:37 onwards). Then silence the piano on the CD and add the left-hand chords in the rhythm indicated. Start your solo where the bass comes in at 0:51, so you have three choruses to play over. See the exercises on p. 67 for help with the co-ordination of left and right hands.

❺ **Pentatonic scales** For the first eight bars the right hand could play any of the following scales, some of which are implied in the melody:

Fig 7.8: Pentatonic scale choices for B♭13

❻ **Quartal patterns** Over A♭13 and G♭13 the following perfect fourth shapes can be used, as in the written melody:

Fig 7.9: Perfect fourths (play an octave higher with chords in left hand)

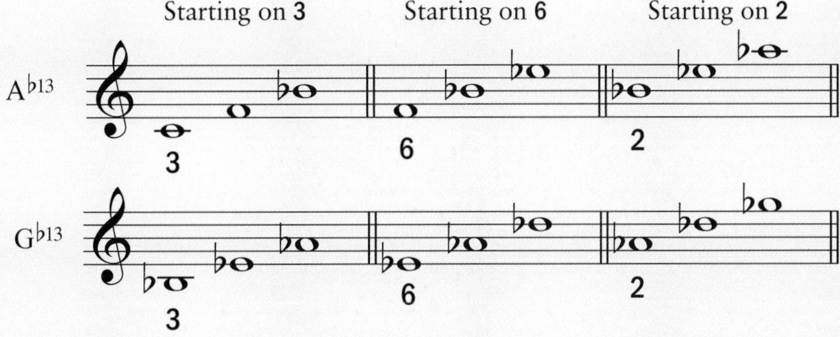

Play around with these shapes, arpeggiating and inverting them if desired (see Vol. 1, Figs 5.14–5.15). They will give you a more contemporary sound than using scales. Notice that the one that starts on B♭ is common to both chords.

The B♭ minor pentatonic/blues scale also works well over both these chords, as in bars 15–16 of the melody.

❼ **II–V patterns** In bars 17–20 the chords move chromatically, so a single scale cannot be used. Many musicians have their own pet phrases or 'licks' for such situations. The melody alternates two of these so that each one appears in two keys, a tone apart. For further examples, see Fig 7.15.

Red Garland, pianist with the Miles Davis Quintet from 1955–58, epitomises the fresh, swinging sound of 1950s jazz, and also developed his own personal style of block chords. Listen to his sparkling soloing on John Coltrane's album 'Traneing In' and on Miles' four classic albums 'Workin'', 'Steamin'', 'Cookin'' and 'Relaxin''.

Playing left-hand chords off the beat

In *Thirteenth Groove*, the first eight bars of the melody contain mainly quarter-notes played on the beat, the rhythmic interest being provided by the left-hand chords, which are almost all off the beat.

This is also a very useful left-hand skill to develop when improvising. As well as being able to play quarter-note lines in the right hand with this type of accompaniment, you should try it with eighth-note lines. Let's start with an ordinary B♭7 scale played with chords that are on the beat. Play in swing eighth-notes and tap your foot on the downbeat:

Fig 7.10: (a) Chords on the beat

Now play the same scale and foot-tap, but move the chords half a beat earlier, so that they come on '2 and' and '4 and', no longer with the foot-tap:

(b) Chords before the beat

When you get used to it, you'll find that this swings much better than the first example. The left hand is now ahead of the right, something which would be even more apparent if the chords changed from bar to bar, as you would anticipate each new chord on the '4 and' instead of playing it on the 'one'. This driving, pushy feel is the cornerstone of many pianists' styles. Listen to Red Garland's left-hand chording for a classic example of this effect.

Now try playing the chords half a beat *later* than the first example, so that they fall on '1 and' and '3 and' giving a more 'laid-back' feel:

(c) Chords after the beat

Although this is less pushy than (b), it still swings much better then (a). This style can be heard on many of Bill Evans' recorded solos.

Actually many pianists use both these devices in order to better control the feel and direction of their improvisations. When listening to and playing jazz, try to become aware of the different ways of left-hand chording – not only harmonically, but also rhythmically.

Short II – V patterns

The chords in bars 17–20 of *Thirteenth Groove* consist of four **II** – **V**s descending in semitones. They are called 'short' **II** – **V**s because each chord only lasts two beats, whereas in a 'long' **II** – **V** they would last a bar each (see Vol. 1, p. 161).

Two different 'licks' were used in the right hand, the first one being very straightforward – it outlines an ascending root position minor seventh chord and resolves onto **3** and **5** of the **V** chord:

Fig 7.11: II – V arpeggio phrase

You'll need to analyse licks in this way in order to memorise them and find them quickly in other keys. Singing them before you play them is also great practice.

In bar 18 another lick was used which is a little more oblique in the way it relates to the underlying chords. Here it is in the same key as above for comparison:

Fig 7.12: II – V lick

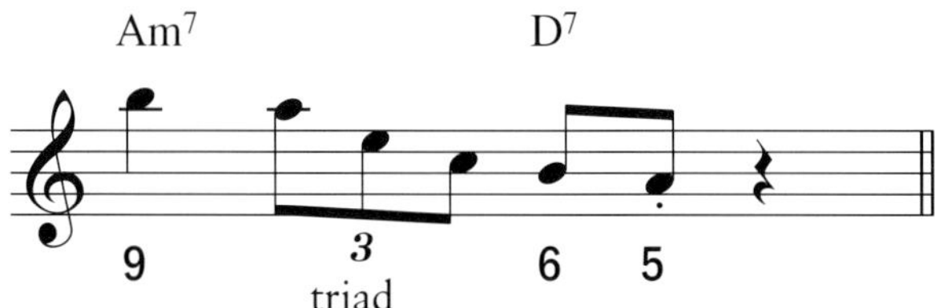

This starts on the ninth of the minor chord (B), goes down the notes of the minor triad, and resolves onto **6** and **5** of the **V** chord. Phrases like this are part of the jazz 'language' and are used by all jazz musicians. Some people overuse licks to the extent that their playing comprises little else, and it is not my intention to lead you down that path! However, an understanding of how these phrases work is a very important part of building a jazz vocabulary.

In order to be able to use licks successfully, without them sounding stilted, they should be practised in all keys so that any technical problems such as fingering are dealt with in advance. It should then be possible to personalise them with your own inflections and to play them with rhythmic variations.

The phrase in Fig 7.12 is very common – once you're aware of it you will probably start to hear it in solos all over the place! In fact it is a dual purpose phrase – not only can you think of it belonging to Am7 or Am7 – D7, but you can also use it for a dominant seventh chord by itself (eg: D7), in which case you must think of it as starting on the sixth (B). Here's an example that includes some rhythmic variation:

Fig 7.13: Using the lick over dominant chords in bars 9–16 of *Thirteenth Groove*

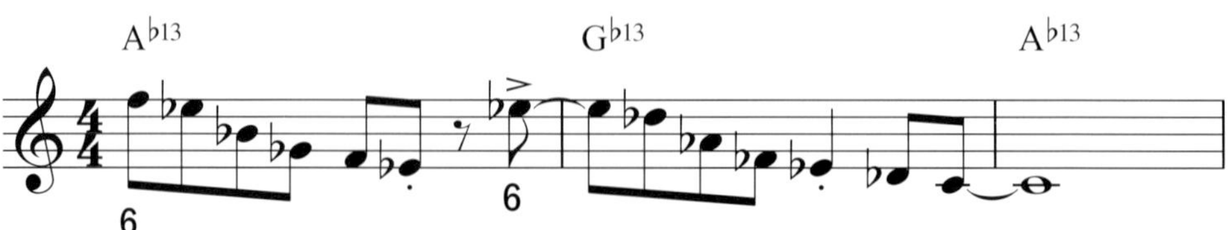

When using **II – V** licks in improvisation, familiarity is the key. If you knew the phrases in Figs 7.11 and 7.12 really well in different keys, you could easily play them the opposite way to the written melody, with the second phrase first, eg:

Fig 7.14: *Thirteenth Groove* melody (bars 17–20 rephrased)

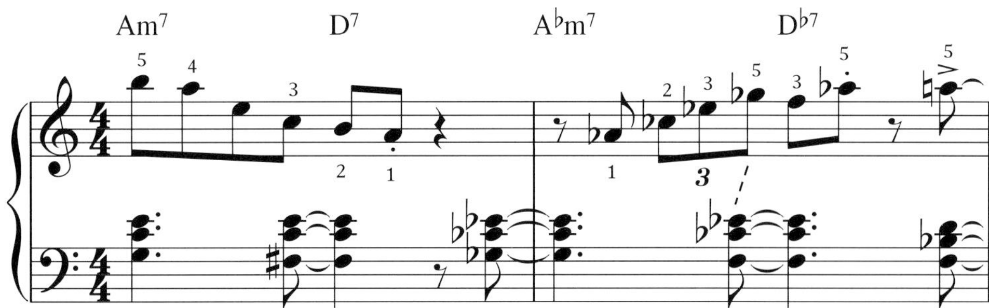

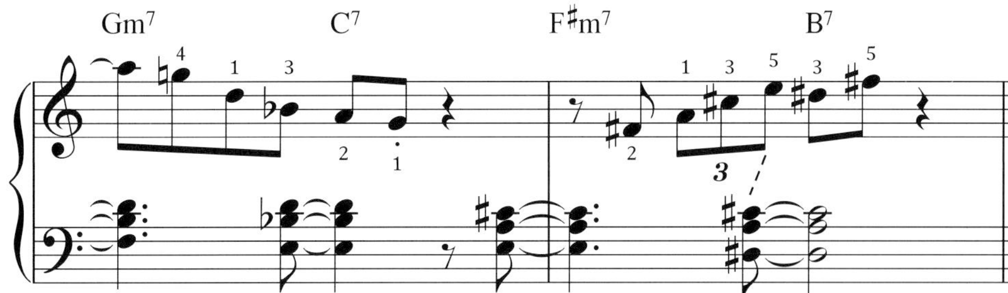

These two licks work well together because each one begins a semitone away from the final note of the previous lick. Quick thinking is required to pull off such smooth transitions between ideas in a solo. Alternating ascending and descending phrases and avoiding ungainly jumps will help your lines to sound musical.

Note the 'pushed' left-hand chords in Fig 7.14 – this illustrates how you can apply the left-hand techniques of Fig 7.10(b) to the playing of patterns as well as scales. This time the chords are held rather than played *staccato*.

Overleaf you'll find some more short **II – V** licks for bars 17–20 of your solo in *Thirteenth Groove*.

Fig 7.15: Short II – V patterns over Am7 – D7

Arpeggio starting on R

Arpeggio played downwards

Downwards arpeggio starting on 5

Downwards triad arpeggio

R235 pattern

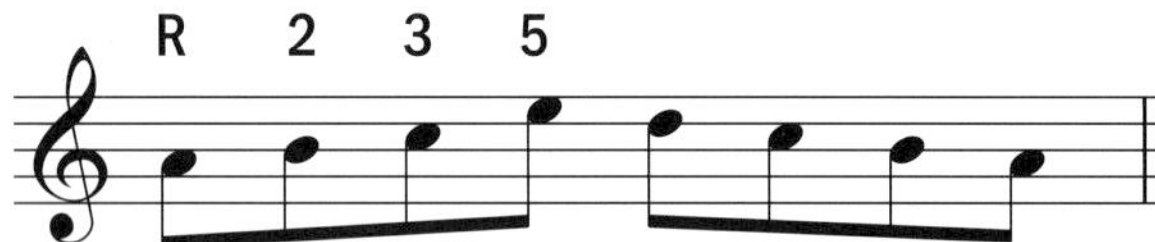

R235 on both chords

Chromatic pattern starting on 4

Triads with chromatic linking note

Same pattern starting on 3 (includes 9th)

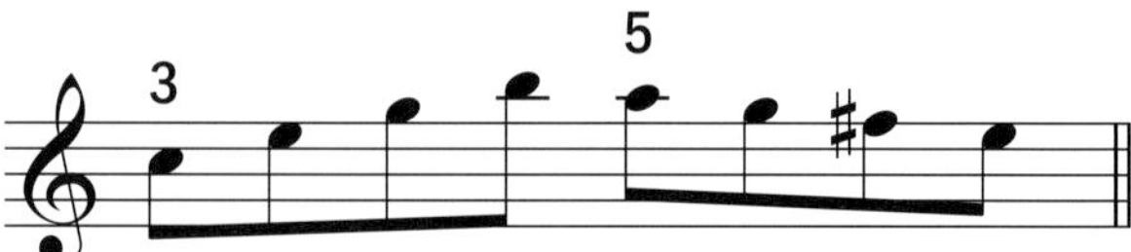

Ascending triad starting on 3

Downwards arpeggio starting on 3

Variation starting on R

Same pattern starting on 3

R235 pattern played downwards

Encircling the third of the V chord

Same pattern starting on 5 (includes 9ths)

Notice that some of the patterns end with a scale up or down from a note of the **V** chord, making them easy to link to other patterns without a break (providing the scale leads to the starting note of the new pattern). Others finish with a quarter-note or rest on the fourth beat. You'll need to develop a flexible approach to each pattern, adapting the ending if necessary so that it flows neatly to the next idea.

The next piece, *Short II – V Workout*, gives practice at using these patterns.

11 with bass & drums
Includes play-along sections

♩ = 120 (swing 8s)

Short II – V Workout

Tim Richards

This piece uses most of the short **II – V** patterns given in Fig 7.15. To give you space to try out your own ideas in all four keys, the repeats are left empty on the CD.

Assignments and Improvisation Tips: Short II – V Workout

❶ **Choose some licks** Review Fig 7.15 and memorise two or three contrasting licks that appeal to you. Don't try to learn all of them at once – your mind will be able to not retain them.

❷ **Join them up** Stay in the same key (Am7 – D7) for now and join your licks together in different ways, playing along with the first eight bars of the backing (CD track 11), as many times as you wish. The written material in bars 1–4 is an example of what you might end up with, although there's no need to play any left-hand chords at this stage. Experiment with altering the register, direction, timing and order of your right-hand notes.

❸ **Other keys** Transpose your memorised licks to the other keys, working out the notes and fingering for A♭m7 – D♭7, Gm7 – C7 and F♯m7 – B7. Practise each key separately until you can improvise fluently, using the **II** – **V** licks alongside other improvised material (eg: Dorian mode patterns, blues scale, arpeggios, etc). When you come to trying this out with the CD (without the piano), you'll have eight bars in each key to try out your ideas.

❹ **Transpose the written material** Now learn the two-bar phrases given for Am7 – D7 and Gm7 – C7 in all four keys, checking the fingering in each key.

❺ **Last eight bars** The last section of the piece changes key in every bar, as in *Thirteenth Groove*. All your practice so far has been leading up to this challenge. Try out the written material, and then your own ideas, in the eight bars that follow it. Strive to find logical and musical ways to connect one lick to another, adapting each one as necessary to what comes before and after.

❻ **Left-hand shells** Underneath your improvisation add the shells, trying out both configurations, ie: **R7** – **R3** and **R3** – **R7**. Strive for rhythmic variety, playing the chords both on and off the beat. (See also Figs 7.10(b) & (c).)

❼ **Rootless chords** When you're comfortable with the shells, try the left-hand voicings given below instead, transposing and memorising them in all four keys. You may need to move the right hand up an octave.

Rootless II – V voicings

In *Thirteenth Groove*, the **II** – **V** chords in bars 17–20 were three-note voicings:

Fig 7.16

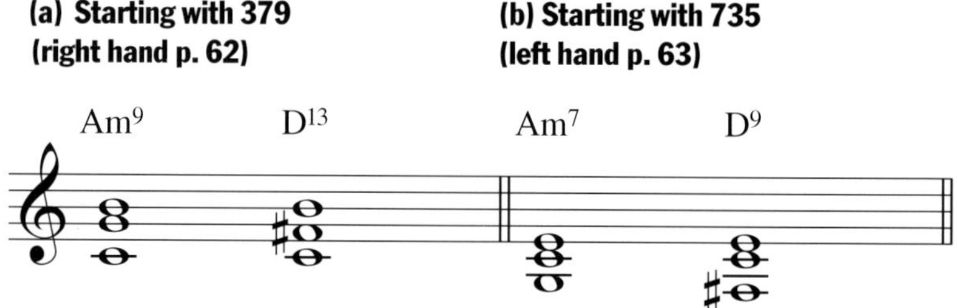

Here are the equivalent voicings using four-notes:

Fig 7.17 **(a) Starting with 3579** **(b) Starting with 7935**

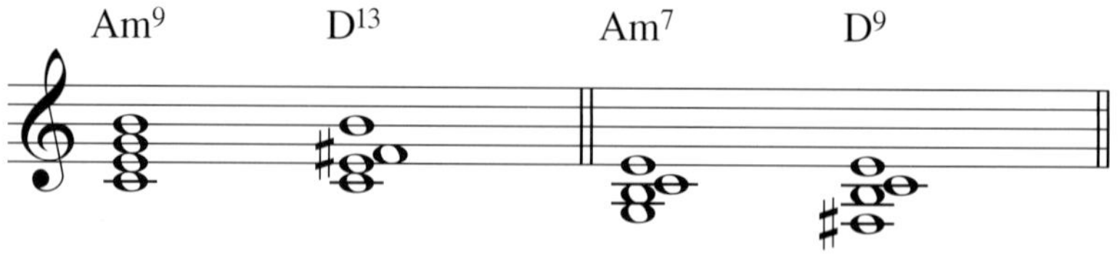

Am9 D13 Am7 D9

You played these **3579** and **7935** minor ninth shapes in *Cloud Nine* (see Vol. 1, pp. 196–197). Retaining the extra notes in the dominant chords gives them more bite.

In all cases there is still only one note difference between the **II** and the **V** chord – the **7** of the minor chord drops a semitone, becoming the **3** of the dominant chord.

Two-handed II – V voicings

R7 and **R3** shells can be used as the basis for a very useful system of two-handed voicings. There are two basic configurations, both using two notes in each hand. Because you are only playing four notes, it is important that none are doubled.

The first configuration has a **R7** shell in the left hand for the minor chord. The right hand fills in the missing notes of the chord, **35**, as in *Open Up!* (Vol. 1, p. 138).

Fig 7.18: II – V voicings starting with R7/35

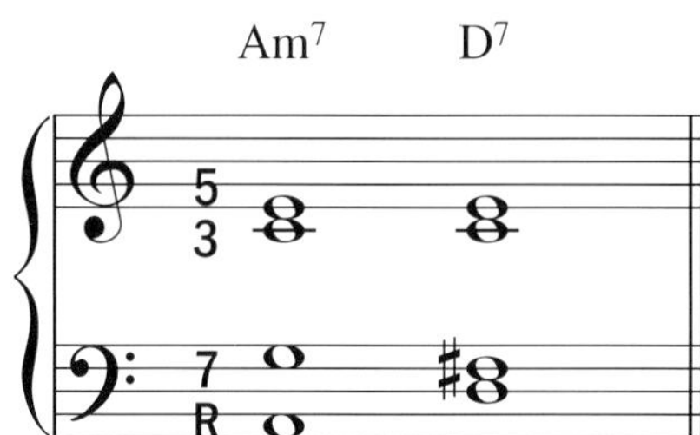

Notice that the right-hand notes do not change when moving from **II** to **V**, as the top note (the fifth of the minor chord) becomes the ninth of the dominant chord.

The second configuration has a **R3** shell for the minor chord. This voicing, with **79** in the right hand, is the same as the one used above for the dominant chord:

Fig 7.19: II – V voicings starting with R3/79

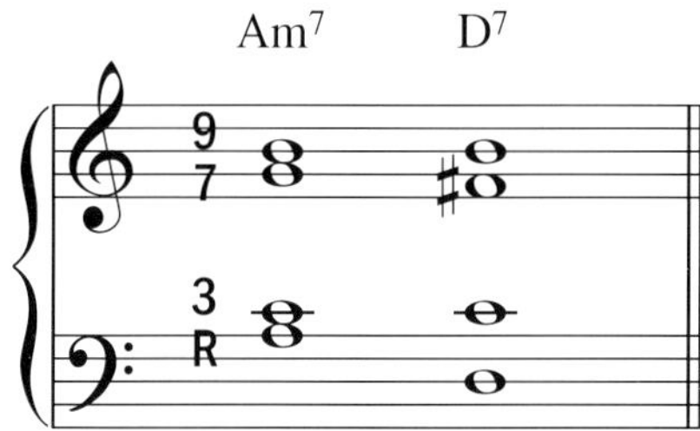

The top note, now the ninth of the minor chord, is again retained and becomes the thirteenth of the dominant chord. The other right-hand note must drop a semitone to make the change from **II** to **V**.

Another thing worth remembering is that in this style of 'comping', the left and right thumbs always play **3** or **7**, sometimes known as the 'guide-tones'.

Both voicings are demonstrated in *II – V Comping* overleaf, which follows the chord sequence of *Short II – V Workout*.

Assignments: II – V Comping

❶ **R7/35** Memorise Fig 7.18 and transpose the chords as necessary, starting with A♭m7, Gm7 and F♯m7, as in *Short II–V Workout*.

❷ **Play along** Play the chords with the backing (track 12), noting the rhythmic variations given. When you are comfortable with them, try out some rhythms of your own. Remember to play in swing eighth-notes!

❸ **R3/79** Repeat steps 1 and 2 with the opposite configuration (Fig 7.19), until you are equally comfortable with both ways of playing the **II** – **V**s.

12 with bass & drums

Includes play-along sections

♩ = 120 (swing 8s)

II – V Comping

Tim Richards

These shapes all have **R7** or **R3** shells in the left hand, either as **R7/35** or as **R3/79**.
Where the chords are not written, supply your own voicings by transposing the given ones.

Playing melodies using two-handed voicings

When reading single-note melodies from lead sheets, experienced pianists will often play the main notes of the tune as two-handed voicings, with the melody note as the top note. In the following example, the melody notes in bars 1, 3 and 5 are the fifth of each chord, signalling the use of a **R7/35** voicing:

Fig 7.20: *Take the 'A' Train* (Vol. 1, p. 64)

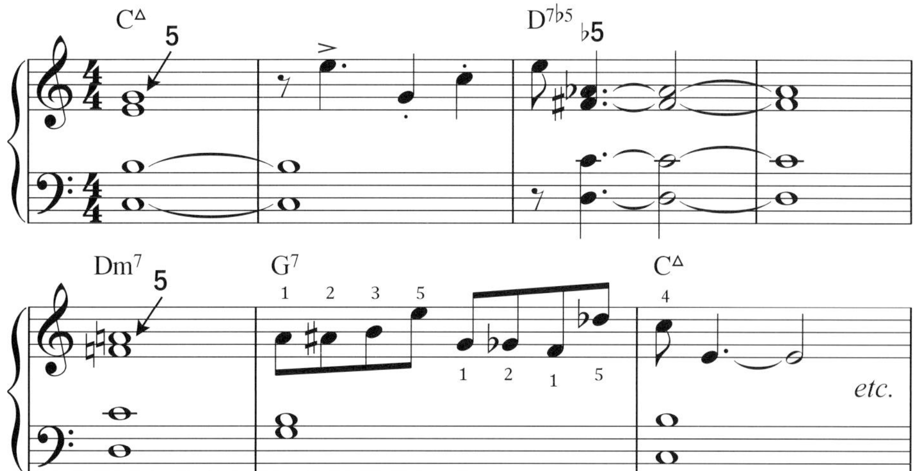

The above example also shows how the voicing can be adapted should the melody fall on the ♭**5** (or **#11**) as in bar 3. In fact there is a whole family of dominant voicings based on **R7/35**, in which only the top note differs:

Fig 7.21: Dominant R7/35 family

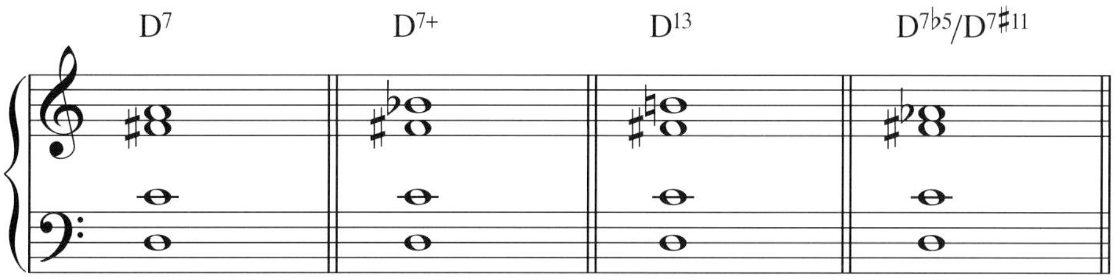

D7 | D7+ | D13 | D7♭5/D7#11

The next example includes three dominant seventh chords with raised fifths:

Fig 7.22: *Someday My Prince Will Come* (see also Fig 7.27)

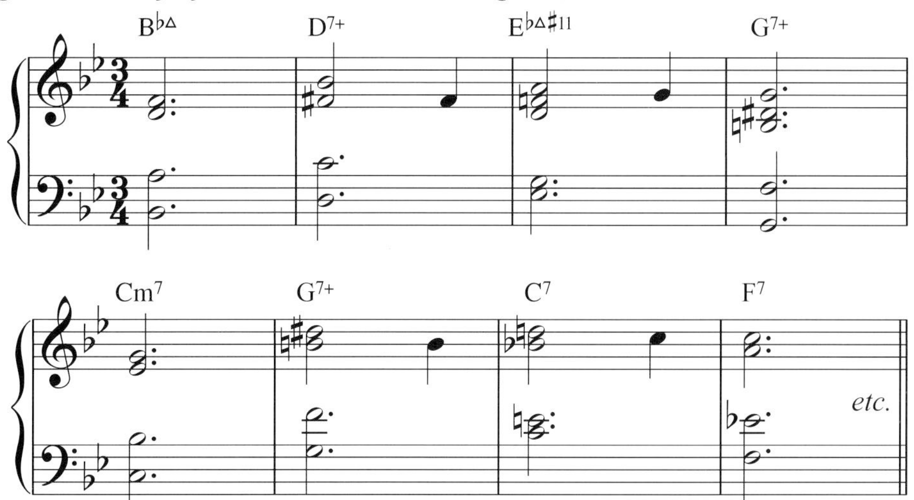

In bar 7, the melody note is the ninth of the C7 chord, indicating the other configuration from Fig 7.19, **R3/79**. In bars 3–4, five notes are played, the melody being played by the little finger above the four note voicings.

- E♭△#11 the melody note (**#11**) is played over a **R3/79** voicing
- G7+ the melody note (**R**) is played over a **R7/35** voicing

To ensure you can successfully incorporate two-handed voicings into your playing of melodies, it is advisable to practise **II – V – I** sequences in various keys, based on the two formats given in Figs 7.18–7.19. Some examples are given below.

Four- and five-note II – V – I voicings

Using the voicings from Figs 7.18–7.19 over a complete **II – V – I** gives us the following set of shapes:

Fig 7.23: Starting with R7/35 (melody note is fifth of minor chord)

Em^{7} A^{9} D$^{\Delta}$ (D^{6})

5 3 7 R

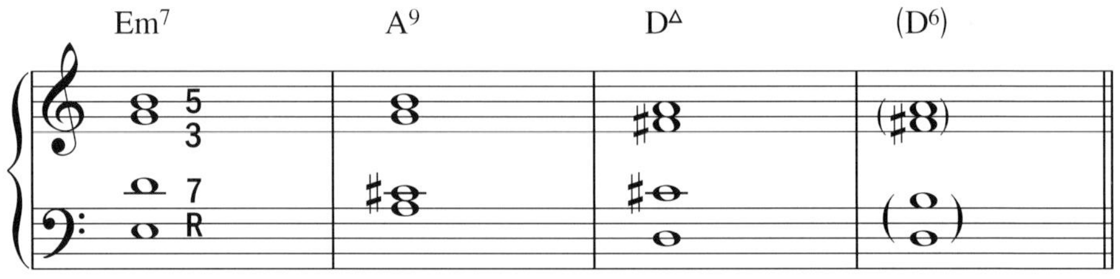

The major voicings in brackets on this page are optional – you can play either or both voicings.

As in any chord sequence whose roots follow the cycle of fifths, left-hand shells for **II – V – I** will always alternate **R7** and **R3**, or vice versa. Here are the opposite shapes:

Fig 7.24: Starting with R3/79 (melody note is ninth of minor chord)

Am^{9} D^{13} G$^{\Delta 9}$ (G6/9)

9 7 3 R

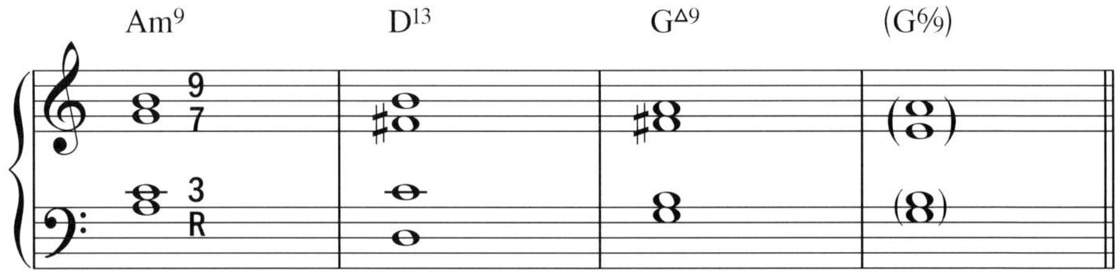

Once you have mastered these in various keys (see Assignments opposite), you could try adding a third note in the right hand. The most commonly used extra notes are the ninth (add above **R7/35**) and the fifth (add above **R3/79**). Here are the two configurations:

Fig 7.25: Five-note voicings starting with R7/359 (melody note is ninth of minor chord)

Em^{9} A^{13} D$^{\Delta 9}$ (D6/9)

9 5 3 7 R

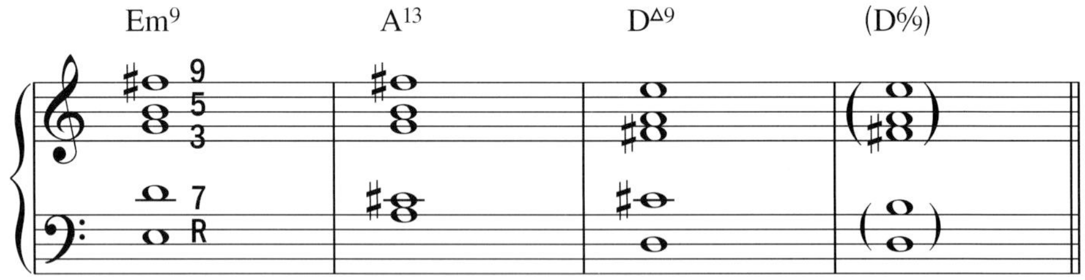

Fig 7.26: Five-note voicings starting with R3/795 (melody note is fifth of minor chord)

Am^{9} D^{13} G$^{\Delta 9}$ (G6/9)

5 9 7 3 R

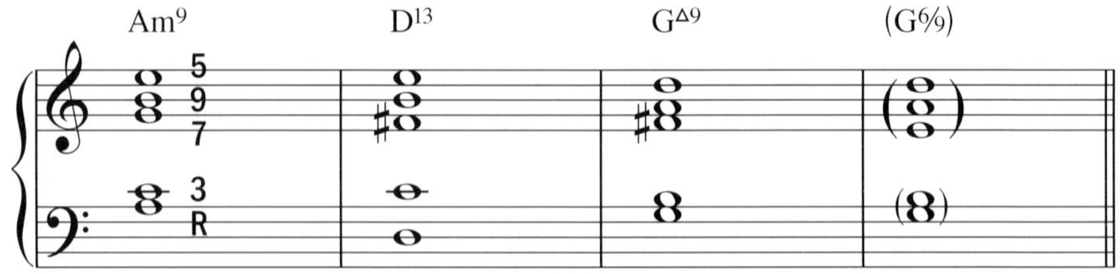

To play two-handed voicings fluently when harmonising tunes you'll need to develop a thorough familiarity with all the shapes above. Use them whenever you spot a melody note that is either **5** or **9** of the chord.

Revisiting Fig 7.22 in the light of the five-note shapes gives an alternative way of voicing the melody in the last three bars:

Fig 7.27: *Someday My Prince Will Come* (bars 5–8)

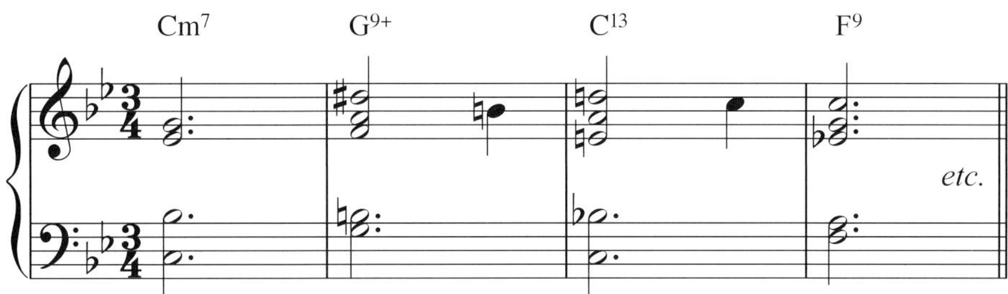

This solution is much more effective, as the previous four-note voicings used for the G7+, C7 and F7 bars were rather high. There is more bass in the sound now, and the addition of the thirteenth to the C7 chord enhances the harmony.

This important way of playing melodies, with the right hand playing three notes on top of left-hand shells, is demonstrated further in the bebop tune *Ladybird* (overleaf), and also in *Misty*, p. 106.

Assignments: II – V – I Cycles

❶ **Four-note voicings – R7/35** Play Fig 7.23 round the following **II – V – I** cycle, which covers six key centres, moving down in tones:

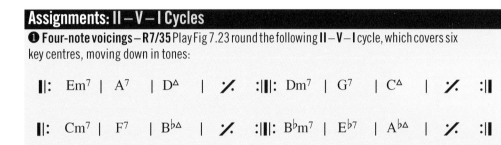

||: Em^7 | A^7 | D$^\Delta$ | % :||: Dm^7 | G^7 | C$^\Delta$ | % :||

||: Cm^7 | F^7 | B$^{\flat\Delta}$ | % :||: B$^\flat$m^7 | E$^{\flat 7}$ | A$^{\flat\Delta}$ | % :||

||: A$^\flat$m^7 | D$^{\flat 7}$ | G$^{\flat\Delta}$ | % :||: F$^\sharp$m^7 | B^7 | E$^\Delta$ | % :||

As you play each shape, say the chord name out loud (tip: don't mix up flats and sharps in the same **II – V – I**). If you have difficulty finding the shapes, practise the left-hand shells alone (see *II – V – I Arpeggio Workout,* Vol. 1, p. 164).

❷ **Four-note voicings – R3/79** Play Fig 7.24 round the second cycle, which takes you through the six keys not covered by the first one:

||: Am^7 | D^7 | G$^\Delta$ | % :||: Gm^7 | C^7 | F$^\Delta$ | % :||

||: Fm^7 | B$^{\flat 7}$ | E$^{\flat\Delta}$ | % :||: E$^\flat$m^7 | A$^{\flat 7}$ | D$^{\flat\Delta}$ | % :||

||: C$^\sharp$m^7 | F$^{\sharp 7}$ | B$^\Delta$ | % :||: Bm^7 | E^7 | A$^\Delta$ | % :||

Aim to memorise both cycles and to play all the chords without any music.

❸ **Repeat with the opposite cycles** Now play Fig 7.23 round the second cycle, and Fig 7.24 round the first. If the chords start to sound muddy, move the voicings up an octave, or switch to the opposite configuration. Being familiar with both configurations allows you to position the chords in the optimum place on the keyboard – not too high, not too low.

❹ **Five-note voicings** Play Figs 7.25 and 7.26 round the same cycles as in steps 1, 2 and 3. With all two-handed voicings, play all the notes together for maximum effect. Don't get into the habit of 'flipping' the shapes or of playing the notes one-by-one. Try to visualise the complete shapes on the keyboard before you play them – eventually your fingers will find the shapes themselves!

Several **II – V – I**s are included in the chord sequence of *Ladybird* overleaf and two pieces based on the same changes, *Swinging Comping #1* and #2.

13 with bass and drums

Includes play-along section

♩ = 168 (swing 8s)

Ladybird

A classic bebop tune from the 1950s, played in two-handed voicings with **R7** or **R3** left-hand shells.

Tadd Dameron
arr. Tim Richards

CΔ | | Fm7 | B♭7
CΔ | | B♭m7 | E♭7
A♭Δ | | Am7 | D7
Dm7 | G7 | CΔ E♭Δ | A♭Δ D♭Δ

Checkpoint: Ladybird

● **Key centres** Whilst starting and finishing in the key of C major, this tune modulates to the key of A♭ major in bars 7–10, as shown by the **II – V – I**, B♭m7 – E♭7 – A♭Δ. There is also a **II – V – I** in C major in bars 13–15.

Other keys are implied by the **II – V** chords in bars 3–4 (Fm7 – B♭7) and 11–12 (Am7 – D7), but these do not resolve to the expected **I** chords (E♭Δ and GΔ respectively), so cannot be considered true modulations.

● **The IV minor** Fm7 is an expression of the **IVm** chord:

Fig 7.28: Simple expression of IVm using triads

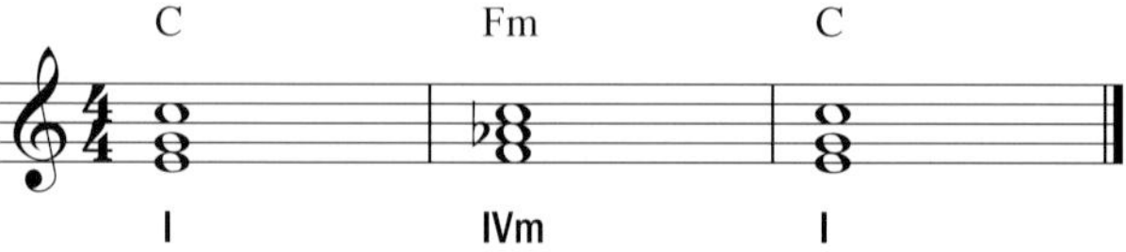

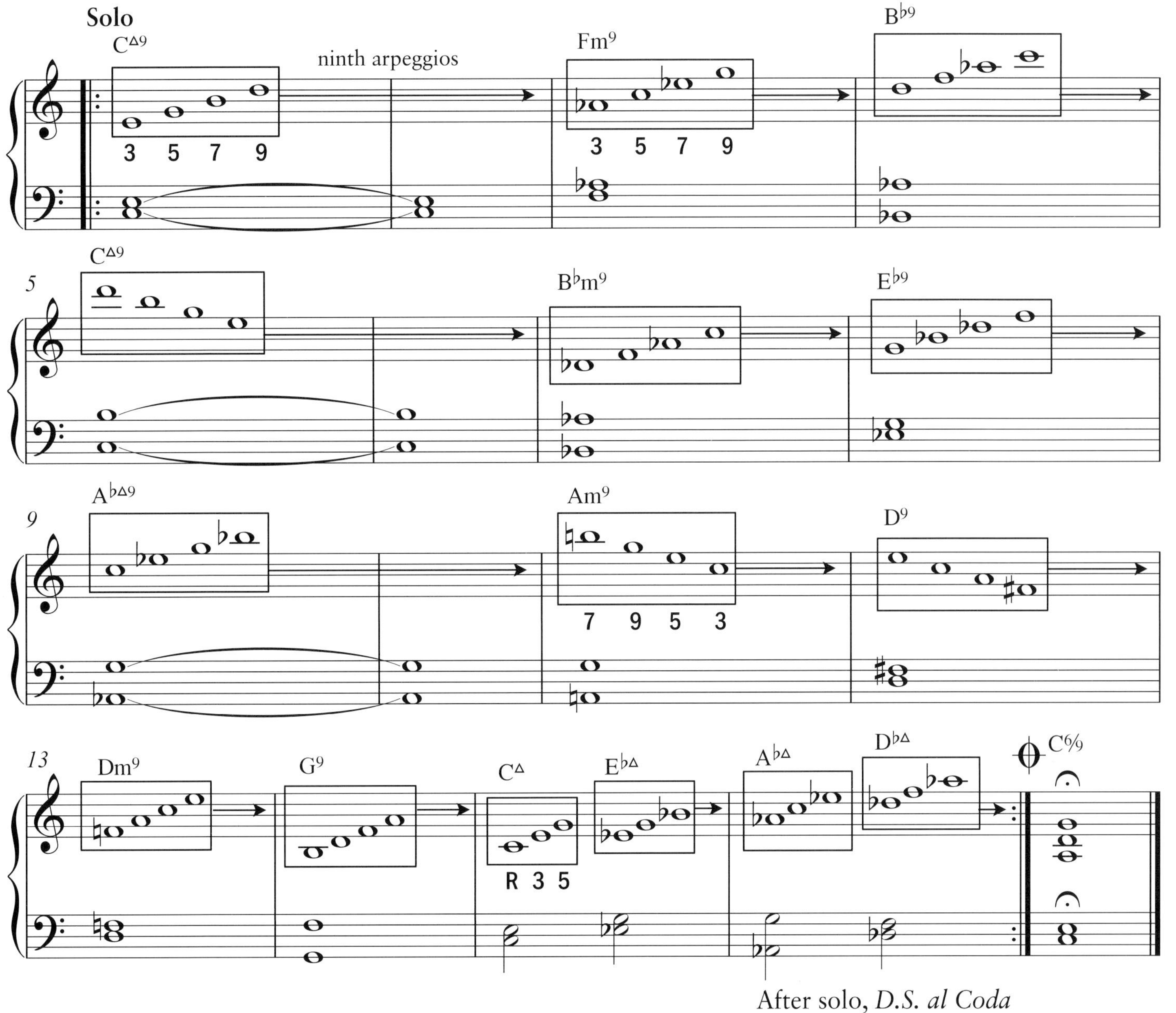

The sequence Fm7 – B♭7 – C∆ is an example of another way of resolving a **II – V**, basing it on **IV** of the major key instead of on **II**.

● **Turnaround** The last three chords go up in fourths from E♭∆, using the cycle of fifths to end up on D♭∆ – a semitone above the tonic. This way of resolving back to C is a modern variation on more conventional turnarounds which end on **V** (G7). Using only major chords gives it a very distinctive sound. Note that the ∆chord symbols have mostly been interpreted as 6/9 chords.

● **Shells** These are retained in the left hand for the solo, which frees up the central area of the keyboard for the right hand. You don't need to play them all on the beat as written – vary the left-hand rhythms as shown earlier (see pp. 64–5, 67, 69 and also Vol. 1, Fig 4.44).

● **Comping** The two-handed voicings played on the CD during the solo section are shown overleaf in Fig 7.29. See also *Swinging Comping #1* and #2 (pp. 81 and 85) for accompaniment styles suitable for use without a bass player.

● **Improvisation** The right-hand arpeggios suggested are all ninth shapes based on the third of each chord (**3579**), played in upwards and downwards directions. In the turnaround, however, triads are suggested as the chords only last two beats each.

More ideas for soloing over *Ladybird* can be found on pp. 86–92. For improvisation assignments, see pp. 89 and 92.

Assignments: Ladybird comping

❶ **Comping** Before learning the melody, play the basic two-handed shapes first, as heard in the solo section (track 13, 0:47 onwards). Ignore the notes in brackets until Assignment 4.

Fig 7.29: Two-handed comping for *Ladybird*

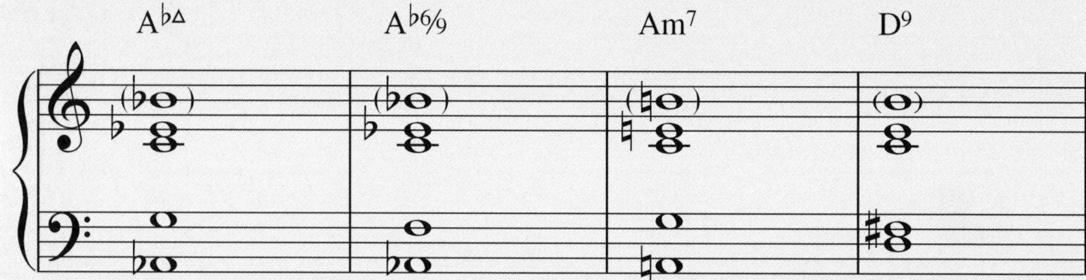

When comping there is no need to place the melody note on top, so you have more freedom of choice concerning what shapes to use.

❷ **Vary the rhythm of the chords** Rather than playing them all on the beat as written, try out different rhythms, playing the chords on and off the beat, like the right-hand chords in *Thirteenth Groove* (see p. 62). Some other rhythms you could try are given on pp. 82–3.

❸ **Accompany a friend** Invite someone to play the melody, or improvise a solo, on any instrument, while you comp behind them, both of you playing with the CD (bass and drums only). Listen to their phrasing so you can compliment it, and try not to overplay – you don't have to play every chord!

❹ **Add the extra note** Adding the note shown in brackets will give you five-note shapes for each chord, as heard in the second chorus on the CD. Repeat steps 1–3 with the extra notes.

❺ **Opposite shapes** Fig 7.29 finishes with a different CΔ voicing from the opening one. Continuing from this chord, work out all the other voicings for the whole tune, using **R3** in the left hand where **R7** is given and vice versa. If the voicings sound too muddy, move them up an octave.

14 with drums

♩ = 168
(swing 8s)

Swinging Comping #1

Tim Richards

The chords from *Ladybird* are played here as three-note rootless voicings, underpinned by a walking bass line – a useful accompaniment style for any swing piece!

Checkpoint: Swinging Comping #1

● **Walking bass line** Play the left hand by itself, *legato*, taking time to check out the fingering which is the key to playing bass lines smoothly. Notice the variety of techniques used, all of which are marked as they occur.

Once you understand how bass lines are put together, you'll be able to play your own variations by combining the elements in different orders (see *Swinging Comping #2* on p. 85. Avoid reading the notes from the book – write yourself a chord chart to follow, or better still, memorise the changes so you don't need any music at all.

● **Run-ups** Notice that the run-ups contain both major and minor thirds (see Vol. 1, Fig 3.43). They can be used with major, dominant and minor chords, as long as the root of the next chord is a fourth above.

● **Chord shapes** Only two voicings are used, with either **7** or **3** on the bottom:

735 – for Fm7, B♭m7, A♭Δ, Am7 and G7 (or **736** to give G13)
379 – for B♭7, E♭7, D7 and Dm7 (or **369** for CΔ, E♭Δ, D♭Δ)

The major (Δ) chords can be played as either **379** or **369**, depending which sound you prefer – I have gone for the 6/9 sound for all of them except A♭Δ.

Comping rhythms

● **The 'on-off' rhythm** This is used for the right-hand chords in *Swinging Comping #1*:

Fig 7.30

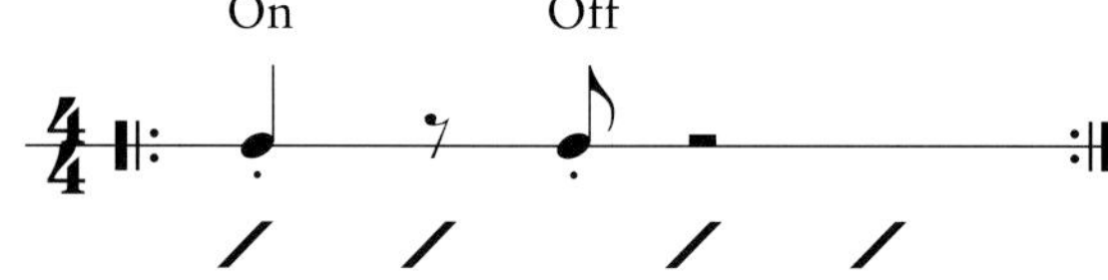

Both chords should be given a crisp *staccato* articulation, without upsetting the pulse of the bass line, which must remain *legato* and steady as a rock!

Remember that in order to swing correctly off-the-beat chords should be played with a triplet feel, ie: slightly later than halfway through the beat (see *Thirteenth Groove* and Figs 7.5–7.7).

● **Pushed chords** The fourth bar of every line features an anticipated (pushed) chord, played on the '4 and' of the previous bar, and held. This long chord contrasts with the *staccato* chords that precede it, and establishes a four-bar rhythmic pattern. Try playing the piece with pushed chords in every bar:

Fig 7.31

(a) Pushing chords once a bar

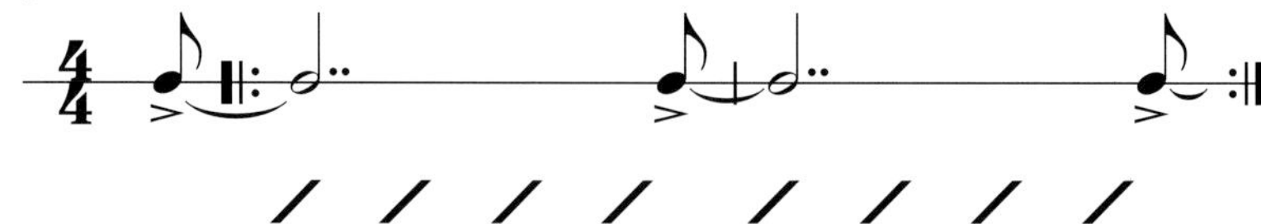

(b) Pushing chords twice a bar

Example (b) above corresponds to the turnaround (bars 15–16) when the pushed chords come on 'four and' and on 'two and'. Both of these rhythms are essential to master for effective swing-feel comping. You should also practise them with *staccato* chords:

(c) Playing pushed chords *staccato*

When a chord symbol is given on the first beat of a bar, the chord is often played on the '4 and' of the previous bar. I have marked the foot-tap (same as the four-to-the-bar bass line) below all examples, so you can see at a glance which chords are played in between the left-hand notes.

● **The 'off-on' rhythm** This is the basis of *Swinging Comping #2* (p. 85). The first chord is off the beat, on 'one and':

Fig 7.32

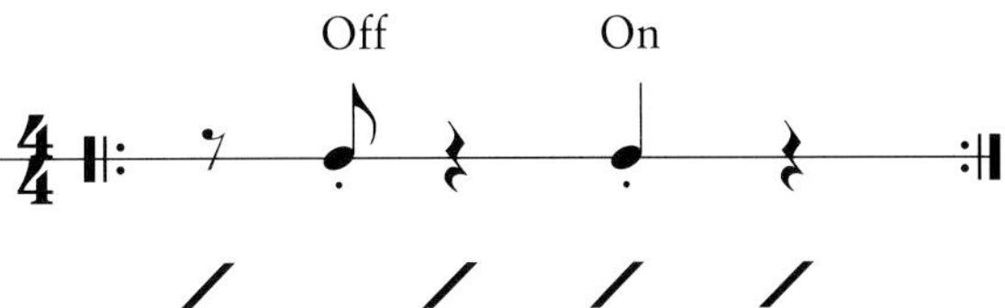

This is combined with the 'on-off' rhythm (Fig 7.30) to give a useful two-bar pattern:

Fig 7.33

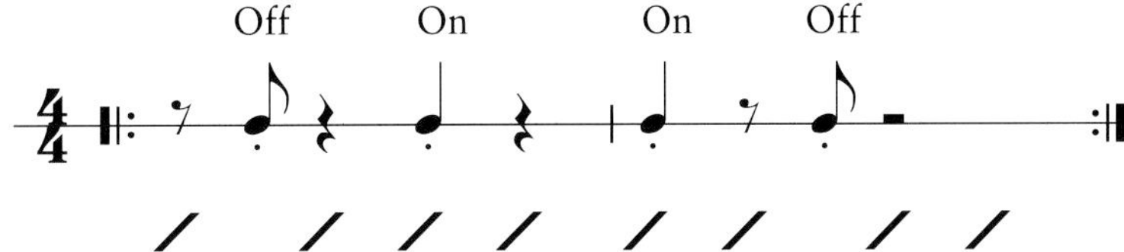

Become familiar with all of these rhythms and practise them for all the swing-feel tunes in this book, with walking bass lines. Cultivate hand independence so you can play off-beat chords with ease. Successful swing comping depends on a combination of factors:

- Mixing on- and off-the beat chords
- Varying the articulation (include both long and short chords)
- Creating a groove by setting up two-, four- or eight-bar patterns
- Playing with a good swing (triplet) feel
- Listening to and fitting in with the soloist

Three- and four-note rootless II – V – I voicings

The right-hand voicings used in *Swinging Comping #1* contain three notes only. Two configurations are in common use:

● The third on the bottom of the minor chord

Fig 7.34: Three-note shapes starting with 379 (play one octave lower)

Dm^{9} G^{13} C$^{\Delta 9}$ C$^{6/9}$

9 7 3

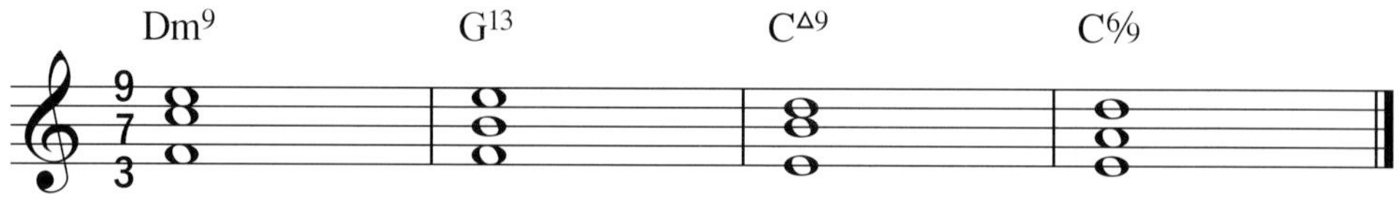

Once you're familiar with these, try the four-note version of the same configuration, obtained from the three-note shapes as follows:

- add the fifth to **379** or **369** voicings
- add the ninth to the **735** or **736** voicings

Fig 7.35: Four-note shapes starting with 3579 (play one octave lower)

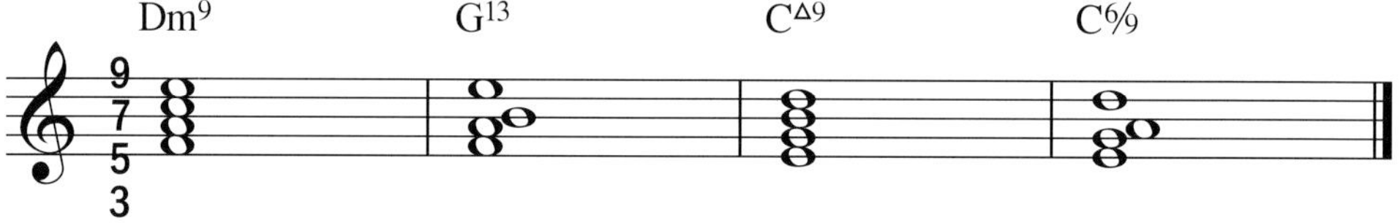

Play both sets of voicings round the cycles on p. 77. Learn them in the right hand first, playing the missing roots low down with the left hand. Say the names of the chords out loud to help you memorise the shapes.

The fourth note adds bite to the voicings, making them more jazzy. However, you can't play them as low down the keyboard as the three-note shapes. If things start to sound muddy, switch to the opposite set of voicings:

● The seventh on the bottom of the minor chord

Fig 7.36: Three-note shapes starting with 735 (play one octave lower)

Am^{7} D^{9} G$^{\Delta}$ G$^{6/9}$

5 3 7

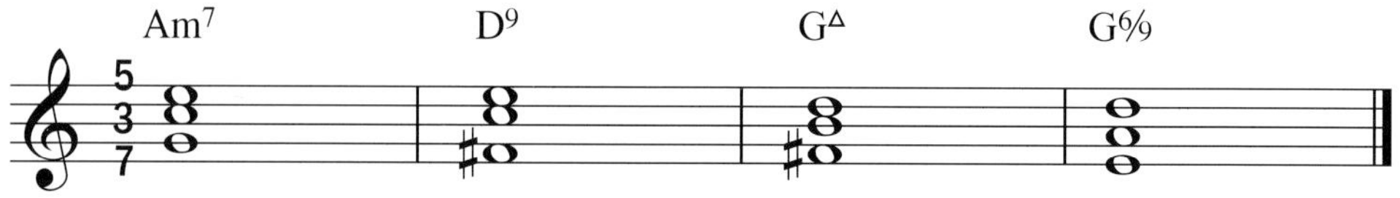

Fig 7.37: Four-note shapes starting with 7935 (play one octave lower)

Am^{9} D^{13} G$^{\Delta 9}$ G$^{6/9}$

5 3 9 7

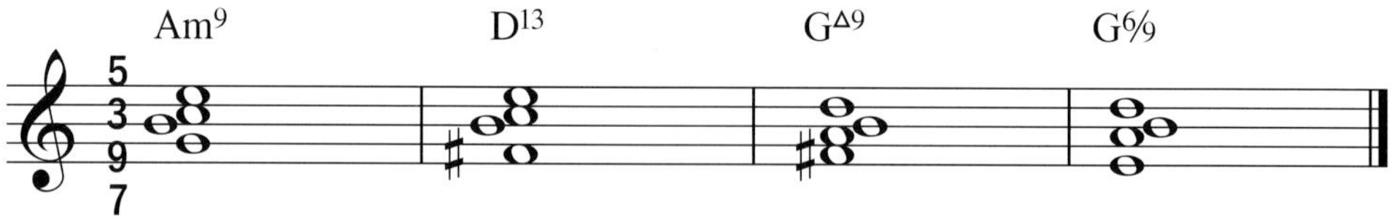

As above, practise both sets of voicings round the cycles on p. 77. When you know the shapes, you can try adding a left-hand bass line as in the next piece. Note that all the voicings on this page have the following in common:

- Only one note changes when moving from **II** to **V**: **7** drops to **3**
- The bottom note alternates between **3** and **7** (or **6** for 6/9 chords)

The two sets of four-note voicings are inversions of each other, ie:

- Major and minor seventh chords: **7935** is an inversion of **3579**
- Dominant seventh chords: **7936** is an inversion of **3679**
- 6/9 chords: **6935** is an inversion of **3569**

15 with drums

♩ = 168 (swing 8s)

Swinging Comping #2

Tim Richards

The chords from *Ladybird* are played here as four-note rootless voicings, with a different walking bass line to the version on p. 81.

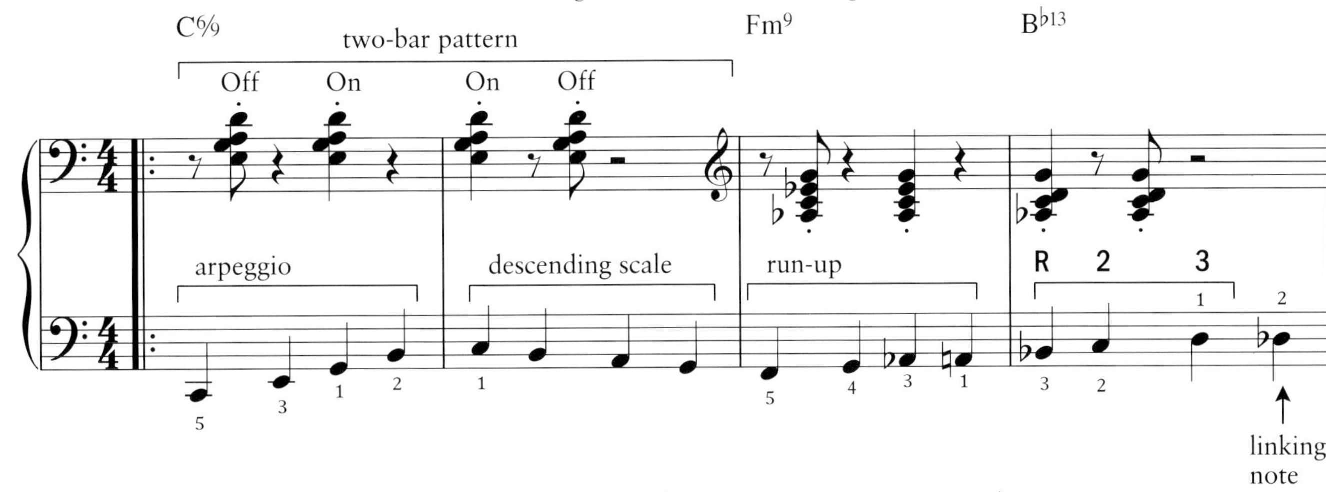

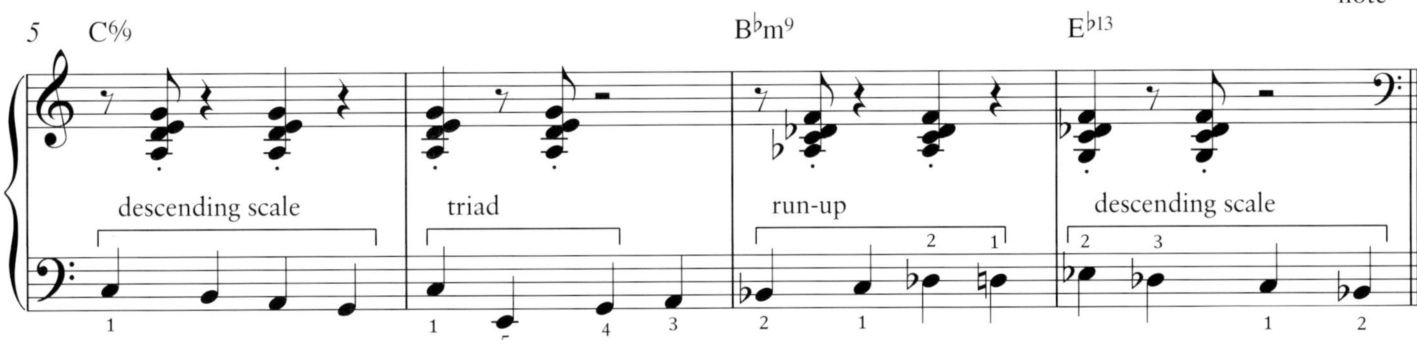

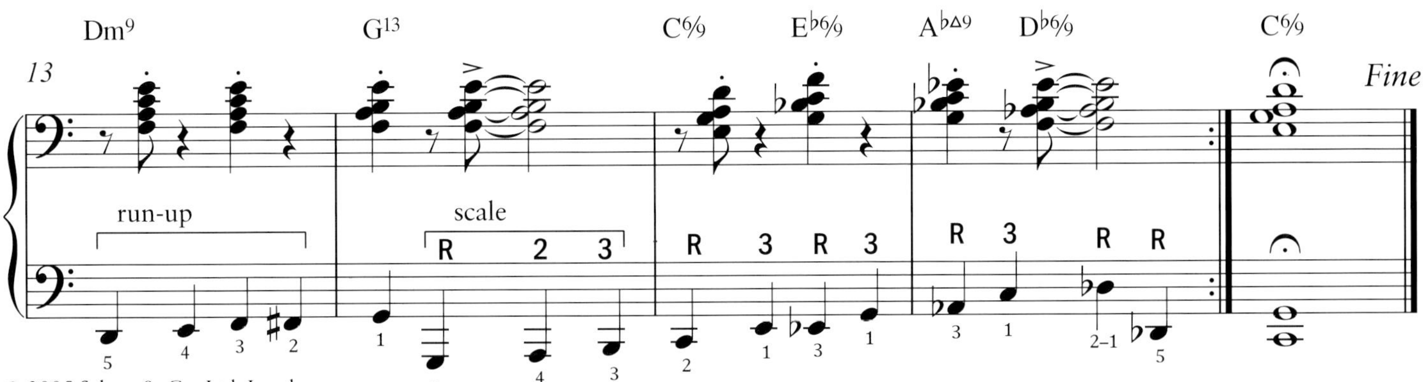

Assignments: Swinging Comping #2

❶ **Play the bass line alone** Compare it with the bass line on p. 81 noting how the same techniques are used, but in different places.

❷ **Memorise the four-note chords** When you're comfortable with the shapes, play the 'off-on/on-off' chord pattern as given every two bars, with the left-hand bass line. The first three chords are always *staccato*, but the fourth one can be sustained whenever you wish to create variety.

❸ **Vary the chordal rhythms** Try out some of the rhythms from pp. 82–3 in place of the given ones. Once you're confident with them, try mixing the rhythms up a little. Use a simpler bass line to start with if you prefer, like **R353** on every chord.

❹ **Vary the bass line** Don't just play what's written! Explore your own variations using the same principles. Get rid of the music and follow the chord chart you wrote earlier. Review the sections on bass lines in Vol .1, pp. 70 and 119 (Fig 3.43).

The four assignments above can all be played with tracks 14 or 15, drums only.

❺ **Left-hand chords** Transfer the three-note chord shapes from p. 81 to the left hand (in the same register) and practise them with the *Ladybird* backing (track 13, bass and drums only), trying out some of the comping rhythms from pp. 82–3. Repeat with the four-note chord shapes on p. 84.

❻ **Add a right-hand improvisation** Further ideas for soloing over the chord sequence of *Ladybird* are given below.

The chord/scale lick

This is a very useful pattern for long **II** – **V**s (one bar on each chord), as in *Ladybird*:

Fig 7.38: Go up the arpeggio and down the scale of each chord

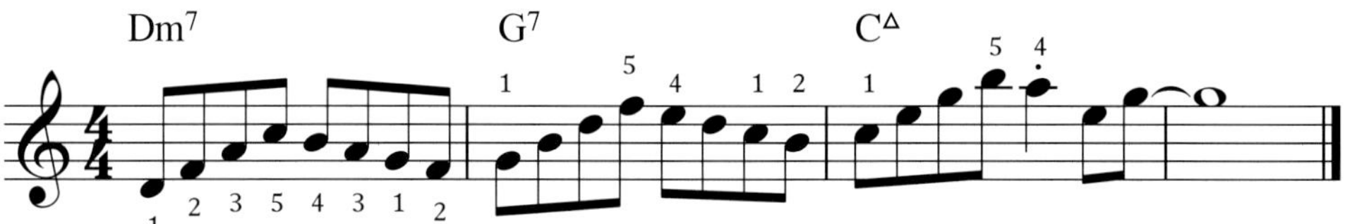

This example uses the root of the chords as target notes on the first beat of each bar. It is also possible to play a similar pattern using the third of each chord as a target note – the first four notes on each chord will now be the **3579** arpeggios suggested in the improvisation boxes of *Ladybird*:

Fig 7.39: Include the ninth by starting on 3

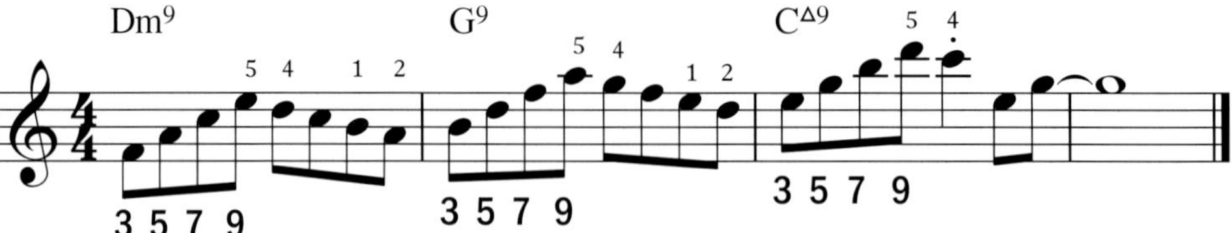

Memorising these exercises and playing them round the cycle of fifths (see Assignments, p. 77), will greatly increase your fluency in different keys. Make sure you pay careful attention to the fingering which will vary considerably from key to key.

Many variations are possible. Here's one that encircles the third of the dominant and major chords by approaching them chromatically from a tone below:

Fig 7.40: Encircle the third of the chords

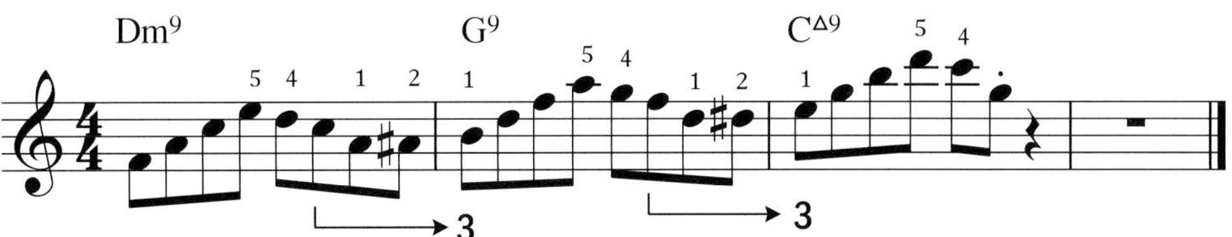

Notice that this ending also encircles the root of the C major chord on the third beat of the bar – another important place to position target notes.

One of the problems with playing this type of pattern round cycle of fifths chord sequences like **II** – **V** – **I** is that the lines move higher and higher up the keyboard. It's a good plan to include some descending phrases to combat this tendency:

Fig 7.41: Include descending lines

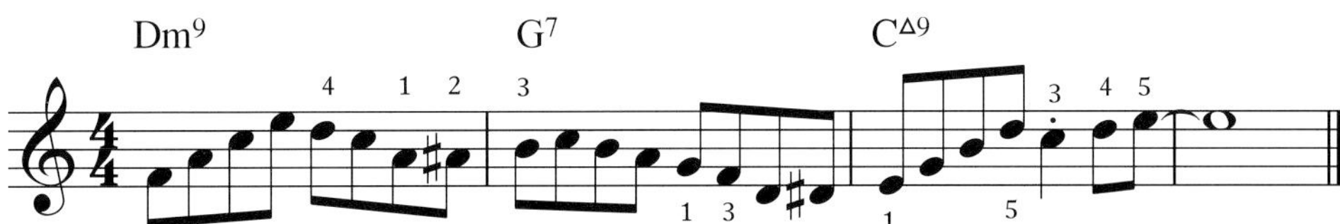

The next example descends from the ninth of the Dm chord, and also includes some triplets for rhythmic variety:

Fig 7.42: Introduce triplets

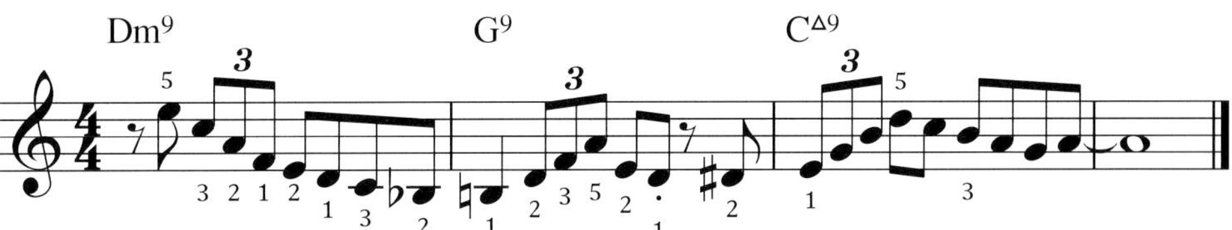

The above phrase also illustrates the importance of 'editing' your lines. The eighth-note rest in the second bar divides the **II** – **V** – **I** into two phrases, thus avoiding a constant stream of eighth-notes.

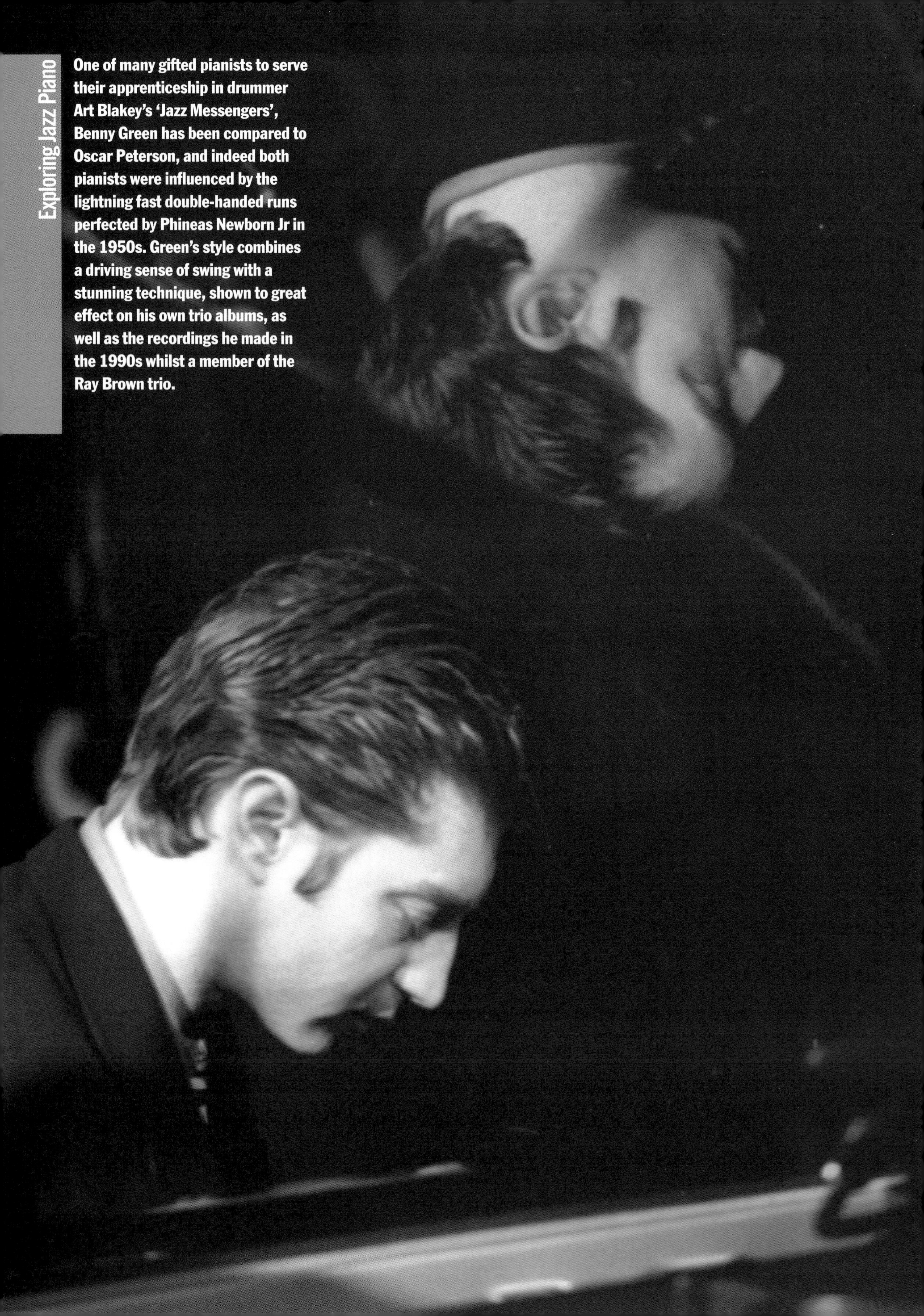

One of many gifted pianists to serve their apprenticeship in drummer Art Blakey's 'Jazz Messengers', Benny Green has been compared to Oscar Peterson, and indeed both pianists were influenced by the lightning fast double-handed runs perfected by Phineas Newborn Jr in the 1950s. Green's style combines a driving sense of swing with a stunning technique, shown to great effect on his own trio albums, as well as the recordings he made in the 1990s whilst a member of the Ray Brown trio.

Encircling notes with arpeggios

Overuse of any idea, even an elegant one such as the chord/scale lick, will result in very repetitive and boring solos! As an improvising musician, you need to develop a large vocabulary, in the same way that a language student does when learning to express concepts in a foreign tongue.

Chords that last for two bars, like the CΔ and A♭Δ chords in *Ladybird*, give you a bit more space than the chords of a **II – V**, which change in every bar. A common trick is to embellish arpeggios of major chords by encircling the root with **9** and **7**:

Fig 7.43: Major ninth arpeggio lick

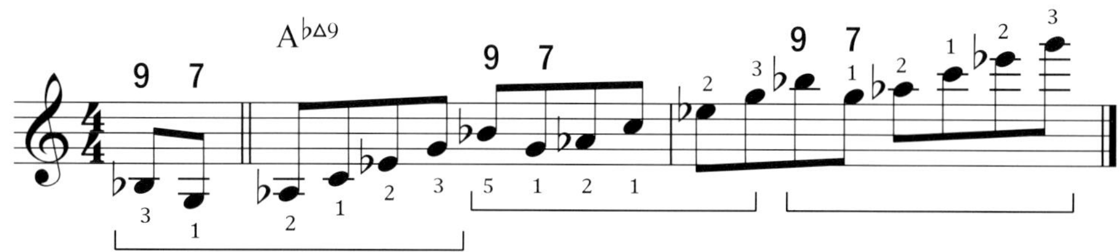

This phrase is actually easier to play over chords like A♭Δ and E♭Δ, than over white-note chords such as CΔ or FΔ, where you'll need to take care with the fingering.

Because the notes of A♭Δ are the same as those of a rootless Fm9 chord, Fig 7.43 will also sound great over Fm7. Note how the phrase repeats every six notes – for this reason it is easily played in triplets and is often used as an ending flourish:

Fig 7.44: Same phrase in triplets

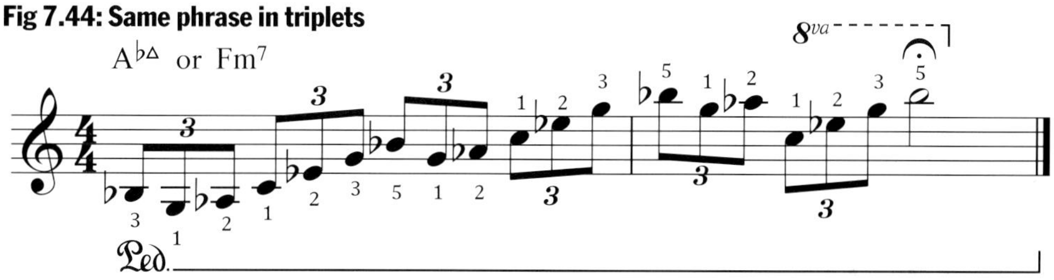

A♭Δ or Fm7

A similar phrase is given in E♭ for the ending fill in *Misty* on p. 107.

When playing phrases like this over a chord containing a ♭**7**, eg: C7 or Cm7, it is effective to encircle the root with the ♮**7**, giving both sevenths in the same lick:

Fig 7.45: Including the major seventh in a Cm9 arpeggio

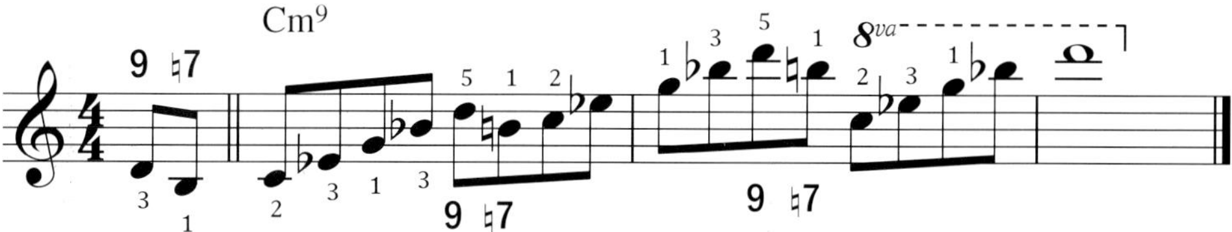

Assignments: Ladybird

❶ **Chord/scale lick** Practise the ideas in Figs 7.38–7.42 over all the **II – V**s and **II – V – I**s in *Ladybird*, with shells in the left hand.

❷ **Arpeggios** Work out the arpeggio ideas above over the same chords, adapting them to minor and dominant chords as well as major ones, and encircling either **R** or **3** of the chords. Play with left-hand shells.

❸ **Combine steps 1 and 2** Work on *Ladybird* in four-bar chunks, experimenting with different combinations – you might play the arpeggio licks in bars 1–2, joining them to a chord/scale phrase in bars 3–4, or vice versa.

❹ **Play along** When you have covered various possibilities for each four-bar line, put them together and practise taking complete solos with the backing (track 13). If you silence the piano on the CD you'll have five choruses to play along with.

How to make scales swing

When improvising in eighth-notes using scales, best results are obtained if you place notes of the chord (**R**, **3**, **5**, **7**, **9**) on the beat.

Fig 7.46 Successful scale phrases

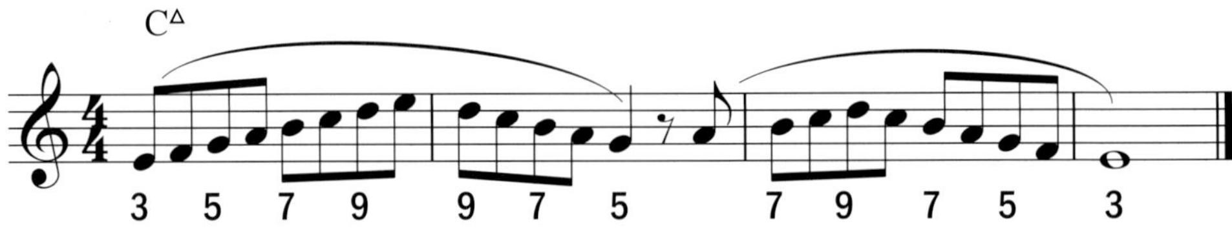

These phrases swing well because the correct pattern of tension and release occurs in every beat. The non-chord notes (**4** and **6**) are all placed on the upbeats (the 'and' of each beat), creating tension which is released when they are followed by a note of the chord on the downbeat.

Fig 7.47: Three ways of playing a descending scale

(a) Incorrect

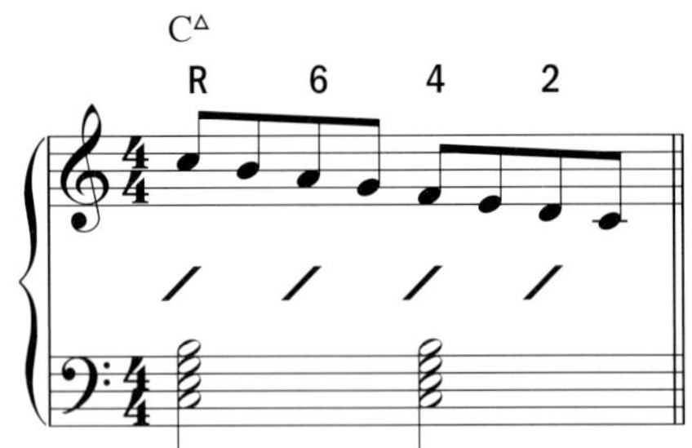

(b) Correct

(c) Correct

(a) starts out on the wrong foot by placing the fourth (F) on the third beat clashing quite badly with the chord. The other two examples avoid this problem by placing the correct notes on the downbeats.

(b) starts the scale half a beat later, on the '1 and',

(c) starts the scale on the ninth instead of the root.

Experienced improvisers often do these things subconsciously, in order to avoid the uncomfortable feeling of playing scale phrases 'back-to-front'. However, problems can still occur when playing in eighth-notes over two or more bars, due to the fact that ordinary scales only have seven notes. So even if you start correctly in the first bar, the second bar can be 'on the wrong foot':

Fig 7.48: The second bar is not acceptable for C△

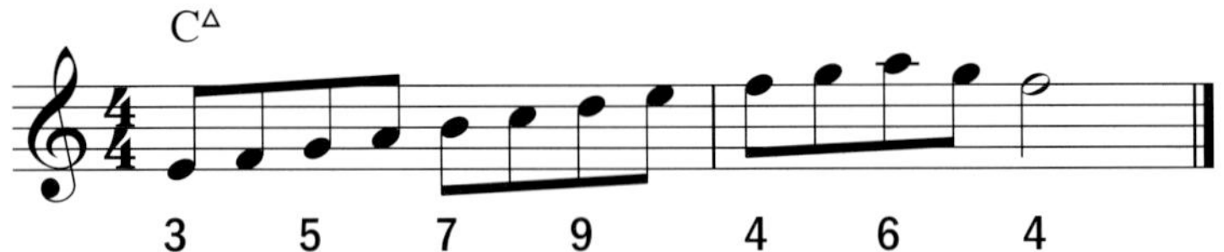

Rather than stressing **R**, **3**, **5** or **7**, the second bar now places **4** and **6** on the beat. If you find that your scale lines often sound awkward, and don't seem to swing, this is almost certainly the reason why!

Over the years, many great players have tackled this problem. A solution adopted by some is to raise the fourth, the main clashing note, turning the major scale into a Lydian scale (see Fig 6.13). Remember that ♯**4** (F♯) is often called ♯**11**:

Fig 7.49: Raising the fourth of the C major scale

The major bebop scale

Whilst Fig 7.49 solves the problem of the clashing fourth, using the **♯11** takes you out of the home key, especially in the context of a **II – V – I**. If you are playing in a conventional or mainstream situation, it may sound a little 'out'.

Another solution shifts the emphasis from **7** to **6**, so that the sixth is now the main chord-note. To make this possible the **♭6** (same as **♯5**) is added to the major scale, making an eight-note scale, generally known as the 'bebop' scale:

Fig 7.50: The major bebop scale over two octaves

Notice that the second bar now contains the same notes as the first. Learn to play both scales up and down (see Assignments overleaf for fingering suggestions).

To use the bebop scale successfully, start phrases on any downbeat, beginning on any note of the chord (ie: **R**, **3**, **5**, or **6**). You can change the direction of the scale at any point, but always insert the **♭6** between **5** and **6**:

Fig 7.51: Major bebop scale phrases starting on a downbeat

In the light of this scale we can now transform the way we use the chord/scale lick over a major chord, adapting it much more successfully for use over two bars:

Fig 7.52: Chord/scale licks with major bebop scale

Check the notes that fall on the downbeats in all the phrases above – they are all notes of the chord. The bebop scale swings automatically!

Assignments and Improvisation Tips: Ladybird improvisation

❶ **Learn the fingering** Practise Fig 7.50 until the eight-note scales no longer feel strange, starting at a slow tempo and building up to 160 bpm. There are two ways of fingering these scales. For C major they are:

123 123 12   *1234 1234*

Try them both before deciding – it depends on the key and the direction of the scale. The following example uses the first fingering going up (starting with *2*), the second one coming down (starting with *3*). To play more than one octave in either direction, repeat the same fingering for the second octave.

Fig 7.53: A♭ major bebop scale fingering

❷ **Major bebop scale licks** Play all the ideas on p. 91, working out notes and fingerings for both A♭∆ and C∆. Also invent some phrases of your own using the major bebop scale, remembering to start the scale with **R**, **3**, **5** or **6** on one of the downbeats. This doesn't mean all phrases must start on the beat – just that the chord-notes should be on the beat.

Fig 7.54: Starting a phrase on the upbeat

❸ **Practise II–V–Is** With chords in the left hand (shells or rootless voicings) improvise some right-hand lines round **II**–**V**–**I**s, using any ideas you like for the **II** and **V** chords, joining them up with bebop scale ideas for the two bars over the major chord. Use the cycles on p. 77 to practise in various keys. For *Ladybird* (p. 78), practise especially over the following sequences:

Dm7 – G7 – C∆   B♭m7 – E♭7 – A♭∆   Fm7 – B♭7 – C∆

❹ ***Ladybird*** Review all the improvisation topics covered so far and apply them to *Ladybird*, playing along with track 13 (with left-hand chords as well). Right-hand ideas should include: related scales and scale patterns (Dorian on minor sevenths), arpeggios and broken chord patterns (eg: **3579**), chord/scale licks, encircling target notes, bebop scales (on major chords), etc.

❺ **Turnaround** The chords in the last two bars change every two beats. Here's a possible phrase using the **R35** (triad) pattern suggested in the solo:

Fig 7.55: Triad pattern

Explore other ways of using this concept by playing the triads in different registers, reversing their directions, or by using other inversions or permutations of the notes. You could also explore patterns like the useful **R235** motif:

Fig 7.56: R235 pattern

See pp. 98–101 for the dominant and minor bebop scales.

Eliane Elias, the Brazilian pianist whose ground-breaking 1989 album 'Plays Jobim' featured a remarkably fresh take on Bossa Nova material by Antonio Carlos Jobim, with Eddie Gomez and Jack DeJohnette on bass and drums. A subtle improviser, capable of holding her own in the most select company.

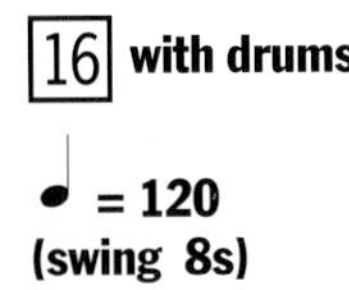

Dominant Seventh Workout #2

Tim Richards

This cycle goes through all twelve keys using three-note ninth and thirteenth shapes in the right hand.

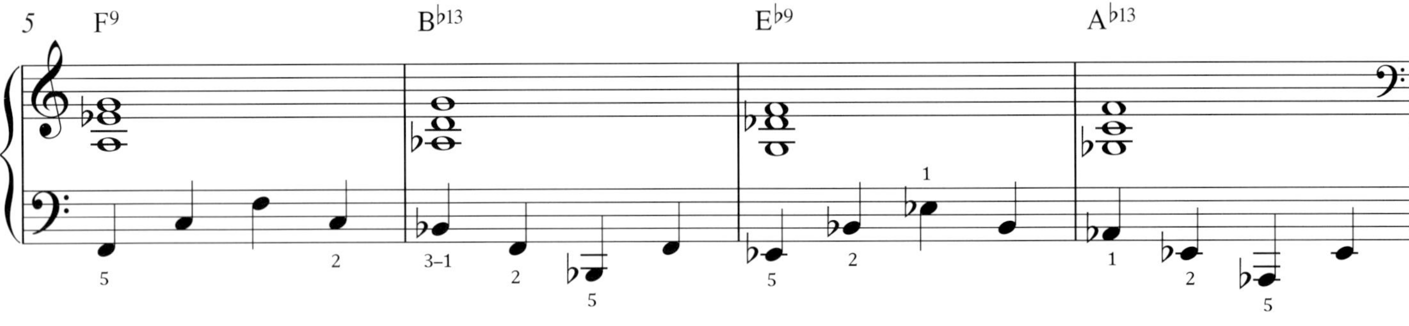

Checkpoint: Dominant Seventh Workout #2

● **Cycle of fifths** This exploits the natural tendency of dominant seventh chords to resolve up a fourth (as in a **V** – **I** cadence). As with any cycle of fifths sequence (eg: **II** – **V** – **I**), the voicings alternate **3** and **7** on the bottom. In fact, see how the bottom two notes are the tritones (**37** or **73**), which descend in semitones throughout the cycle (see Vol. 1, Fig 3.41).

● **Bass line** The walking bass line uses a **R** – **5** – **R** – **5** configuration on each chord, alternately up and down. Be sure to practise the fingering to enable you to handle the octave displacements smoothly. Try it with your eyes closed!

● **Chord shapes** We first encountered these three-note shapes in *Thirteenth Groove*, pp. 62–3 (see also Figs 7.4 and 7.16). If you compare them with the shapes used in *Dominant Seventh Workout #1* (Vol. 1, p. 118), you'll see that the top note has been raised by a tone, giving the ninth on top (**379**), or the thirteenth on top (**736**).

● **Right-hand rhythm** On the CD the chords are played 'straight' first time, with a typical comping pattern on the repeat:

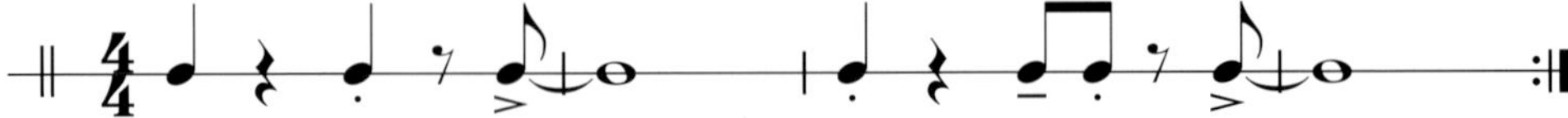

The dominant seventh cycle

Dominant seventh chords following a cycle of fifths are featured heavily in the next few pieces as well as in both *Dominant Seventh Workouts*. Being familiar with the cycle will enable you to recognise parts of it when they occur in other tunes. Here are just a few examples:

● **Rhythm Changes** *I Got Rhythm* and other tunes with the same chords (eg: *The Theme*, Vol. 1, p. 122) feature the cycle in the bridge, with two bars on each chord:

(Key: B♭) || D^7 | ⁒ | G^7 | ⁒ | C^7 | ⁒ | F^7 | ⁒ ||

See also *Bebop Bridge*, p. 103, and *Rhythm Changes Comping*, pp. 192 and 196.

● **Blues** Four chords from the cycle occur for a bar each in bars 8–11 of a twelve-bar blues, and again in the turnaround, twice as fast:

(Key: F) || F^7 | $B^{\flat 7}$ | F^7 | ⁒ | $B^{\flat 7}$ | ⁒ | F^7 | D^7 | G^7 | C^7 | F^7 D^7 | G^7 C^7 || F^7

See *Tension & Release Blues #1*, p. 159, and *Tritone Blues*, IBP, p. 117.

● ***Yesterdays*** This well-known number by Jerome Kern (p. 230) features the cycle during the last eight bars:

(Key: Dm) || A^7 | D^7 | G^7 | C^7 | Cm^7 F^7 | $B^{\flat\Delta}$ | Em^7 | $E^{\flat 7}$ || Dm

● ***Sweet Georgia Brown*** The first twelve bars of this tune are a dominant seventh cycle with four bars on each chord:

(Key: A♭) || F^7 | ⁒ | ⁒ | ⁒ | $B^{\flat 7}$ | ⁒ | ⁒ | ⁒ | $E^{\flat 7}$ | ⁒ | ⁒ | ⁒ | $A^{\flat\Delta}$

● ***Caravan*** The sixteen-bar bridge of *Caravan* (p. 144) is identical to the chords for *Sweet Georgia Brown* above.

Assignments: Dominant Seventh Workout #2

❶ **Memorise the three-note voicings** Practise the right-hand chords with the CD (track 16), trying out the comping rhythm shown, and the ones given in Figs 7.5–7.7 and 7.30–7.33. Then try this with drums only, adding the left-hand bass line. If you want more time to explore the rhythms without changing chord, practise away from the CD, staying for 2, 4 or 8 bars on each chord.

❷ **Opposite shapes** Play the whole cycle a semitone lower, starting with A♭9 (**379**) and D♭13 (**736**). Although you'll be covering the same twelve chords, you'll be using the opposite shapes, ensuring you know them both in all keys.

❸ **Vary the bass line** Play a ♭**5** on the fourth beat, immediately before the root of a new chord, thereby approaching it from a semitone above:

Fig 7.57

In place of some of the **R** – **5** – **R** – **5** patterns, try playing run-ups or run-downs (see Vol. 1, Fig 3.43) – these always sound good in walking bass lines.

❹ **Four-note shapes** Repeat steps 1–3 with the chord shapes from *Bossa Nova Comping #2* overleaf, still using the walking bass line.

The Bossa Nova

The next piece uses a bass line similar to that in *Bossa Nova Comping #1* (Vol. 1, p. 145), based on the **R** and **5** of each chord. In the earlier piece, the right hand played the same chordal rhythm in every bar:

Fig 7.58: One-bar comping rhythm

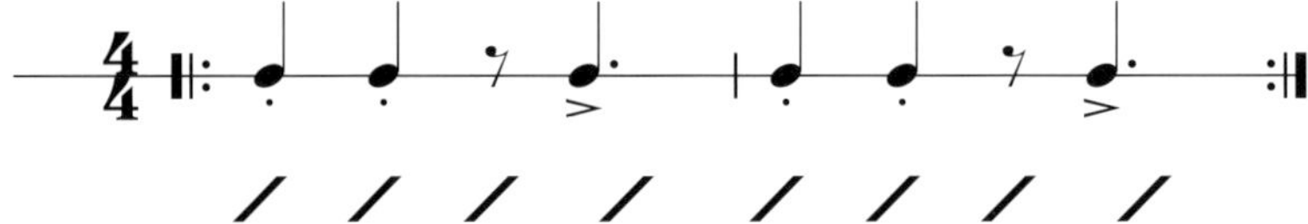

Latin rhythms often follow a two-bar pattern, the 'clave' (pronounced 'clar-vay'), after the percussion instrument upon which it is often played:

Fig 7.59: Brazilian clave

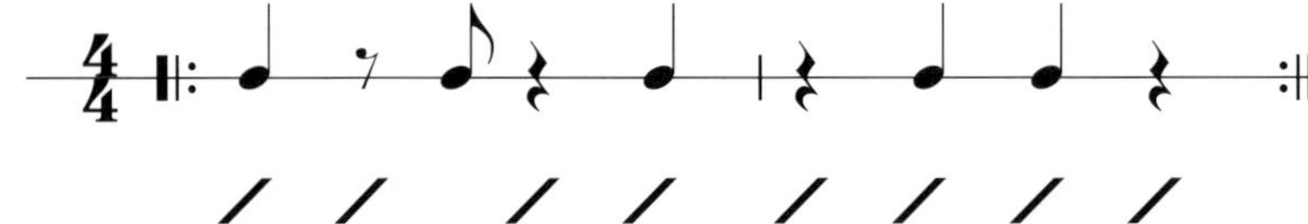

In jazz, the clave is often played slightly differently, with the last note half a beat later. This is the rhythm used for the chords in *Bossa Nova Comping #2*:

Fig 7.60: Bossa Nova (jazz) clave

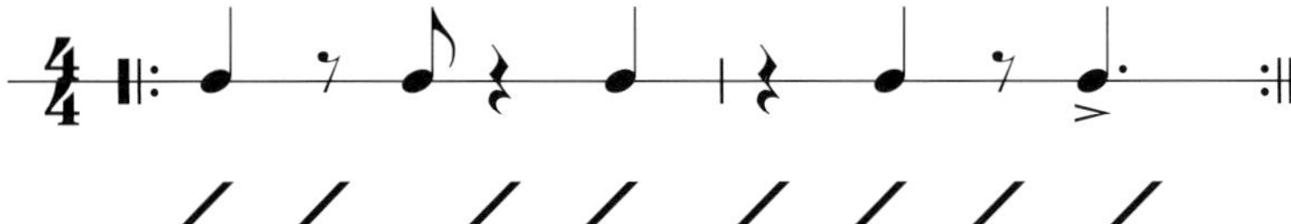

Clap or tap both these rhythms against a foot-tap or metronome until you can feel them without needing to read the notes. Jazz drummers often play the clave on the snare drum when accompanying in bossa style.

Both these claves are known as '3–2' because the first bar has 3 notes, the second bar has 2. If you start with the second bar instead, it is called a '2–3' clave. Try clapping it this way round as well until you can feel it both ways.

Fig 7.61: 2–3 Clave

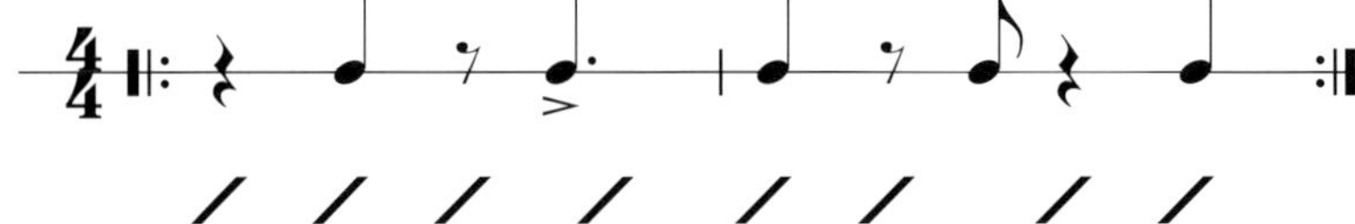

Bossa Nova Comping #2 features a 3–2 clave in the right hand, following a cycle of dominant sevenths like the previous piece. Once established in a piece of music, the clave is not usually interrupted or reversed. For a particular tune, in order to determine whether to use a 3–2 or a 2–3 clave, try them both to see which best fits in with the rhythm of the melody.

Assignments: Bossa Nova Comping #2

❶ **3–2 clave** Clap and memorise the Bossa Nova clave, then play the first two bars over and over, with the bass line, until you have mastered the co-ordination (no chord changes yet). Play slowly at first, and note that only the first two right-hand chords coincide with the left hand.

❷ **Memorise the chord shapes** Without reading the rhythm, play the complete cycle, with the bass line as written. If you wish you could do this first with the three-note shapes from *Dominant Seventh Workout #2*, p. 94. In the early stages you could also stay longer than two bars on each chord.

❸ **Play along** Drop the bass line and play the chords in either hand with the CD (track 17), keeping to the 3–2 clave throughout.

❹ **2–3 clave** Repeat steps 1–2 with the rhythm given in Fig 7.61 instead.

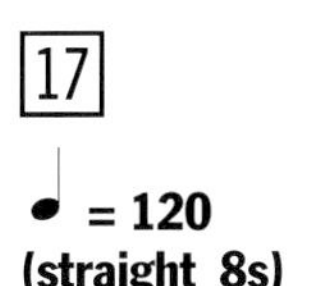

Bossa Nova Comping #2

Tim Richards

The cycle of dominant sevenths from the previous piece is played here with a Latin bass line, this time with four-note rootless thirteenth chords in the right hand.

A13 3–2 clave (9 7 6 3) D13 (6 3 9 7)

5 G13 (9 7 6 3) (rhythm *simile*) C13 (6 3 9 7)

9 F13 B♭13

13 E♭13 A♭13

17 D♭13 G♭13

21 B13 E13

The dominant bebop scale

When we created the major bebop scale by adding an extra note to the major scale (the ♭**6**), we diverted the emphasis from the seventh to the sixth of the chord. Whilst this worked well for major chords, it is not appropriate for a dominant seventh, as the ♭**7** is an essential note in the chord.

The corresponding scale for use with dominant chords is identical to the Mixolydian scale, with an extra note, the 'natural' seventh, between the root and the ♭**7**:

Fig 7.62: The dominant bebop scale

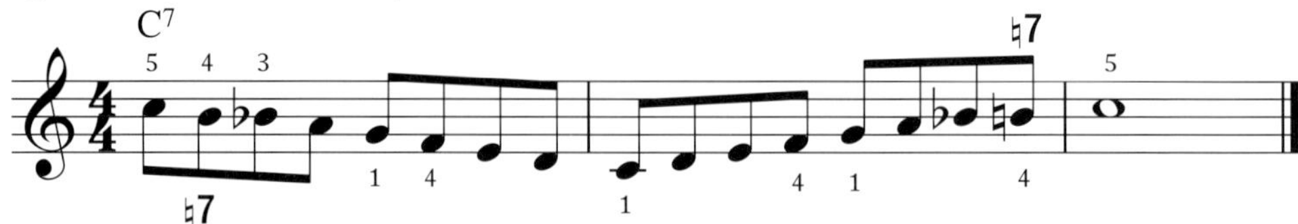

Starting this scale with **R**, **3**, **5** or ♭**7** on a downbeat will ensure that all the other notes of the chord also fall on a downbeat, even when the scale is played over several octaves. As before, you can change direction at any point:

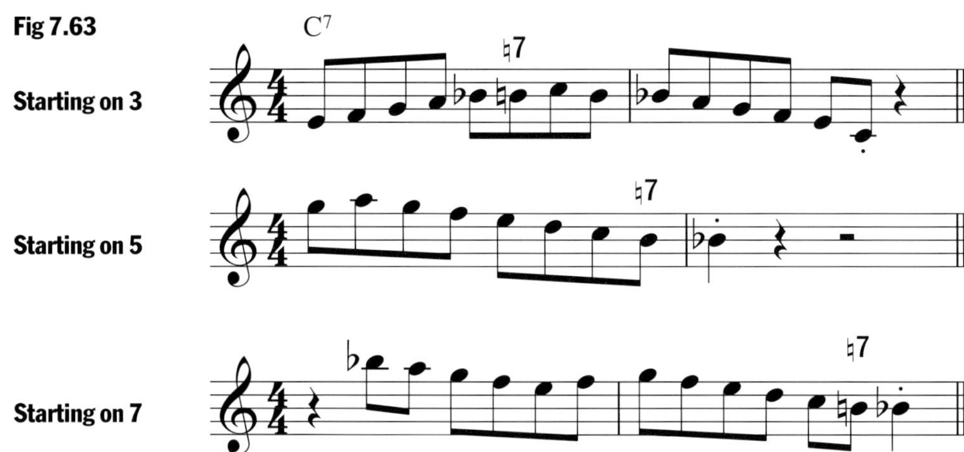

If you follow this rule when improvising with dominant scales, your lines will always swing, as the correct patterns of tension and release are built into them. This applies to eighth-note lines in any style, not just swing, but also straight-eight feels such as Latin, rock, funk, etc.

The fingering of bebop scales can take some getting used to as most people are conditioned from an early age into playing scales with seven notes, rather than eight. However, the fact that you can reverse the direction of the scale at any point can be a lifesaver if you suddenly find you have run out of fingers in the middle of a line!

The next piece, *Dominant Bebop Scale Workout*, gives you a chance to familiarise yourself with the fingering of the dominant bebop scales in various keys, by playing them round the cycle of fifths. The cycle is the same as in the last two pieces, but starts in a different place:

C7	F7	B♭7	E♭7
A♭7	D♭7	F♯7	B7
E7	A7	D7	G7

The **7936** and **3679** rootless thirteenth chords from *Bossa Nova Comping #2* have now been transferred to the left hand.

18 with bass & drums

♩ = 144 (swing 8s)

Dominant Bebop Scale Workout

Tim Richards

This is the first half of a cycle of dominant sevenths – complete it yourself for the remaining six chords.

Assignments and Improvisation Tips

❶ **Memorise the left-hand chords** Practise them with the CD (bass and drums only) round the whole cycle (not just the six chords given above).

❷ **Comping rhythms** Explore different rhythms for the chords (on the beat, off the beat, one-bar patterns, two-bar patterns, etc). When you find a rhythmic pattern you like, take it through the whole cycle. Remember also to vary the articulation, playing both short (*staccato*) and long (held) chords.

❸ **Bebop scale fingering** Memorise the bebop scale phrases given, taking care with the fingering in all keys, including those not written above. Play this and all the assignments that follow with left-hand chords, with the CD (bass and drums only). Review 'Playing left-hand chords off the beat', p. 67.

❹ **Reverse the direction** Play the C7 scale ascending, the F7 scale descending, and so on through the cycle. Also try changing the direction of the scales at any point in mid-phrase.

❺ **Don't always start on the root** Go through the cycle again, starting bebop scale phrases on **3**, **5**, or **7** of the chords, in both directions as above.

❻ **Don't always start on the first beat** Alter the phrasing by starting on the second, third, or fourth beats of the bar. Providing you start with **R**, **3**, **5** or **7** on a downbeat your line will be ok. You can also start phrases on an upbeat, but the next note must be one of the above to conform with this rule.

❼ **Improvise freely!** Mix other phrases in with the bebop scale. You might try deliberately alternating ideas, one or two bars each, eg:

- arpeggios – bebop scale
- bebop scale – major pentatonic
- chord/scale lick – broken chords
- scale patterns – blues scale

Don't forget to leave some space too!

Encircling the fifth of the dominant chord

We'll now look at another technique that you can use when improvising over the twelve chords in *Dominant Bebop Scale Workout*, to give you an alternative to the bebop scale.

By now you should be quite used to encircling the root and third of a chord during the course of your improvisations (see 'Encircling notes with arpeggios', p. 89). The fifth is also a favourite note for encircling, especially with dominant chords. This is often accomplished by using a pick-up:

Fig 7.64

Example (a) encircles the fifth chromatically, by preceding it with **♯5** and **♭5**. In example (b), and in Fig 7.65, there are two upper notes, **6** and **7**.

As long as the fifth is still the target note (ie: on a downbeat), the encircling notes can also appear at the beginning of the bar. The next example starts with the same four notes as the pick-up used in (b) above:

Fig 7.65:

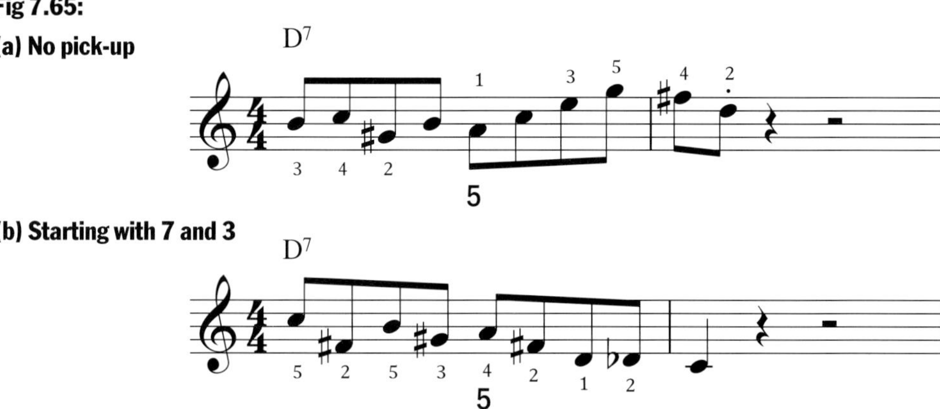

Accomplished players often encircle the fifth in the middle of a phrase, thus adding interest to ordinary scales, breaking up the line and introducing chromaticism:

Fig 7.66: Scale phrases with encircled fifth

(a) Ascending line

(b) Descending line

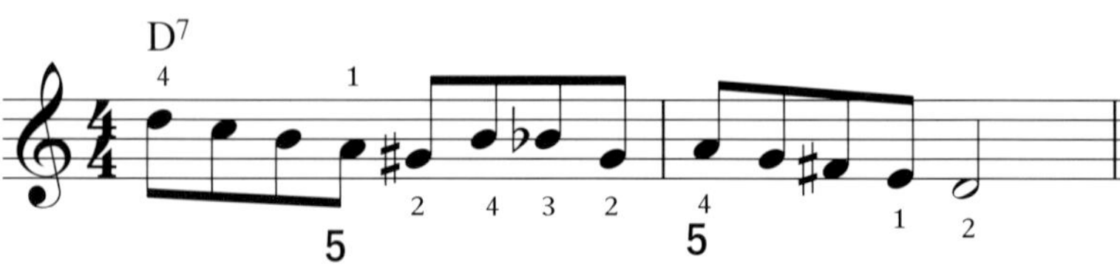

Assignments: Encircling the fifth

❶ **Cycle of fifths** Memorise one of the phrases from Fig 7.64 and work it out in all twelve keys, following the cycle at the bottom of p. 98. To help with this focus on the fifth of each chord to find the encircling notes for the pick-up. Sing each phrase before you play it.

❷ **Play along** When you've worked out the fingerings in all keys, play the phrases with the *Dominant Bebop Scale Workout* backing (track 18), remembering to start each pick-up on the fourth beat of the bar before the new chord.

❸ **Add left-hand chords** Repeat step 2, adding the rootless thirteenth voicings given on p. 99. Try out different left-hand rhythms.

❹ **Repeat steps 1–3** Choose another lick from p. 100 and repeat the process. When you're familiar with different ways of encircling the fifth, try varying the endings of the phrases at will, making up similar phrases of your own.

❺ **Bebop scale** Combine these ideas with the dominant bebop scale. To incorporate it into the phrases on p. 100, play the bebop scale up or down from the fifth straight after encircling it.

Alternatively, you could use the bebop scale on some chords, the phrases on p. 100 on others, perhaps alternating them to give contrast and variety.

The minor bebop scale

When improvising over a **II** – **V**, we've seen how the Dorian scale used for the **II** chord has the same notes as the Mixolydian scale used over **V**, because they are both modes of the parent key (**I**) (see Vol. 1, pp. 141, 161–163 , 172 and Fig 4.31).

This principle also applies to bebop scales in a **II** – **V**, so that the dominant bebop scale used for the **V** chord can also be played over the **II** chord that precedes it:

Fig 7.67: The F7 dominant bebop scale fits over Cm7 – F7

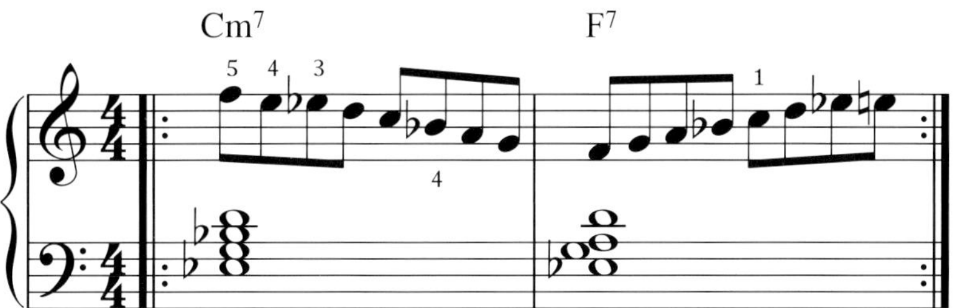

This works because it's ok to play the fourth of a minor chord on the beat, unlike with major or dominant chords. From the point of view of minor chords, the bebop scale is the same as the Dorian mode, with an extra note between ♭**3** and **4**. This note is the major third, but it sounds fine because it is always played on the upbeat.

The correct starting notes for a minor chord will be the same notes that work for the related **V** chord – **R**, **3**, **5** and **7**. Thinking from the root of the minor chord, these notes become **4, 6, R** or **3**. It is safe to go up or down from any of these, as long as you place them on the downbeat:

Fig 7.68: Bebop scale over Am7 (these phrases also fit D7)

Starting on 4

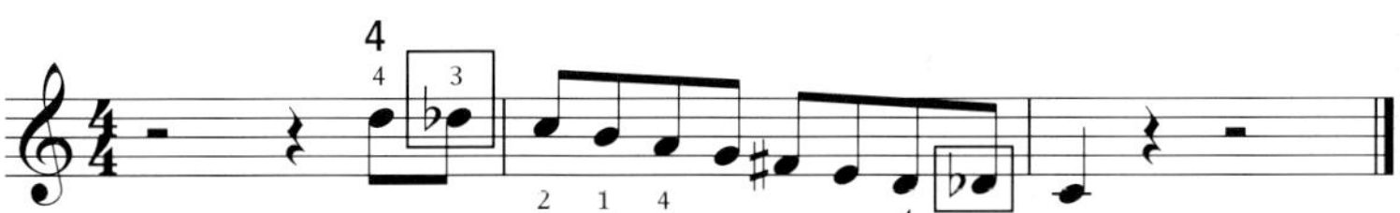

Starting on 6

Starting on R

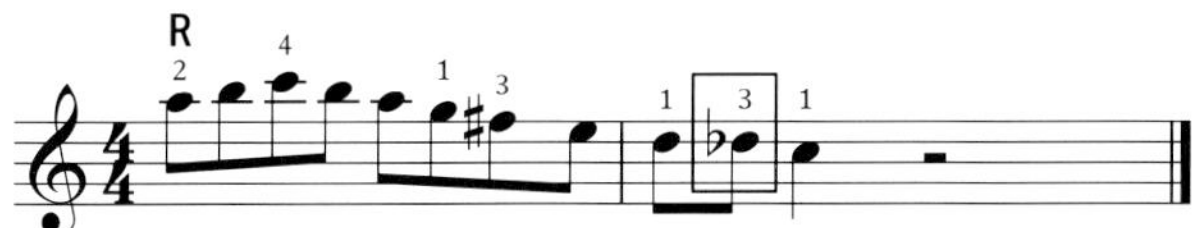

Starting on 3

Revisiting the bridge of 'Rhythm Changes'

Countless tunes have been written using the chord sequence of *I Got Rhythm*, featuring the cycle of fifths bridge we saw in *The Theme* (Vol. 1, p. 122). The last chord of the bridge must be the **V** chord of the key, in this case F7 (key of B♭).

The following two-handed voicings have **R3** or **R7** shells in the left hand, using the same format as the **II** – **V** – **I** voicings shown on p. 76. Play two bars on each chord to make the eight-bar bridge:

Fig 7.69

(a) Four notes starting with R7/35

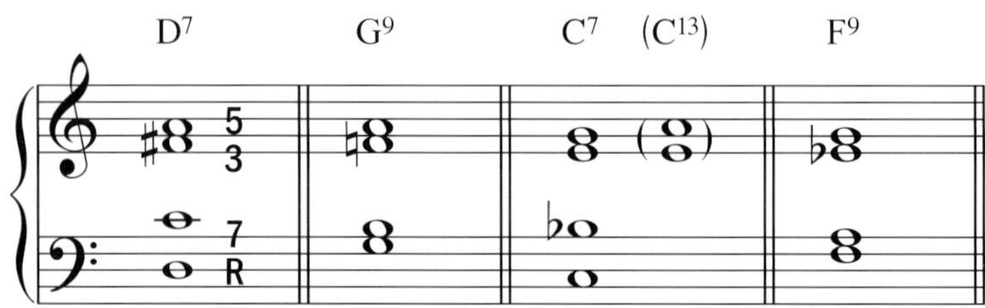

(b) Four notes starting with R3/79

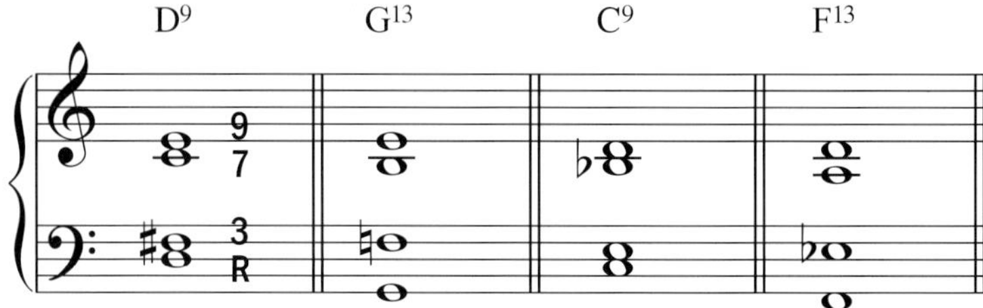

Once you've memorised the above, try adding a third note in the right hand:

Fig 7.70

(a) Five notes starting with R7/36R

D13 G9 C13 F13

R 6 3 7 R

(b) Five notes starting with R3/795

D9 G13 C9 (C13) F13

5 9 7 3 R

Rather than playing for two bars on each chord, many musicians convert some of the dominant chords into **II** – **V**s, by replacing the first bar with a minor chord a fourth below. This can take place on any of the chords, eg:

Original bridge:	D7	⁒	G7	⁒	C7	⁒	F7	⁒
II chord before D7 and C7:	**Am7**	D7	G7	⁒	**Gm7**	C7	F7	⁒
II chord before G7 and F7:	D7	⁒	**Dm7**	G7	C7	⁒	**Cm7**	F7
II chord before all four chords:	**Am7**	D7	**Dm7**	G7	**Gm7**	C7	**Cm7**	F7

Bebop Bridge opposite uses the eight chords of the last example, the first four of which are the same as bars 11–14 of *Ladybird* (p. 78).

19 with bass & drums

♩ = 160 (swing 8s)

Bebop Bridge

Tim Richards

This will give you practice at playing **II – V**s over a 'Rhythm Changes' bridge in B♭. Play the scales and arpeggios up and down, not just in the directions suggested.

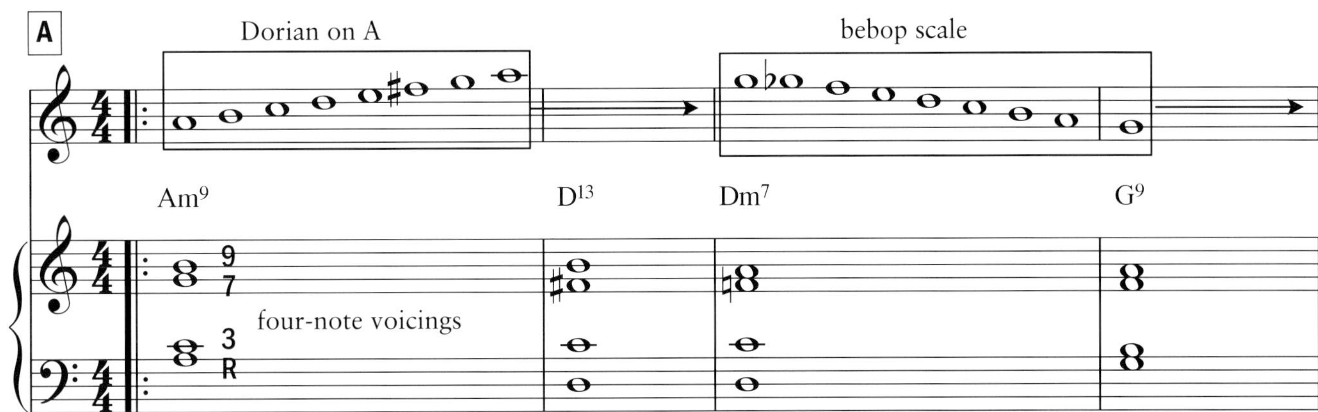

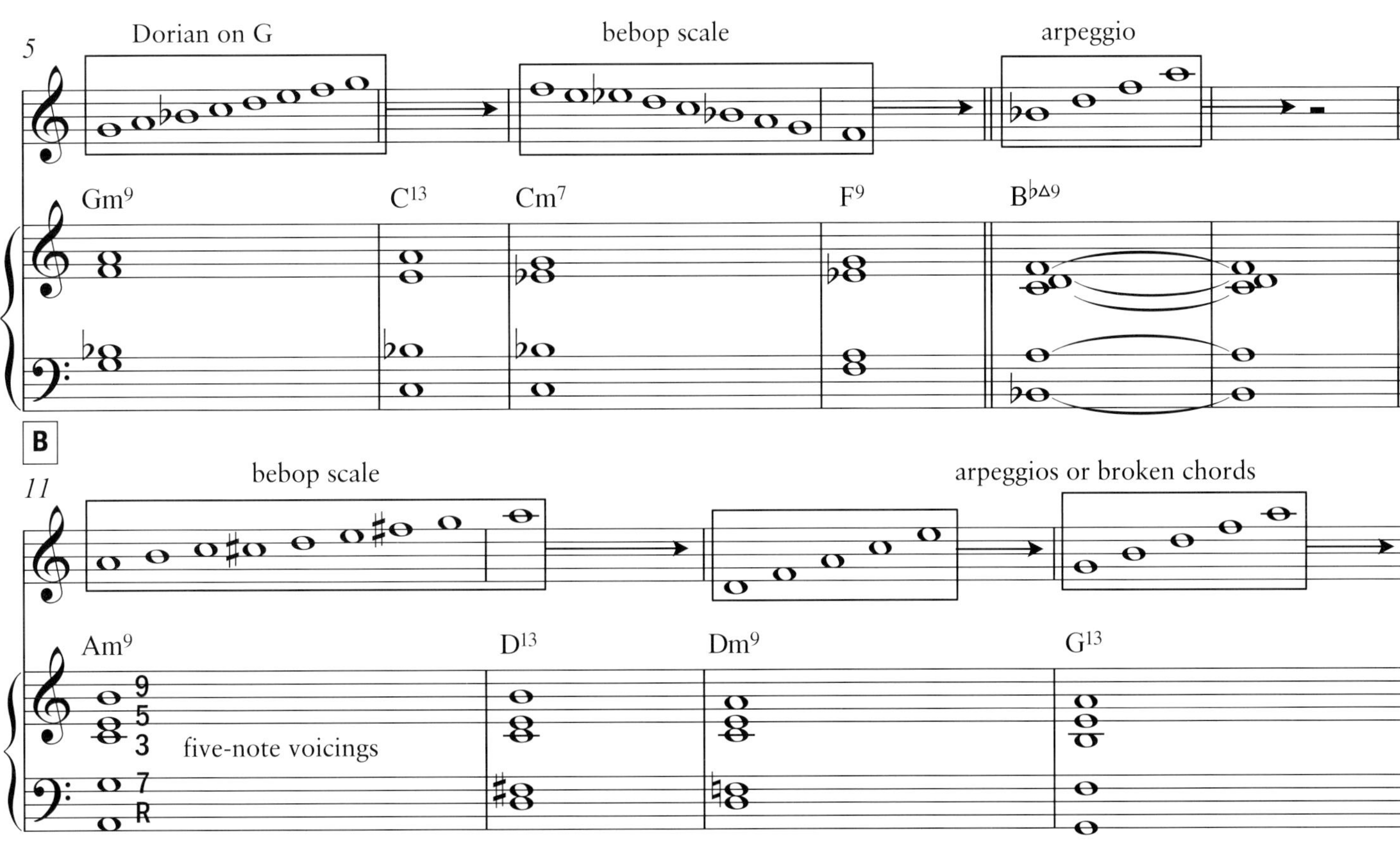

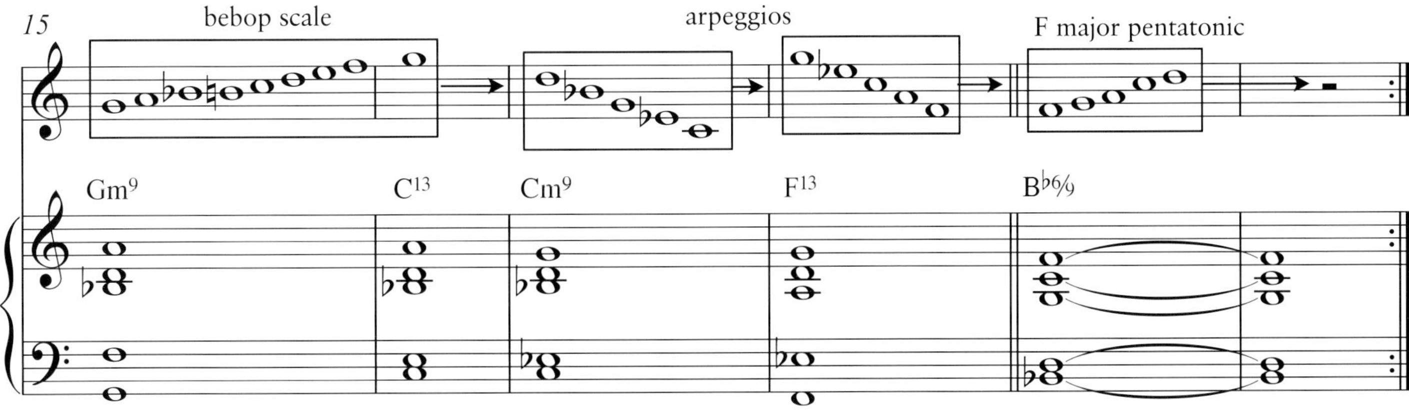

Assignments: Bebop Bridge

❶ **Comping – two-handed voicings** Play the first set of voicings at 'A', with the CD (track 19, bass and drums only), exploring the comping rhythms given on pp. 64 and 82–3. Notice that the shapes stay around the centre of the keyboard and give a pleasantly light sound.

❷ **Five-note voicings** When you are comfortable with the above, try the second set of chords at 'B', which use the opposite shells. Although each chord has the same top note as the four-note voicing, they sound much 'beefier' due to the extra note and the lower register of the bottom four notes. Familiarity with both sets will give you the ability to vary the weight and texture of your comping without altering the top note – an important skill.

❸ **Improvisation** Accompanying yourself with the left-hand shells, improvise in the right hand using the scales or arpeggios suggested. Try both sets of shells – the ones at 'B' free up the area of the piano around middle C for use by the right hand.

❹ **Rootless voicings** Memorise the shapes below for the eight chords (see Figs 7.35 and 7.37) and play them in the right hand against a walking bass line. The example below shows how you might sound if you were accompanying somebody in this style (without a bassist). Notice the pushed right-hand chords:

Fig 7.71: Accompaniment style

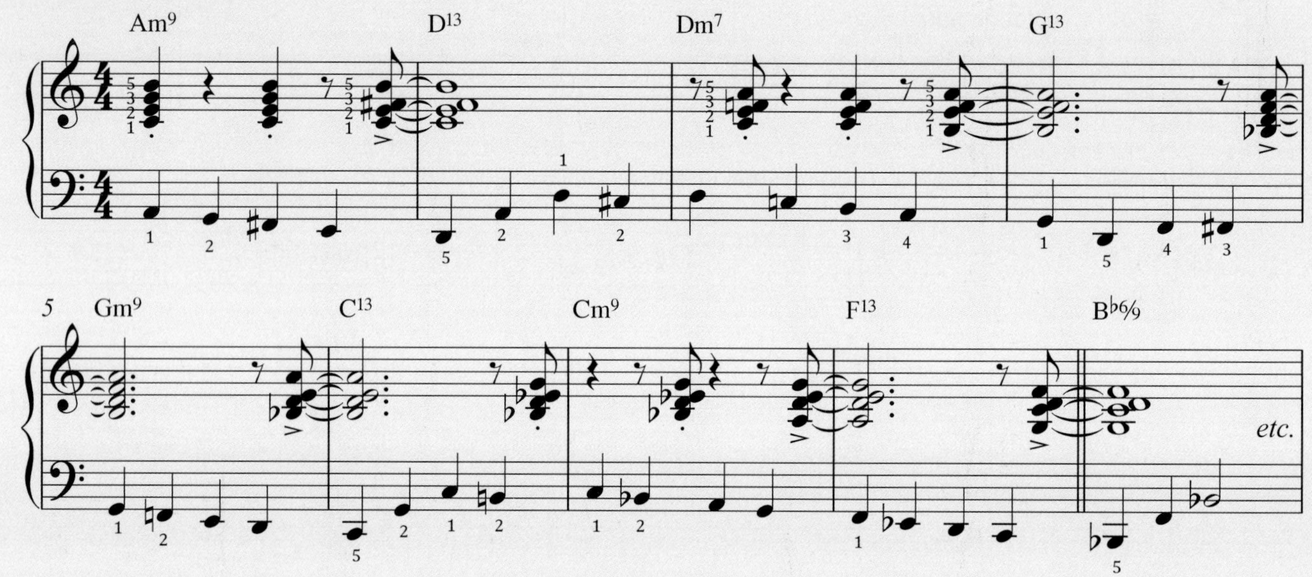

Vary the right-hand rhythms, and make up your own bass lines using a combination of scale and chord patterns in both directions (see Vol. 1, Fig 3.43).

❺ **Opposite shapes** Now learn the opposite set of shapes to Fig 7.71, and practise them in the left hand with the CD (bass and drums only).

Fig 7.72

Use these shapes to accompany your right-hand improvisation, instead of the shells.

❻ **Complete the cycle** Extending it beyond the eight bars of the bridge gives a complete sequence of twenty-four chords, passing through all twelve keys:

Am7 – D7	Dm7 – G7	Gm7 – C7	Cm7 – F7
Fm7 – B♭7	B♭m7 – E♭7	E♭m7 – A♭7	A♭m7 – D♭7
C♯m7 – F♯7	F♯m7 – B7	Bm7 – E7	Em7 – A7

Repeat all the steps above round this complete cycle – it's a great practice routine which will accelerate your ability to play in different keys.

Long II – V patterns

Most jazz musicians have a repertoire of **II – V** patterns that helps them to improvise convincingly in the jazz idiom. Many of these patterns are heard so frequently, across many different styles of jazz, that they have become 'public domain'.

I have dealt with short **II – V** patterns earlier in this chapter (pp. 68–70). When the chords last a bar each, a long **II – V** pattern is required:

Fig 7.73: Typical long II – V pattern played in eighth-notes

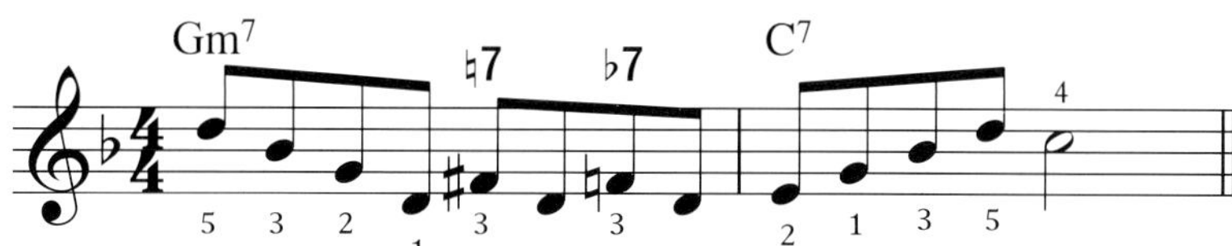

This phrase, or variations on it, has been used by countless jazz musicians, including John Coltrane, Oscar Peterson, Bill Evans, Charlie Parker, to name just a few. Notice that the F♯ (not a note of the Gm7 chord) is used to delay the resolution to E (the target note for C7).

If the same pattern is played in sixteenth-notes, it will fit a short **II – V**:

Fig 7.74: Same pattern in double time

Here are two more useful long **II – V** patterns suitable for either situation, both of which include the extra note (B) from the C dominant bebop scale:

Fig 7.75

(a)

(b)

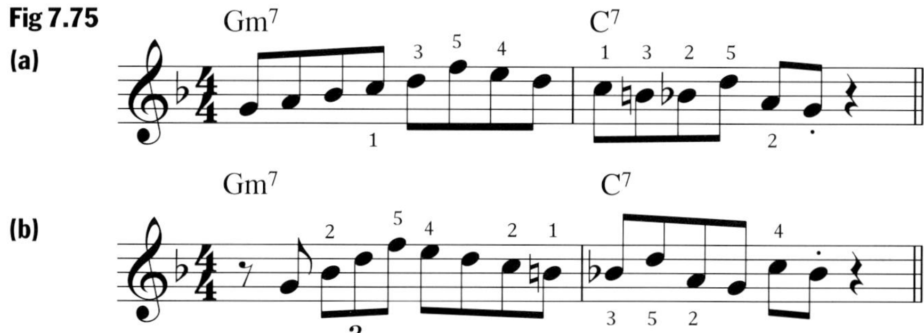

Assignments and Improvisation Tips: Long II – V patterns

❶ ***Ladybird*** Memorise one of the patterns above, and try playing it during your solo, using track 13 as a backing. You'll need to have prepared patterns and worked out the fingering for the four long **II – Vs** that occur in this tune (see p. 78):

Fm7 – B♭7 B♭m7 – E♭7 Am7 – D7 Dm7 – G7

Make each **II – V** pattern join up with the notes in the following bar, so that they blend in with the rest of your improvisation.

❷ ***Dominant Bebop Scale Workout*** Return to this piece (p. 99), replacing some of the written right-hand material with long **II – V** patterns. Because each dominant chord last two bars, you can treat the first bar as a minor (**II**) chord for the purposes of your solo: two bars of C7 will therefore become Gm7 – C7. There's no need to do this on every chord, give yourself some space between **II – V** patterns, improvising with the bebop scales as suggested.

❸ ***Bebop Bridge*** Incorporate long **II – V** patterns in some of the bars of this piece (p. 103), in place of the suggested scales or arpeggios. You might try this in bars 1–2 and 5–6, or in bars 3–4 and 7–8. Try to run each lick into the material in the following bar so that you obtain a good flow, rather than playing a series of short phrases.

❹ ***Short II – V Workout*** Return to this piece (p. 71), incorporating some of the patterns you have learnt, playing them in *double time* as in Fig 7.74. There's no need to swing the sixteenth-notes, even when playing in a swing-feel piece.

20

Misty

♩ = 76
(swing 8s, except where marked)

Erroll Garner
arr. Tim Richards

Garner's popular ballad is still an essential item in many jazz pianists' repertoires.

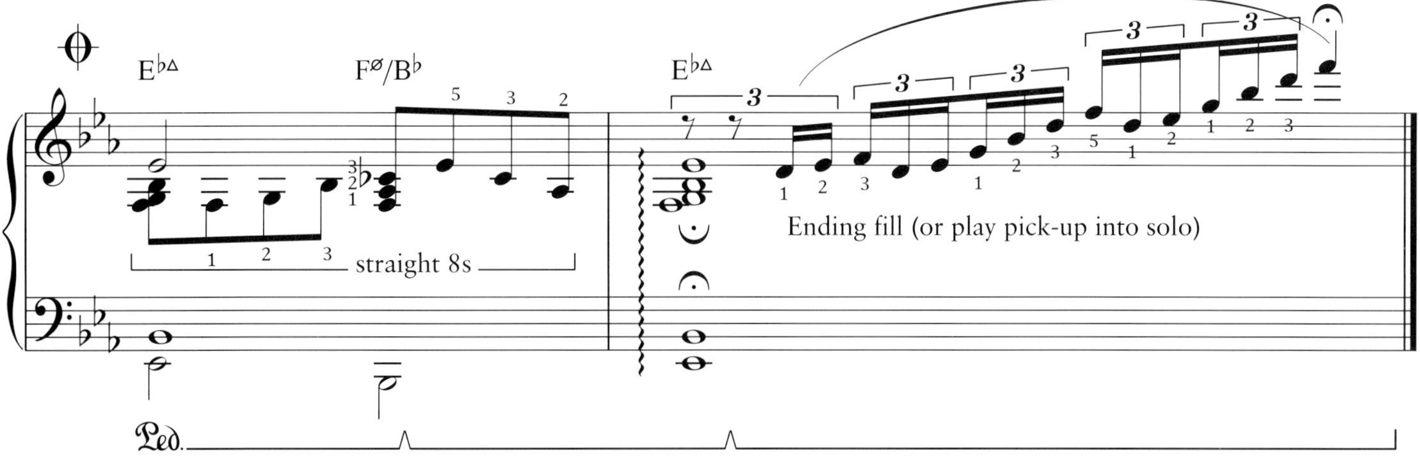

Checkpoint: Misty

● **AABA form** *Misty* has the common 32-bar song form with 'A' and 'B' sections lasting 8 bars, like *Take the 'A' Train, The Theme, In a Sentimental Mood* (Vol. 1), and *Impressions* (p. 38). As usual with chord charts and lead sheets, it is laid out as concisely as possible to save space. On the repeat of the first 'A', remember to replace bars 7–8 with the second time bars to lead into the bridge ('B'). After the bridge repeat the first 'A', jumping to the coda at the sign. The AABA form must be strictly adhered to during the improvised solos as well.

● **Two-handed shapes** This arrangement demonstrates the technique of placing the melody note at the top of a two-handed voicing. This is especially useful for the **II – V**s in bars 2 and 4, when the melody note is the ninth of the minor chord:

Fig 7.76: R7/359 shapes

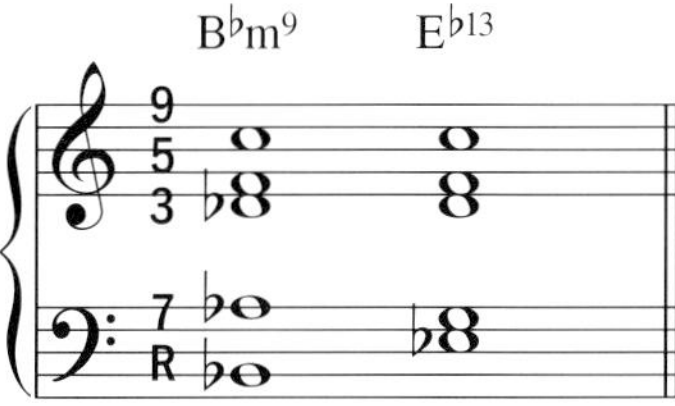

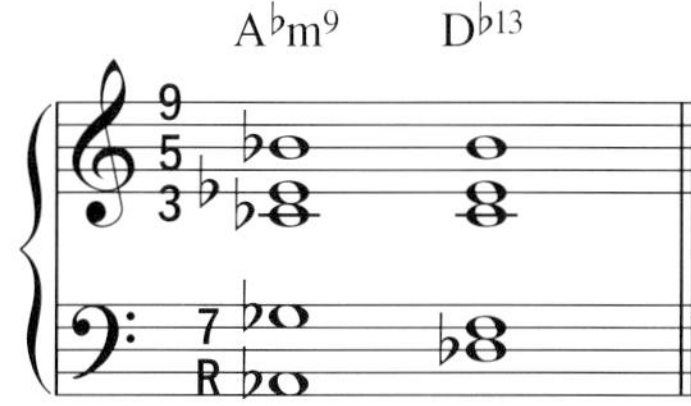

● **Pseudo-stride in bridge** In contrast, the melody in bars 16–22 is played in single notes or octaves against a left hand that imitates stride piano, the 'pseudo-stride' style (see p. 109), similar to the left hand in *Autumn Leaves* (Vol. 1, p. 150).

● **Pentatonic scales** The right-hand E♭Δ octaves that lead to the bridge and the similar A♭Δ phrase four bars later both follow major pentatonic scales based on the chords. Note that the A♭ scale starts on the fifth (E♭):

Fig 7.77

(a) E♭ major pentatonic (bar 16) **(b) A♭ major pentatonic (bar 20)**

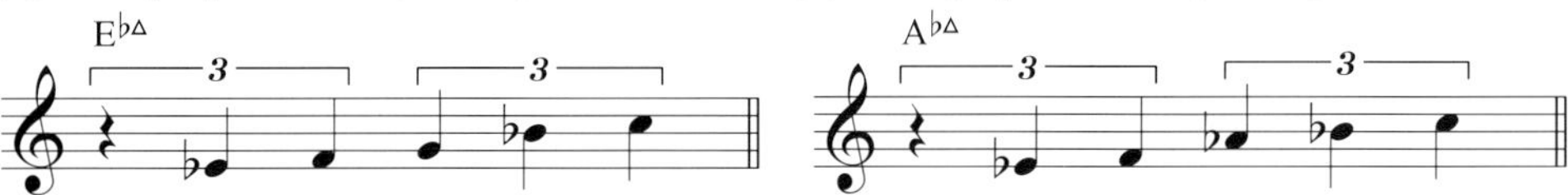

● **Quarter-note triplets** The ability to play 'three against two' is very important in bars 16, 18, 20 and 22. Practise tapping the polyrhythm on your knees:

Fig 7.78: Three against two

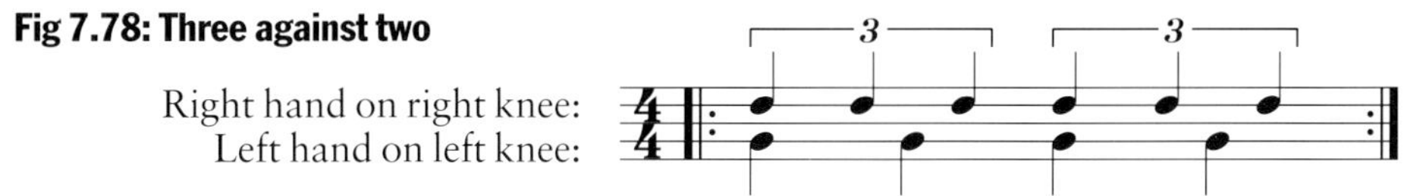

Both hands must spread their notes evenly across the bar. Listen alternately to the left hand (count '1, 2, 3, 4') and the right hand (count '1, 2, 3, 4 , 5, 6'), and check that this is the case. See also 'Polyrhythms' (p. 25), *Blueberry Hill* (IBP, pp. 186–187) and *Honky Tonk Train Blues* (IBP, pp. 235–239).

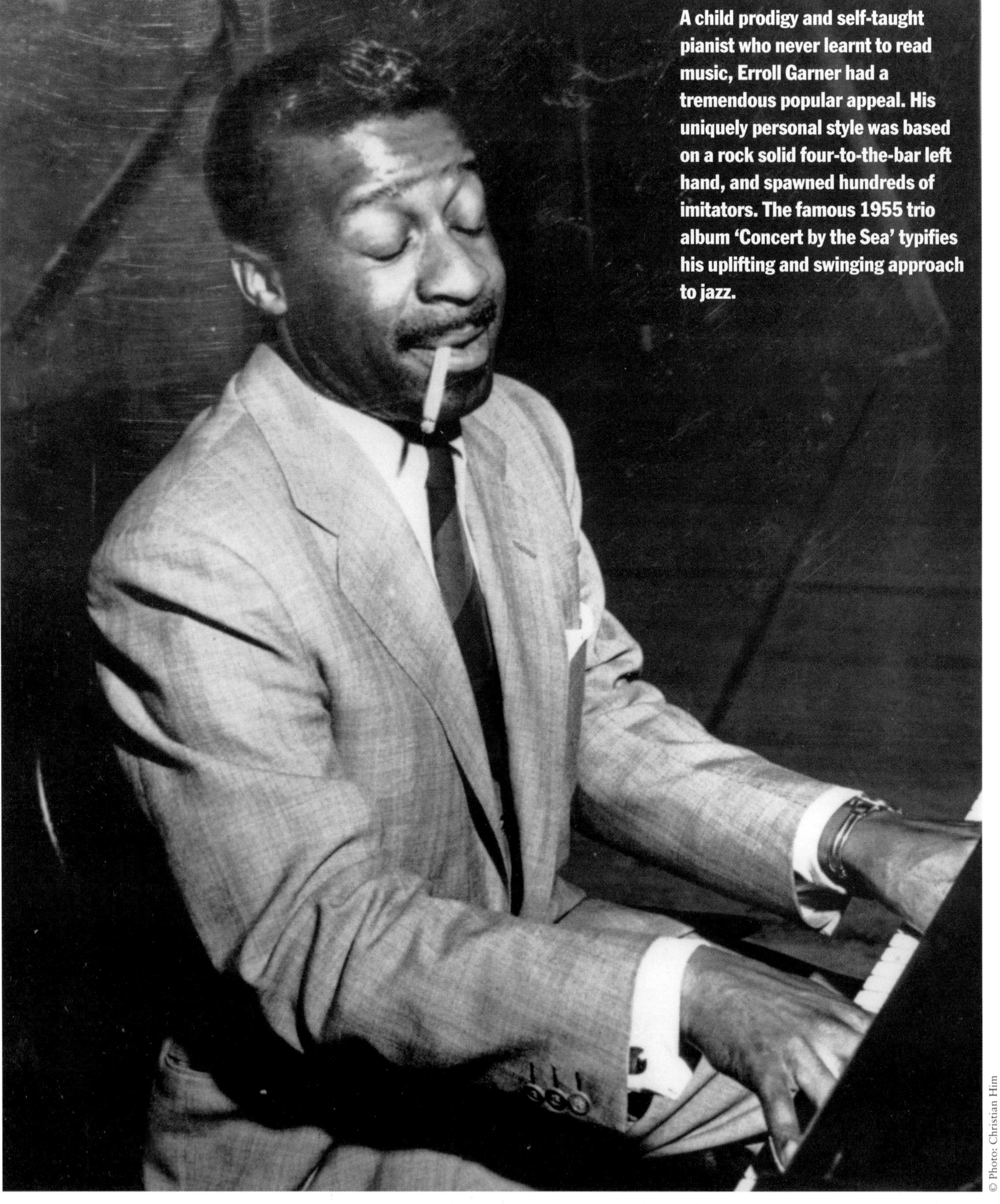

A child prodigy and self-taught pianist who never learnt to read music, Erroll Garner had a tremendous popular appeal. His uniquely personal style was based on a rock solid four-to-the-bar left hand, and spawned hundreds of imitators. The famous 1955 trio album 'Concert by the Sea' typifies his uplifting and swinging approach to jazz.

● **Coda** Bar 31 has exactly the same chord shapes as bar 15 (the second time bar of the 'A' section), but I have written the right hand in an arpeggiated style to fill out the rhythm. You could use the same arpeggiated technique in other places where the melody is static, eg: the Gm7– G♭7 – Fm7 chords in bars 7–8.
● **Ending fill** The E♭Δ9 right-hand lick encircles the root of the chord in the manner described in Fig 7.44. Only play this at the end of the piece – if you are going to improvise over the AABA form, lead into your solo here instead.

Some stride piano techniques

The 'pseudo-stride' left-hand used in the bridge of my arrangement of *Misty* involves relatively little hand movement and with practice can be played without looking at the left hand, by feel alone.

When a chord lasts a whole bar, the little finger alternates **R** and **3** in the bass, as in the lead-in to the bridge (bar 16), and the A♭Δchord in bars 19–20:

Fig 7.79: Pseudo-stride pattern

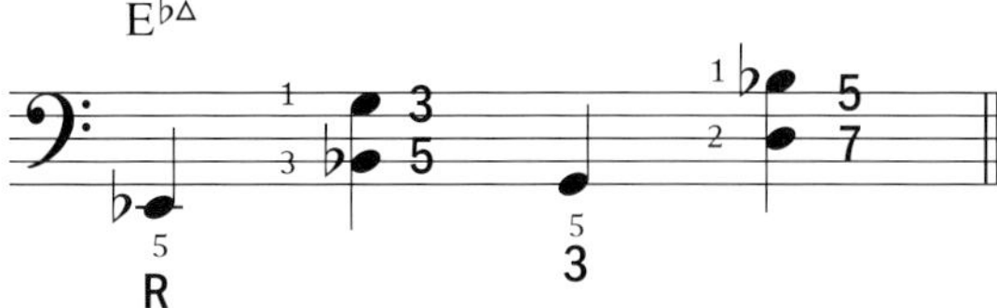

Pseudo-stride gives the effect of the stride piano style, but with less of the up-and-down arm movement. In genuine stride, a chord lasting a whole bar usually alternates a deep **R** and **5** in the bass with an inversion in the centre of the piano:

Fig 7.80: Genuine stride pattern

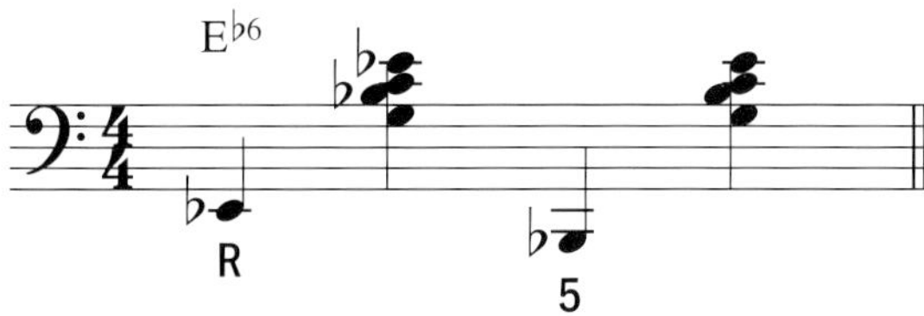

Stride piano is a style that dates right back to the days of ragtime, and is basically a solo piano style – the left hand pumps out a four-to-the-bar bass line and chords, making a rhythm section unnecessary. James Johnson, Fats Waller, Earl Hines and Art Tatum were some of the masters of this style in the 1930s and 40s.

The pianists of this era would generally play the central chord shapes as ordinary four-note inversions, such as the E♭6 in Fig 7.80, without ninths or other extensions. However, pianists like Thelonious Monk and Jaki Byard continued to play stride in the 1950s, 60s and later, updating it with their own more modern chord shapes, which might include clusters, whole-tone voicings or ♭**5** chords.

The following sample left hand does include some ninths and thirteenths, as most of the central chords are rootless, avoiding the 'old-fashioned' sound of Fig 7.80:

Fig 7.81: Stride left hand for the first eight bars of *Misty*

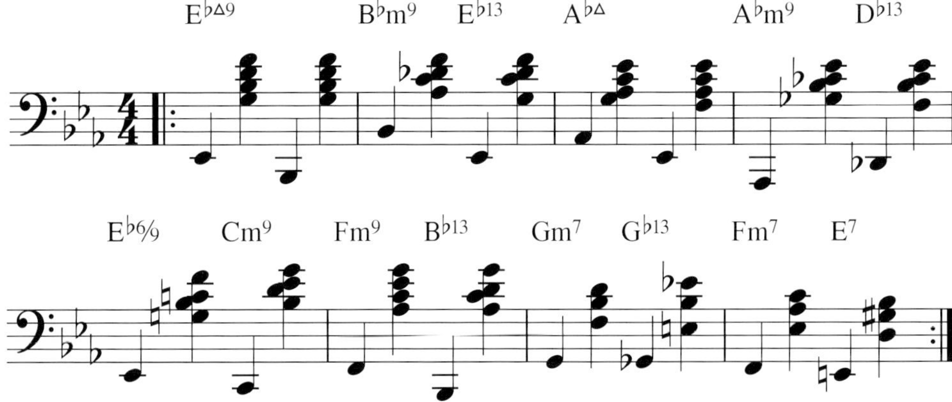

Note that **5** only appears in the bass if a chord lasts a whole bar (as in bars 1 and 3). When the chords change every two beats, only the roots are played.

Stride is still an important solo piano style today. Feel free to change some of the shapes to suit yourself – your choice of voicings will determine whether you sound contemporary or traditional.

Tenths

A common stride technique is to play a tenth (**R** and **3**) on the first beat of the bar, especially with major chords. The fifth is often included in the middle, making an open triad (**R53**):

Fig 7.82: Tenth on first beat

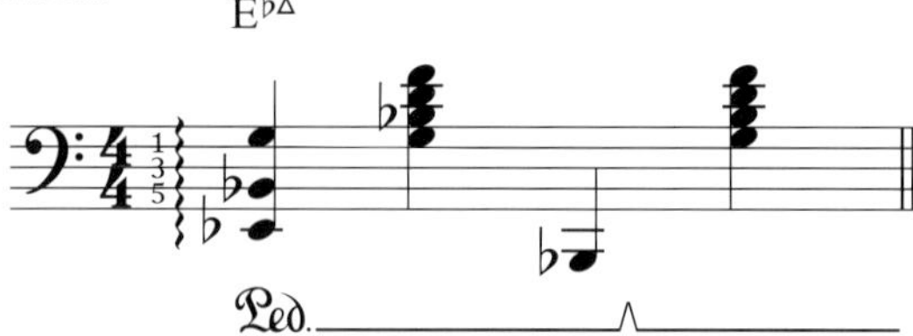

If you have large hands, you may be able to play all the notes of the tenth together, as Art Tatum would have done! (see Vol. 1, Fig. 4.32). Most people will have to 'flip' them, from the bottom note up, using the sustain pedal so that all three notes sound together. You'll need to keep a loose, flexible wrist as you move your hand and arm rapidly from left to right, keeping your third finger on the middle note. Always place the top note (G in this case) on the first beat of the bar.

Here is another very common stride device, often played in place of two bars on a major chord. It is shown here in pseudo-stride style:

Fig 7.83: Pseudo-stride left hand for two bars of E♭Δ

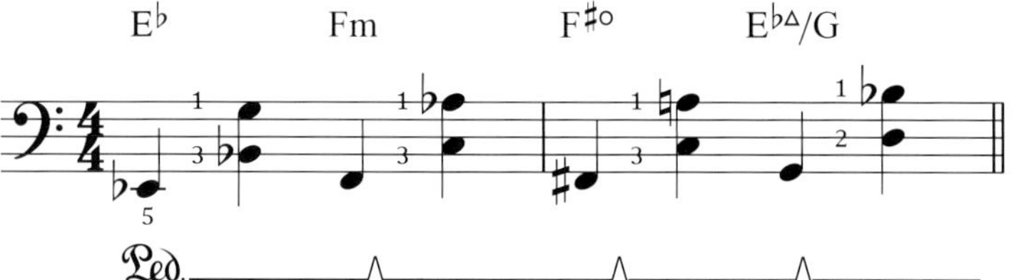

We've added two passing chords, Fm and F♯° (F♯ diminished), in the middle of the two bars of E♭Δ. This is often possible in passages of static harmony, as long as there is no clash with the melody. (See Chapter 8 for more on diminished chords, and Figs 8.4–8.6 for other ways of playing this sequence.)

Fig 7.83 could be played in bars 15–16 of *Misty*, in place of the E♭ – Fø – E♭ chords given. In another context, the same four chords might be condensed into one bar, and played as 'walking' tenths, without the middle note:

Fig 7.84: Walking tenths for one bar of E♭Δ or E♭7

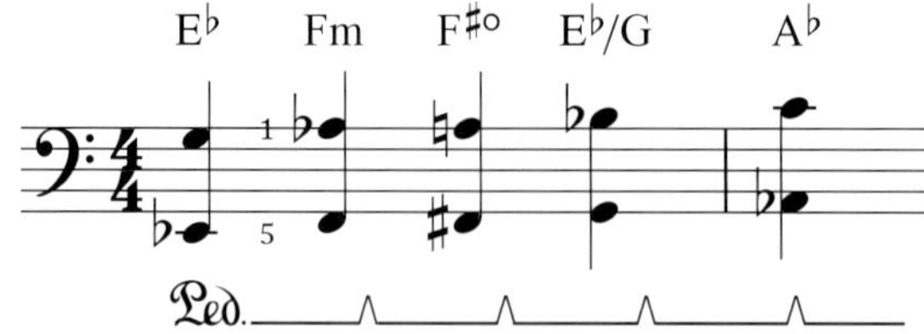

As before, you'll probably have to flip the tenths, placing the top notes on the beat, and changing the pedal with each pair of notes as marked.

Fig 7.84 is really a harmonised version of the run-up found in walking bass lines when the chords move up in fourths (see *Swinging Comping #1* and #2, pp. 81 and 85). Notice how all the notes move up in semitones, apart from the first two bass notes which are a tone apart.

In a long **II** – **V** – **I**, you can play these walking tenths for the **V** chord, and sometimes for **I** as well. Apply this to the E♭7 chord in bars 17–19 of *Misty* as follows:

Instead of: || B♭m7 E♭7 | B♭m7 E♭7 | A♭Δ | ⁒ |

Play: || B♭m7 | E♭7 | A♭Δ | ⁒ |

Assignments and Improvisation Tips: Misty

❶ **Melody** Play the arrangement and memorise the tune and chord sequence.

❷ **Add right-hand fills** Many pianists like to add their own personal flourishes, especially in ballads, at points where there are gaps in the melody. Whilst this can lead to an over-flowery result, it is effective in moderation. The following examples both use just two notes – **3** and **7** of the E♭Δ and A♭Δ chords:

Fig 7.85: Fills in bars 1 and 3 of *Misty*

The fills must not interrupt the timing of the melody or left-hand chords. Tap your foot as shown, use a metronome, and count, to help you come in at the right time with the next phrase after each fill. The fill in bar 3 has less notes than in bar 1 because the right-hand melody enters a beat earlier with the triplet pick-up.

❸ **Improvisation: 'A' section** Memorise the left-hand shells from the first eight bars, and use them to accompany a right-hand solo over the same chords, playing the same eight bars round and round.

In the right hand, use either arpeggios or the related scales of the chords. Try to avoid using the same approach every time. For the first 'A' you might play arpeggio patterns over the four chords E♭Δ – Cm7 – Fm7 – B♭7; for the second 'A' you could play an E♭ major pentatonic, because they are **I** – **VI** – **II** – **V** in the key of E♭. Further ideas over these chords are shown in the next piece, *Turnaround Workout #1.*

❹ **Stride piano** Play Fig 7.81 over and over until you know it from memory. When you're confident with it, add the melody (section 'A') in the right hand in single notes, moving it up an octave.

Next, repeat your solo ideas from step 3 over the stride left hand. It will help if you keep your right-hand ideas very simple to start with – leave plenty of gaps and make your first priority not to interrupt the left-hand pulse.

❺ **Improvisation: Bridge** Memorise the pseudo-stride left hand given on p. 106, and try to construct a right-hand solo over it, just as you did for steps 3 and 4. The first four bars (B♭m7– E♭7 – A♭Δ) could all have the same scale (Dorian on B♭, or A♭ major), or you could play arpeggios, **II** – **V** patterns, bebop scales, etc.

❻ **AABA form** Now play a complete improvisation over the whole 32-bar form, piecing together your ideas from steps 3–5. At the end of the second 'A' section, remember to play the pseudo-stride pattern from Fig 7.83 in place of bars 7–8, to take you to the bridge.

❼ **Solo piano** The secret of being a successful solo pianist lies in having a strong left hand. Work on all the stride and pseudo-stride techniques discussed in the last few pages, practising the left-hand variations over and over to get a smooth result, before attempting to add any right hand.

❽ **Variety** Try things differently, eg: learn to play the bridge with a genuine stride pattern, or with shells. Or work out a pseudo-stride left hand for the 'A' section as an alternative to the genuine stride pattern given in Fig 7.81.

During one chorus of melody or improvisation (32 bars), there will be three 'A' sections, so don't be lazy and play them all exactly the same, even though it's written that way. Remember that the chart is just a starting point!

21 with drums
Includes play-along sections
♩ = 100 (swing 8s)

Turnaround Workout #1

Tim Richards

This features six different styles of left-hand accompaniment and six suggestions for improvisation, all for the same four chords in the key of E♭ – a kind of summary of the concepts covered so far. Try out each right-hand suggestion with all six left-hand patterns.

Checkpoint: Turnaround Workout #1

● **The turnaround** Each line of this piece has the same chords, **I** – **VI** – **II** – **V** in E♭, containing only notes from the scale of E♭. This sequence is called a turnaround because it is often found in the last two bars of a tune, the **V** chord sending you back to the **I** chord at the start. In *Misty*, however, the chords appear in bars 5–6.

● **Right-hand ideas** Play your improvisations in eighth-notes. Stay as long as you like on each right-hand approach, taking time to master the co-ordination with the various left-hand styles.

Two four-bar examples of each approach are given on the CD (track 21), with a four-bar gap after each for you to repeat the phrase, or insert your own ideas.

Assignments and Improvisation Tips

❶ **Arpeggios** Explore different permutations and inversions of the four arpeggios. When you're comfortable with the basic shapes, add ninths by starting on the third of each chord instead of the root. Also add chromatic passing notes to link one arpeggio to the next, as in *II – V – I Arpeggio Workout* (Vol. 1, p. 164).

❷ **E♭ major pentatonic** Use this 'horizontally' across all four chords – an approach that contrasts with the vertical sound of the arpeggios in step 1. Explore pentatonic patterns (Vol. 1, pp. 182–3), and don't forget to add colour by sometimes including the ♭**3** (G♭) in front of the major third of the scale.

❸ **E♭ major scale** This gives you the modes of E♭ for each chord. Explore scale patterns, as shown in Vol. 1, pp. 98–9. Even when playing horizontally, it's always good to relate scales to the underlying chords by targeting the notes of the prevailing chord (**R**, **3**, **5**, **7**). For that reason, you may wish to treat the second bar as a Dorian scale on F (same notes as E♭major). See 'How to make scales swing', p. 90.

❹ **R235 patterns** We first saw this pattern in the turnaround for *Ladybird* (Fig 7.56). It's just one of many four-note patterns that can be used to play 'vertically' round changes. Take care to play the ♭**3** for minor chords. Experiment with altering the order and direction of the notes for some of the chords. We'll be developing this idea further in *Turnaround Workout #2*, pp. 138–41, and on pp. 250–51.

❺ **Chord/scale and II – V patterns** Note how the **VI** chord, Cm7, has the same notes as E♭6, which is almost the same as the **I** chord, E♭Δ. The right hand can therefore play the first bar as if there's no chord change, which is why the E♭Δ chord/scale pattern works well over both chords. Also try starting it on the third of the chord (G) instead of the root (see Fig 7.39).

The **II** – **V** pattern shown for Fm7 – B♭7 is a variation on one of the short patterns given on p. 70. Try your own favourite short pattern(s) here instead.

❻ **Bebop scales** I have suggested the E♭ major bebop scale for the first two chords, treating the Cm7 like E♭6 as above. The second bar uses the B♭7 dominant bebop scale over both chords of the **II** – **V** (see Fig 7.67).

Over the next few pages we'll look at ways of moving your improvisation up a gear, by playing in triplets and sixteenth-notes.

Chord substitution

The chords of *Turnaround Workout #1*, like those in bars 5–6 of *Misty*, contain nothing but notes from the scale of E♭ major (the key of the tune):

E♭Δ – Cm7 – Fm7 – B♭7 – E♭Δ
I – VI – II – V – I

● **Creating secondary dominants** Because all the chords are diatonic the overall sound of these two bars is rather bland, with no surprises. In order to add interest, jazz musicians and composers often turn the **VI** chord into a secondary dominant, giving C7 instead of Cm7:

E♭Δ – **C7** – Fm7 – B♭7 – E♭Δ

This also strengthens the sequence, since C7 is the dominant of Fm7 and resolves perfectly to it. However, any substitution should only be used if the melody note sounds ok with the new chord – this is often a question of taste.

● **Replacing the I chord with III** The tonic (**I**) chord can often be replaced by a minor seventh chord built on the third – the **III** chord, giving Gm7 in place of E♭Δ. Bars 5–6 then become a cycle of fifths right from the start:

Gm7 – Cm7 – Fm7 – B♭7 – E♭Δ
III – VI – II – V – I

This works because Gm7 is the top part of an E♭Δ9 chord – **3579** in fact. If you were playing E♭Δ as a rootless voicing, you might play a Gm7 shape anyway; the difference is that we are now specifying a G root, rather than an E♭ one.

Applying this substitution as well as the C7 secondary dominant gives alternating minor and dominant chords a fourth apart, and two **II – V** sequences in a row:

Gm7 – **C7** – Fm7 – B♭7 – E♭Δ

● **Tritone substitution** The third type of substitution used in *Misty* applies to dominant chords in any cycle of fifths situation. It is called tritone substitution because the dominant chord is replaced with another one whose root is a tritone (♭**5**) away. Applying this to the C7 in the above sequence gives:

Gm7 – **G♭7** – Fm7 – B♭7 – E♭Δ

This works because C7 and G♭7 share **3** and **7** (the third of C7 is the seventh of G♭7, and vice versa). Applying this substitution to B♭7 as well would give:

Gm7 – **G♭7** – Fm7 – **E7** – E♭Δ

These are the chords in bars 7–8 of *Misty*, essentially the same as those in bars 5–6 with substitutions. Notice that the roots of the chords now descend chromatically:

III – ♭IIIx – II – ♭IIx – I

(NB: The **x** in the roman numerals indicates a dominant chord, as **II** and **III** chords would normally be minor sevenths.)

Tritone substitution transforms the cycle of fifths sequence, allowing you to voice chords with, for instance, consecutive left-hand **R7** shells down in semitones, rather than alternating **R7** with **R3** as in a regular cycle. In Chapter 9 we'll examine in greater detail how tritone substitution works.

Playing in triplets

Once you've gained the ability to improvise lines in eighth-notes, you could move on to playing in triplets. Triplets will always swing, because the swing feel is based on dividing the beat into three. However they do present a greater technical challenge, as you'll need to play up to twelve notes in a bar, rather than eight.

Practise all your major scales in triplets, over three octaves, accenting every third note. If you do this correctly there will be an accent at the very top of the scale:

Fig 7.86: C major scale in triplets over three octaves

The fingering given is normal C major fingering: *123 1234*. Note that the accent falls on different fingers in turn – an excellent exercise in finger independence. The natural tendency is to play the strongest accent with the thumb, but you mustn't allow this unless the thumb falls on the first note of a group of three. Don't be tempted to adapt the scale fingerings for playing in triplets.

Here are some triplet lines round the chords of *Turnaround Workout #1*. Try each one with the CD (track 21), with any of the left-hand accompaniments given on p. 112.

Fig 7.87: Triplet lines for I – VI – II – V in E♭ major (horizontal)

(a) E♭ major scale (with scale pattern in bar 2)

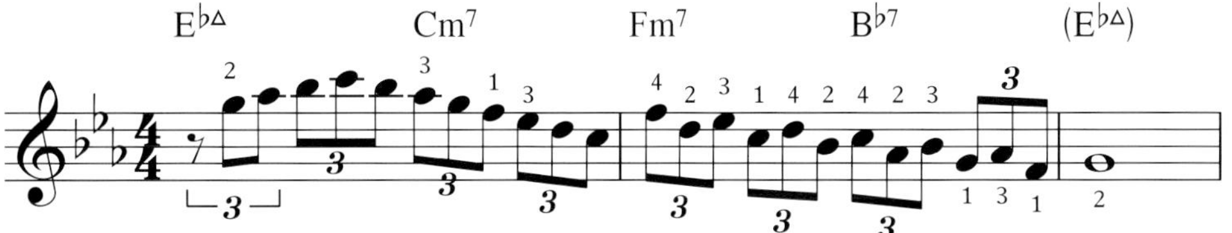

(b) E♭ major pentatonic (includes ♭3 in bar 2)

Both of the above demonstrate a horizontal approach to improvisation, with the same scale being played across all four chords. The next three examples show a vertical approach, in which each chord symbol generates its own six notes:

Fig 7.88: Triplet lines for I – VI – II – V in E♭ major (vertical)

(a) Arpeggios (including the ninth on some chords)

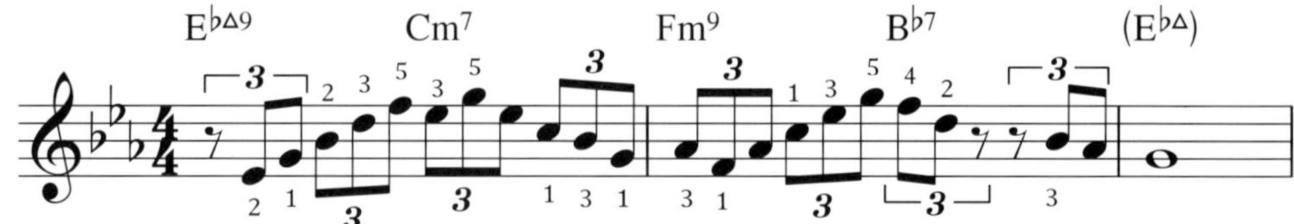

(b) R235 patterns on each chord

(c) R235 patterns with permutations

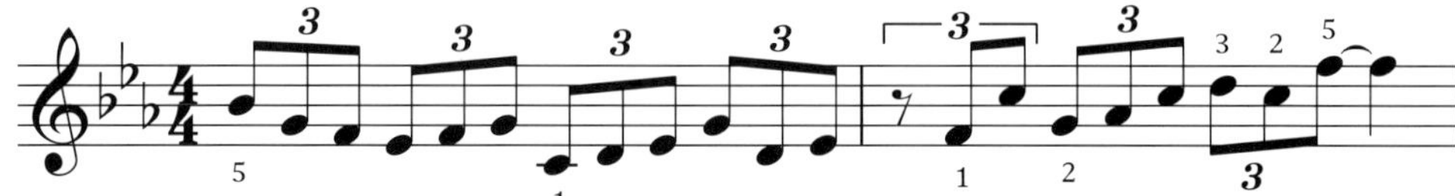

Bebop scales should not be played in triplets – because they have eight notes it will not work out and the incorrect notes will be placed on the beat. As we'll see on p. 117, bebop scales really come into their own with double-time playing.

Assignments: Playing in triplets

❶ ***Turnaround Workout #1*** Apply the triplet ideas above to this piece (p. 112), playing along with the CD, track 21.

❷ **Chord substitution** Repeat step 1 over Gm7–G♭7–Fm7–E7–E♭Δ, adapting both hands to fit. In the right hand, since you're now playing over non-diatonic chords, 'vertical' ideas will probably work best (arpeggios, **R235** patterns). To avoid clashes with the left hand on the CD, play along with drums only.

❸ **Play *Misty*** Improvise over this tune again (p. 106), playing triplet lines alongside regular eighth-note lines, with left-hand accompaniment.

Playing in double time

Playing lines in sixteenth-notes (up to sixteen notes per bar) represents the ultimate technical challenge for the improvising musician and is an important skill in both swing and straight-eight feels. To develop fluency, practise your ordinary scales in sixteenths, over four octaves, with an accent every eight notes. Unlike with triplets, there will not be an accent on the top note:

Fig 7.89: F major scale in sixteenth-notes over four octaves

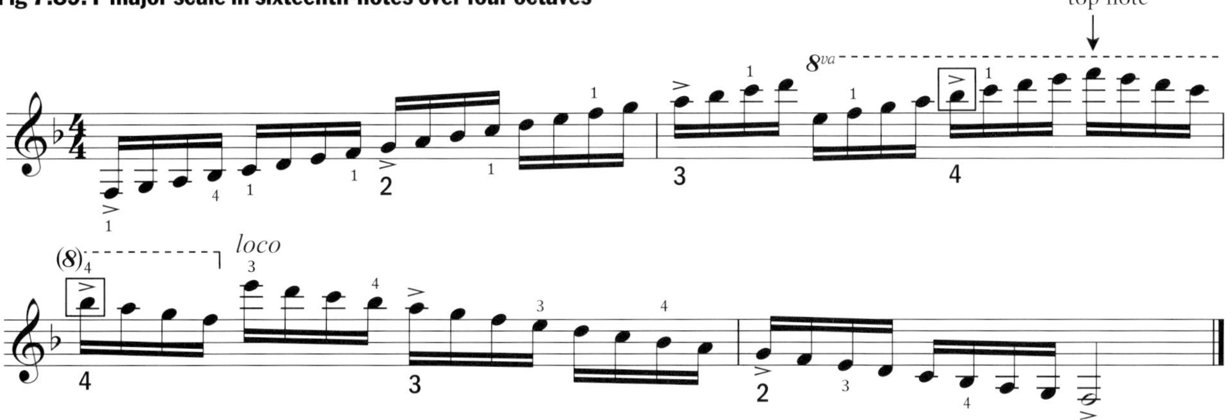

Using regular F major fingering (*1234 123*) results in **2**, **3** and **4** being accented by the second, third and fourth fingers respectively, in both directions. This will not work out so conveniently in all keys!

Whilst this is a great technical exercise, it highlights the problems of using ordinary scales to improvise over chords. If you play Fig 7.89 over 4 bars of F∆, you'll be stressing unsuitable notes in the second and fourth octaves, which are 'on the wrong foot', especially where the B♭ falls on the first or third beat (boxed notes).

This can be easily remedied by playing the eight-note bebop scale instead:

Fig 7.90: F major bebop scale (use with F∆ or F6)

Successive bars now contain the same notes, and each octave of the scale is on the same 'foot'. Don't forget that with dominant chords, the extra note falls between the **R** and the **♭7** of the Mixolydian scale:

Fig 7.91: F dominant bebop scale (use with F7 or Cm7)

Pacing your solo

The ability to step up a gear in your right hand is a useful tool if you hold it in reserve, especially in ballads. Experienced players will often hold back from going into double time in their solo until a significant place in the form, such as the bridge, or the start of the second chorus of 32 bars (if taking a longer solo).

Listen to jazz solos on records (by any instrument) and see if you can spot passages of triplet or double-time playing. Although some players with impressive techniques (eg: Bud Powell, Oscar Peterson, Benny Green) do often play long streams of sixteenth-notes, to start with you'll want to confine yours to short bursts, mixing them in with ordinary eighth-note phrases.

Here are some points to bear in mind:

- Don't swing sixteenth-notes. Even in swing numbers, double-time passages are usually played with a straight feel
- Never sacrifice the pulse or groove for the sake of playing more notes in the right hand
- Guard against rushing – practise with a metronome (see p. 200)
- The secret of building successful solos lies in use of space and contrast, rather than in trying to play as many notes as possible.

For inspiration, listen to Red Garland's incredible solo at the end of Coltrane's *Traneing In*, on the album of the same name. Having already played a very long and elegant solo at the start of this 'B♭ Blues with a Bridge', he turns in another one after the bass solo, beginning at 8:35:

8:35	'A1'	12 bars (blues)	Eighth-note lines
8:52	'A2'	12 bars	Sixteenth-note lines
9:09	'A3'	12 bars	More sixteenth-notes!
9:26	'A4'	12 bars	Block chords
9:44	'B'	8 bars (bridge)	More block chords
9:55	'A5'	12 bars	Yet more block chords!

John Coltrane must have been inspired, since he also takes a second solo immediately afterwards, before returning to the head. Self-indulgent, perhaps, but who can blame him?

Notice how Red Garland alters the content of his solo to mark the different sections, improvising in block chords as the climax. His block chord style is examined in Chapter 9, pp. 188–9.

For further examples of sixteenth-note lines, check out the transcribed solos later in this book by Oscar Peterson (p. 214), Hampton Hawes (p. 232) and Wynton Kelly (p. 240).

Assignments: Triplets and double-time playing

❶ **Review *Ladybird*** Improvise over the chords of this tune again, using the triplet and double-time concepts discussed on pp. 115 and 117.

There's no need to keep streams of fast notes going – long lines will come with practice. Intersperse your triplet and double-time ideas with bars of ordinary eighth- or quarter-note playing.

To start with, stay with a simple two- or four-bar phrasing concept (such as those in Vol. 1, p. 81), until you can negotiate the form confidently. Don't forget to use repetition (rhythmic and melodic), variation, motifs, rests, pick-ups, etc.

❷ **Review *Misty*** To get a double-time feel in any tune, mentally double the number of bars on every chord. Here are the first eight bars of *Misty* (p. 106):

|| E♭ | B♭m⁷ E♭⁷ | A♭Δ | A♭m⁷ D♭⁷ |

| E♭Δ Cm⁷ | Fm⁷ B♭⁷ | Gm⁷ G♭⁷ | Fm⁷ E⁷ ||

Inserting bar-lines turns this into a sixteen-bar sequence:

|| E♭ | ⁒ | B♭m⁷ | E♭⁷ | A♭Δ | ⁒ | A♭m⁷ | D♭⁷ |

| E♭Δ | Cm⁷ | Fm⁷ | B♭⁷ | Gm⁷ | G♭⁷ | Fm⁷ | E⁷ ||

If you play in eighth-notes over these changes, the first two bars will contain sixteen notes, which is the same as playing in double time over one bar of E♭Δ at the original tempo. You can dip in and out of a double-time feel whenever you like, secure in the knowledge that the actual time spent on each chord is the same either way.

❸ **Review *Dominant Bebop Scale Workout*** Incorporate double-time bebop scales into this tune (p. 99), and others such as *Blue Bossa* (p. 224), *Bebop Bridge* (p. 103), *Dominant Seventh Workout #2* (p. 94), *Bossa Nova Comping #2* (p. 97), etc.

Daily practice routine

To help achieve a high level of fluency with scales, try the following routine on a different note every day, with your metronome set to 100 bpm (for example). First choose a scale or mode (Dorian, Mixolydian, etc), and a starting note no higher than middle C. Play the scale in the right hand, up and down as follows:

1 in eighth-notes over 2 octaves
2 in triplets over 3 octaves
3 in sixteenth-notes bebop scale over 4 octaves

Take care with the fingering for the bebop scale which will differ from the previous steps. It is important to play all three scales at the same tempo – if you cannot execute the last step comfortably, set your metronome slower to start.

If you wish to develop a comparable left-hand technique, you should practise the above assiduously with both hands together, one or two octaves apart, in all keys.

Appendix VII, 'Practice Routines' (p. 282) contains further suggestions for systematic practice of the material covered in this book.

Chapter Seven – Final Checkpoint

● **Cycles** In this chapter you have consolidated your playing of **II – V – I** sequences using three- or four-note rootless voicings, including ninths and thirteenths. We've seen how one of the best ways to learn these voicings is to practise them systematically through the cycle of fifths. Here's a summary of the various cycles mentioned in this book:

● II – V – I cycle (six keys)

|| Em^7 | A^7 | D$^\Delta$ | % || Dm^7 | G^7 | C$^\Delta$ | % ||

|| Cm^7 | F^7 | B$^{\flat\Delta}$ | % || B$^\flat$m^7 | E$^{\flat 7}$ | A$^{\flat\Delta}$ | % ||

|| A$^\flat$m^7 | D$^{\flat 7}$ | G$^{\flat\Delta}$ | % || F$^\sharp$m^7 | B^7 | E$^\Delta$ | % ||

Repeat starting on Am for the remaining six keys (see p. 77).

● II – V cycle (six keys)

|| Em^7 | A^7 || Dm^7 | G^7 ||

|| Cm^7 | F^7 || B$^\flat$m^7 | E$^{\flat 7}$ ||

|| A$^\flat$m^7 | D$^{\flat 7}$ || F$^\sharp$m^7 | B^7 ||

Repeat starting on Am for the remaining six keys.

● Dominant seventh cycle (all keys)

|| E^7 | A^7 | D^7 | G^7 |

| C^7 | F^7 | B$^{\flat 7}$ | E$^{\flat 7}$ |

| A$^{\flat 7}$ | D$^{\flat 7}$ | F$^{\sharp 7}$ | B^7 ||

This goes through all keys without the need for a second cycle. The same is true of the following **II – V** cycle, obtained by adding a minor chord in front of each dominant chord above:

● II – V cycle (all keys)

|| Bm^7 | E^7 | Em^7 | A^7 | Am^7 | D^7 | Dm^7 | G^7 |

| Gm^7 | C^7 | Cm^7 | F^7 | Fm^7 | B$^{\flat 7}$ | B$^\flat$m^7 | E$^{\flat 7}$ |

| E$^\flat$m^7 | A$^{\flat 7}$ | A$^\flat$m^7 | D$^{\flat 7}$ | C$^\sharp$m^7 | F$^{\sharp 7}$ | F$^\sharp$m^7 | B^7 ||

Use these cycles constantly to practise just about everything, eg:

- Bass lines (two-feel, walking, Latin)
- Left-hand shells (or tritones for dominant sevenths)
- Rootless voicings (three or four notes) in either hand
- Stride piano (left hand only)
- Two-handed voicings

With the right hand you should practise arpeggios, scales, bebop scales, pentatonics, patterns, **II – V** licks, etc, to fit each chord, played in eighth-notes, triplets and sixteenth-notes. Eventually practise the cycles hands together, combining the various left- and right-hand techniques in as many ways as you can.

Chapter Eight
Diminished chords and scales

In this chapter we'll not only be exploring diminished chords, but also the chords with which they are inextricably linked – dominant sevenths with flattened or sharpened ninths.

So far in this book we have concentrated on four main types of seventh chord – major, dominant, minor and half-diminished (m7♭5). Compared to a major seventh, a half-diminished chord has **♭3**, **♭5** and **♭7**. If we flatten the seventh of this chord again, we'll get a diminished seventh (**♭♭7**). The interval between the top and bottom note of the chord is now the same as a sixth.

Fig 8.1 shows the five chord-types in root position – each chord is derived from the previous one by flattening the note indicated:

Fig 8.1: The five main chord-types on a C root

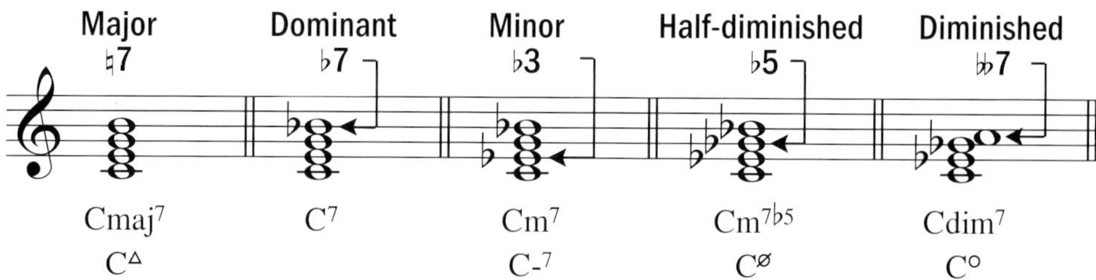

Note the variety of chord symbols in use. In this book I use ° to indicate both diminished triads and sevenths. Some writers use °7 for a full diminished seventh, but in practice most musicians include **♭♭7** anyway whether it is given or not.

Practise the five chord-types on other roots as well, so that you can find the five shapes quickly in all keys, without having to read them. Also play all five chords in the left hand, adding the correct arpeggios in the right hand over two octaves. Keep time with the left hand on the 'one' as shown below:

Fig 8.2: Diminished seventh arpeggio

Use *1234* fingering for all five chords, saving the fifth finger for the top note (see Vol. 1, Fig 3.66).

The diminished seventh is the only one of the five chords that is symmetrical – the notes are all a minor third apart. When the chord is inverted, it doesn't change shape, but becomes another diminished seventh chord, a minor third up:

Fig 8.3: Inversions of D diminished seventh chord

This is a 'family' of diminished chords, all of which contain the same notes. To learn all twelve chords, you just need to become familiar with the other two families:

C° – E♭° – F♯° – A° E°– G° – B♭° – C♯°

The diminished seventh as ♭III° in a major key

Although a diminished *triad* is found on the seventh of the major scale (see Vol. 1, Fig 2.29), diminished sevenths do not occur naturally in major keys. They are, however, frequently used as linking chords, eg: between **II** and **III**:

Fig 8.4: The diminished chord as ♭III°

Instead of resolving to **III** as above, the final chord is often played as a first inversion **I** chord:

Fig 8.5: Resolving back to the tonic

The next piece, *Crossing the Tracks*, features these chords over and over in the key of C, also transposing them for the **V** chord, G. You have already played this sequence in the key of E♭ in the pseudo-stride left-hand option for *Misty* (Figs 7.83–7.84, p. 110).

Crossing the Tracks

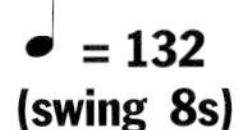

Tim Richards

This tune in the key of C is based on two chords – C and G.
All the other chords are passing chords, inserted to add harmonic interest.

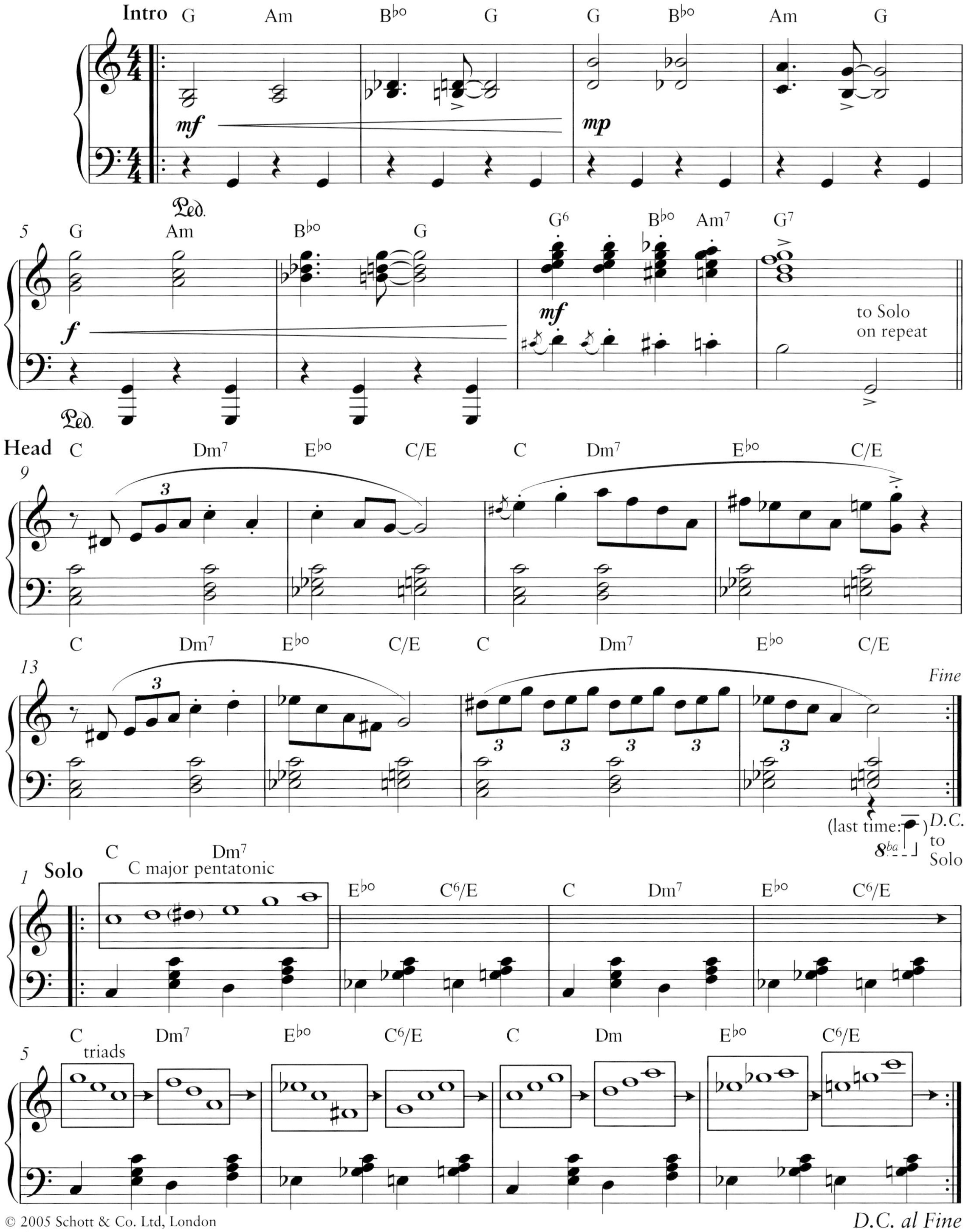

Intro G Am B♭o G G B♭o Am G

mf mp

Ped.

5 G Am B♭o G G6 B♭o Am7 G7

f mf

to Solo on repeat

Ped.

Head C Dm7 E♭o C/E C Dm7 E♭o C/E

9

C Dm7 E♭o C/E C Dm7 E♭o C/E

13

Fine

(last time: 8ba) *D.C. to Solo*

1 Solo C Dm7 C major pentatonic E♭o C6/E C Dm7 E♭o C6/E

5 C triads Dm7 E♭o C6/E C Dm E♭o C6/E

D.C. al Fine

Fats Waller emerged from the 1920s world of prohibition and rent parties to become one of the foremost entertainers of the day. A pupil of the famous 'Harlem School' stride pianist James P. Johnson, his style influenced in turn pianists like Art Tatum and Count Basie (who studied organ with him). Waller's career peaked in the 1930s, when his light-hearted and witty vocal style became popular. Also a prolific composer, his best known tunes are *Honeysuckle Rose* and *Ain't Misbehavin'*.

Assignments: Crossing the Tracks

❶ **Solo section** Explore right-hand ideas, devoting some practice time to improvising horizontally (eg: C major pentatonic) and some to playing vertically (eg: triad shapes and arpeggios, changing with each chord). The suggested left-hand accompaniment staggers the root and chord – if you find this hard, revert to the straight chords at first, as given for the head.

❷ **Varying the left hand** Here's a few alternative accompaniments for the solo section. You can hear (b) in the second half of the solo, at 1:01. Choose a couple and practise them (left hand alone) until you no longer need to look at the keyboard.

Fig 8.6: Ways of playing I – II – ♭III° – I

(a) Sixths

(b) Pseudo-stride

(c) Tenths

(d) Genuine stride

Now try your improvisation again over the new left hand. Remember that the **♭III°** chord has the same notes as a diminished seventh on **I** (ie: E♭° is the same as C°).

❸ **Pick another key** Repeat steps 1 and 2 in a new key every day!

Other uses of the diminished seventh

The chord sequence given in *Crossing the Tracks* and Fig 8.6 can be adapted for use with dominant seventh chords by including a **♭7** on the **I** chord:

Fig 8.7: Substitute chords for two bars of C7 (pseudo-stride)

● **Cycle of dominant sevenths** If the middle note is omitted, the sequence works equally well for major or dominant chords. Here it is in tenths:

Fig 8.8: Bridge of *I Got Rhythm* ('Rhythm Changes') in B♭

This time-honoured way of fleshing out the harmony is also found in bars 47–8 of *Caravan* (p. 145).

● **Endings** The **♭III°** chord is implied in the so-called 'Count Basie' ending, often played at the top end of the piano with just a couple of notes:

Fig 8.9: 'Count Basie' endings (play one octave higher)

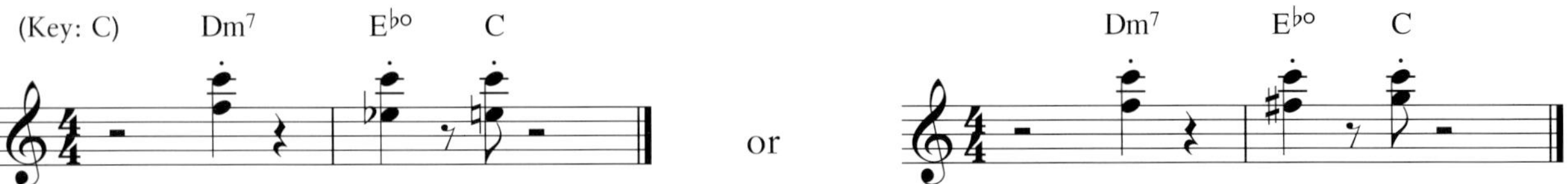

● **As a link between I and II** This often occurs in the first bar of 'Rhythm Changes', as shown on p. 191.

Fig 8.10: The diminished seventh as ♭II° (Key: B♭)

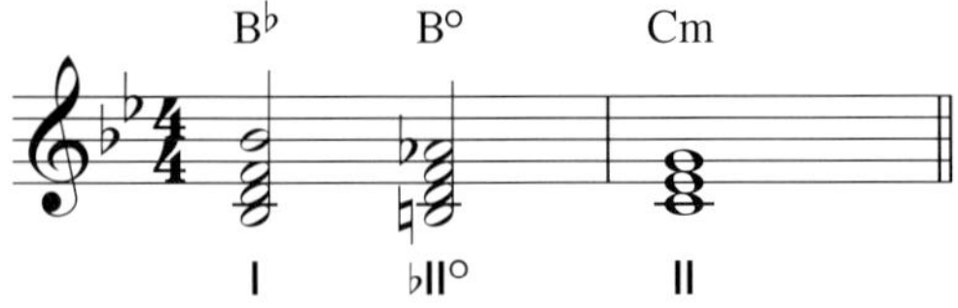

● **As a link between IV and I** This can occur in bar 6 of a blues, as in *Blue Monk* (IBP, p. 108) and *Tension & Release Blues #2*, p. 180.

|| B♭7 | E♭7 | B♭7 | ⁒ | E♭7 | E° | B♭ | B♭7 | F7 | ⁒ | B♭7 | ⁒ ||
I IV #IV° I

The **♯IV°** chord is typical of many gospel numbers (eg: *Just a Closer Walk with Thee*, IBP p. 194), and also occurs in the following jazz tunes:

- *St Thomas* (Sonny Rollins), bar 14
- *Honeysuckle Rose* (Fats Waller), bar 6
- *Scrapple from the Apple* (Charlie Parker), bar 6
- 'Rhythm Changes', bar 6 (see p. 191).

Fig 8.11: The diminished seventh as #IV° (Key: C)

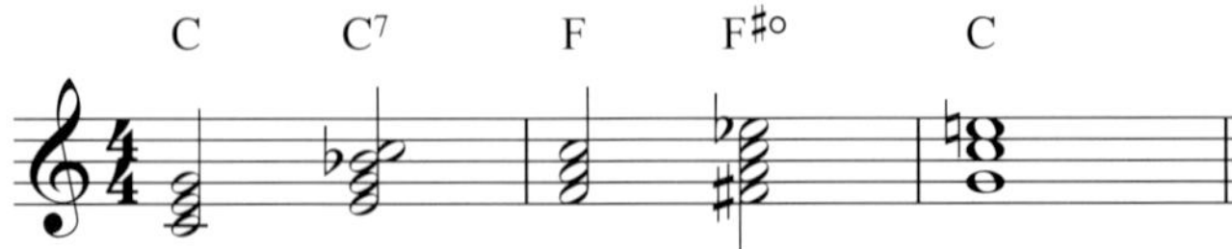

It also crops up in the following tune *Don't Stop the Carnival.* (For further examples of diminished chords as **♯IV°** and **♭III°** see IBP, Chapter 5.)

23 with drums
Includes play-along section

♩ = 152 (straight 8s)

Don't Stop The Carnival

This catchy calypso number has been recorded by Sonny Rollins and McCoy Tyner.

Traditional
arr. Tim Richards

Checkpoint: Don't Stop the Carnival

● **Chord sequence** The melody is played twice, making sixteen bars in all, formed by repeating the same four-bar chord sequence. The last two bars are a **I – VI – II – V** turnaround in C (see *Turnaround Workout #2*, p. 139).

● **#IV° diminished chord** In the accompaniment section, the F♯° chord is played in two different ways (bars 10 and 14). These three-note shapes can be formed from any inversion of F♯° by leaving out the note next to the bottom note:

Fig 8.12: Three-note shapes for F♯°

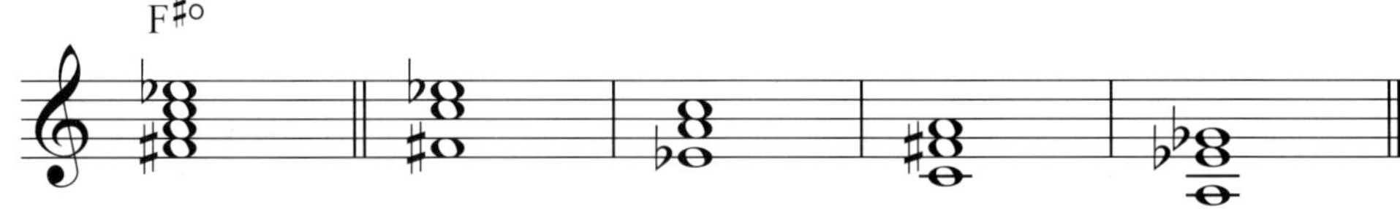

● **Slash chords** C7/E means a C7 chord with E in the bass; likewise C/G indicates a C triad with a G bass note. The information given by these slash chords relates purely to the bass line. When playing the solo accompaniment, with the bass in the left hand, you don't need to worry about placing these notes at the bottom of the right-hand chords – a variety of inversions can be used.

● **Left-hand harmony line** The final head is played with both hands together. The left hand is generally a tenth below the melody, although some other intervals are also present, such as the sixths in bars 20 and 23–24.

Assignments and Improvisation Tips: Don't Stop the Carnival

❶ **Melody** Learn this in the right hand alone to start with, playing it with the CD and checking the rhythm carefully, especially any off-beat notes like those found in bars 2, 4, 6 and 8. When you've memorised it, add the 'two-feel' bass line in the left hand and try it without the backing CD.

❷ **Accompaniment** Get a friend to play the head or improvise (on another instrument, or the top half of the piano) while you play the backing. The solo can be open length, so repeat the eight bars over and over, as many times as you like.

❸ **Inversions** Notice that the second four bars of the solo accompaniment use different shapes for the same chords. Because the sequence repeats so often, I recommend you practise the inversions of all the chords in the piece so that you can play them in other positions too, not just as written.

❹ **Your solo** As with *Crossing the Tracks* (p. 123), you have the option of playing vertically or horizontally. For the latter, a C major or ♭3 pentatonic will work over all the chords, providing you don't play an E over the F♯°.

For a more vertical approach, practise the arpeggios of all the chords and use them to link one chord to the next as musically as you can. In the following example, the boxed F♯ is a chromatic passing note.

Fig 8.13: Vertical improvisation using only the notes of each chord

The flattened ninth chord

Diminished seventh and dominant seventh chords differ by one note only. To illustrate this, raise the root of any dominant seventh chord by a semitone – the result will be a diminished seventh:

Fig 8.14: F7 becomes F#° by raising its root

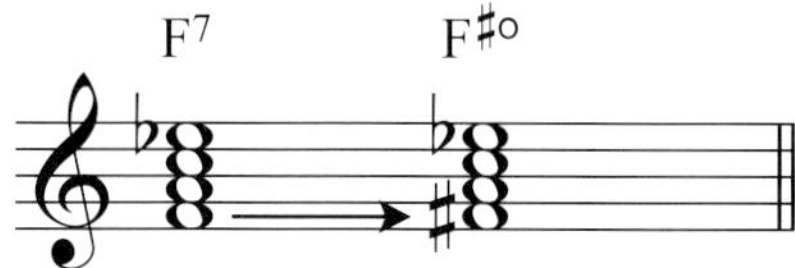

This diminished chord can be considered as part of the original dominant seventh if the F♯ is thought of as a flattened ninth (G♭). This is clearer if the F♯° is played in first inversion, ie: as A°:

Fig 8.15: Dominant seventh chord with flattened ninth

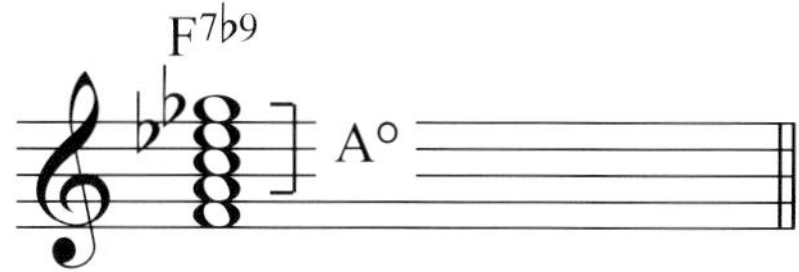

The chord symbol F7♭9 is sometimes written F7–9. Both are usually pronounced 'F seven flat nine'.

Because it is difficult to play all five notes of Fig 8.15 in one hand, A° is often used as a **3579** rootless voicing for F7♭9, the root of the chord (F) being played in the left hand, or by a bass player. Compare this with the equivalent voicing for F9:

Fig 8.16: 3579 rootless voicings

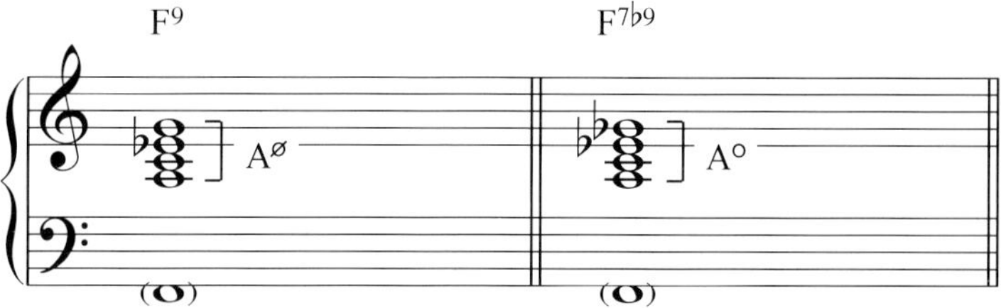

To find the correct diminished chord for any dominant flat ninth chord, you must base it on the third of the chord. The **3579** voicing has become **357♭9**. Don't forget, however, that any diminished chord is part of a family that also includes three other diminished chords, a minor third apart (see Fig 8.3). For F7♭9 you can therefore play A°, C°, E♭°, or F♯°, because they all have the same notes.

In practice, therefore, as well as basing your diminished chord on **3** of the flat nine chord, you can base it on **5**, **7** or **♭9** instead. To give an example in a different key, here are the four possibilities for G7♭9:

Fig 8.17: Flat nine voicings using four diminished chords

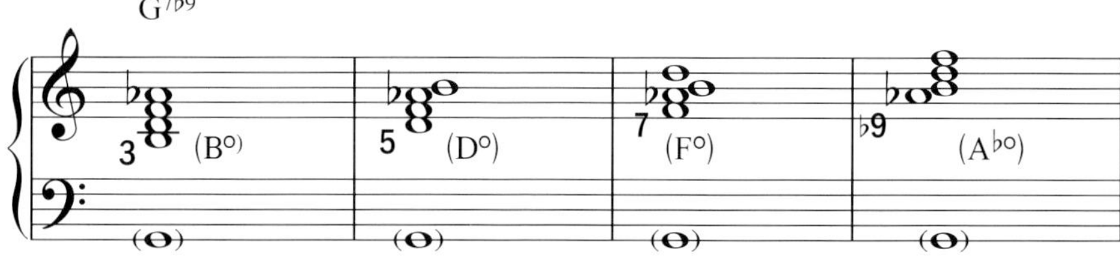

This works because all the diminished chords in Fig 8.17 have the same notes – you're really just playing inversions of B°.

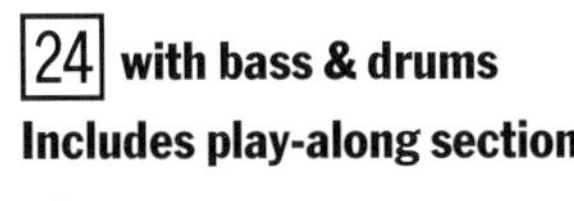

♩ = 100
(swing 8s)

Summertime

One of the most famous jazz standards, written for Gershwin's 1935 opera 'Porgy and Bess'.

George Gershwin
arr. Tim Richards

Intro Am7 (On) E7♭9 (Off) | Am7 E7♭9 | Am7 E7♭9 | Am7 E7 𝄋

Head
Am E7 | Am E7 | Am E7 | Am A7

5 Dm A7 | Dm E♭o | E7 B⌀ | E7

Ped.

9 Am E7 | Am E7 | Am E7 | Am G7

13 C Am | B⌀ E7+ | Am E7 (Coda) | Am

Ped.

Solo over 16-bar form then *D.S. al Coda*

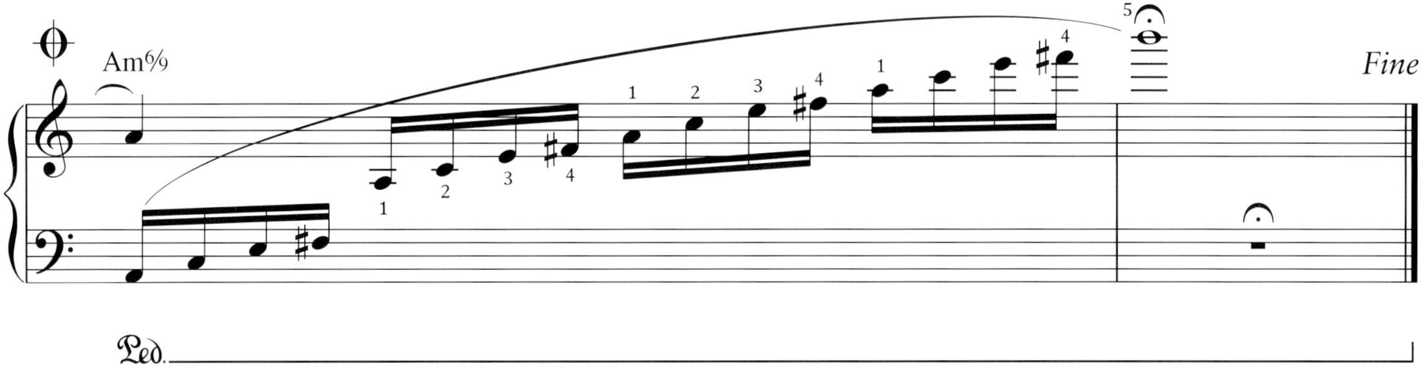

Checkpoint: Summertime

● **Chord sequence** The sixteen-bar sequence opens like a blues in A minor, moving to Dm in bar 5. Two bars later, however, unlike a blues, it moves straight to **V** (E7). The second half of the tune echoes the beginning, but moves to **III** (the relative major, C) in bar 13 before returning to Am. Ignoring the passing chords, the main harmonic movement is as follows:

● **Key of A minor** Dominant (**V**) chords in minor keys often include **♭9**, rather than a regular ninth, like the E7 chords in the intro:

Fig 8.18: E7♭9 looks like G#°

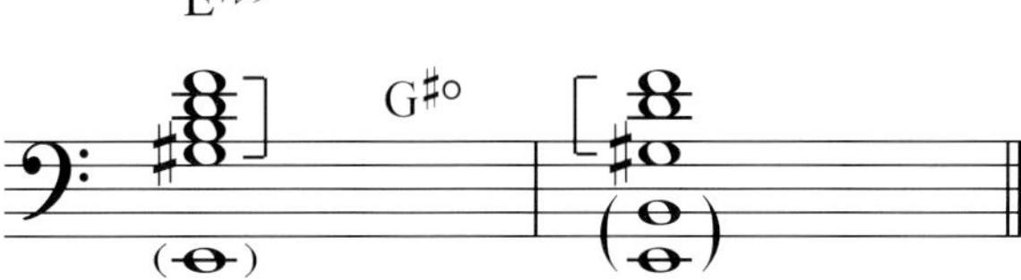

The **V** chord can also have a raised fifth, as in bar 14, where the **#5** (C) is in the melody too. The chords in bars 14–15 form a **II – V – I** in A minor:

Fig 8.19: Three-note shapes for II – V – I in A minor

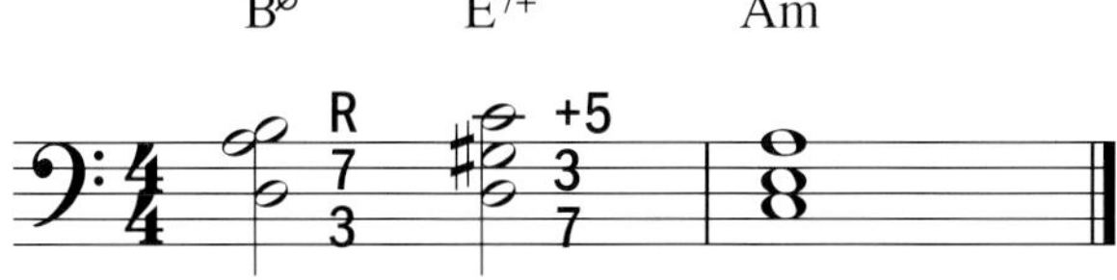

See Chapter 10 for more on minor **II – V – I**s.

● **Melody** With one exception in bar 7 (B), all the notes of this tune belong to the A blues scale, reinforcing the blues flavour of the piece.

Fig 8.20: Blues scale on A

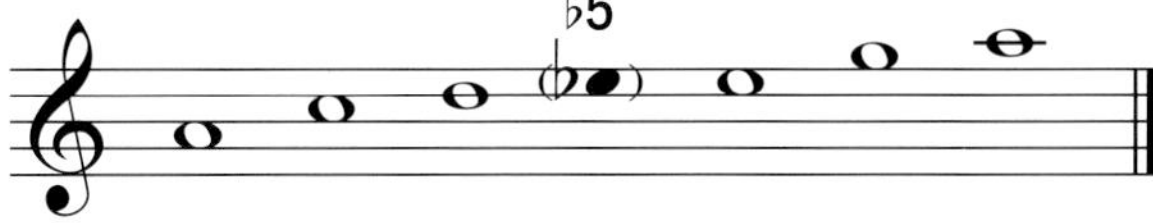

In bar 14, the first melody note (E) is sometimes played (or sung) as an E♭, the **♭5** of the blues scale.

● **Left-hand chords** This arrangement uses three-note chords in a four-to-the-bar style. A variety of inversions has been chosen to enable the shapes to move as smoothly as possible, usually by step. Triads are used for Am, Dm and C. Watch the E♭° passing chord in bar 6 – as in *Don't Stop the Carnival* (p. 127) it is based on **#IV** of the key.

Varying the left-hand accompaniment

Once you've memorised the melody with the left hand as written, try some of the following left-hand variations, so you don't end up playing it the same way every time.

● **Left-hand chords on and off the beat** Explore 'on-off' and 'off-on' rhythms for the left hand. The following two-bar pattern combines both these rhythms:

Fig 8.21: Melody (bars 1–5) with 'off-on/on-off' chord pattern

Retain the same two-bar pattern for the whole melody, practising each four-bar section over and over if necessary, until you have mastered the co-ordination. For more on 'off–on' and 'on–off' rhythms, see 'Comping rhythms' (pp. 82–3), and *Barrelhouse Blues* (IBP, p. 63).

● **Arpeggios in left hand** This approach gives a more lyrical, classical feel, effective as an intro, or for a solo piano performance. You can hear it during the final head in track 24, for which the bass and drums drop out. Play both hands in straight eights, *rubato* if desired:

Fig 8.22(a): Arpeggio accompaniment for *Summertime* (as played at 2:38)

Note the variation in bars 7–8, in which E7– F7 – E7 replaces E7 – Bø – E7. Since Bø and F7 are a ♭**5** apart, this is a form of tritone substitution (see p. 114).

● **Pseudo-stride** The arpeggios above use the same shapes as this useful left-hand style that we encountered in *Misty* (pp. 106–110) and other tunes. Unlike the arpeggios, pseudo-stride allows the right hand to play swing eighth-notes:

Fig 8.22(b): Pseudo-stride accompaniment (as played at 2:04)

This left hand is heard for sixteen bars on track 24, as the last chorus of comping before the return of the head. It is suitable for accompanying both the melody and a right-hand improvisation.

Assignments and Improvisation Tips: Summertime – horizontal

❶ **Memorise melody and chords** You'll be using the same left hand to accompany your solo as in the melody. Make sure you know the chord shapes very well, playing them on every beat as on p. 130, or using rhythmic variations such as the one shown in Fig 8.21.

❷ **Harmonic minor scale** During the bars which alternate Am and E7, the A minor harmonic scale is a good option for soloing, as it includes F and G♯ (♭**9** and **3** of E7 respectively). When using this scale, try to ensure these two notes are played during the second half of each bar, to coincide with the E7 left-hand chord. You can hear this in action in the first four bars of my solo on track 24:

Fig 8.23: A harmonic minor scale over bars 1–4 (as played at 0:51)

See Vol. 1, Fig 4.18 for an example of this principle at work in *Fly Me to the Moon*.

❸ **Blues scale** Taking a cue from the melody, use the blues scale or minor pentatonic on A (Fig 8.20) to improvise horizontally over the whole piece. To avoid any clashes take care to end phrases on a note of the prevailing chord. You can hear the blues scale during the last four bars of my solo on track 24.

Fig 8.24: Blues scale on A over bars 12-16 (as played at 1:19)

See Vol. 1, Fig 4.35 for an example of this principle at work in *Autumn Leaves*.

Vertical improvisation over *Summertime*

So far I've suggested playing your solo 'in the key' using either the blues scale or the harmonic minor scale on A throughout.

Now focus on the chords themselves. First of all, the top notes of the alternating Am and E7 chords in *Summertime* can actually be made to form a complete scale, passing through all four inversions of Am7:

Fig 8.25: Alternating I and V to make a scale

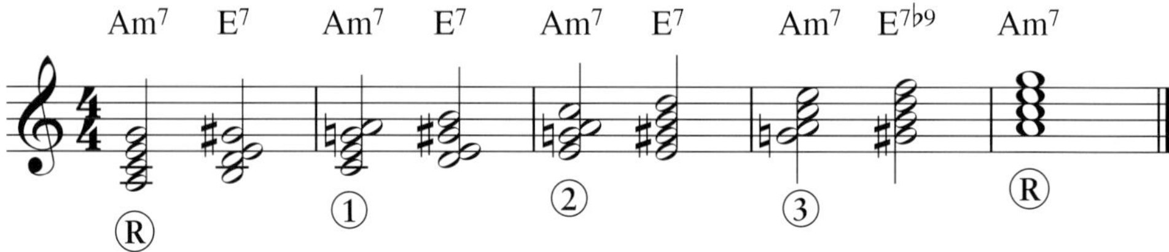

Play Fig 8.25 up and down. Try it in the left hand as well, until you're familiar with each four-note shape. These hand positions will be invaluable when improvising in eighth-notes, since that requires you to play four notes on each chord.

Providing you keep track of where you are, it is not necessary to outline every single chord, sometimes just a couple of notes are fine, or you can omit some chords entirely. The following example avoids a continuous stream of notes, by incorporating rests and phrasing:

Fig 8.26: Using notes of the chords over bars 1–9

Playing dominant sevenths as diminished chords

The last E7 chord in Fig 8.25 is actually a diminished shape – G♯°, based on the third of E7♭9. It is possible to play all the E7 chords as diminished chords, by moving the roots up a semitone (ie: by replacing every E with an F).

Fig 8.27: Playing rootless ♭9 chords for E7

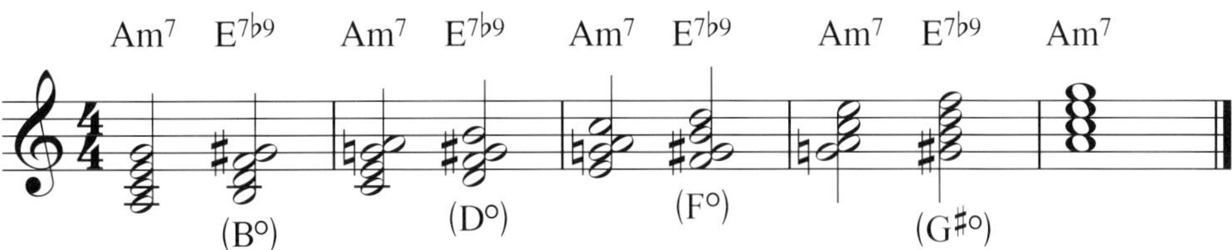

The E7s have now been treated as rootless **♭9** chords, using the G♯° inversion 'family': G♯° – B° – D° – F°. Note how much smoother the progression sounds as a result.

We can also apply this principle to the right-hand improvised line. Here is an example with a simple left-hand accompaniment:

Fig 8.28: Using diminished arpeggios over bars 5–13 (as played at 1:01)

Assignments and Improvisation Tips: Summertime - vertical

❶ **Using notes of the chords** Continue the improvisation begun in Fig 8.26 round the whole sixteen-bar sequence, using similar right-hand ideas. This approach relies on familiarity with the arpeggios of every chord, in all inversions, so that you have the flexibility to go to the nearest shape whenever the chord changes.

❷ **Vary the left hand** Repeat step 1 with another left-hand style.

❸ **Include diminished arpeggios** Extend the improvisation shown in Fig 8.28 over the whole tune, seeking out the diminished arpeggios for the dominant chords where possible. Improvise several choruses in this way.

❹ **Work out an arrangement** Your solo must be framed by the melody before and after. Try to include at least two different left-hand styles in your performance, to provide contrast. During the improvisation, play both horizontal and vertical ideas – you might try a chorus of each, for instance.

❺ **Play along** Try all the steps above (and those in the 'horizontal' Assignments, p. 133) with the CD (track 24), silencing the piano to play with bass and drums only. This will give you three sixteen-bar choruses for your solo before the rhythm section drop out. Work out a plan! Here's a possible example:

First chorus	Embellish the melody, add fills, etc
Second chorus	Play notes of the chords, including diminished arpeggios
Third chorus	Play A harmonic minor and/or blues scale

The chord/scale lick for flat nine chords

We first used the chord/scale pattern over the chords of *Ladybird* (p. 78). When starting on the third of a dominant seventh chord, the **♭9** can be included as the top note of the ascending arpeggio:

Fig 8.29: Chord/scale lick over C7♭9

Notice how the root of the chord (C) is encircled by **7** and **♭9**.

In *Dominant Seventh Flat Nine Workout* opposite, the chords are joined together in pairs. The ending of Fig 8.29 has been altered to make it encircle the starting note of the next chord, the third of F7 (A):

Fig 8.30: Joining dominant seventh chords

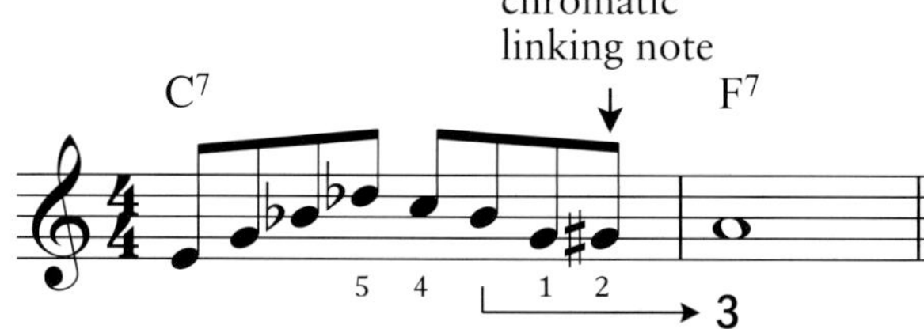

For the second time through the cycle at 'B', a variation of Fig 8.29 is used:

Fig 8.31: Jumping straight to the ♭9

This way of incorporating the **♭9** into an improvised line is a very important part of the jazz idiom, and is used by soloists on all instruments. You can hear it all the time when listening to pianists from the bebop and hard bop schools, such as Bud Powell, Bobby Timmons, Hampton Hawes, Phineas Newborn Jr, Wynton Kelly and many others, right up to the present day.

Assignments: Dominant Seventh Flat Nine Workout

❶ **Chord/scale lick** Memorise the right-hand phrases in section 'A', observing how the fingering varies from key to key, and how use of the thumb on black notes is avoided. Where there is no written material, work out the notes and fingering for yourself.

❷ **Play along** Play the phrases with the CD (track 25, bass and drums only), until you are comfortable with all twelve chords. Don't read from the music! If necessary use the chord chart at the bottom of p. 98 to guide you round the cycle.

❸ **Section 'B'** Repeat steps 1–2 for the phrase in bars 13–14. If you're secure with the chord/scale lick, you should find this variation comes quite easily.

❹ **Start on F7** Pair up the chords the opposite way, joining F7 to B♭7, E♭7 to A♭7, etc.

❺ **Introduce variations** Personalise the exercise by experimenting with the rhythm and/or notes of the left-hand chords. Also incorporate some improvised ideas of your own over some of the chords, mixing them in with the **♭9** licks suggested.

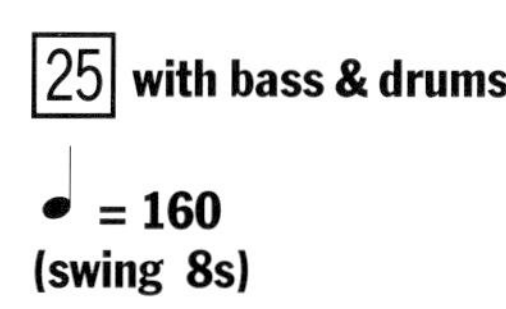

Dominant Seventh Flat Nine Workout

Tim Richards

These flat nine 'licks' round all twelve keys are supported in the left hand by a combination of shells (**R7**), tritones (**73** or **37**) and three-note voicings (**37♭9** or **735**). Vary these as you wish.

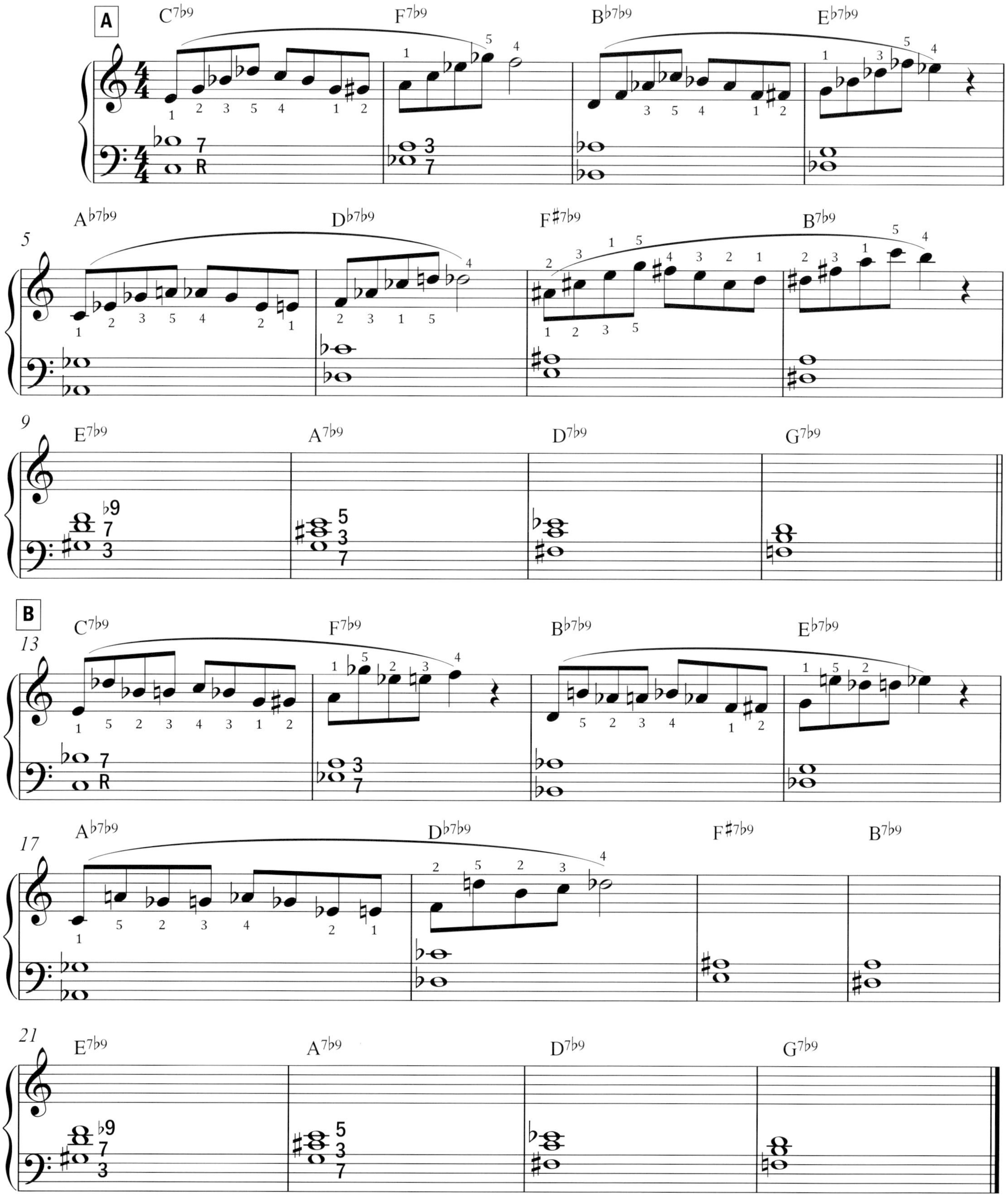

A

C7♭9 | F7♭9 | B♭7♭9 | E♭7♭9

5 A♭7♭9 | D♭7♭9 | F♯7♭9 | B7♭9

9 E7♭9 | A7♭9 | D7♭9 | G7♭9

B

13 C7♭9 | F7♭9 | B♭7♭9 | E♭7♭9

17 A♭7♭9 | D♭7♭9 | F♯7♭9 | B7♭9

21 E7♭9 | A7♭9 | D7♭9 | G7♭9

Vertical improvisation with R235 patterns

In *Turnaround Workout #1* (p. 112), one of the suggested right-hand options was to play a **R235** pattern starting on the root of each chord. For a diatonic turnaround in C this gives the following phrase:

Fig 8.32: I – VI – II – V turnaround with R235 patterns

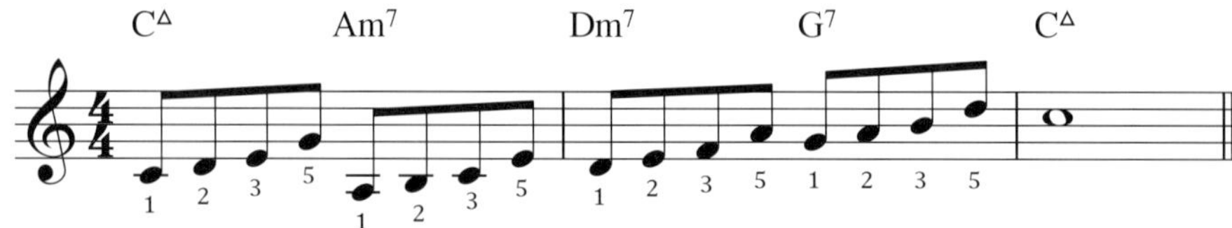

Turnaround Workout #2 features a secondary dominant on the **VI** chord – A7. This necessitates the inclusion of C♯ in the A pattern:

Fig 8.33: Same line with dominant chord on VI

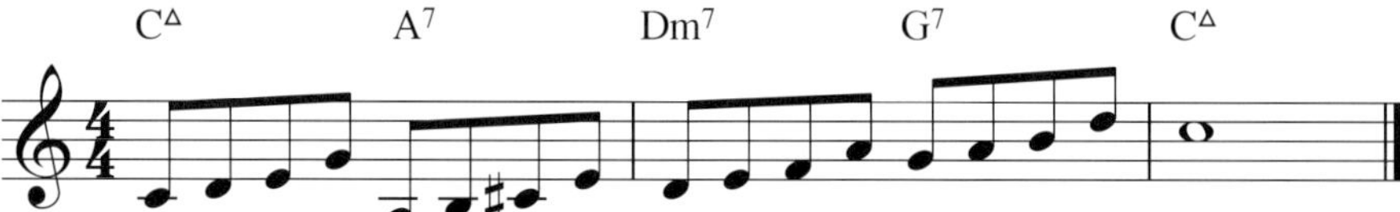

Either of the dominant chords can have a **♭9** if desired. As this note is the same as **♭2**, the **R235** pattern therefore becomes **R ♭2 3 5**:

Fig 8.34: Same line with ♭9 pattern on G7

To add interest, try varying the order of the notes, so that the motif doesn't always start on the root. There are actually 24 different ways of playing a **R235** group:

Fig 8.35: Permutations of D major R235 pattern

Checkpoint: Turnaround Workout #2

- **Key of C** The written line uses the same **R235** shapes as Fig 8.34, with a **♭9** on the **V** chord – G7. The order of the notes has been changed, however, using some of the permutations given in Fig 8.35.
- **Key of F** Both left and right hands play a **♭9** over the **VI** chord – D7. If the left hand plays a **♭9** chord, the right hand must follow suit or there'll be a clash.
- **Key of B♭** The pseudo-stride left hand given contains no ninths, so the right hand is free to play either **9** or **♭9** over the dominant chords.

Further ideas for **R235** patterns are given overleaf. For Assignments see p. 142.

26 with bass & drums

Includes play-along sections

♩ = 100 (swing 8s)

Turnaround Workout #2

Use this **I – VI – II – V** sequence to practise your **R235** patterns and their permutations.
The left-hand accompaniments are interchangeable – transpose each one to all three keys.
Space has been left blank for you to write down some of your right-hand ideas.

Tim Richards

Developing the R235 pattern

Further variations can be arrived at by learning the corresponding patterns that start on **3** and **5** of the chords, giving a choice of three shapes for each chord:

Fig 8.36: R235 choices following the scale of each chord

Choosing **R235** motifs based on different notes of the chord saves you having to move the patterns up a fourth when playing round cycle of fifths chord sequences:

Fig 8.37: Turnaround with gradually ascending R235 motif

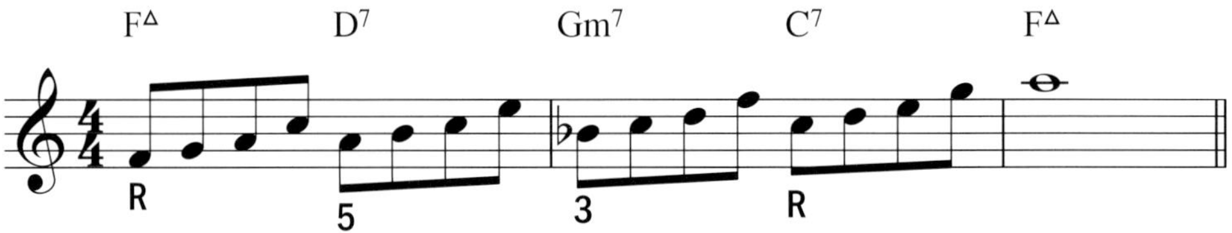

For ♭**9** chords, the patterns can follow a Mixolydian scale with a ♭**9**:

Fig 8.38: Mixolydian ♭9 scale with R235 patterns

Because each four-note group can be played 24 ways, that makes a total of 72 possible patterns for each chord! Practise all the above hand positions until you are completely familiar with them for each type of chord shown. Here's a practice pattern that is great for strengthening the little finger:

Fig 8.39: R235 patterns (played backwards) based on R, 3 and 5

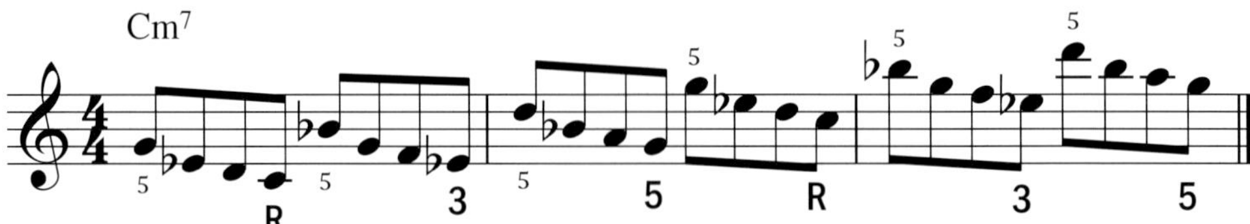

As with any pattern, you could also displace the accent:

Fig. 8.40: Same pattern with accent on second note

Play Figs 8.39 and 8.40 descending as well, and adapt them to different chord types (eg: C7, CΔ) by changing **3** and **7** as necessary.

Octave displacement can be applied to one of the notes in a four-note group – this is very useful if you run out of fingers in the middle of a line!

Fig 8.41: Octave displacement

(a) Bar 9 of *Turnaround Workout #2*

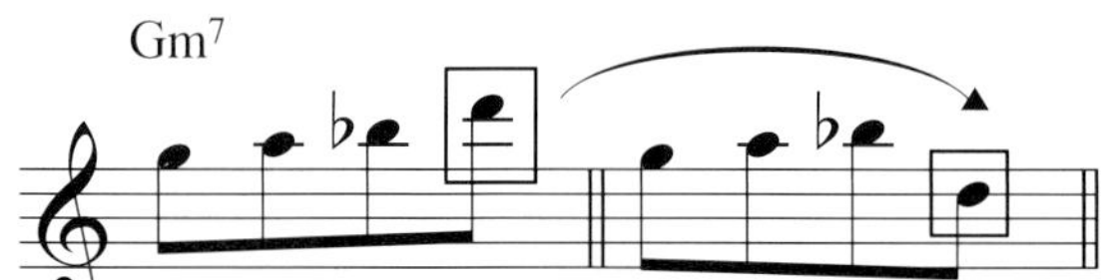

(b) Bar 13 of *Turnaround Workout #2*

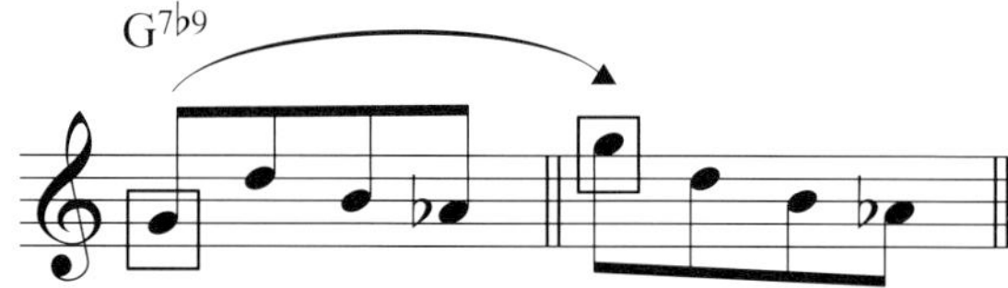

Double-time playing with R235 motifs

The **R235** pattern really comes into its own when playing in sixteenth-notes. Many elegant licks can be constructed by combining just two of the hand positions from Fig 8.36:

Fig 8.42: Combining R235 patterns based on R and 5 of chord

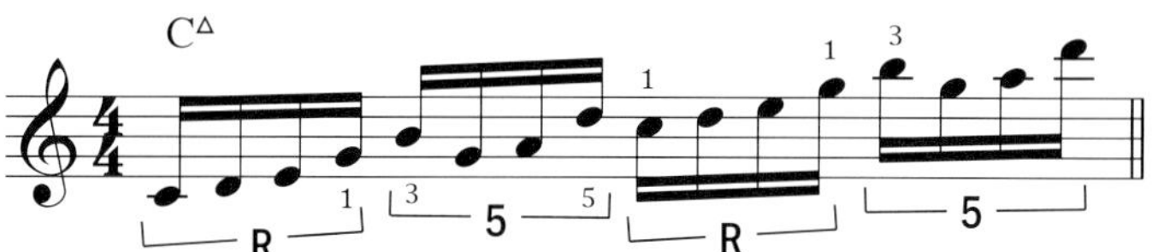

Fig 8.43: Similar pattern descending

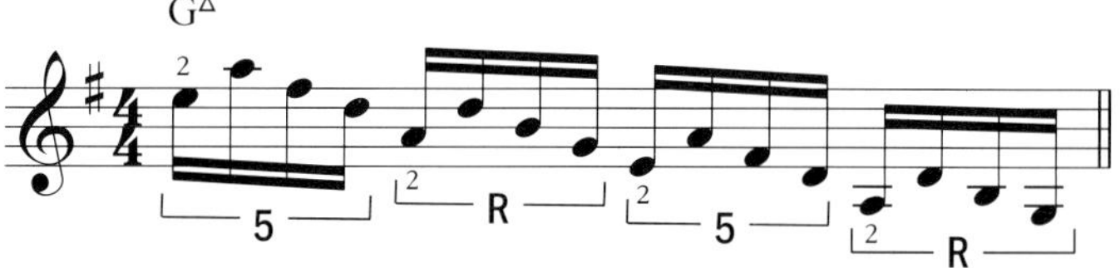

Practise both the above patterns over dominant chords as well (flatten **7**), and over minor sevenths (flatten **7** and **3**).

In order to play double time in a turnaround, with chords lasting two beats each, you need to play eight notes per chord. Here's an easy way to do this using root position **R235** shapes (watch the octave displacement in the Gm7 bar):

Fig 8.44: Playing the same pattern twice on each chord

A much more interesting sound is obtained if two different patterns are combined on each chord. Here are two examples, both using the same hand positions, but with different permutations:

Fig 8.45: Playing a variety of R235 patterns on each chord

When playing in double time, try to visualise groups of four notes, rather than thinking of one note at a time. This gives you a big advantage, as there's very little time for thought when improvising at fast tempos. Practising the hand positions on these pages will help you find the required shapes for each chord as quickly as possible.

Assignments and Improvisation Tips: Turnaround Workout #2

❶ **R235 Patterns** Get used to playing these in eighth-notes round the turnaround chords in the right hand only, using the shapes based on the root of each chord. Explore various permutations of each shape to create a variety of lines, like the examples given.

You don't need to play continuous streams of notes all the time, introduce rests every couple of bars, or leave some of the chords out completely.

❷ **Shells in left hand** Work these out for all three keys and use them to accompany your lines from step 1.

❸ **Rootless voicings** Work these out for all three keys and add your right-hand lines from step 1.

❹ **Pseudo-stride** Practise this in all three keys until the left hand can play without looking. Then add the right-hand lines from step 1.

❺ **Vary the right-hand patterns** Start to include **R235** patterns based on **3** and **5** of the chords as described on p. 140. Play these over all three types of left hand as in steps 2–4.

❻ **Double time** Work on playing in sixteenth-notes, using **R235** patterns as described on p. 141. Practise slowly at first, gradually increasing the tempo. When you're confident, add your preferred left-hand accompaniment.

❼ **Bebop scales** Incorporate these into your double-time improvisation over some of the chords, along with other devices such as arpeggios or broken chords, **II** – **V** patterns, chord scale licks, etc.

Over **II** and **V**, remember to use the dominant bebop scale that fits the **V** chord (think of starting on **4** of the minor chord).

❽ **Triplets** Improvise in triplets over *Turnaround Workout #2,* adapting the ideas from Chapter 7 (p. 115–16) to the key of C.

❾ **Other pieces** Review any of the swing pieces covered so far, applying all the techniques listed above, including triplets and double-time improvisation in the right hand. I would suggest the following tunes:

Take the 'A' Train – Vol. 1, p. 64
Autumn Leaves – Vol. 1, p. 150
Ornithology – Vol. 1, p. 156
Short II–V Workout – Vol. 2, p. 71
Ladybird – Vol. 2, p. 78
Misty – Vol. 2, p. 106

Now that you're dealing with multiple rhythmic levels in your solos, here are some important points to remember:

- Always strive to be clear in your subdivision of the pulse – know whether you're playing eighth-notes, triplets or sixteenth-notes
- Tap your foot, play with a metronome, or both
- Aim for clarity by practising lines slowly at first – this also enables you to spend time working out good fingerings
- Triplets do not sit easily in a straight 8 or 'Latin' feel
- Sixteenth-notes are generally played straight, even in a swing context.

The sharpened ninth chord

As well as lowering the ninth of a dominant seventh chord, we can also raise it, giving the sharpened ninth (**♯9**), often pronounced simply 'sharp nine'.

Fig 8.46: Three types of dominant ninth chords

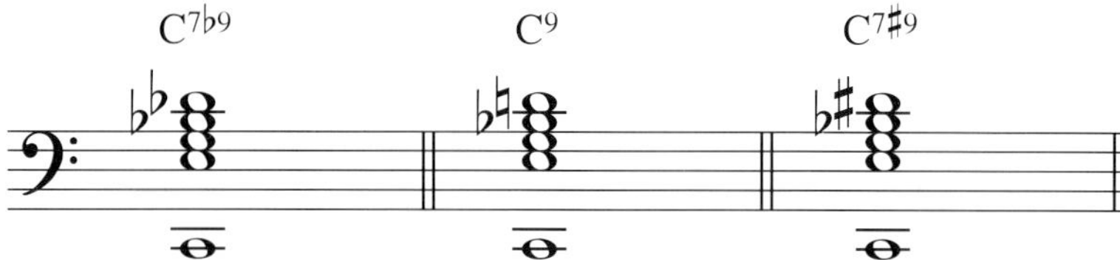

The sharpened ninth of C7 can be written as either D♯ or E♭, whichever is convenient. It is sometimes referred to as a 'flattened tenth', especially by older musicians. The fifth of the chord is often omitted, giving the following three-note shape:

Fig 8.47: Rootless 379 voicing for C7#9

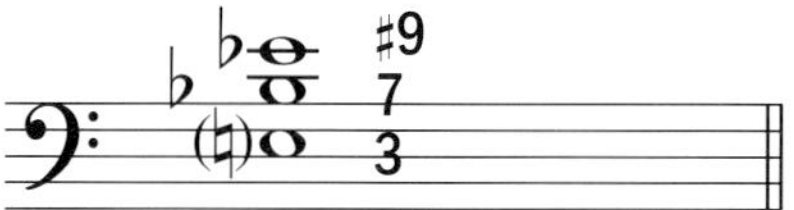

Sharp nine chords are often interchangeable with flat nine chords. If you see C7♭9 on a chord chart, you can often play C7♯9 instead, or as well, melody permitting.

In a **II** – **V** – **I**, jazz musicians often play a **♭9** or a **♯9** on the dominant (**V**) chord to make the harmony more interesting, as long as there is no clash with the melody:

Fig 8.48: Rootless II – V – I shapes

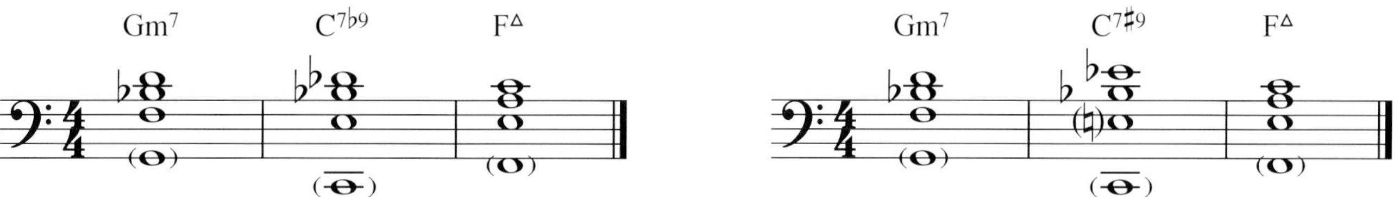

It is quite common to use both, giving two sounds for the **V** chord:

Fig 8.49: Rootless II – V – I with both #9 and ♭9

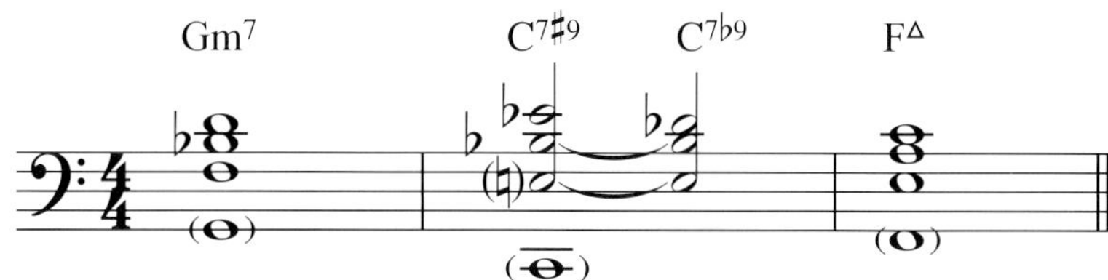

The C7♯9 shape above can also be used for E°, as a way of making the ordinary diminished shape more interesting:

Fig 8.50: Moving the top note of a diminished chord up a tone

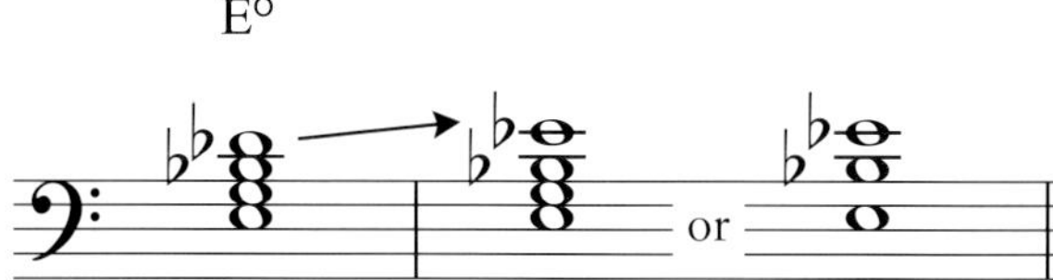

Forming a new diminished shape by moving the top note up a tone will work with any inversion of the chord: E°, G°, B♭°, or C♯°.

27 with drums

♩ = 184

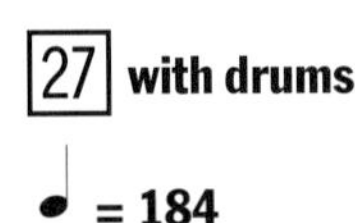

Caravan

Duke Ellington & Juan Tizol
arr. Tim Richards

Co-written by the valve trombonist in Duke's orchestra, this number alternates 'Latin' and swing feels. It is an ideal tune for practising diminished harmony, as each C7♭9 chord lasts for 12 bars.

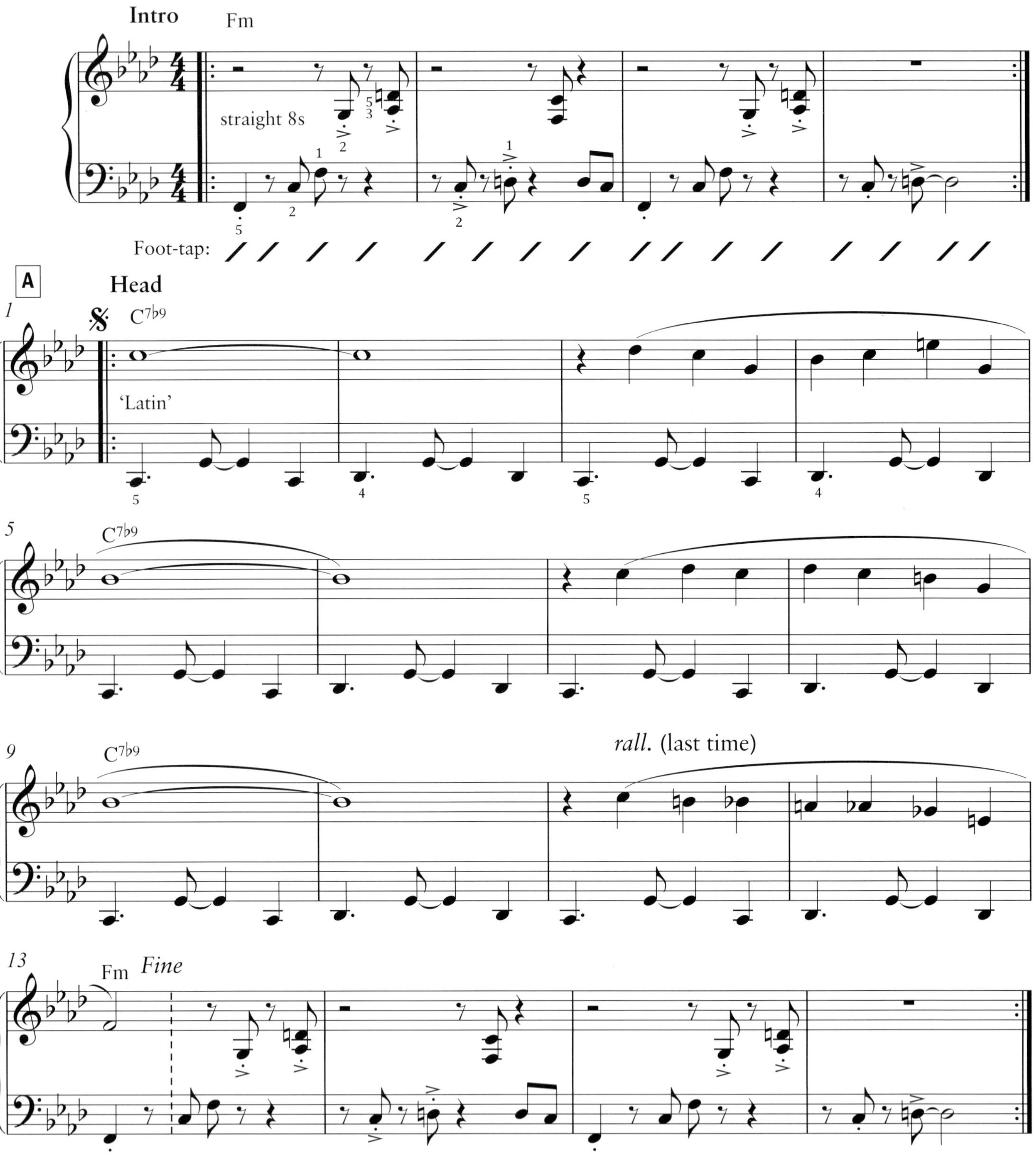

Intro
Fm
straight 8s
Foot-tap:
A
Head
C7♭9
'Latin'
C7♭9
C7♭9
rall. (last time)
Fm
Fine

D.S. al Fine

Checkpoint: Caravan

● **Fm riff** The notes of the introduction are shared between the hands and imply an Fm6 chord. Repeat the four-bar pattern to set up the groove and tempo. At the end of the 'A' sections (bar 13) the same riff returns for another four bars.

This riff is not present in any of Duke's many recorded versions of this tune – it is particular to this arrangement, as played on my trio CD 'The Other Side' (33Jazz037). If you wish you may substitute any other 'Latin' riff at these points, as long as it fits over Fm6 or Fm7 and lasts for four bars.

● **Long AABA form** Like *Take the 'A' Train* (Vol. 1, p. 64), the structure of *Caravan* follows the common AABA form. However, it is unusual in that each section is 16 bars long, rather than 8 bars, giving a total length of 64 bars for one chorus (head or solos).

● **Bridge** The middle section ('B') comprises a cycle of dominant sevenths (F7 – B♭7 – E♭7) culminating in A♭Δ, the relative major, all played with a swing feel. Remember to revert to a 'Latin' (straight 8) feel for the final 'A' to complete the form, in both head and solos.
● **Bass lines** The 'Latin' bass line given at 'A' is one way you might interpret the chord symbol C7♭9 as a solo pianist – see how the bottom note alternates **R** and **♭9** (D♭). In the bridge a walking bass line establishes the swing feel. If playing with a bass player (or the backing CD), play left-hand chords in both sections instead. (See overleaf for suggestions.)
● **Neutral chords** The rhythmic figure in the end of the bridge (bars 47–48) sets up the Latin groove for a repeat of the 'A' section. The left and right hand are a tenth apart, exactly as in Fig 8.8. Although only C7 is given as the chord symbol, added passing chords create harmonic interest, implying the following chord sequence:

C – Dm – E♭° – C

● **Thickening the melody** The right hand in the 'A' section is given as it would appear in a fake book or lead sheet – single notes with chord symbols. At 'B' however, some notes of the chords have been added below the melody to thicken it. Overleaf we'll look at various ways of achieving this for both sections.

Interpreting lead sheets

The single-note 'melody and chord symbols' style of most fake books puts the responsibility on *you* to devise your own personal arrangement based on the information given. The result will differ according to the context in which you intend to play, eg:

- Solo piano
- Singing the melody, accompanying yourself at piano
- Duo or trio without bassist (eg: with sax, flute, guitar, vocals etc)
- In a band (any line-up with bassist)

Over the next few pages we'll look at *Caravan* in detail, exploring various options which will enable you to prepare this tune for either solo or band playing.

Duke Ellington, leader of the most long-lived and probably the most revered big band in jazz, pictured in his dressing room. Composer of such timeless classics as *Mood Indigo, Satin Doll* and *Solitude*, Duke's harmonic concept was way ahead of his time. His piano style was also highly original, consisting of dark chords, cascading arpeggios and percussive effects, often prefiguring later modernists such as Thelonious Monk.

BABY
POWDER

Caravan as a solo piano piece

● **'A' sections** The bass line suggested is effective as a solo piano left hand, because it fulfils two essential functions: it implies the harmony through its inclusion of the **♭9** (in alternate bars), and it provides the required 'Latin' setting, which is lacking in the melody itself, consisting as it does of whole- and quarter-notes only.

Feel free to play other bass lines for these twelve bars. Here is a selection to try out; work on them with the right-hand melody until you can play both together:

Fig 8.51: Alternative 'Latin' bass lines for C7♭9

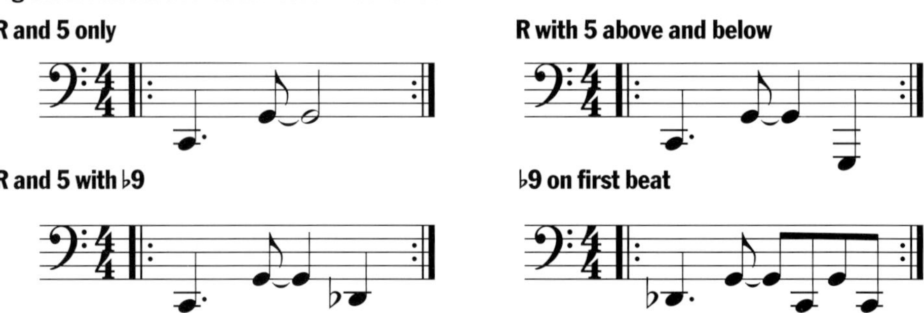

● **Right hand** Now let's look at two important ways of adding texture when stating the melody above a bass line. The first of these consists of adding notes of the prevailing chord below the main notes of the melody, as shown in the bridge on p. 145.

For the 'A' sections, you can add notes from a C♯° chord (same as E°), since C7♭9 contains the notes of this diminished chord. You can hear this in the right hand on the CD (track 25), during the second 'A' section:

Fig 8.52: Adding notes below the melody (as played at 0:32)

The second approach consists of adding an unchanging note above the melody, often the **R** or **5** of the chord, to give 'top harmony'. You can hear this in the right hand during the final 'A' section:

Fig 8.53: Adding notes above the melody (as played at 1:11)

The top harmony technique derives from blues piano, but is an important part of many jazz pianists' styles too (see *Funky Two-Five*, Vol. 1, p. 188 and Figs 5.21–5.23). It is also used at the end of the bridge, the root of the C7 chord being played in the right hand above the moving notes (bars 47–48).

● **Bridge** If you decide to play a bass line in the bridge, start off learning the melody (single notes at first) over a simple, repetitive bass pattern such as a triad (**R353**) or sixth chord (**R356**) in every bar. When you have mastered this, you could graduate to a bass line like the one given, which includes scale passages and run-ups (see Vol. 1, p. 70 and Fig 3.43). It's important not to have to read the bass line from the page – if necessary memorise it first, four bars at a time.

● **Changing the register** In the 'B' section, the melody is given an octave lower than the original, producing a richer sound. Changing the register of the melody is one way of personalising it! Moving it down was only possible because the walking bass stays at the low end of the keyboard, only rarely venturing into the octave below middle C.

● **Pseudo-stride** Instead of the walking bass line given, try the following left-hand pattern for all the chords, up to and including A♭Δ (see Fig 7.79):

Fig 8.54: Pseudo stride pattern for bridge

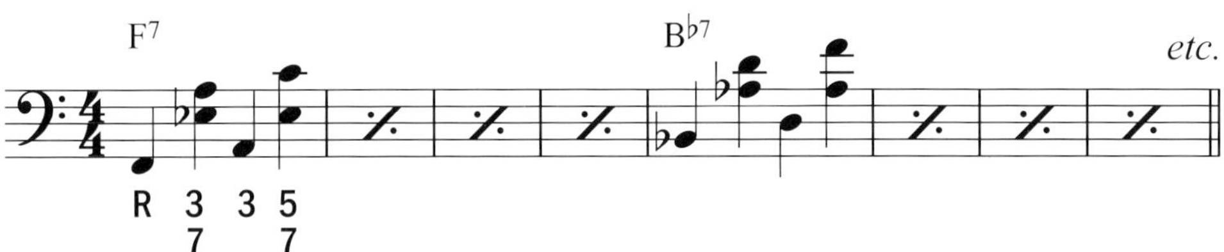

To avoid the hands overlapping, you'll need to play the right hand given on p. 145 an octave higher than written.

● **Rhythmic alterations** The melody in bars 34, 38 and 42 of the bridge has been slightly changed – the three accented notes are played half-a-beat earlier than the original. 'Pushing' notes that are written on the beat is common practice, and many jazz musicians phrase this way when reading 'straight' melodies without even being aware of it. The anticipated notes make the music swing (see *Autumn Leaves,* Vol. 1, p. 150 and Fig 4.25(a)).

Finally, notice how I've written the two E♭ chords in bar 44 as *staccato* quarter-notes, whereas the original had two long notes here. This is another example of personalising the melody – if you don't like it, don't do it!

Assignments: Caravan – solo piano

❶ **Melody** Prepare the melody for solo performance as described on the previous pages, choosing an appropriate left-hand accompaniment for each section, and memorising it. Don't forget to thicken the right hand in places.

❷ **Improvisation** Using the same left hand as in step 1, practise improvising over each section of the tune in turn. Some suggestions for the right hand are given on p. 152. When you are comfortable with each section, put them together so that you can take a solo over the complete AABA form without any interruptions.

❸ **Arrangement** Prepare a complete performance, like this:

Intro – Melody – Solo – Melody – Ending
AABA AABA AABA

Most jazz performances would include more than just the one chorus of improvisation – in a group, several musicians might take turns, playing several times round the AABA form each.

If you'd rather shorten your arrangement, solo over the first two 'A' sections only, then play just the second half of the melody, from the bridge to the end:

Intro – Melody – Solo – Melody – Ending
AABA AA BA

A variation on this is to play one and a half choruses of improvisation:

Intro – Melody – Solo – Melody – Ending
AABA AABA AA BA

Occasionally (usually in ballads), the recurring AABA form is not preserved, and the first two 'A' sections are simply omitted from the last head. In a group situation this requires a cue from the leader to go straight to the bridge:

Intro – Melody – Solo (eg: 2 choruses) – Melody – Ending
AABA AABA AABA cue: BA

Caravan as a group piece

The techniques that follow are suitable for any situation where a bassist is present, including playing with the backing track on the CD. The left hand now doesn't need to state the bass line or chord roots, and can be freer rhythmically.

● **'A' sections** The left-hand chords shown below are similar to those used earlier in the right hand (Fig 8.52). There are several ways of supporting a melody by playing chords in the left hand; in this example the melody is strengthened by playing the chords in the same rhythm as the right hand:

Fig 8.55: Reinforcing the rhythm of the melody

This approach leaves all the gaps between the melody notes empty, giving space for the rhythm section or backing to be heard. You might also try the opposite approach, in which left and right hands engage in a kind of dialogue:

Fig 8.56: Left-hand chords in gaps between phrases of melody

● **Quartal C7 shapes** As well as the ♭**9**, the chords in Fig 8.56 include the ♯**9** (E♭) and ♯**11** (F♯). All have the same interval structure – tritone below, perfect fourth above. The boxed chords are passing chords a semitone away from the C7 shapes.

The C7 shapes are derived from the family of diminished chords that belong to C7♭9, ie: E° and its inversions, by moving the top note of each chord up a tone:

Fig 8.57: Derivation of three-note C7 shapes from E°

Notice that the chord shapes in Fig 8.57 go up in minor thirds, and imply different types of dominant seventh chord, all of which are compatible with C7♭9:

Fig 8.58: Quartal dominant shapes going up in minor thirds

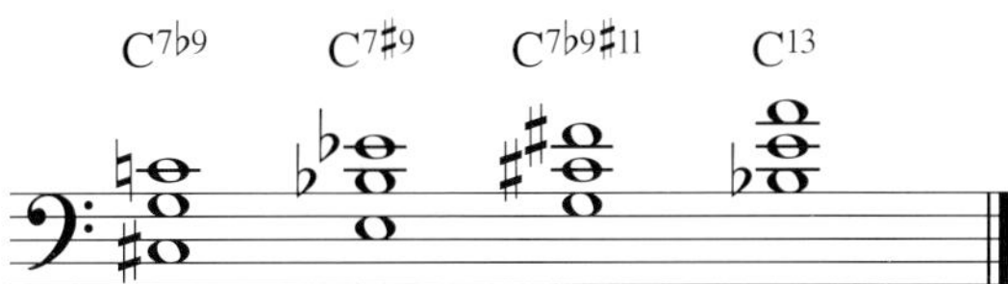

Although the C13 shape was not used in Fig 8.56, all four shapes are included in the left hand of the next piece, *Diminished Scale Workout* (p. 154).

● **Bridge** The usual way of playing a melody when a bassist is present is to play rootless voicings in the left hand, single notes in the right:

Fig 8.59: Rootless voicings in left hand

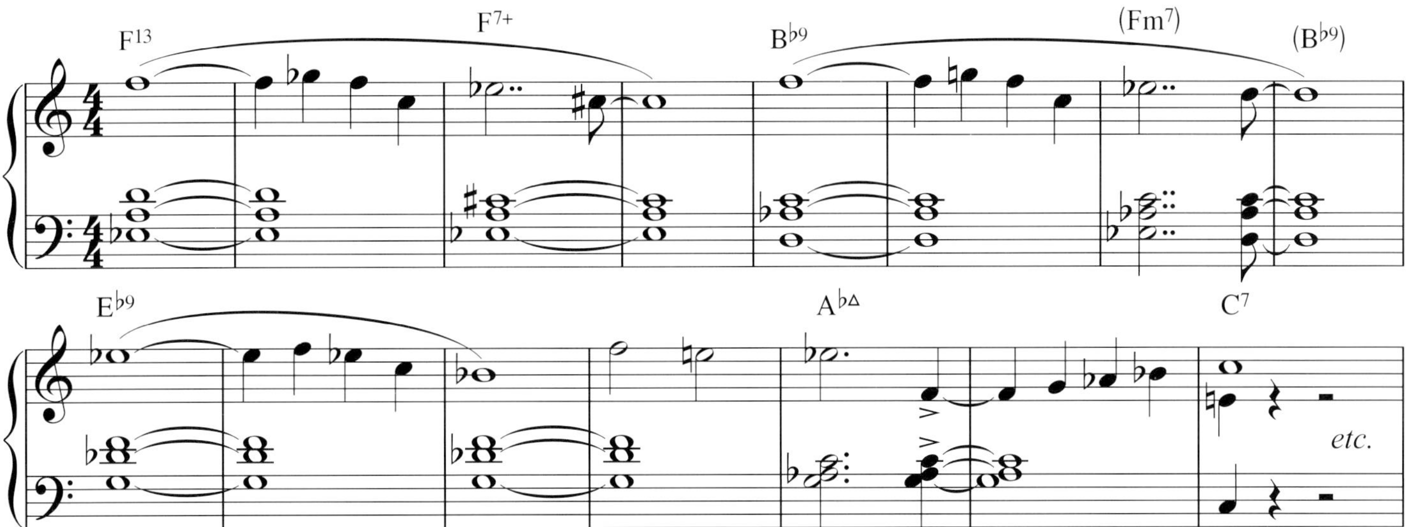

● **Thickening the texture** With melody notes that last several beats, you can add notes between the left-hand voicing and melody. The following example also includes some four-note left-hand chords to thicken things even more:

Fig 8.60: Two-handed voicings for the bridge

In deciding which notes to add underneath the melody, wherever possible avoid doubling the notes already present in the left hand. Notice the perfect fourth structures in the right hand for F13, B♭13, E♭13 and A♭Δ – these often sound good above rootless voicings.

The ♭9 pentatonic scale

When improvising over C7♭9 in *Caravan* you can of course use arpeggios or broken chord patterns based on E°, G°, B♭° or C♯°, all of which contain the same notes. However, if you add the root (C) to any of the above, an interesting five-note scale is formed:

Fig 8.61: C7♭9 pentatonic scale

It is important to be confident about changing to Fm at the correct place. If you find that you get lost counting the 12 bars of C7, there are various strategies to help prevent this.

Firstly, see how the melody divides into three four-bar phrases, each of which has the same rhythm. Emulate this in your solo by playing variations on the following phrase, changing the notes but keeping roughly the same rhythm:

Fig 8.62: Four-bar phrase (rhythmic template)

Now try breaking each four-bar phrase into two. You'll need to play six two-bar phrases before the change to Fm. Starting each one with a pick-up so that they go across the bar-lines will give your solo much better forward motion, as shown below over bars 8–13 of section 'A'. The target note of each pick-up is indicated below by ❋.

Fig 8.63: Two-bar phrases with forward motion

Assignments and Improvisation Tips: Caravan

The following suggestions for right-hand improvisation apply both to playing *Caravan* by yourself (solo piano), and to playing it with a band (or with the CD backing).

❶ **'A' sections** Practise your improvisation round the first sixteen bars over and over, by playing along with track 28, *Diminished Scale Workout* (p. 154). This is at a slower tempo, and never goes to the bridge. The right hand can explore the C7♭9 pentatonic scale (Fig 8.61) or the diminished scale, shown opposite. When you reach Fm (last four bars), you can choose between the Dorian scale on F, the F minor pentatonic or blues scale, and the ♭3 pentatonic on F (see Vol. 1, Fig 5.22).

❷ **Bridge** Practise improvising round the sixteen bars of the 'B' section over and over. Here are some of the right-hand techniques you could try:

- Arpeggios and broken chord patterns (Vol. 1, pp. 118–121)
- Mixolydian scale patterns (for dominant seventh chords)
- Bebop scales (Vol. 2, pp. 91–2 and 98)
- Major pentatonic scales (based on the root of each chord)
- Encircling the fifth of the dominant chord (Vol. 2, p. 100)
- Upper and lower neighbours (Vol. 2, p. 218)
- Chord/scale lick (use the flat nine licks on p. 136 to lead into each new chord)
- Whole-tone scales (Vol. 1. p. 111)

The whole-tone scale is implied by F7+ (bars 35–36), but you could use it over B♭7 and E♭7 as well, as long as you adjust the left-hand chords to fit (ie: raise or lower **5**).

❸ **AABA** When you're ready, put the 'A' and 'B' sections back together, improvising a complete 64-bar solo, either by yourself or with the CD (track 27, drums only), depending which style you've been practising.

The diminished scale

On the previous page you improvised over C7♭9 using the notes of the chord: C, E, G, B♭ and D♭. The top four notes make an E diminished chord.

We have seen how moving the top note of a diminished chord up a tone gives an alternative shape for the chord (Figs 8.50 and 8.57). Because C7♭9 can be thought of as G°, B♭° and D♭° as well as E°, these can all have raised top notes too. Including the four raised notes alongside the original E° notes gives an eight-note scale:

Fig 8.64: E diminished scale (also fits C7♭9)

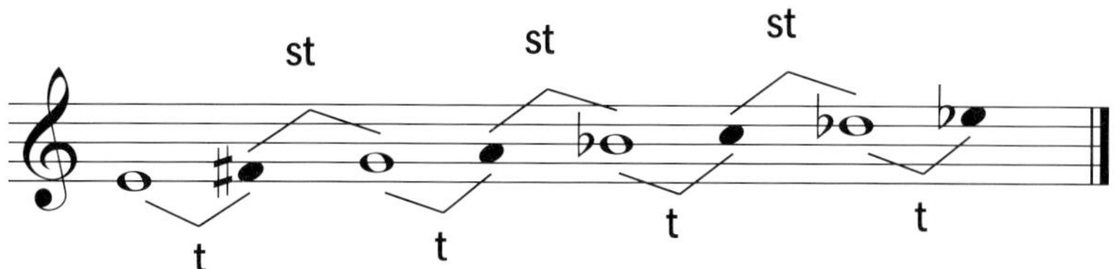

The white notes above are the notes of the E° chord. The notes in black are each one tone up from these, and outline a second diminished chord – F♯°.

The scale therefore alternates tones and semitones. Unlike most other scales, it is symmetrical. Here's a good way to practise it that highlights this:

Fig 8.65: Diminished scale practice pattern

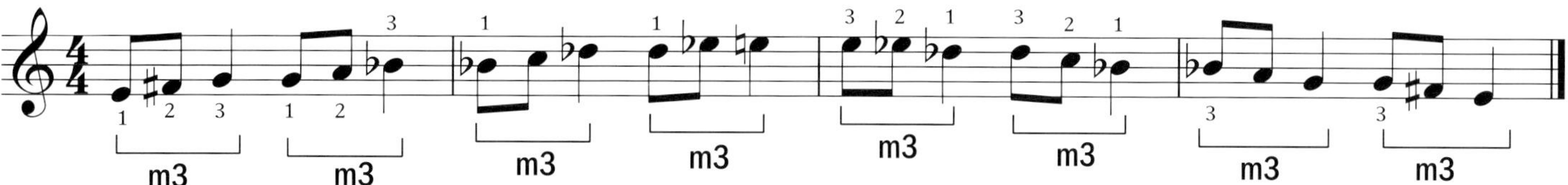

The above scale contains the same notes whether you start it on E, G, B♭ or D♭. For that reason, it can actually be used over all of the following chords:

E°	$C^{7\flat9}$	$C^{7\sharp9}$
G°	$E\flat^{7\flat9}$	$E\flat^{7\sharp9}$
B♭°	$G\flat^{7\flat9}$	$G\flat^{7\sharp9}$
C♯°	$A^{7\flat9}$	$A^{7\sharp9}$

If you want to play a diminished scale over a dominant seventh chord, remember to base the scale on the third of the chord, and to play it 'tone first'.

Once you have got used to the fingering, you'll find this a fascinating scale to play. Most jazz players have their own favourite diminished scale patterns that exploit the minor third symmetry in different ways. A few of these are given below, and can be found (with others) in *Diminished Scale Workout* overleaf.

Fig 8.66: Useful diminished scale patterns (E° or C7)

(a)

(b)

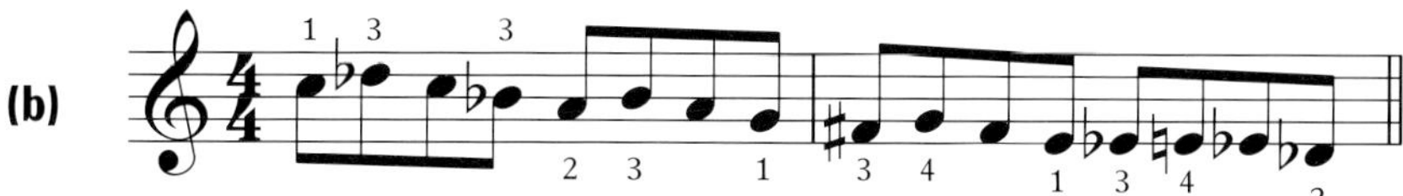

(c)

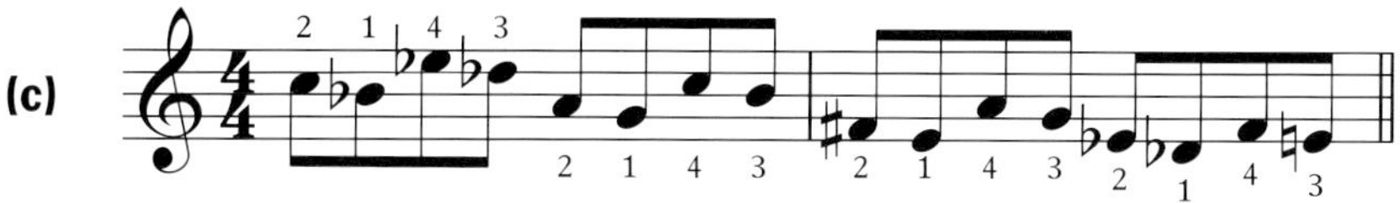

28 with bass & drums

♩ = 160
(straight 8s)

Diminished Scale Workout

Tim Richards

This piece provides practice at using a variety of E diminished scale patterns over the 'A' sections of *Caravan*. Memorise some of the patterns and develop them in your own improvisations.

25
29
Fm9
♭3 pentatonic on F
Fm6/9
Fm9
Fm6/9
A3
C7♭9
33
Repeat phrase here or continue up in minor thirds
37
Repeat phrase here or continue down in minor thirds
41
45
Fm9
F blues scale
Fm6/9
Fm9
Fm6/9
Fade on Fm

Getting to know diminished scales

Just as an E° chord has the same notes as G°, B♭° and C♯°, so with the scales. That means that there are actually only three diminished scales to learn, each of which fits four possible diminished chords:

Fig 8.67: The three diminished scales (tone/semitone alternating)

As we have seen in *Caravan*, the most important use of diminished scales is with dominant seventh **♭9** chords, eg: the E° scale with a C7♭9 chord, starting the scale on the third of the chord.

Some authors and musicians advocate playing the diminished scale starting on the root of the dominant chord, rather than the third. To make this work it is necessary to play the semitone first. Let's compare these two options for C7:

Fig 8.68: E diminished scale played over C7

(a) tone first (starting on 3)

(b) semitone first (starting on R)

I do not personally advocate learning your scales as in (b), for two reasons:

1 You'll need to learn two types of diminished scale, rather than just one. This gives you twice as much work and leads to unnecessary confusion!
2 Playing up from the root in eighth-notes places the notes of the related dominant chord (**3**, **5**, **7**, **♭9**) on the upbeats, rather than the downbeats as in (a), and makes the scale harder to visualise.

Learn your scales from the third of the dominant chord, playing a tone first, as in (a). Note that the scale includes the **♯11** (F♯) as well as the **♭9** and **♯9** of the C7 chord, but not the **♯5**. The chord symbol that most completely expresses this is:

$$C^{13\flat9\sharp9\sharp11}$$

This is too cumbersome for general use, but if you see the symbol C7♭9, C7♯9 or C13♭9, that's more or less telling you the diminished scale is a good choice.

Resolving diminished scale patterns

It is unusual for a dominant **♭9** or **♯9** chord to last as long as twelve bars before resolving, as in *Caravan*. In most tunes, you will only have a bar or so before needing to resolve to the next chord.

● **Minor third symmetry** Any diminished scale pattern can be started in four different places, the starting notes being a minor third apart.

When practising diminished patterns over the **V** chord in a **V** – **I** situation, get into the habit of exploring all four starting points, resolving each phrase to the nearest note of the **I** chord (the 'target' note, usually **R**, **3** or **5**) on the first beat of the bar:

Fig 8.69: Four ways to resolve the same diminished pattern

See how the last two examples elegantly encircle the target note.

If you have two bars on the **V** chord, you could double the length of the phrase (start a tritone higher). Or you could play these sixteen notes in double time, to make them fit one bar again.

Try transposing any of the examples in Fig 8.69 to E7♭9 – Am and playing them in bars 8–9 of your solo in *Summertime*, for instance.

● **Tritone symmetry** From the minor third symmetry, it also follows that any diminished scale phrase can be played a tritone (**♭5**) away without departing from the scale. Here is a simple example of this:

Fig 8.70: Descending from the root of the dominant chord

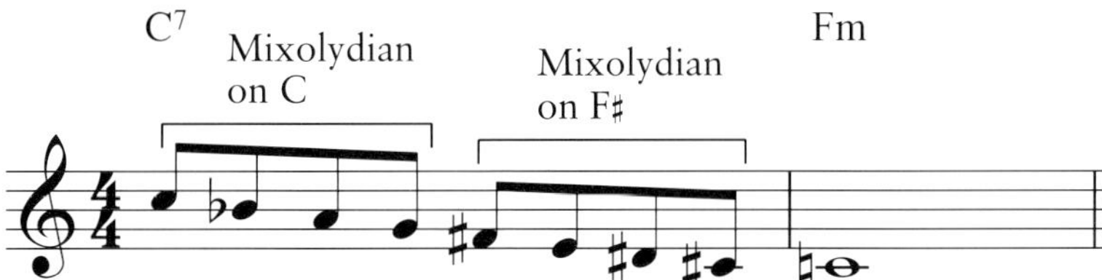

The first four notes are the same as the Mixolydian mode; the next four are like a Mixolydian mode descending from the **♭5**. This ties in with the fact that the diminished scale which fits C7 also fits its tritone substitute, F♯7 (and the chords a minor third away too: E♭7 and A7).

Three ways to end a blues

The most basic twelve-bar blues sequence contains just three chords – **I**, **IV** and **V**. In its simplest form, the last four bars of this sequence feature only **V** and **I**:

Blues in F:	C^7	C^7	F^7	F^7 ‖
	V		**I**	

Jazz twelve-bars that feature this simple ending include Monk's *Straight No Chaser* (Vol. 1, p. 108) and *Blue Monk* (IBP, also p. 108 – synchronicity at work?!) Equally common is the following ending, which also features the **IV** chord, as in John Coltrane's *Bessie's Blues* (original in E♭):

C^7	$B^{\flat 7}$	F^7	F^7 ‖
V	**IV**	**I**	

Most rock or blues musicians would finish off a twelve-bar blues in one of these two ways. In jazz it is more common to play a **II – V** in bars 9–10:

Gm^7	C^7	F^7	F^7 ‖
II	**V**	**I**	

Don't forget that whatever the style, all three sequences often feature a turnaround during the last two bars, which is not shown above. The simplest turnaround just consists of a **V** chord in the final bar, as in *Tension & Release Blues #1* opposite. We'll be looking at other types in *Bird Blues Comping* and *Blues Turnaround Workout* (pp. 161 and 164–5).

The diminished scale and the blues

The sequence given below probably represents the most popular (simple) set of blues changes used by the average jazz musician. Notice that the **II – V** given in the third example above is preceded by the **VI** chord (D7) in bar 8:

‖ F^7	$B^{\flat 7}$	F^7	[F^7]
$B^{\flat 7}$	$B^{\flat 7}$	F^7	[D^7]
Gm^7	[C^7]	F^7	[C^7] ‖

The dominant chords in boxes all resolve up a fourth, as in a **V – I** cadence. There are four main places where this occurs:

- bar 4: F7 to B♭7
- bar 8: D7 to Gm7
- bar 10: C7 to F7
- bar 12: C7 to F7

B♭7 to F7 (bar 2 and bar 6) does not fit into this category as B♭7 is not the dominant of F. This is a **IV – I** cadence instead.

The boxed bars are the best places to play **♭9** and/or **#9** chords, and to use the diminished scale in your right-hand improvisation. Because these devices use notes outside the 'home' (Mixolydian) scale of the chords, they create tension which is resolved when you arrive at the next bar. I wouldn't recommend doing this straight away for the F7 in bar 1 (even though it does resolve as expected to B♭7 in bar 2) because you need to establish the 'home' tonality at the start of the sequence. By bar 4, however, the ear is ready to be diverted!

Take care not to use the diminished scale over chords containing a **#5**, as there will be a clash with the regular fifth in the scale. If you find yourself playing sharp five chords in any of these bars, the right hand should use a whole-tone scale (as in bar 4 opposite), or the altered scale, which we'll deal with in Chapter 9.

Tension & Release Blues #1 opposite is a simple twelve-bar in F, with examples of diminished or whole-tone phrases in the four places mentioned above.

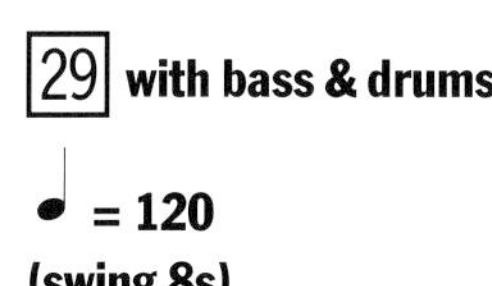

Tension & Release Blues #1

Tim Richards

This piece provides practice at using the diminished or whole-tone scales at tension points in the blues sequence: bars 4, 8, 10 and 12.

Head

F13 | B♭9 | F13 | F7+ whole-tone scale

5 B♭9 | | F13 | D7♯9 diminished scale

9 Gm7 | C7♯9 ♭9 lick | F13 | C7♯9 diminished scale

Solo

1 F13 Improvise ad lib. | B♭9 | F13 | F7♯9 diminished scale

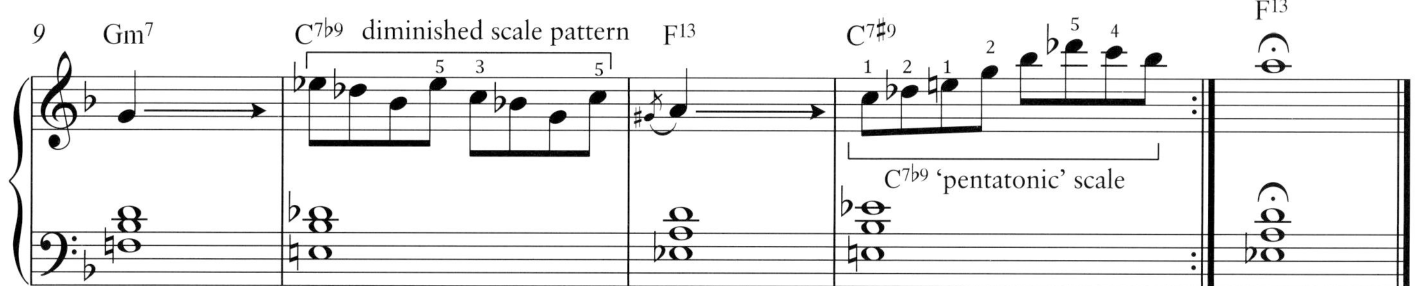

Assignments: Tension & Release Blues #1

❶ **Memorise the left-hand chords** Watch the dominant chords in bars 4, 8, 10 and 12 – they can be played with **♭9**, **#9** or **#5**. The choice is yours.

❷ **Play the head** Make sure you understand how to find the correct scales in the bars mentioned above, and how to resolve them onto target notes in the next bar. Remember that **#5** chords should take the whole-tone scale.

❸ **Improvise** For the solo section, improvise your own phrases in the empty bars, incorporating the written material in bars 4, 8, etc. Don't use the diminished or whole-tone scale outside of these bars. Eventually aim to use your own diminished patterns or other ideas to create tension in these bars, in a more spontaneous fashion.

By silencing the piano on the CD (track 29), you'll have four choruses of bass and drums to play along with.

❹ **Comping** From the third chorus (2:50) onwards you can hear two-handed voicings, obtained by adding right-hand notes to the rootless chords given for the left hand. Work out similar voicings by ear and practise them with the backing track.

There's a play-along track with similar chords in IBP: *Tritone Blues* (p. 117, track 42).

Two-handed voicings for ♭9 and #9 chords

In bars 9–11 of the previous piece the left hand played three-note rootless shapes for **II – V – I**s with **♭9** or **#9** on the **V** chord (see also Fig 8.48). Here are some two-handed versions for the same changes:

Fig 8.71: Major II – V – I with shells in the left hand

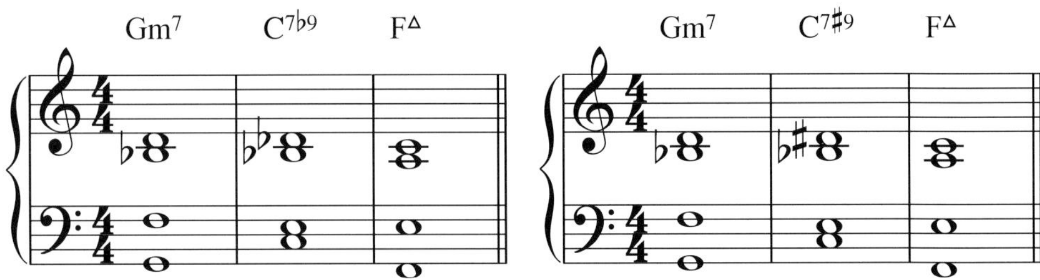

Whilst raising or lowering the ninth is optional for the dominant chord in a major **II – V – I**, in minor keys it is the norm, just as the **II** chord normally has a **♭5**. The equivalent voicings to the above for the key of F minor are as follows:

Fig 8.72: Minor II – V – I with shells in the left hand

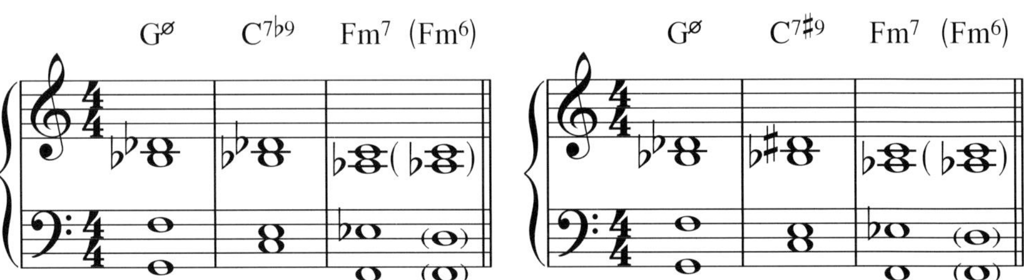

In minor keys, the **V** chord often has **#5** as well. This will be apparent when you play voicings with opposite left-hand shells to above (ie: starting with **R3** in the left hand):

Fig 8.73: Minor II – V – I with opposite shells

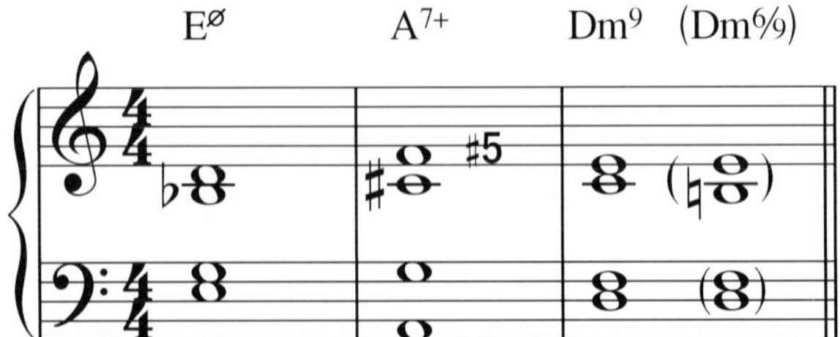

Note that the half-diminished chord doesn't have the usual **R3/79** voicing, but is played as **R3/57** instead, to avoid the rather discordant sound of the ninth. Most of the voicings above appear in *Bird Blues Comping* opposite.

30 with bass & drums

♩ = 160 (swing 8s)

Bird Blues Comping

Tim Richards

This chord sequence for a twelve-bar blues was introduced by the influential alto saxophonist Charlie Parker ('Bird'). Tunes written over these changes include his well-known *Blues for Alice*.

Diminished chords and scales

Checkpoint: Bird Blues Comping

● **Major seventh chord as I** These Parker changes are recognisable as a blues in F by the movement to the **IV** chord (B♭7) in bar 5, and the **II – V – I** (Gm7 – C7 – F) in bars 9–11. However, there are some radical differences that set them apart from a more conventional twelve-bar:

- Use of FΔ as the **I** chord rather than the usual dominant sound of F7
- Cycle of fifths in first four bars starting with the **VII** chord, Eø
- Chromatically descending **II – V**s, starting in bar 6 with the **IVm**, B♭m7

● **Two-handed voicings** All have **R7** and **R3** shells in the left hand, both configurations being used over the two choruses. Look out for **♭9**, **#9** and **#5** on the dominant chords – these are used when they resolve up a fourth. Don't alter the ninths or fifths of other dominant chords (eg: in bars 5–8).

♭9 and #9 polychords

Another way of playing two-handed voicings with five notes is to play major triads in the right hand, like we did for sharp 11 chords in Chapter 6 (Fig 6.11). Here are two ways of doing this for a **II – V – I** with left-hand shells:

Fig 8.74: Gm7 – C7 – FΔ played as polychords

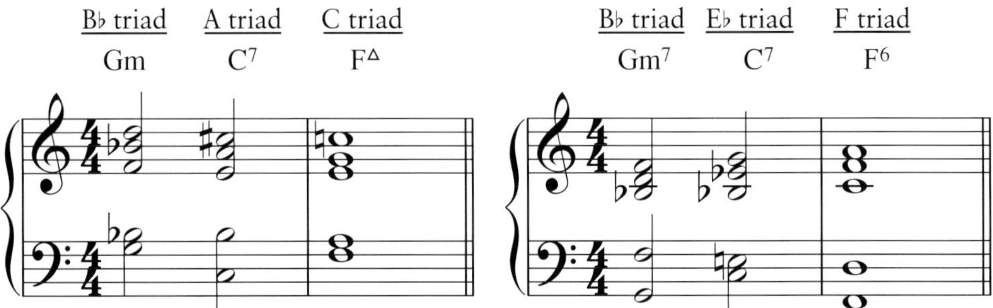

The first of these examples gives C7♭9 as the **V** chord, the second gives C7#9. For a summary of the formation of the dominant polychords, see p. 167. For the Gm7 and FΔ chords, note the following:

- Minor seventh chords have a major triad on **♭3** (B♭/Gm)
- Major seventh chords have a major triad on **5** (C/FΔ) or on **R** (F/F6).

Assignments: Bird Blues Comping

❶ **Memorise the changes** Once you know the chord sequence by heart learn the two-handed voicings so that you no longer need to read the music.

❷ **Play along** Comp with the CD (track 30, bass and drums only), using both sets of voicings as given at 'A' and 'B'. Vary the rhythms of the chords.

❸ **Expand the voicings** Add a third note to some of the chords with the right-hand little finger. This procedure is shown in Figs 7.25–7.26 for **II–V–I** chords. For the minor **II – V – I** in bar 2, Eø – A7 – Dm, see Fig 10.62.
You could also play the **♭9** and **#9** chords as polychords, as described above and on p. 167.

❹ **Take a solo** Improvise in the right hand, using mainly arpeggios of the chords, linking them as musically as you can. When you can do this fairly fluently, accompany yourself with the left-hand shells given (try both sets) and play along with the backing track.

❺ **Rootless voicings** Shells are often the best option for bebop-style tunes with rapidly changing chords, like *Blues for Alice* and *Ornithology* (Vol. 1, p. 156). However, you could update the left hand by working out a set of three- or four-note rootless voicings, following the examples given in Figs 7.16–7.17.

❻ **Push the boundaries** Try out other ideas in the right hand, such as **R235** patterns (pp. 138–41) and the short **II – V** patterns given in Fig 7.15. Include some of these in your solo, with shells or rootless chords in the left hand.

❼ **Key of B♭** It's important to be familiar with the blues sequence in several keys, and B♭ is one of the most popular. Adapt both 'Bird Blues' and regular blues changes (p. 159) to this key, trying out the latter with the *Tension & Release Blues #2* backing, track 33 (p. 180).

I – VI – II – V turnarounds

The simplest way to send a sequence back to its starting point is to go to the **V** chord in the last bar (assuming the first chord is **I**). This was the turnaround in *Tension & Release Blues #1* (p. 159), and *Straight No Chaser* (Vol. 1, p. 108), the last two bars of which were:

Blues in F: | F | C^7 :‖
I **V**

The last two bars of *Bird Blues* featured the diatonic turnaround that we have already seen in *Misty* and *Turnaround Workout #1* (pp. 106 and 112):

| F$^{\Delta}$ Dm^7 | Gm^7 C^7 :‖
I **VI** **II** **V**

As we saw in 'Chord substitution' (p. 114) variations can be applied to this basic turnaround by introducing secondary dominants. In *Turnaround Workout #2*, (p. 139), the **VI** chord was transformed from minor to dominant:

| F$^{\Delta}$ **D7** | Gm^7 C^7 :‖

● **Cycle of dominant sevenths** In a blues sequence, unless you are playing 'Bird Blues' changes, the **I** chord will be dominant too. The Gm7 can also become G7:

| **F7** D^7 | **G7** C^7 :‖

We now have a dominant seventh cycle starting on D7, finishing on F7. The easiest way to play these chords is as tritones (see Vol. 1, p. 107):

Fig 8.75: Tritones descending in semitones from D7

Adding a third note above the tritones gives three-note rootless shapes:

Fig 8.76: 735 and 379 shapes

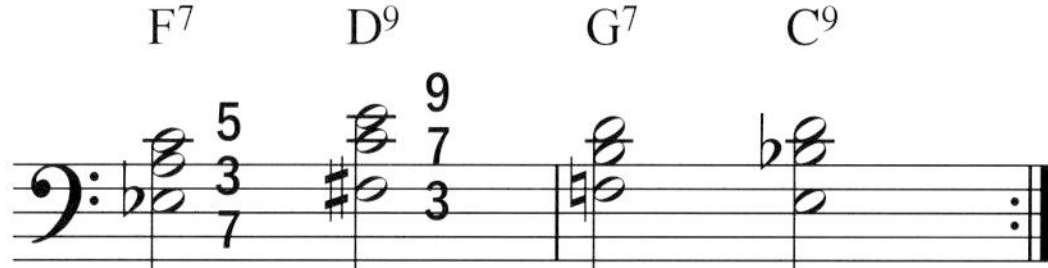

● **Descending in semitones** By altering some of these chords, we can make the shapes go down in semitones from D7, just like the tritones we started with:

Fig 8.77

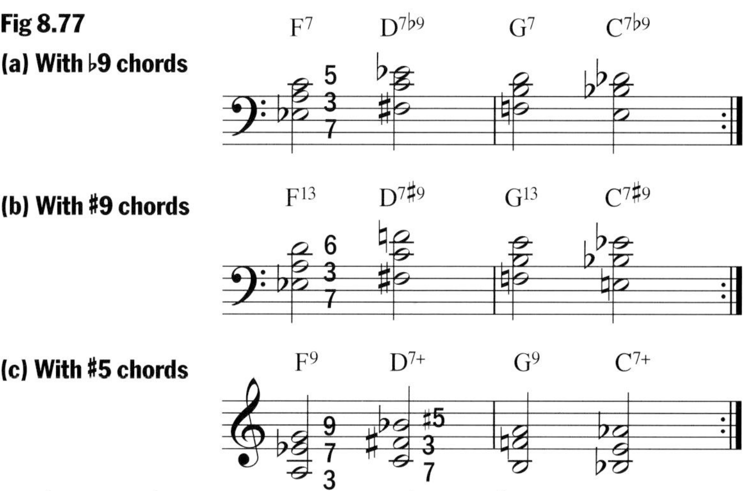

Each example in Fig 8.77 uses only one shape:

- ● To get the D7 shapes, move the F7 shapes up a minor third
- ● The C7 shapes are a semitone above the F7 shapes they resolve back to.

Blues Turnaround Workout overleaf gives practice with these shapes in both hands.

31 with drums
Bass enters for second page

♩ = 120
(swing 8s)

Blues Turnaround Workout

Tim Richards

On this page rootless chords are played in a variety of rhythms, the shapes descending in semitones from D^7 (see p. 163). The walking bass notes on beats 1 and 3 are always the roots of the chords. Linking-notes are played on beats 2 and 4 – where these are chromatic (ie: not a note of the chord, **R**, **3**, **5** or **7**) these are shown in a box.

A Tritones in right hand (73 or 37)

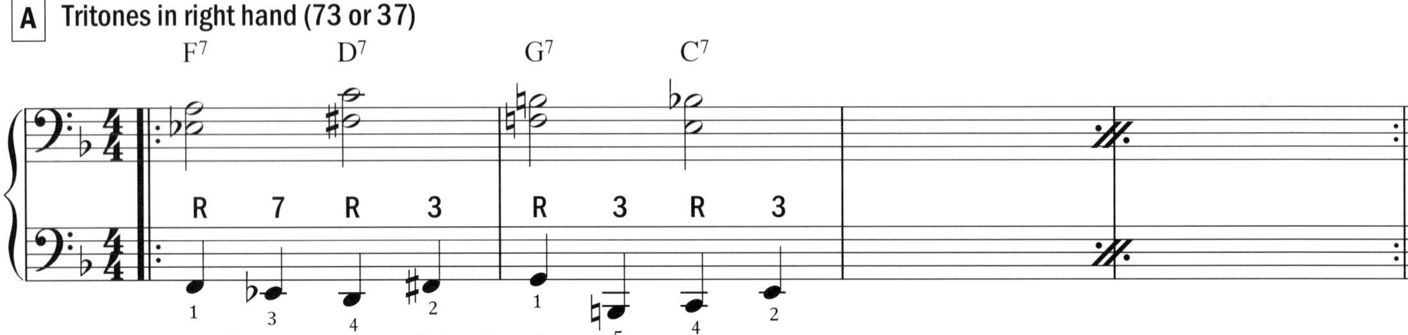

Bass line uses notes of chords only

B Right hand plays 'on-off' rhythm (three-note shapes)

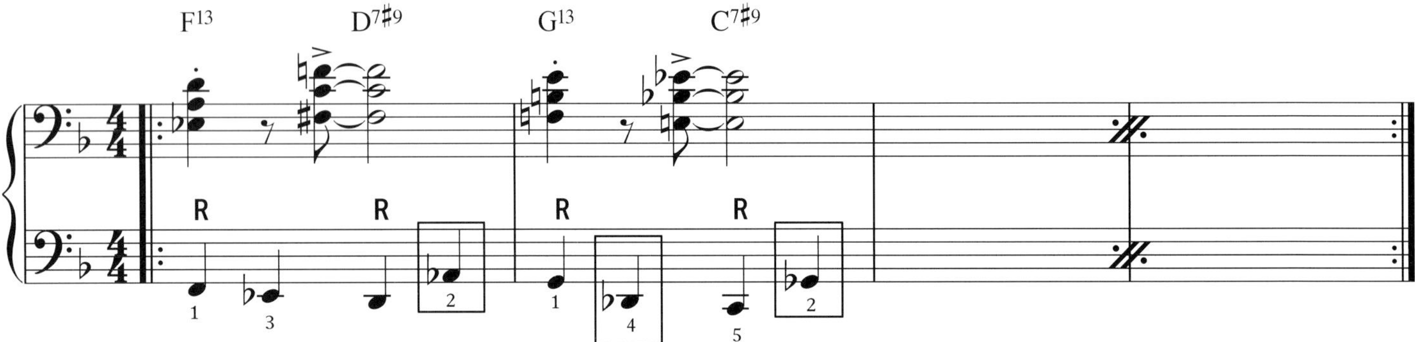

Bass line uses linking-notes a semitone above roots of chords

C Right-hand chords played half a beat 'early'

Bass line uses linking-notes a semitone below roots of chords

D Right-hand chords played half a beat 'late'

Bass line uses linking-notes a semitone above and below roots of chords

The chordal rhythms from the first page are now transferred to the left hand, beneath horizontal or vertical improvisation in the right.

Bass enters at 1:08

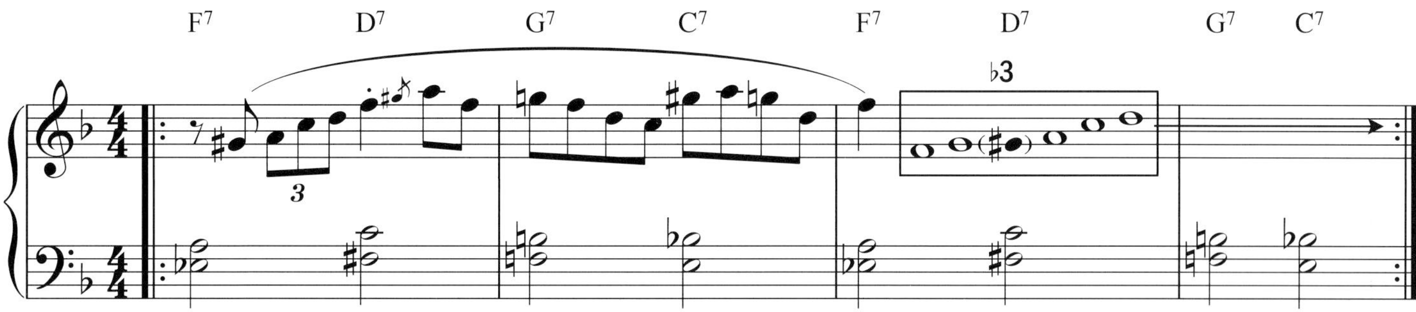

B Blues scale (minor pentatonic with ♭5)

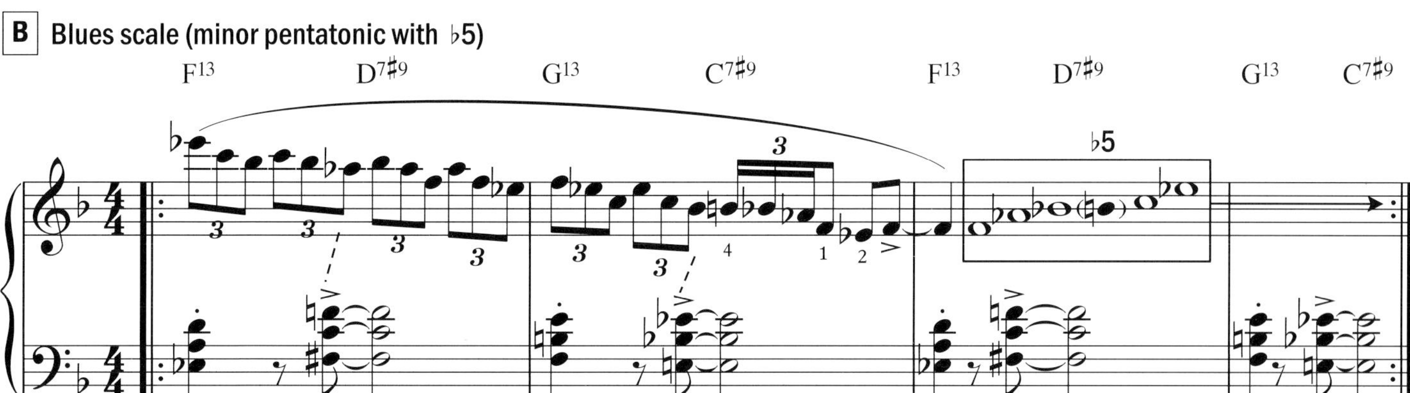

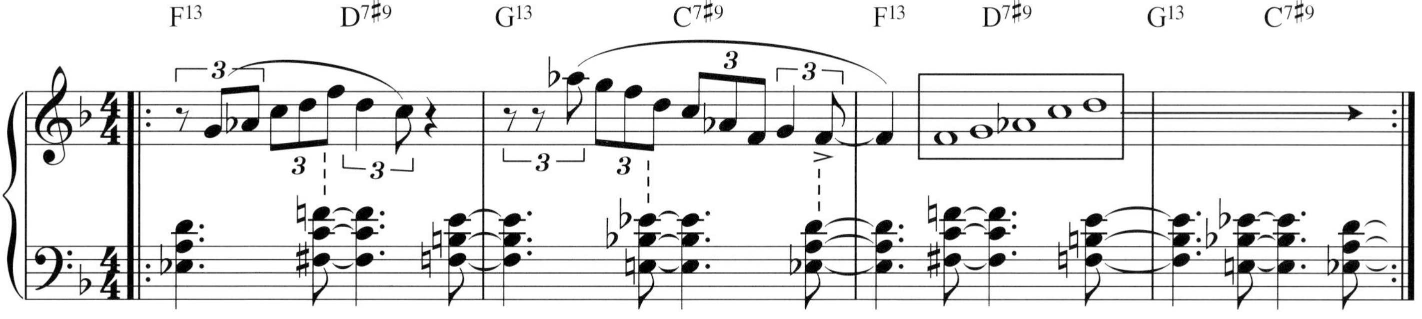

Assignments and Improvisation Tips: Blues Turnaround Workout

❶ **Comping (first page)** Memorise the notes and fingering for each of the bass lines. Vary the bass line ad lib. using chromatic linking notes as shown – without reading the notes! Next explore the various chord shapes and rhythms shown. Get a friend to sing or play the improvisation while you accompany them in this way.

❷ **Horizontal improvisation (second page)** Choosing one of the scales shown at 'A', 'B' or 'C', work on playing each left-hand chordal rhythm in turn beneath your improvisation, playing along with track 31 (from 1:08, bass and drums only). Then repeat with another scale. Review 'Playing left-hand chords off the beat' (p.67).

❸ **Vertical improvisation** Mix up arpeggios, **♭9** licks and **R235** patterns in your lines, trying them with each left-hand rhythm in turn. Also try adapting *Dominant Seventh Flat Nine Workout* (p. 137) by playing it in sixteenth-notes to fit this turnaround.

❹ ***Tension & Release Blues #1*** Incorporate the blues turnaround into bars 11–12 of every chorus (p. 159), playing along with track 29 (bass and drums only).

❺ **Solo piano** Repeat steps 2–3 with just the walking bass line in the left hand. Practise it by itself with your eyes closed to prepare you for adding a right-hand solo.

Aged only 17 when he took over Benny Green's piano chair in Art Blakey's 'Jazz Messengers', Geoff Keezer rose magnificently to the occasion. His hard bop credentials thus secured, he went on to join bassist Ray Brown's swinging trio in 1997. A virtuoso stylist with a very distinctive touch and an amazing time feel, his playing sometimes displays a classical influence, especially on more recent recordings and those under his own name.

Chapter Eight – Final Checkpoint

● **Diminished chords and scales** In this chapter we've seen how diminished seventh chords can function as **♭II°**, **♭III°** or **#IV°** in major keys, where they act as linking chords.

We've also seen how they form the top part (**3579**) of a dominant seventh flat nine chord. That's why the diminished scale (tone/semitone alternating) fits a dominant seventh chord by starting on the *third* of the chord. The scale contains **#11**, **♭9** and **#9**.

We'll return to diminished chords and scales in the context of minor keys in Chapter 10.

● **Polychords – summary** We've also extended our repertoire of polychords, playing major triads in the right hand for two-handed **♭9** and **#9** voicings (Fig 8.74). We'll compare these below to the polychords we used in Chapter 6 for sharp 11 and sus 4 chords:

Fig 8.78: Polychords for dominant sevenths

(a) Sharp 11 – tone up
Play a major triad on 2

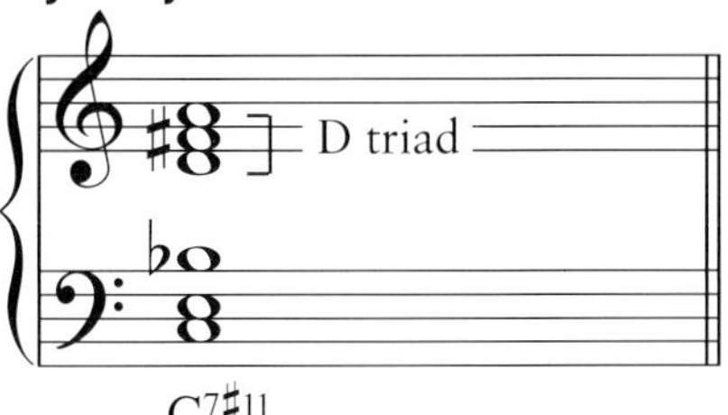

(b) Sus 4 – tone down
Play a major triad on ♭7

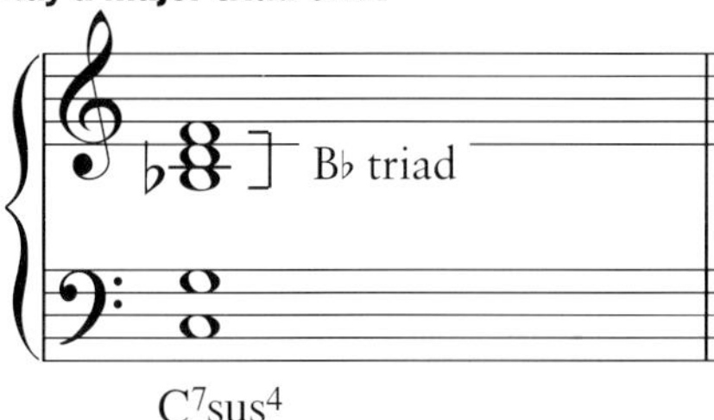

(c) Sharp 9 – m3 up
Play a major triad on ♭3

(d) Flat 9 – m3 down
Play a major triad on 6

The above triads can be played in any inversion, although the second inversion often sounds best, as shown for the **♭9** voicing, A/C7.

> Tip: Instead of thinking of the A triad as based on **6** of the C scale, count down three semitones (minor third down).

With all the above voicings be careful not to omit **3** or **7** (except in a sus 4 chord, when **3** can be omitted). If you omit the E♮ from the left hand of the **#9** voicing it will sound like a Cm chord! Another option is to play tritones (**37** or **73**) in the left hand instead.

Final Assignments: Polychords

❶ ***Dominant Seventh Flat Nine Workout*** Play along with track 25 (bass and drums only), comping with the **♭9** and **♯9** polychords shown above. If you alternate the two chord-types, the triads will descend in semitones:

Fig 8.79: Polychords for cycle of dominant sevenths

❷ ***Blues Turnaround Workout*** Play along with track 31 (bass and drums only), applying the polychord principle to the dominant seventh cycle in the blues turnaround:

Fig 8.80: I – VI – II – V turnaround with shells in left hand (Key: F)

Chapter Nine
Altered chords and scales

This chapter focuses on dominant chords with raised or lowered fifths and ninths, usually referred to as altered chords, and the scale that they imply.

In the previous chapter we looked at various ways of playing dominant chords that contain ♭**9** or ♯**9**, including polychords with major triads in the right hand (see Fig 8.78). Not only is the polychord concept a useful way of visualising complex voicings, it is also an invaluable tool when harmonising melodies.

To get a handle on this way of voicing chords you need to be very familiar with triads and their inversions, in order to find the correct shapes quickly. For any given melody note, there are three possible major triads that contain that note – it will be the **R** of one triad, **3** of another, and **5** of the third one.

● **Dominant seventh ♭9 chords** Let's take as an example a C7 chord with a D♭ melody note, the ♭**9** of the chord. D♭ can be found as:

- the root of a D♭ triad
- the third of an A triad (C♯)
- the fifth of a G♭ triad

Play these three triads above a C7 left hand, keeping the hands fairly close together and choosing triad inversions with the D♭ on top:

Fig 9.1: C7 polychords containing the ♭9 (D♭ or C♯)

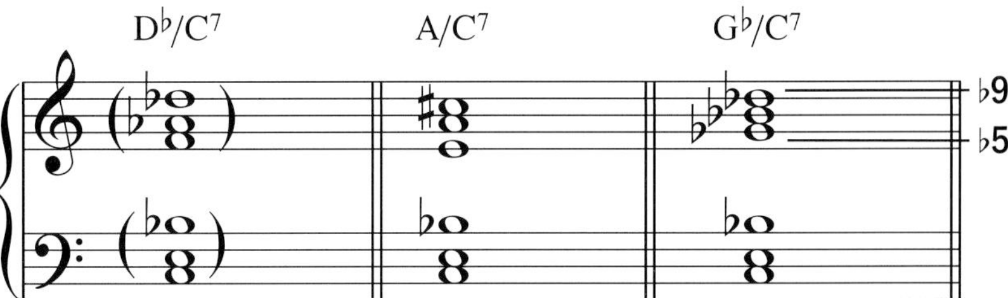

The D♭ triad is too discordant for normal use because it includes the fourth of the C7 chord (F) which clashes with **3** in the left hand (E). But hear how exciting the other two polychords sound!

We came across the A/C7 polychord voicing in the last chapter (Fig 8.78), but G♭/C7 is a new combination, containing not only ♭**9** but also ♭**5** (G♭). Because both the fifth and ninth have been lowered, this type of dominant chord is called an 'altered' chord. The conventional chord symbol for G♭/C7 would be:

$C^{7\flat9\flat5}$ or $C^{7\text{-}9\text{-}5}$ or C^{7}alt

and is pronounced 'C seven flat nine flat five', or simply 'C seven altered'.

● **Dominant seventh ♯9 chords** As a second example let's take a C7 chord with an E♭ melody note, the **♯9** of the chord. E♭ can be found as:

- the root of an E♭ triad
- the third of a B triad (D♯)
- the fifth of an A♭ triad

Play these three triads over a C7 left hand, choosing inversions with E♭ on top:

Fig 9.2: C7 polychords containing the ♯9 (E♭ or D♯)

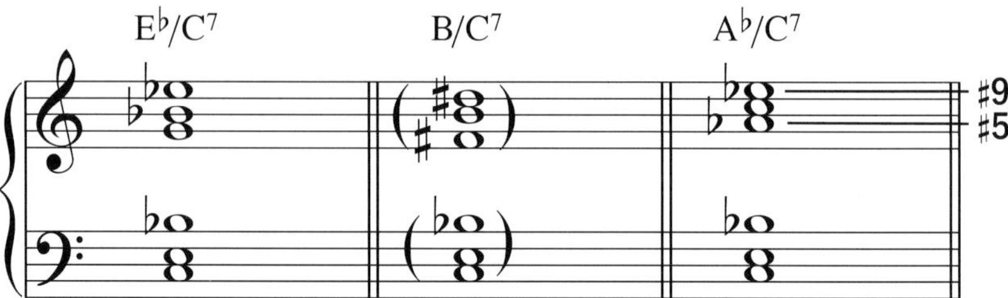

The B triad is not acceptable for a C7 chord owing to the presence of the B natural which clashes with the **♭7** in the left hand (B♭).

We've seen the E♭/C7 polychord in the previous chapter (Fig 8.78), but A♭/C7 is a new combination, giving not only **♯9** but also **♯5** (A♭, sometimes referred to as **♭6**). Because both the fifth and ninth have been raised, this can also be called an 'altered' chord.

The conventional chord symbol for A♭/C7 would be:

$C^{7\sharp9\sharp5}$ or $C^{7\sharp9}_{+}$ or $C^{7}alt$

and is pronounced 'C seven sharp nine sharp five' or, as before, simply 'C seven altered'.

Altered chords

The expression 'altered' is usually reserved for dominant seventh chords. **♭5**, **♯5**, **♭9** and **♯9** can appear in any combination, giving rise to four possible configurations:

$C^{7\sharp9\sharp5}$ $C^{7\flat9\flat5}$ $C^{7\sharp9\flat5}$ $C^{7\flat9\sharp5}$

The first two of these can be played as polychords as we've seen above, but this system does not extend to the third and fourth chord types, at least not with major triads in the right hand.

Many musicians prefer to use $C^{7}alt$ in place of the above chord symbols, as it's less of a mouthful to say and easier to write. It also has the advantage of being non-specific – as long as you raise or lower both **9** and **5** (without omitting either) the result qualifies as an altered chord.

'Altered', therefore, is a blanket term describing a range of dominant sounds. The use of this chord symbol gives more choice to the performer – you may wish to try out all four options to decide which sound you like best.

The most common way of interpreting an altered chord is with a **♯9** and **♯5** (A♭/C7). Often the melody note will be the deciding factor in helping you make your choice.

The easiest way to find the two altered polychord voicings is to think of playing triads based on the ♭**5** and ♯**5** (♭**6**) of the dominant chord:

Fig 9.3: Polychords for C7alt

(a) Play a major triad whose root is ♭5 of the chord

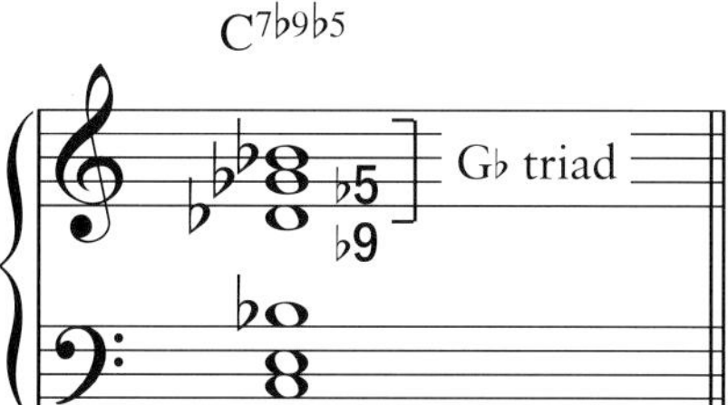

(b) Play a major triad whose root is ♯5 of the chord

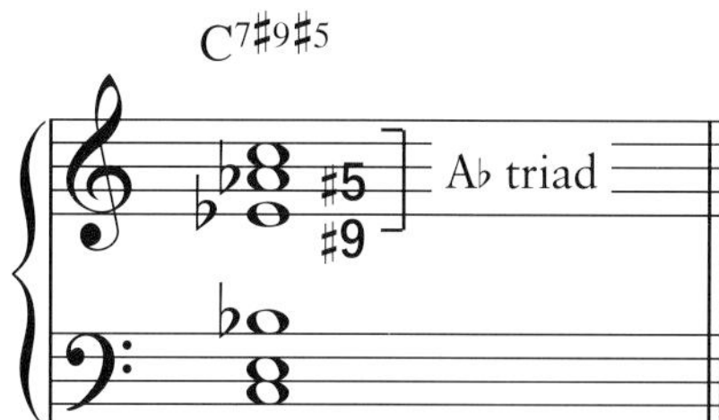

The triads here have been played in second inversion, rather than in root position as in Figs 9.1 and 9.2. Note that the two triads A♭ and G♭ are one tone apart. In some situations you can play both triads for the same chord symbol:

Fig 9.4: D7alt voiced with two triads a tone apart (B♭ and A♭)

Most of the melody notes in *Blue in Green* can be voiced as polychords, as shown overleaf. Before turning the page, try the Assignments below.

♩ = 63 (swing 8s)

Blue in Green

Miles Davis & Bill Evans

The melody is given here in lead sheet format, as you might find it in a fake book.

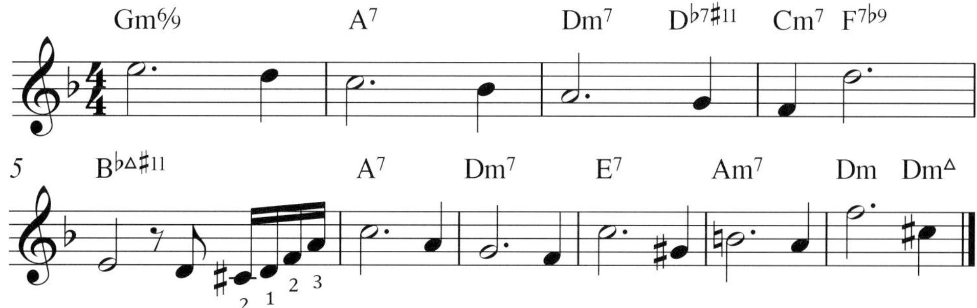

Assignments: Blue in Green

❶ **Play the melody** Accompany yourself with simple left-hand chords (eg: **R37**).

❷ **Polychords** Now work out which major triads you could include in the right hand to create polychords for the main melody notes. Each triad must have the melody note as its top note. One possible solution is given on the next page.

32 **with bass & drums**

♩ = 63 (swing 8s)

Blue in Green

Miles Davis & Bill Evans
arr. Tim Richards

This beautiful ballad can be heard on Davis' famous 'Kind of Blue' album, although the melody given here is closer to Evans' trio version on 'Portrait in Jazz'. Note the unusual ten-bar form.

Checkpoint: Blue in Green

● **Polychords** These are used for every chord symbol, demonstrating the technique for major and minor as well as dominant chords. The major triads in brackets are the right-hand part of the polychords. Many of the triads have been inverted to place the melody note on top. Here's a summary of the voicings, counting from the roots of the chords:

bar 1	**m6** chord	triad on **4** (includes **11**. NB: **9** in left hand)
bars 2, 6 and 8	**alt** chords	triad on **♯5**
bars 2 and 4	**♭9** chords	triad on **6** (m3 down from root of chord)
bars 3 and 10	**m7** chords	triad on **♭3** (m3 up)
bars 3 and 5	**♯11** chords	triad on **2** (tone up)
bars 4, 7 and 9	**m11** chords	triad on **♭7** (tone down)
bar 10	**mΔ9** chord	triad on **5**

● **Left hand** Notice the variety of shapes used, including **935** fragments (Gm6/9, DmΔ9), **73** tritones (A7, F7), **R3** shells (Dm7, D♭7, Cm7), **R5** (B♭Δ♯11), **R37** (A7, E7), and **R59** arpeggios (Am9, Dm9).

In a polychord, if the right-hand triad doesn't include **3** and **7** of the chord (or **6** for a 6/9 chord), play these notes in the left hand.

Bill Evans came to prominence as a result of his impressionistic playing on Miles Davis' 1959 'Kind of Blue' album, quickly establishing himself as a tremendously influential innovator. His lightness of touch and singing tone were drawn from his classical roots, and are best heard in the many outstanding trio records he made with various bassists and drummers until his death in 1980. The subtlety of his harmonic and rhythmic concept has rarely been equalled.

The altered scale

We saw on p. 158 how the diminished scale is unsuitable for chords with raised fifths. So far we've dealt with these chords using the whole-tone scale, as in bar 4 of *Tension & Release Blues #1* (p. 159). Let's compare the two scales:

Fig 9.5

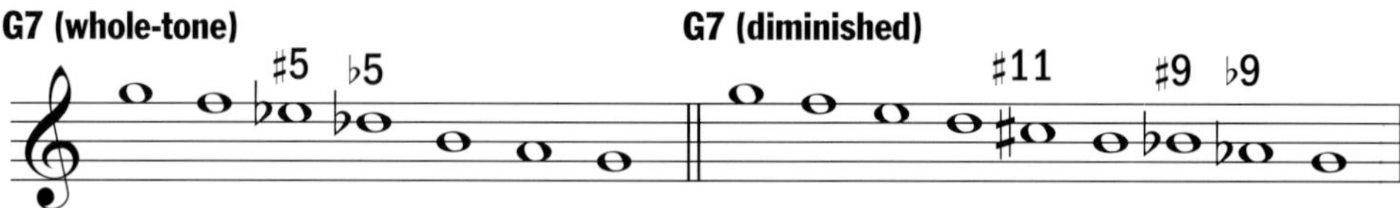

We have defined an altered chord as a dominant seventh containing any combination of ♭**5**, ♯**5**, ♭**9** and ♯**9**. The whole-tone scale will not work over this type of chord because it contains a regular ninth (the note A in Fig 9.5).

The ideal scale for an altered chord contains all four altered notes. This can be achieved by combining the top and bottom halves of the two scales above:

Fig 9.6: The altered scale or 'diminished/whole-tone' scale

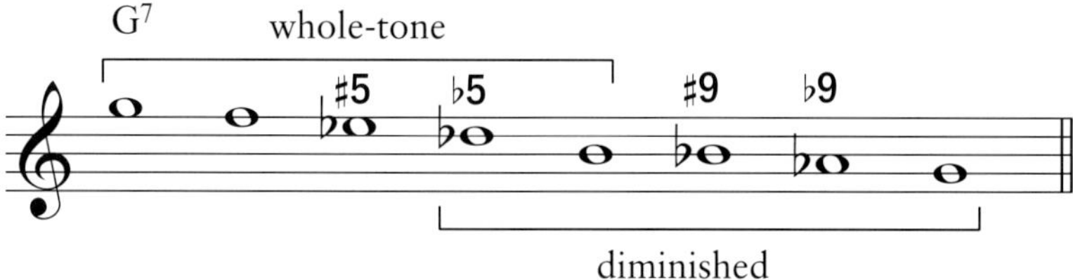

This derivation of the scale is reflected in its alternative name. It is unlike any seven-note scale we have seen so far, in that it contains both the major and minor third of the chord (♭**3** is the same note as ♯**9**).

In fact the scale in Fig 9.6 has the same notes as A♭ melodic minor – the altered scale is a mode of the melodic minor, starting on the seventh. This becomes very clear if you play a C melodic minor scale, starting on B to give a B7 altered scale:

Fig 9.7: C melodic minor and its seventh mode

When you need to work out an altered scale, thinking up a semitone to the relevant melodic minor can help you find the correct notes. Compare this approach with the one we used for half-diminished chords (see Vol. 1, Fig 4.31):

Eø think up a semitone to F major – gives notes of Locrian scale on E
E7alt think up a semitone to F melodic minor – gives notes of altered scale on E

If you're not used to it, the altered scale can sound very exotic. Do persevere, however, as it is an important part of the contemporary jazz sound. Many players use licks derived from it, rather than playing the scale as such – the following example starts on ♯**9** and ♭**9**:

Fig 9.8: Altered scale lick

If you recognize the sound of this phrase, that's because we used it over a minor chord and as a short **II** – **V** lick in Chapter 7 (Figs 7.12–7.14). Apart from the last note, the right hand of Fig 9.8 fits over B♭m – a semitone up from A7–just like the B♭ melodic minor scale from which the A7 altered scale is derived.

Improvising over *Blue in Green*

Although the chords appear quite complex, it is possible to improvise melodically with just two scales, and some arpeggios in bars 3–4:

Fig 9.9(a): Simple improvisation (play with left hand given on p. 172)

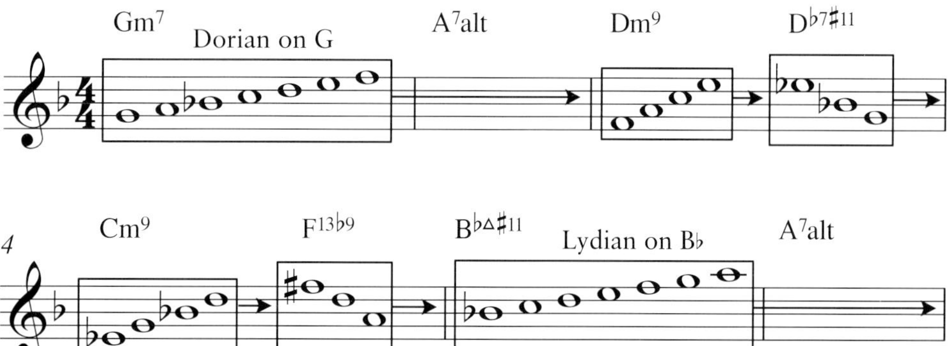

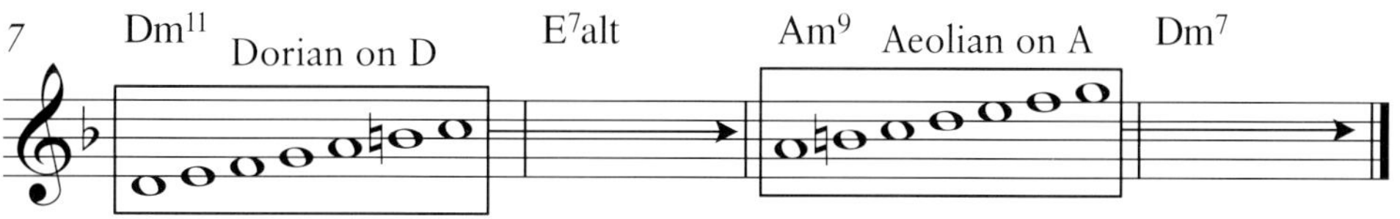

Four scales are named above, but the first two have the same notes, as do the last two:

Dorian on G = Lydian on B♭
Dorian on D = Aeolian on A

The Dorian scale on G is extended over A7alt, becoming in effect a Phrygian scale on A (see Vol. 1, p. 212 and *Orinoco*, pp. 210–11). This gives the ♭**9** (B♭), **#9** (C) and **#5** (F) of A7, as well as the regular fifth, but not the major third. This method of using scales 'horizontally' is also applied in bars 5–6 over B♭Δ#11 – A7alt, and in bars 7–8 over Dm7 – E7alt.

Any bar could also feature broken chords or arpeggios of the major triads which make up the right-hand part of the polychords discussed earlier (see Fig 8.78). This can be seen in bars 3–4 above: E♭ triad for D♭7#11 (tone up), D triad for F13♭9 (m3 down).

Once you've tried Fig 9.9(a) a few times, move on to a more 'vertical' improvisation, bringing altered and/or diminished scales into play for the dominant chords:

Fig 9.9(b): Vertical improvisation with rootless left-hand chords

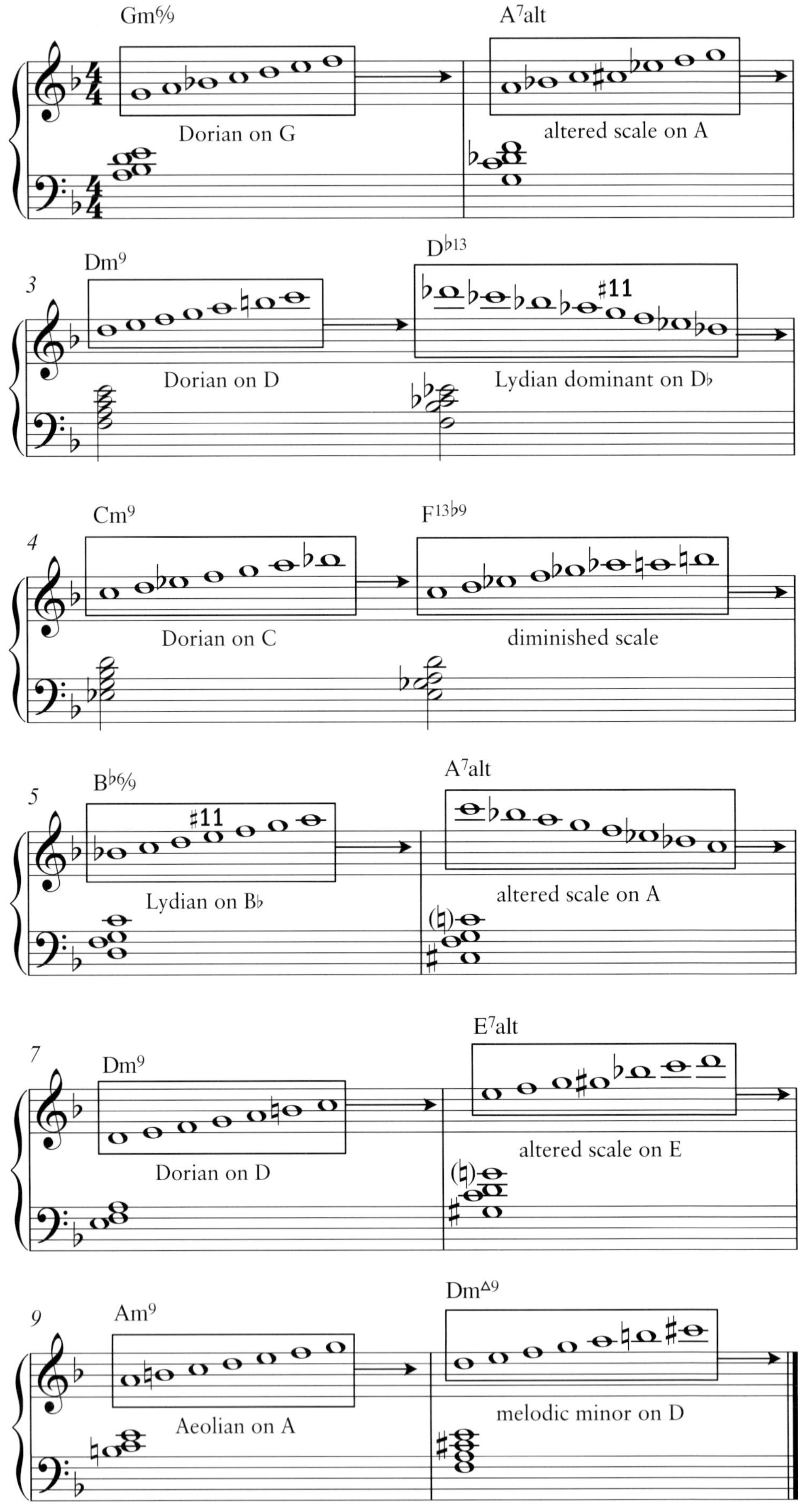

Rootless voicings for altered chords

In Fig 9.9(b), the left hand plays the altered chords as rootless voicings. To play a fully altered chord in one hand, at least four notes are required, not including the root. The notes will be **3**, **7**, **♯5** and **♯9** (or **♭5**, **♭9**). As with other rootless shapes, two positions are in common use, **3579** and **7935**:

Fig 9.10(a): Four-note voicings for A7alt (A7♯9♯5)

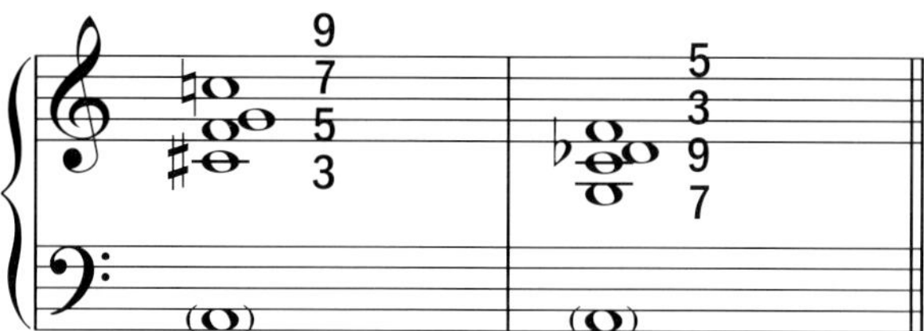

The second shape is simply an inversion of the first, with **7** at the bottom of the chord instead of **3** (and C♯ notated as D♭). Note that the two central notes are a semitone apart.

You can still interpret altered chords as three-note rootless voicings if you wish, using **379** and **735** voicings with **9** and **5** raised accordingly.

Fig 9.10(b): Three-note options for A7alt

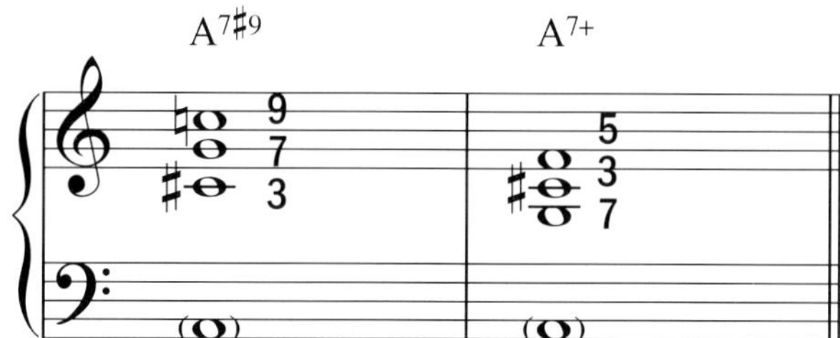

Neither of these options gives the full sound of the altered chord, however, as each voicing contains only one altered note.

Assignments: Blue in Green

NB: On the 'Kind of Blue' and 'Portrait in Jazz' recordings the tempo is doubled after the repeat of the head, so that the solos are taken at about 126 bpm. This is not just a double-time feel, *as mentioned in Chapter 7 in connection with* Misty *(Assignment 2, p. 111). In this case the chords are actually moving twice as fast, which is more unusual. On the CD, however, we have kept the tempo the same for head and solos, to keep it in ballad feel throughout.*

❶ **Melody with polychords** Play this with the CD (track 32, bass and drums only), as on p. 172, and memorise the chord sequence and voicings.

❷ **Rootless left-hand shapes** You can hear the chords in Fig 9.9(b) throughout the solo on the CD. They'll give you a richer sound than the basic left-hand chords on p. 172, and are more suitable for use with a bass player. Memorise the shapes and use them to accompany your solo when playing along with the CD.

❸ **Improvise** Play your solo straight after the melody (p. 172), without a break. Alternatively, if you improvise from the start, you'll have four whole 10-bar choruses to try out the ideas on pp. 175–6.

Tritone substitution

A tritone – a pair of notes three tones (a ♭**5**) apart – can be interpreted as two different dominant seventh chords:

Fig 9.11: G7 and D♭7 share the same tritone

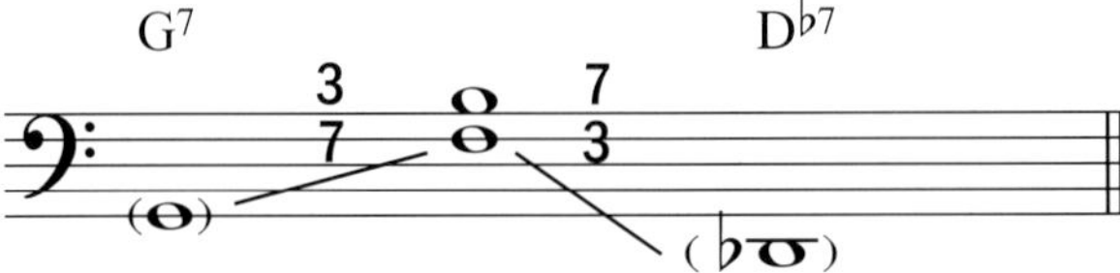

As you can hear, either bass note can function as the root of the tritone, depending on whether it is interpreted as **73** or as **37**. Notice that the roots of the two chords, G and D♭, are also a tritone apart.

Bass players often substitute the bass note a tritone away for a dominant seventh in a cycle of fifths, such as a **II** – **V** – **I**, making the roots descend in semitones, eg:

Dm7 – G7 – CΔ

becomes

Dm7 – **D♭7** – CΔ

This substitution can be seen in bar 3 of *Blue in Green,* resolving to Cm instead of CΔ. See also *Misty* bars 7–8 (p. 106) and 'Chord substitution' (p. 114).

From the point of view of the pianist, if G7 is played as G7♭5 (root position, without a ninth), it contains exactly the same notes as D♭7♭5:

Fig 9.12: G7♭5 and D♭7♭5 are inversions of each other

If it is played as a rootless G7♭9, using B diminished or one of its inversions, this will also be compatible with D♭7:

Fig 9.13: G7♭9 and D♭7♭9 contain the same notes

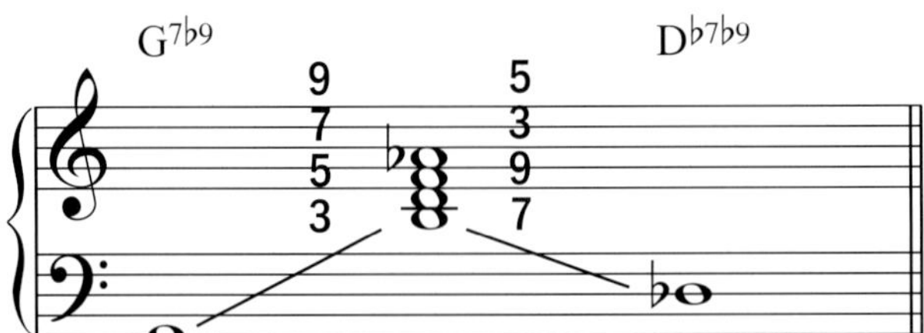

This does not always work out so conveniently – with most other dominant chord shapes the new bass note will change the quality of the chord. This is what happens with other four-note rootless shapes:

Fig 9.14: Thirteenth and ninth chords become altered chords

Three-note rootless shapes for dominant chords also change quality when the bass note is substituted a tritone away. They are shown below in the context of a **II – V – I** in F major:

Fig 9.15

(a) Ninth chords become ♯5 chords

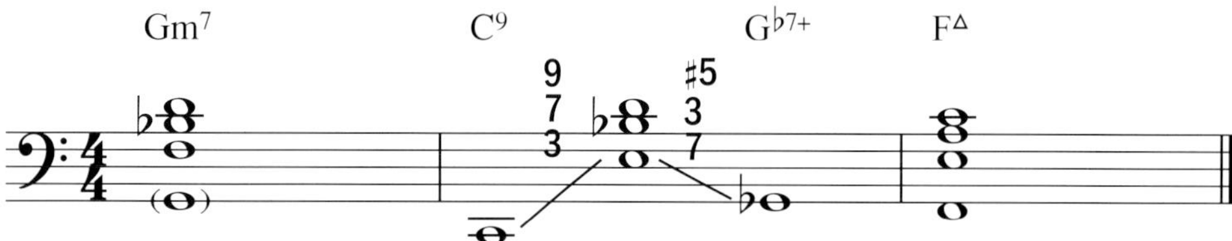

(b) ♭9 chords become ordinary sevenths

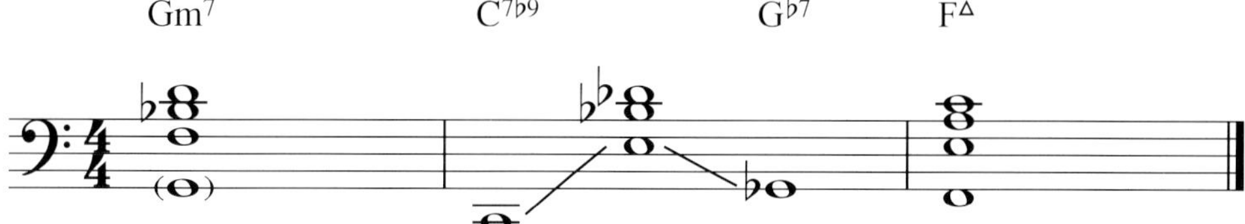

(c) ♯9 chords become thirteenth chords

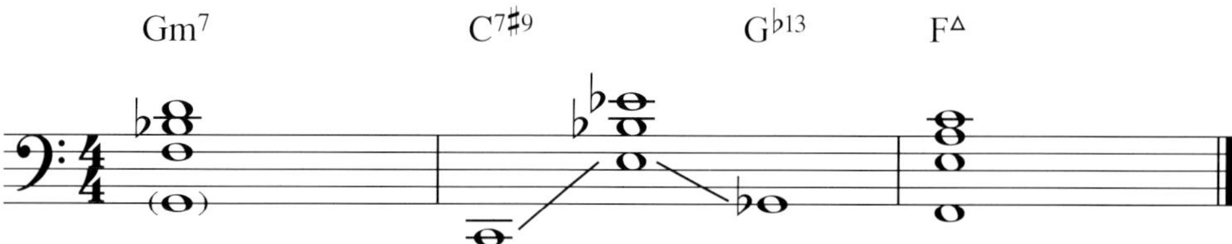

Play these chords first with C as the bass note for the **V** chord, then with G♭, noting the effect of the substitution:

II – V – I

becomes

II – ♭IIx – I

In a roman numeral, **x** indicates a dominant seventh.

The next piece, *Tension & Release Blues #2*, uses four-note altered chords in left and right hands.

33 with drums
Bass enters for head

♩ = 176
(swing 8s)

Tension & Release Blues #2

Tim Richards

Like its counterpart in F on p. 159, this B♭ blues explores areas of tension in the twelve-bar sequence (bars 4, 8, 10 and 12), this time using altered chords and scales.

Checkpoint: Tension & Release Blues #2

● **Intro** The first twelve bars is a backing figure with a walking bass left hand – use it over several choruses to accompany a friend playing the head or taking a solo.

● **Tritone substitution** The altered chords can all be considered as thirteenth chords with roots a ♭**5** away (see Fig 9.14):

B♭7alt = E13   G7alt = D♭13   F7alt = B13

Including these substitutions gives the following sequence:

‖: B♭13 | E♭13 | B♭13 | **E13** |

| E♭13 | E° | B♭13 | **D♭13** |

| C13 | **B13** | B♭13 | **B13** :‖

This does not affect the rootless chord shapes, just the way you think of them. Note how the **R** and **5** of the new chords figure prominently in the left hand in bars 4, 8 and 10, as marked.

● **Turnaround (bars 11–12)** This is a **I** – **VI** – **II** – **V** turnaround (see p. 163):

B♭13 – G7alt – C13 – F7alt

Ignoring the written bass line, the right-hand shapes could also be interpreted as:

B♭13 – **D♭13** – C13 – **B13**

Tritone substitution has made the roots go down in semitones from D♭, rather than round the cycle from G, without changing any of the chord shapes. We can also substitute the C13 chord (so far unchanged), returning the bass line to a cycle of fifths, a tritone away from the first example:

B♭13 – D♭13 – **G♭7alt** – B13

● **Head** For the first seven bars the left-hand chords are identical to the right-hand ones played in the intro. However, from G7alt onwards the opposite (lower) voicings have been chosen, to create room for the right-hand melody.

The turnaround this time is just a simple **I** – **V** (bars 11–12), although you can continue to play **I** – **IV** – **II** – **V** during your solo, as heard on the CD.

● **Rootless voicings** The left hand plays mainly thirteenth shapes, **7936** or **3679**. For the altered chords, **6** becomes **♯5** and **9** becomes **♯9**.

● **Altered patterns** Four different right-hand patterns are given. Memorise them and practise each one in all three keys (over B♭7alt, G7alt and F7alt), with left-hand chords. Use these patterns when you improvise over this blues, after the head.

Assignments

❶ **Play along** Practise the rootless voicings with the CD (track 33, bass and drums only) until you know them in either hand, without reading the shapes. Try the head and improvisation, using altered right-hand patterns in the bars indicated. Silencing the piano will give you four choruses from when the bass enters at 0:20.

❷ **Turnarounds** Work on improvising over the turnaround in B♭, using the techniques given in *Blues Turnaround Workout* (p. 164). Transposing this to the key of B♭ will give you three-note left-hand shapes in place of the four-note ones in bars 11–12. For more on turnarounds and tritone substitution, see IBP, pp.165–166.

❸ ***Tension & Release Blues #1*** Review this blues in F (p. 159) applying the altered patterns you have learned in place of the diminished ones given. Everything you do in B♭ you should be able to do in F (and vice versa), although you may find that because of the change in register the opposite chord voicings often sound better (eg: **7** on bottom instead of **3**, etc).

Two-handed rootless voicings

So far in this book, most two-handed voicings have had shells in the left hand, which by definition have the root on the bottom. Some musicians will avoid using these when playing with a bassist, mistakenly in my view, as you can prove by listening to records by almost any well-known pianist, right up to the present day.

However, the more voicing techniques you have at your fingertips, the more variety you can bring to your solos and accompaniments. Amongst contemporary pianists, a style of comping using two notes in each hand has become popular:

Fig 9.16: Rootless II – V – I voicings (two notes each hand)

(a) starting with 37/95

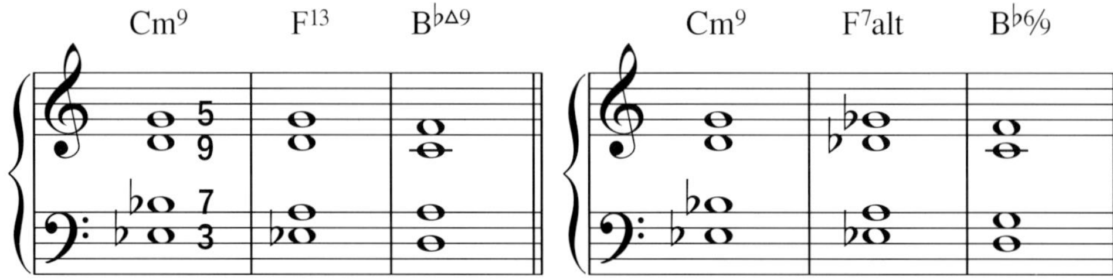

(b) starting with 73/59

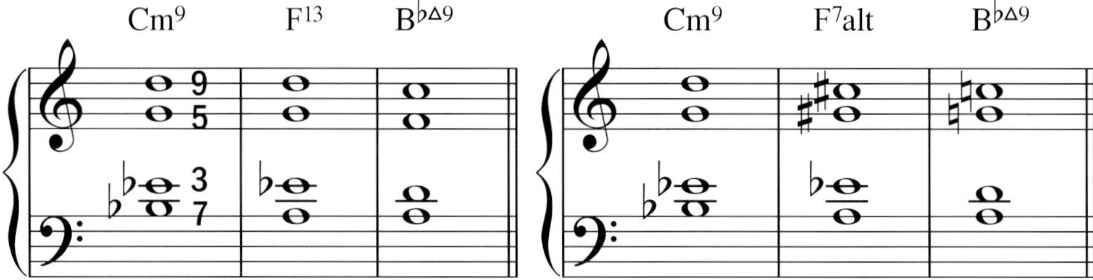

These voicings are great for comping, as their light sound will not overshadow the soloist. They are also very useful for up-tempo numbers, when your fingers may not have time to find larger shapes, as in section 'B' of *Tune Up* opposite.

An excellent way to practise them is to play the following cycle, previously seen in *Bebop Bridge* (p. 103):

Fig 9.17: Bridge of 'Rhythm Changes' (Key: B♭)

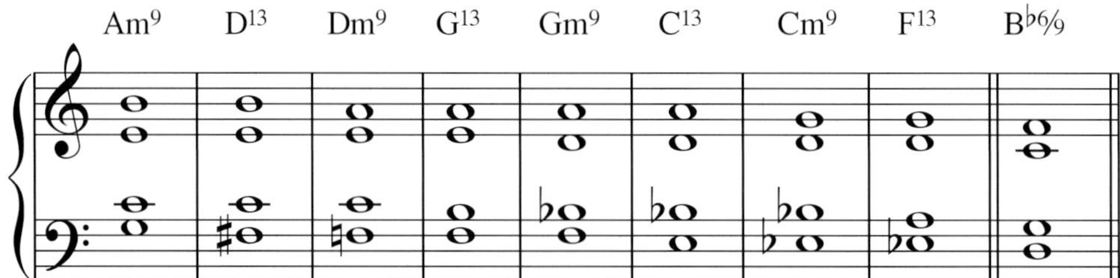

When playing a blues turnaround, the **I** chord can have the root on top:

Fig 9.18: I – VI – II – V turnaround in B♭

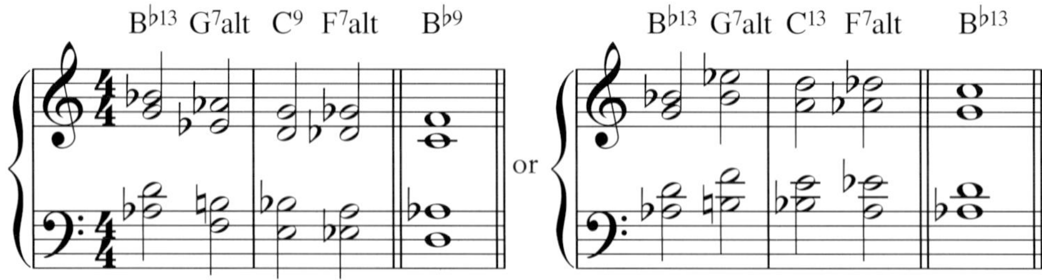

See *Four-Finger Blues* (IBP, p. 214) for an example of a complete blues in B♭ voiced in this way, and *C Jam Blues* (IBP, p. 216) for its application to playing melodies.

34 **with bass & drums**

♩ = 200 (swing 8s)

Tune Up

Miles Davis
arr. Tim Richards

This up-tempo tune can be heard on Miles' 1957 album 'Cookin', and also on Sonny Rollins' 'Newk's Time'. The first twelve bars follows the cycle of fifths, with **II – V – I**s descending in tones.

A Head

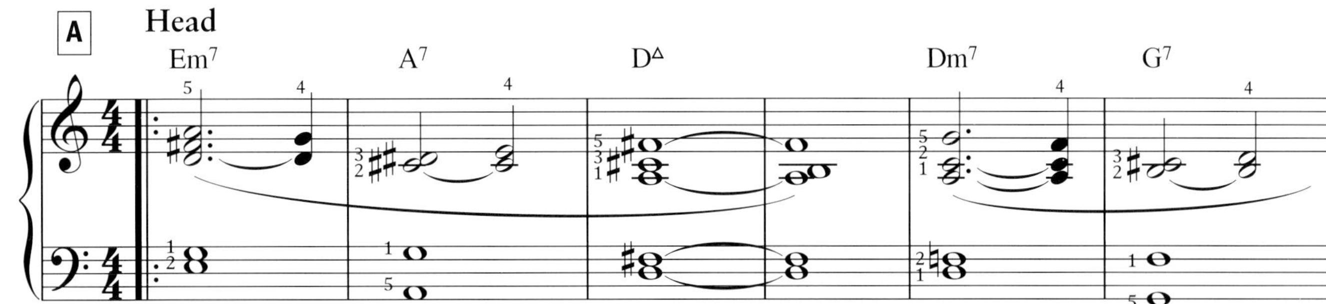

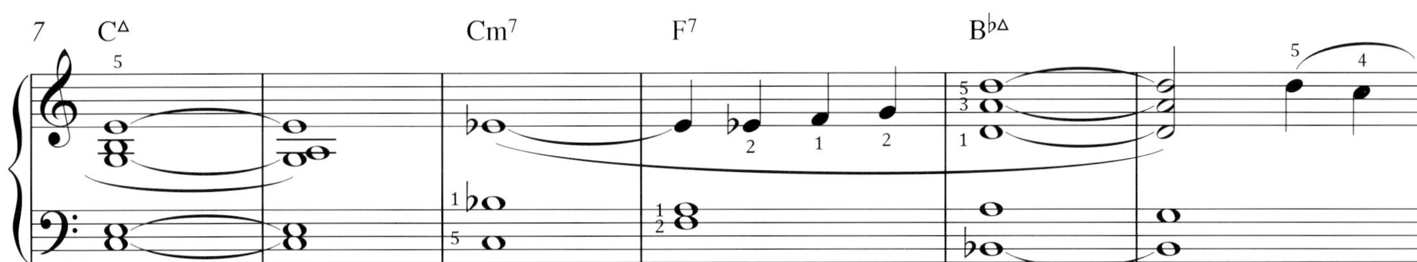

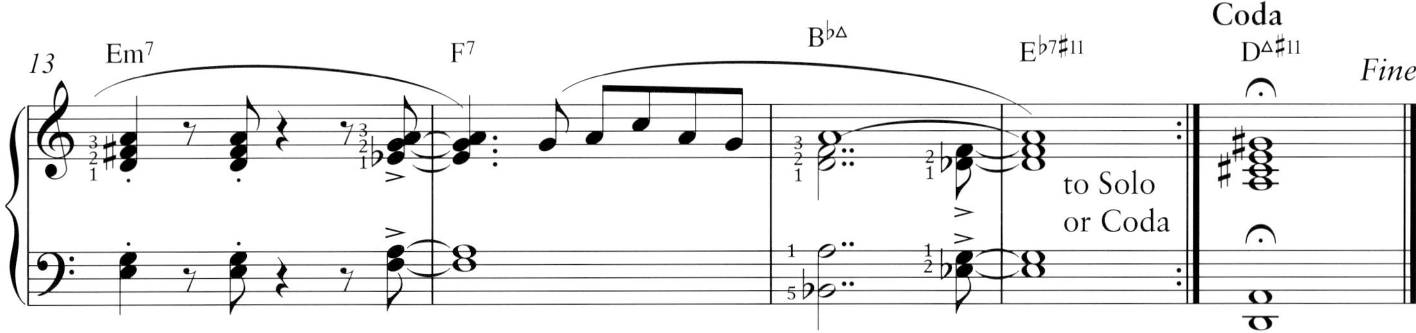

B Rootless comping voicings (backing for Head or Solo)

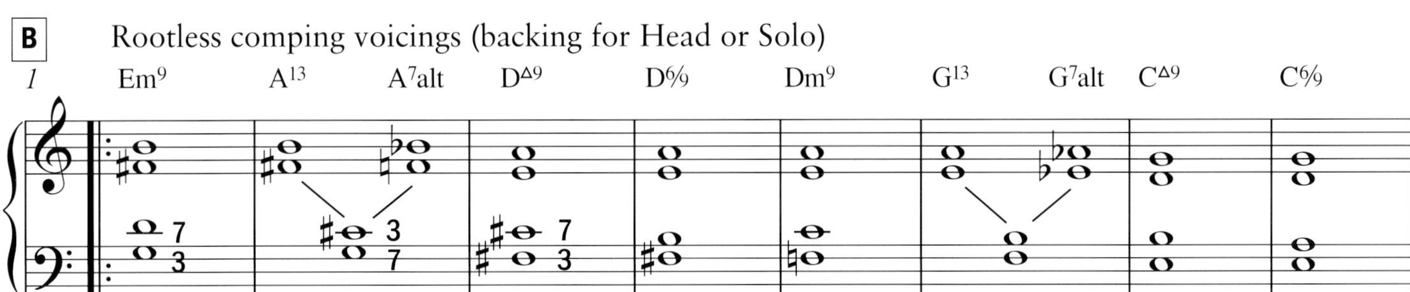

Improvise (or play melody) with rootless voicings in left hand

C N.B.: Play altered chords in Solo only.

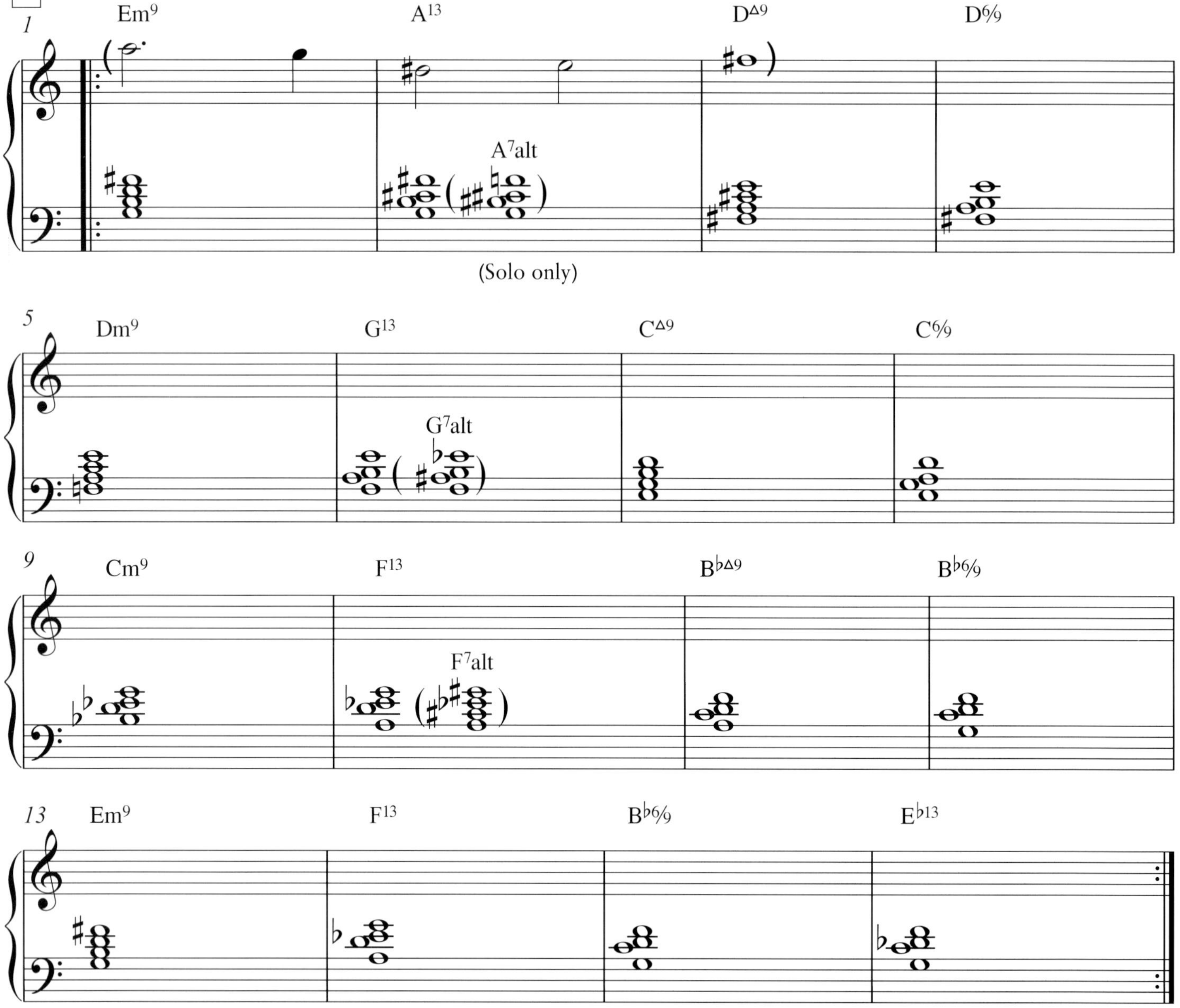

1 Em9 A13 (A7alt) D∆9 D6/9

(Solo only)

5 Dm9 G13 (G7alt) C∆9 C6/9

9 Cm9 F13 (F7alt) B♭∆9 B♭6/9

13 Em9 F13 B♭6/9 E♭13

(after Solo) *D.C. al Fine*

Checkpoint: Tune Up

● **Minor eleventh chords** The Em7 and Dm7 chords both have the fourth as the melody note, and could be given the chord symbols Em11 and Dm11 (see Fig 6.29). Note the two different voicings used, which are interchangeable:

Fig 9.19: Five-note eleventh voicings

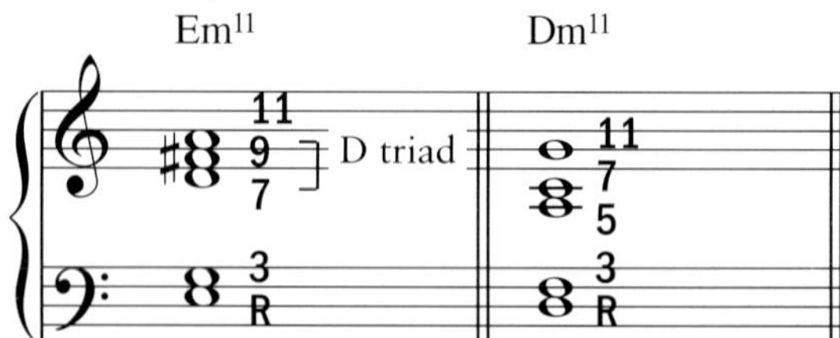

The **R3/7 9 11** voicing is also used for the E♭7♯11chord in bar 16.

● **II – V – Is** The chords in the first twelve bars are straight out of the cycle of fifths, exactly as in *II – V – I Arpeggio Workout* (Vol. 1, p. 164). The key centres go down in tones from D major to B♭ major. Note that bars 13–16 are not a **II – V – I**.

● **Head** This is played at 'A' with two-handed voicings, shells in the left hand, the right hand adding notes beneath the melody to fill out the chords – a style we've used before with *Ladybird* (p. 78) and *Misty* (p. 106).

When working out which notes to add in the right hand, it's best not to double any notes that are already present. Check for missing thirds and sevenths, and if necessary change the left hand from **R3** to **R7**, or vice versa. It is permissible to double the melody note, as in bars 3, 7, 11 and 14–15.

At 'C' the melody should be played in single notes, an octave higher where necessary, above rootless left-hand chords (ignore the altered chords in brackets).

● **Sharp eleven chords** The melody over the dominant chords in bars 2 and 6 includes both ♭**5** (♯**11**) and **5**, implying a sharp eleven chord:

Fig 9.20: Bars 1–3

● **Altered chords and scales** During the solos you are no longer constrained by the melody, so you can play altered dominant chords (which contain ♯**5**), as suggested in sections 'B' and 'C'. These should not be played with the melody, as the ♯**5** in the chords clashes with the regular fifth in the tune. See Figs 9.23–4 overleaf for some tips on including altered (or diminished) chords and scales in your improvisation.

● **Comping voicings** Section 'B' is for playing with a bassist in a group situation, behind another soloist. As shown in Fig 9.16, there are two basic voicing configurations, always with two notes in each hand:

- **37/95** (or **36/95** for 6/9 chords)
- **73/59** (or **73/69** for dominant thirteenth chords)

In this style the right-hand notes are always a perfect fourth or a perfect fifth apart – the quartal flavour reinforces the contemporary sound of the voicings.

Building bebop lines

Tune Up is the ideal tune for practising improvisation round **II** – **V** – **I** sequences. Here's a few different ways you could approach your solo:

● **Horizontal improvisation** This involves playing in the key centres, using a single scale (or patterns based on that scale) for each **II** – **V** – **I**:

bars 1–4	D major scale (start as Dorian on E for Em7)
bars 5–8	C major scale (start as Dorian on D for Dm7)
bars 9–12	B♭ major scale (start as Dorian on C for Cm7)

You still need to keep track of the left-hand chords throughout – either playing the shells from section 'A' or the rootless voicings from 'C' (no altered chords for now).

The last four bars are not so easy, as not all four chords are in the same key. However, F7 – B♭Δ is clearly **V** – **I**, so both these bars can have the same scale (Mixolydian on F, or B♭ major). The melody in the final bar includes a ♯**11**, implying an E♭ Lydian dominant scale (Mixolydian with raised fourth – see p. 19). This scale is only one note (D♭) different from the scale for the two preceding chords, as shown in Fig 9.21 overleaf:

Fig 9.21: Scale choices for bars 14–16

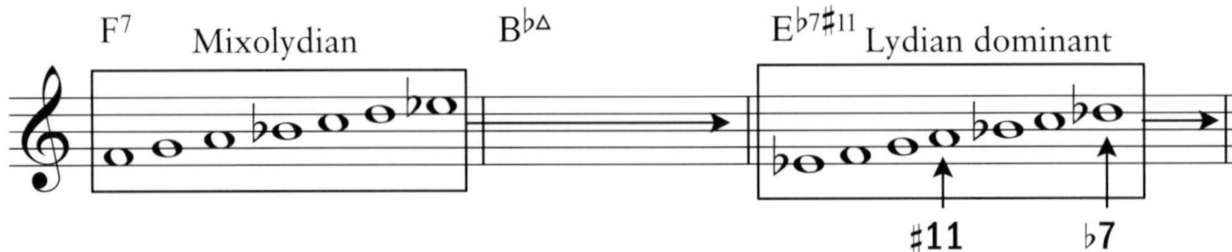

Sometimes it is best not to think in terms of scales. You could just try to find one or two notes that sound good with all the chords, like the melody in bars 13–16, which is based around the note A. An F major triad arpeggio or broken chord would also fit over all three chords in Fig 9.21.

● **Vertical improvisation** Become familiar with the arpeggios of all the chords, using them to improvise lines that join the chords together musically – this will be a challenge at this tempo!

The following example uses many previously-discussed techniques, eg: starting on the third of the chords, including the ninth, linking chords via chromatic passing notes, encircling target notes, using pick-ups, varying the rhythm, incorporating triplets, etc. Notes outside the prevailing chord are in boxes:

Fig 9.22: Sample improvisation using notes of the chords

NB: If the left hand plays altered chords on A7, G7 or F7, the right hand must follow suit by avoiding the regular fifth and/or ninth. A simple solution to this is to play an augmented triad arpeggio (F7+), as shown above in bar 10.

● **Altered scales** Many people are under the impression that vertical improvisation involves using arpeggios, and horizontal involves scales, which is not always the case. When playing an altered scale over the **V** chord in a **II – V – I**, you are improvising vertically because the chord symbols are guiding your choice of notes, rather than the key centre.

Even when using several different scales, try to combine them in a single phrase that connects **II** to **V** and **V** to **I**:

Fig 9.23: Incorporating an altered scale into the flow of a II – V – I phrase

● Diminished scales Providing you adjust the left hand accordingly, changing **#5** to **6** (the thirteenth), you could also use a diminished scale for the **V** chord:

Fig 9.24: Incorporating a diminished scale into the flow of a II – V – I

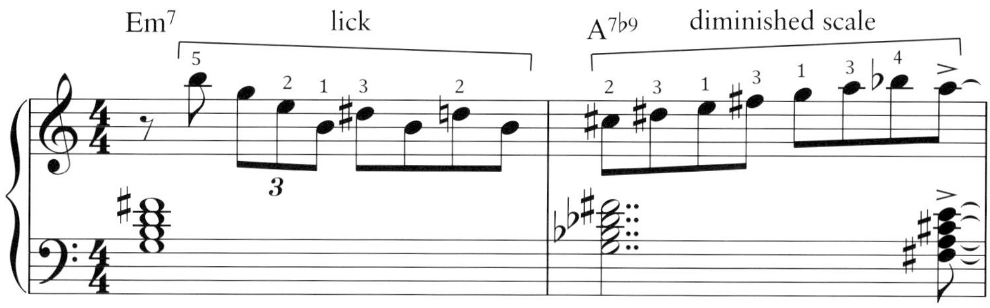

Assignments and Improvisation Tips: Tune Up

❶ Head Play the melody in the two styles shown at 'A' and 'C', as described in the Checkpoint (p. 185), playing along with bass and drums only (track 34). Memorise the shells and rootless voicings for the left hand.

❷ Rootless comping Practise the two-handed voicings given in section 'B' until you can play them up to tempo with the backing track, exploring comping rhythms such as those on pp. 82–3. At fast tempos it is best to keep these rhythms quite simple, repeating them every two or four bars, as in Fig 9.25 overleaf. Also practise four-note comping for other tunes, eg: *Ladybird* (p. 78). As you only have two notes in each hand, remember to avoid doubling.

❸ Improvise Play Fig 9.22 with the CD (track 34, bass and drums only), with shells or rootless left-hand chords, and try creating your own lines using similar arpeggio techniques. Then repeat with some of the horizontal and vertical ideas discussed above. Silencing the piano and improvising from the start of track 34 will give you six 16-bar choruses to solo over before the head returns for the last time through.

Thicker textures

On the Miles Davis version of *Tune Up*, Red Garland plays the following chords immediately after John Coltrane's saxophone solo at 3:22:

Fig 9.25: Red Garland's comping

The chords are alternately on and off the beat, in a two-bar pattern that repeats across the changing chords. They are also played with alternating short (*staccato*) and long articulation.

These new two-handed voicings still have shells in the left hand, but the right hand plays four notes instead of three:

- minor chords: **R3/ 5 7 9 11**
- dominant chords: **R7/♭9 3 ♯5 R**

Red Garland uses the chords in Fig 9.25 in other rhythms too – listen to the last chorus of Coltrane's solo for an example.

Seven-note block chords

The following block-chord technique, developed by Red Garland and used by countless pianists since, features four-note rootless chords in the left hand, with three notes added in the right hand above. Horace Silver does something similar at the end of his solo in *Song for my Father* (Vol. 1, p. 206).

Red Garland's right-hand notes are always an octave apart, with a third note a perfect fifth up from the lower note. Many different configurations are possible:

Fig 9.26: Red Garland-style block chords

(a) II – V– I with unchanging right hand

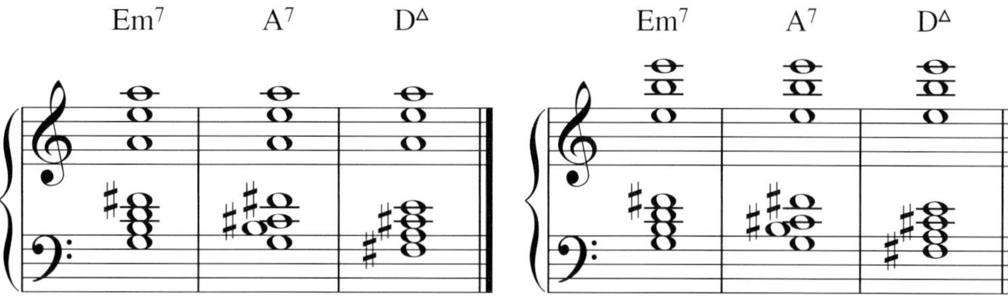

(b) II – V – I with moving right hand

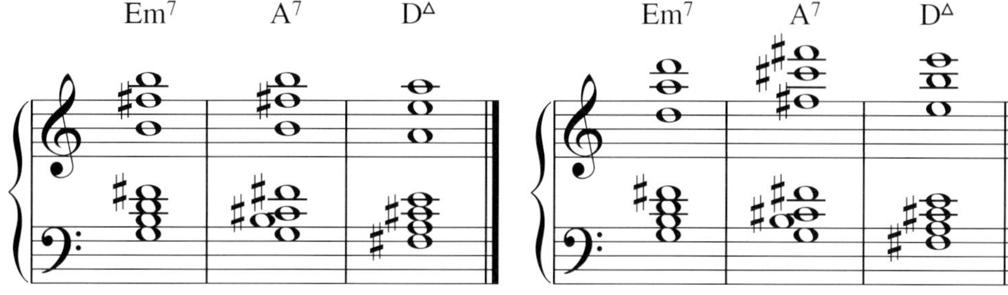

(c) II – V – I with altered dominant chords

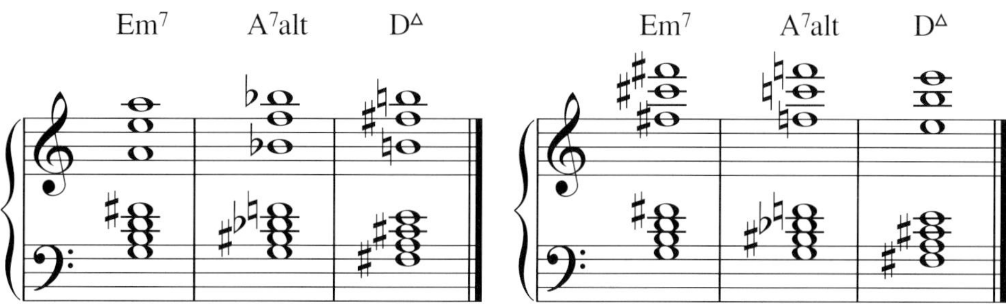

Experiment with other sets of right-hand notes that are compatible with the chord symbols, using your ears to decide whether they sound good with the left hand. The right hand can often move stepwise if you choose the notes carefully:

Fig 9.27: Playing melodies in block-chord style

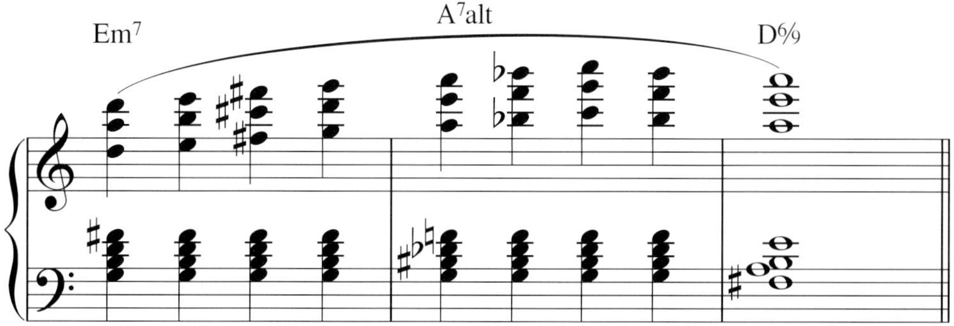

Because the middle right-hand note is always the perfect fifth of the octave, 'incorrect' voicings can occasionally result, like the first right-hand chord in the A7 bar above, which includes the regular fifth of the chord, E. Theoretically this note shouldn't be included as part of an altered chord; in practice, the ear often tolerates such discrepancies, as long as they are part of a moving line.

After classical studies in Canada, Renee Rosnes moved to New York in the 1980s and toured extensively with Joe Henderson, Wayne Shorter, and others. Signing with the Blue Note record label in 1988, her recent albums have showcased her exceptional improvisational and compositional abilities.

Rhythm Changes

We return now to this 32-bar chord sequence, based on the chords of the Gershwin composition *I Got Rhythm*. After the blues, 'Rhythm Changes' are probably the most popular vehicle for improvisation used by jazz musicians.

In *The Theme* (by Miles Davis, Vol. 1, p. 122) we treated the 'A' sections as eight bars of B♭ major, with no chord changes. In reality, the first eight bars of any 'Rhythm Changes' tune are based on a simple diatonic turnaround in B♭: **I – VI – II – V**, with a variation in bars 5–6 (a temporary modulation to the **IV** chord, E♭):

- Original (basic) sequence: modulation to E♭

||B$^\flat$ Gm^7 | Cm^7 F^7 | B$^\flat$ Gm^7 | Cm^7 F^7 | B$^\flat$ B$^{\flat 7}$/D | E$^\flat$ E° | B$^\flat$/F Gm^7| Cm^7 F^7 ||
I VI II V IV

Over the years, the following important variations have come into common use:

- In place of Gm7, play G7 (a secondary dominant):

||B$^\flat$ **G7** | Cm^7 F^7 | B$^\flat$ **G7** | Cm^7 F^7 | B$^\flat$ B$^{\flat 7}$/D | E$^\flat$ E° | B$^\flat$ **G7** | Cm^7 F^7 ||

- In place of G7 in bar 1, play B° (equivalent to G7♭9).

||B$^\flat$ **B°** | Cm^7 F^7 | B$^\flat$ G^7 | Cm^7 F^7 | B$^\flat$ B$^{\flat 7}$/D | E$^\flat$ E° | B$^\flat$ G^7 | Cm^7 F^7 ||

This gives the bass line you played in the left hand of *The Theme*. (See overleaf for comping suggestions using these changes.)

- In place of E° in bar 6, play E♭m, the **IV** minor. Either chord acts as a link between E♭ and B♭:

||B$^\flat$ B° | Cm^7 F^7 | B$^\flat$ G^7 | Cm^7 F^7 | B$^\flat$ B$^{\flat 7}$/D | E$^\flat$ **E$^\flat$m** | B$^\flat$ G^7 | Cm^7 F^7 ||
IVm

- In place of B♭ in bars 3 and 7, play Dm7 (the **III** chord) giving a **III – VIx – II – V** turnaround (see *Misty*, p. 106, for another example of this substitution):

||B$^\flat$ B° | Cm^7 F^7 |**Dm7** G^7 | Cm^7 F^7 | B$^\flat$ B$^{\flat 7}$/D | E$^\flat$ E$^\flat$m |**Dm7** G^7 | Cm^7 F^7 ||
III VI II V III

- In place of F7 in bar 2, play A7♭9 or C♯°. This resolves much better to Dm7:

||B$^\flat$ B° |Cm^7 **C♯°**| Dm^7 G^7 | Cm^7 F^7 | B$^\flat$ B$^{\flat 7}$/D | E$^\flat$ E$^\flat$m | Dm^7 G^7 | Cm^7 F^7 ||

- In bar 5, play Fm7 – B♭7, a **II – V** into E♭, and add A♭7 in place of E♭m in bar 6:

||B$^\flat$ B° |Cm^7 C♯°| Dm^7 G^7 | Cm^7 F^7 | **Fm7 B♭7** |**E♭$^\Delta$A♭7** | Dm^7 G^7 | Cm^7 F^7 ||
II V I

Some comping suggestions for this final sequence are given on p. 196. Although I have singled out the third and final sequences for further study, to play 'Rhythm Changes' well it helps to be familiar with all the variations above.

Aside from *The Theme,* countless tunes have been written over these changes, especially in the bebop era. Here are some well-known ones:

Lester Leaps In (Lester Young)
Anthropology (Charlie Parker)
Oleo (Sonny Rollins)
Serpent's Tooth (Miles Davis)
Fungi Mama (Blue Mitchell)
Flintstones Theme (Hannah/Barbera)
Moose the Mooche (Charlie Parker)
Rhythm-a-Ning (Thelonious Monk)
Cookin' at the Continental (Horace Silver)
The Eternal Triangle (Sonny Stitt)

35 with bass & drums

♩ = 168
(swing 8s)

Rhythm Changes Comping #1

Tim Richards

These two-handed chords follow the bass line of *The Theme* (Vol. 1, p. 122). The first half uses rootless voicings (**3**, **6** or **7** on the bottom). From the bridge, shells are used in the left hand instead.

Checkpoint: Rhythm Changes Comping #1

● **Rootless voicings** These are similar to those used in *Tune Up* on p. 183, with two notes played in each hand. The concise nature of these voicings makes them ideal for 'Rhythm Changes' numbers, which are usually played very fast.

● **Major chords** Including the 6/9 option gives quite a few possible shapes:

Fig 9.28: Major and 6/9 possibilities

B♭6/9 B♭Δ6/9 B♭Δ9 B♭6/9

9 6 | 3 7 | 7 3 | 6 3

● **Diminished chords** These can be played as two tritones a minor third apart, one in each hand. The first tritone is formed by **R** and ♭**5**, the second by **3** and **7**. Both of these tritones can be inverted, or swapped from one hand to the other.

Fig 9.29: Possibilities for B° using tritones

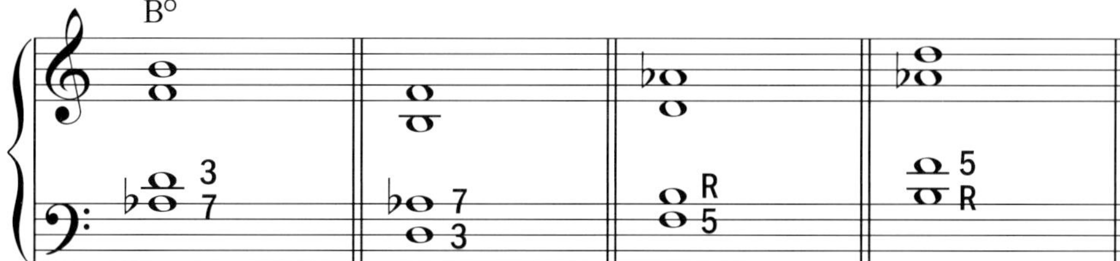

● **Second 'A' section** The second eight bars uses the opposite voicings to the first – the left hand will now be **37** instead of **73**, or vice versa. It is important to explore both ways of playing the changes, enabling you to vary your comping during the many repetitions that make up a complete performance. It also gives you greater flexibility when deciding what register to play the chords in.

● **Bridge: tritone substitution** Each of the four dominant sevenths, D7, G7, C7 and F7, is followed by its tritone substitute a ♭**5** away, which in turn is a semitone above the next chord. This device gives you two chords 'for the price of one', and can be used even if the bass player does not follow suit.

Improvising at fast tempos

Although *The Theme* and *Rhythm Changes Comping #1* are played on the CDs at 168 bpm, tempos of up to 300 bpm are common. In order to deal with such rapidly changing chords, various strategies may be helpful:

- Relax!
- Tap your foot on 'one' and 'three' only (not on every beat)
- Play short phrases, leaving plenty of gaps
- Play less (don't attempt long lines of eighth-notes)
- Include horizontal as well as vertical improvisation
- Simplify the left hand (don't feel obliged to state every chord)

To develop vertical ideas, play simple motifs such as **R2** or **R23**, adapting them to each chord. Here's an example with shells and tritones in the left hand:

Fig 9.30: Vertical improvisation using two- and three-note motifs

As well as the motifs used above, you might try some of the following:

- Two notes: **R3, 35, 57, R5, 7R**
- Three notes: **R35, 357, R75**

Thinking creatively at fast tempos is a challenge. Constant practice is required to be able to improvise successfully in a vertical style over 'Rhythm Changes'.

It is not necessary to adopt a vertical approach all the time – contrast it with passages of horizontal playing, in which the right hand plays in B♭, as in Fig 9.32. The left hand can be simplified by leaving out the middle two chords of the **I** – **VI** – **II** – **V** turnaround, so that only **I** and **V** remain:

Fig 9.31: Simplified left-hand possibilities for bars 1–4 and 7–8

The bassist will still play all the changes, but you'll only play one chord per bar:

Fig 9.32: Horizontal improvisation with simplified left hand

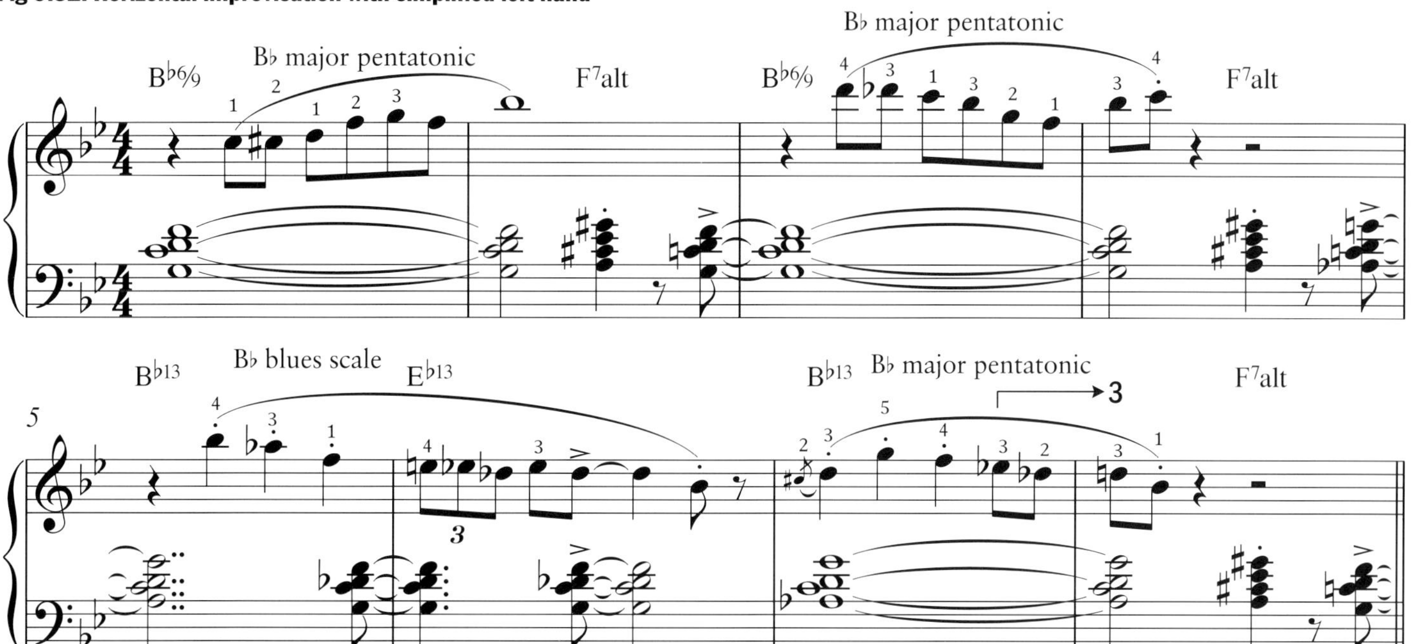

From bar 5 the **I** chord is played as B♭7 (or B♭13), giving a more bluesy sound, and enabling the right hand to play a B♭ blues scale which fits over E♭7 too. Some people like to treat the **I** chord as B♭7 throughout, playing the blues scale for the whole eight bars.

Figs 9.30 and 9.32 both use a dominant chord in bar 6 – E♭7 (E♭13) – in place of the original E♭6/9. Because E♭7 and E° are almost the same (E° is contained in an E♭7♭9 chord), you can omit the E°, as in the example above.

Changing chords from major to dominant is usually fine if you're just playing with a bass player. If the line-up includes a guitarist or other chordal instrument, however, listen carefully to each other and be on the alert for harmonic clashes. One easy way of avoiding problems is to arrange it so that you never comp at the same time!

Assignments: Rhythm Changes Comping #1

❶ **Comping** Play the first eight bars of two-handed chords on p. 192 over and over, until you no longer need the music. Repeat with the three other eight-bar sections until you have the whole 32 bars memorised.

Now play the complete form with the CD (track 35, bass and drums only), or against the piano and drums backing in the solo section of *The Theme* (Vol. 1 CD, track 24, 0:48 onwards). When you're comfortable with this, experiment with the rhythm of the chords, introducing 'on-off' and 'off-on' rhythms, two-bar patterns, etc.

❷ **Vertical improvisation** Play Fig 9.30 with the backing track, hands separately at first. You may omit some of the shells/tritones, or play them in a different rhythm. For the second eight bars, remember that bars 7–8 are different, as they go to the bridge rather than back to B♭. Instead of a turnaround, play B♭ – F7 – B♭ here.

Try some of the other two-and three-note motifs suggested below Fig 9.30, taking each one through all the chords. Vary the choice of notes and experiment with different rhythms until you find something you like. Also, revise the short **II** – **V** patterns on pp. 68–70, and select a couple that you can start to use in the Cm7 – F7 bars.

❸ **Horizontal improvisation** Play Fig 9.32 with the backing track, hands separately at first. Improvise two whole choruses in this style, using your own horizontal ideas in the 'A' sections against left-hand chords such as those suggested in Fig 9.31.

❹ **Solo piano** Away from the CD, practise improvising over the two-feel bass line from *The Theme* (Vol. 1, p. 122), or with shells in the left hand (as in Fig 9.30).

❺ ***The Theme*** Plan a complete performance of the melody, followed by several choruses of improvisation, using all the techniques described above.

36 with bass & drums

♩ = 240 (swing 8s)

Rhythm Changes Comping #2

Tim Richards

This is a more contemporary version of 'Rhythm Changes' with many substitute chords. Left-hand shells are used for the first half, with rootless voicings from the bridge onwards.

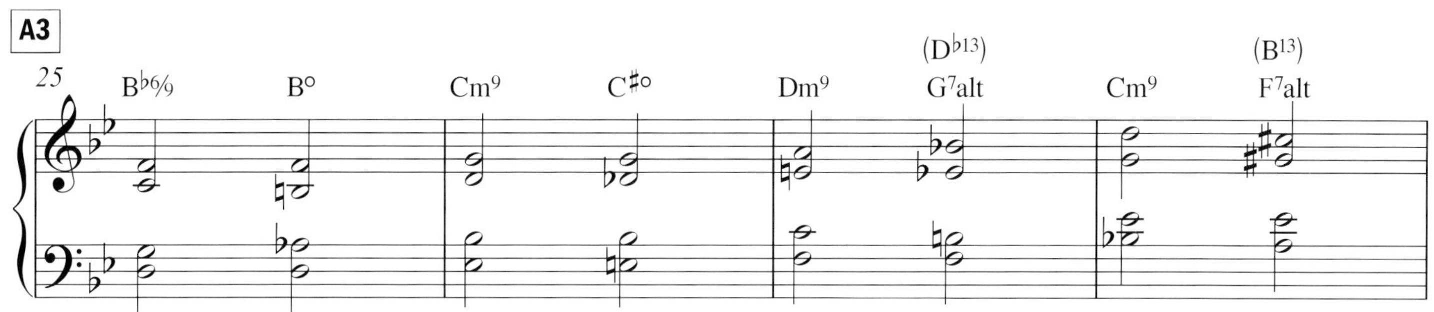

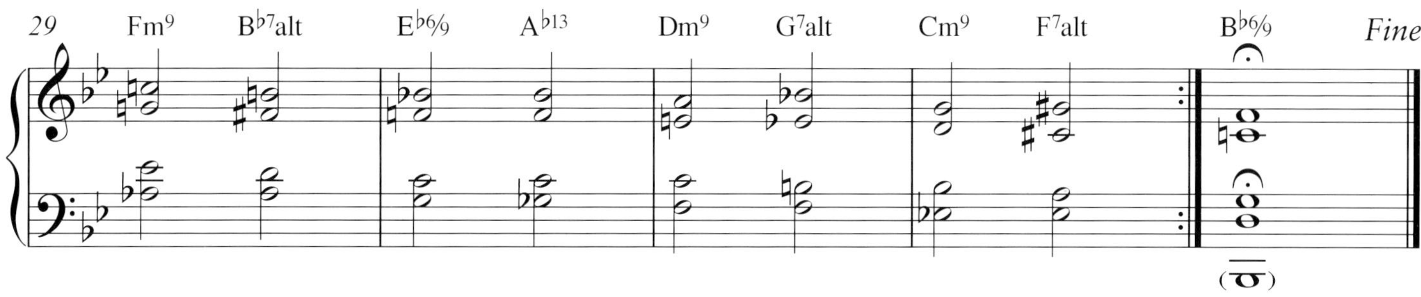

Checkpoint: Rhythm Changes Comping #2

● **Tritone substitutes** The turnaround in bars 3–4 has been altered from the one on p. 192:

Dm7 – G7 – Cm7 – F7

has become

Dm7 – **D♭7** – Cm7 – **B7**

Although this version of the turnaround is only given the first time, you could play it like this whenever it appears, if you think it is appropriate. It reappears in rootless form in bars 27–28 and 31–32:

Dm7 – **G7alt** – Cm7 – **F7alt**

● **Shells** A **R7** shell is used for every chord in the first four bars. This is because there are no cycle movements, the roots of the chords moving up or down in semitones. If you wish you can make this work with **R3** shells in the second 'A' section by playing the substituted turnaround from bars 3–4 in bars 11–12.

● **Diminished chords** The voicings for B° and C♯° in the first two 'A' sections contain notes not found in an ordinary diminished seventh chord. These have been arrived at by moving the top note of the regular voicings up a tone:

Fig 9.33: Making diminished voicings more interesting

The new notes are always part of the diminished scale (see Figs 8.57 and 8.64).

● **Second time bars** Observe the new way of playing bars 15–16, leading to the bridge:

B♭7 – F7 – B♭7

has become

Cm7 – F7 – B♭7

Building lines for 'Rhythm Changes'

In Assignment 2 on p. 195, you improvised vertically on the 'A' sections of *Rhythm Changes Comping #1* by moving a simple two- or three-note motif such as **R2** or **R23** through the chords, as illustrated in Fig 9.30.

You'll need to apply this technique to the new sequence of *Rhythm Changes Comping #2*. Here's an example with shells in the left hand:

Fig 9.34: Vertical improvisation using R3 motif

In Chapter 8 we looked at a four-note motif, **R235** (pp. 138–42), which would also be ideal for use when improvising over 'Rhythm Changes'. Try it now, using the same left hand as the example above. When you've worked out all the **R235** patterns and strung them together, try varying and inverting some of them.

Another useful and important motif is an ordinary triad, **R35**. To keep an eighth-note line going, you need four notes per chord, so you can repeat one of the notes of the triad. There are many ways of doing this; here are just a few:

Fig 9.35: Four-note permutations for B♭ major triad (root position)

See how effective it is to play just one of these motifs over the first five chords:

Fig 9.36: Root position triad pattern

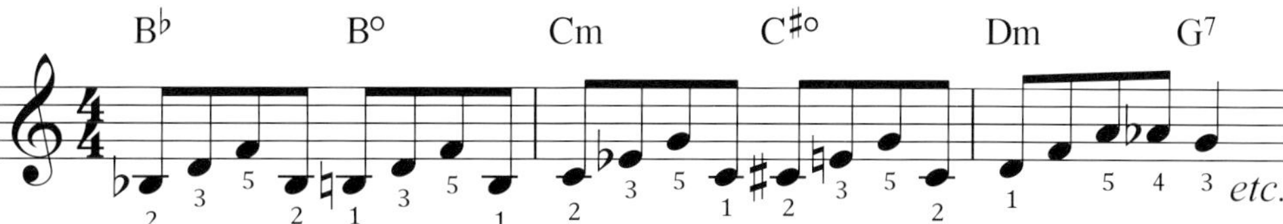

Inverting the triad motifs gives a whole range of new possibilities:

Fig 9.37

(a) First inversion patterns

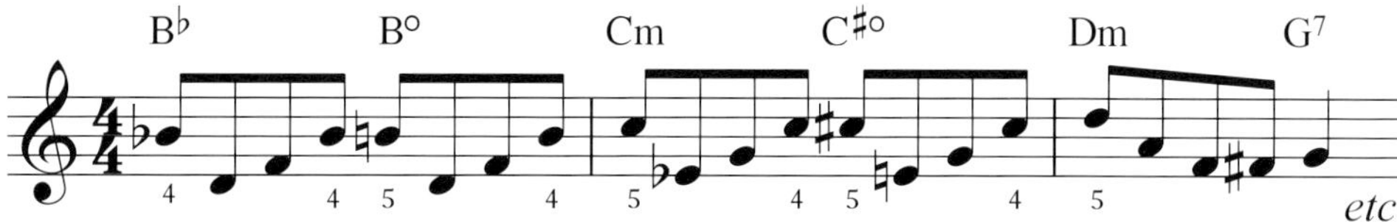

(b) Second inversion patterns

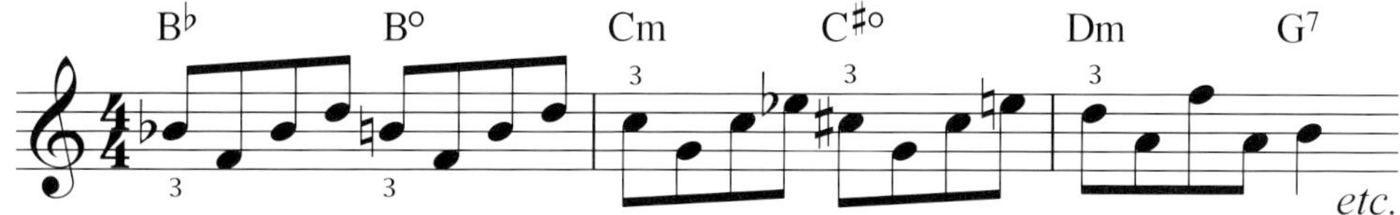

Once you're familiar with these hand positions, mix up different inversions and motifs in the same phrase. Here's a complete 'A' section demonstrating this:

Fig 9.38: Using triad motifs over every chord

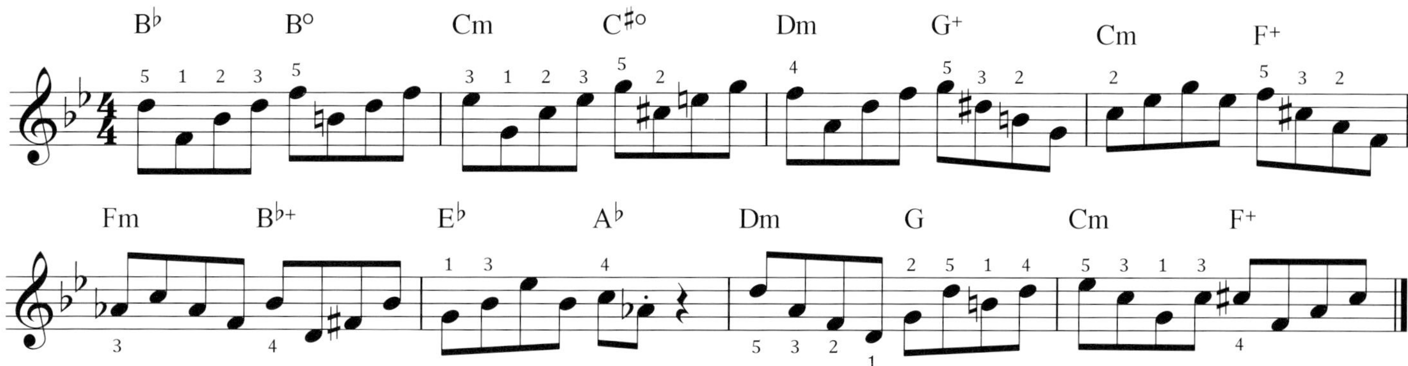

Note that the dominant chords can be played as augmented triads (G+, F+, B♭+, A♭+). This preserves the triad concept and sounds more interesting than using ordinary major triads – the raised fifth provides a little tension and makes up for the lack of a seventh.

At present Fig 9.38 sounds a little like a technical exercise, due to the lack of phrasing, with only one rest. Once you have lines like this under your fingers you'll need to edit them to get a jazzier result, introducing rests, pick-ups, syncopation, etc:

Fig 9.39: The same eight bars after editing

What we're doing with these patterns is a form of minimalism – we're focusing on very basic and familiar aspects of each chord (**R3**, **R35** etc) to facilitate playing at high speeds. The secret lies in learning to connect the chords effectively. Don't turn your nose up at basing your improvisations on such simple concepts. Analysis of solos by some of the greatest improvisers in jazz shows frequent use of triad phrases, for a very good reason – they sound great and are easy to play!

Short II – V patterns with 'Rhythm Changes'

I suggested using short **II** – **V** licks for Cm7 – F7 when soloing over *Rhythm Changes Comping #1* (see Fig 9.30). The new version of the changes includes Dm7 – G7 and Fm7 – B♭7 as well, providing plenty of opportunities for this approach:

Fig 9.40: Bars 3–5, combining two different short II – V licks

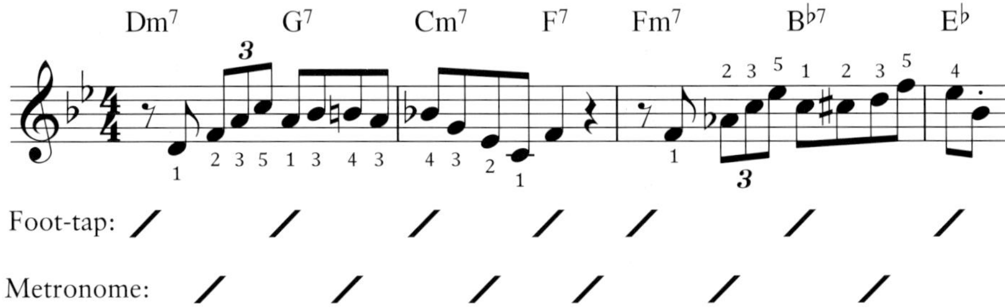

The foot-tap and metronome are marked as suggested above, with the metronome on 'two' and 'four'. Tapping the foot on 'one' and 'three' only gives a much more relaxed feel at fast tempos.

The following example is derived from the ♭**9** lick shown in Fig 8.31:

Fig 9.41: Bars 3–5, short II – V lick with ♭9

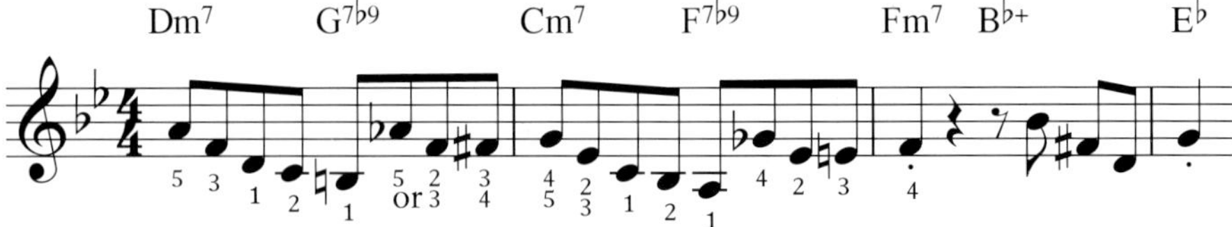

Using the metronome

Practising with a metronome is an essential way to develop a good sense of time. Not only does it help you play in time, it shows you immediately if you speed up or slow down. Speeding up or rushing is a natural tendency which often manifests itself in difficult passages. Once you're aware of it happening, you're in a better position to correct it by consciously holding back.

Digital metronomes can be purchased quite cheaply and usually have a headphone socket. Some models have a range of tones and can be set up to play a different sound on the first beat of the bar (eg: a bell), an invaluable aid when learning a tune or improvising in time signatures such as 3/4, 5/4, 7/4, etc.

With fast 4/4 tempos it is best to tap your foot on 'one' and 'three' only, rather than on every beat. Likewise, set the metronome to click twice a bar only (eg: for 240 bpm, set your metronome to 120 bpm). These devices tell you immediately if you drop a beat, as the click will cross over onto the wrong 'foot'.

Jazz musicians like to set the metronome to click on 'two' and 'four', keeping 'one' and 'three' for the foot-tap, as shown in Fig 9.40 above. This may be off-putting at first, but it's worth persevering as it mimics the typical 'two' and 'four' of the drummer's hi-hat and enhances the swing feel.

Use the metronome also to keep a record of the tempo at which you've practised something, whether it is a technical exercise (eg: 'Daily practice routine', p. 119) or a fast tempo number such as 'Rhythm Changes'. Starting at a medium pace and gradually increasing the tempo by a notch at every practice session will help you build your technique step by step.

Improvisation over up-tempo 'Rhythm Changes' is one of the most challenging skills demanded of the jazz musician, and is often used as a 'testing ground' in jam sessions. Because of the popularity of the sequence, many players regularly devote hours of practice time developing and maintaining their fluency over the chord changes, to enable them to meet this challenge without floundering.

In contrast to 'Rhythm Changes', the next piece, *Seventh Heaven*, contains only three chords: DΔ, B♭Δ and A7alt.

Assignments and Improvisation Tips: Rhythm Changes Comping #2

❶ **Memorise the two-handed voicings** Set the metronome to a slow or medium tempo (eg: 120 bpm) and practise each four- or eight-bar section over and over until you no longer need the music. When you're ready, practise the comping for the whole AABA form. Gradually increase the tempo over a period of time until you can play it with the metronome at 240 bpm.

❷ **Play along** Comp with the bass and drums on track 36, varying the rhythm of the chords, and grouping them together in different ways. Don't worry about leaving the occasional chord out.

❸ **Improvise** In the right hand only, practise the simple motifs suggested on pp. 196–7. As above, play with the metronome at a slow tempo to start with, increasing it gradually over a period of time. As a reminder, here are some of the right-hand motifs we've looked at so far:

R2, R3, R5, 35, 57, R7
R23, R35, 357, R75, R235

Don't forget to invert, vary and combine them, in as many different ways as you can. When you can improvise at 240 bpm, try playing with the backing track.

❹ **Other right-hand techniques** Remind yourself of the arpeggio and short **II – V** lick in Fig 9.30. Try mixing in the occasional arpeggio with the motifs you've played so far over the new chord sequence, remembering that altered dominant chords can be expressed as augmented triads.

Also review the short **II – V** licks given in Fig 7.15 and incorporate some of them over Dm7 – G7, Cm7 – F7 and Fm7 – B♭7, as demonstrated in Figs 9.40 and 9.41.

❺ **Add a bass line** Repeat steps 3–4 at 120 bpm, accompanying yourself with a simple bass line using roots of the chords only:

Fig 9.42: Two-feel bass line for first sixteen bars

For the bridge you'll need to play **R** and **5** of every chord as they last a whole bar each. Alternatively, you could step it up to four notes per bar, using a walking bass like the one given for *Bebop Bridge* (Fig 7.71).

❻ **Left-hand shells** Repeat steps 3–4 with shells in the left hand (as given in the first sixteen bars and in Fig 9.34). Use your own rhythms for the shells, and leave some of them out if you wish. When you're up to tempo try this with the backing track.

37 **with bass & drums**

♩ = 120
(straight 8s)

Seventh Heaven

Tim Richards

Play the intro crisply *staccato* where marked, contrasting with the head which can have plenty of sustain pedal, especially in the D major sections which should have an open, bell-like sound. The original recording can be heard on the 1994 'Spirit Level' CD 'On The Level' (33Jazz021).

Repeat ad lib. and fade to finish

Checkpoint: Seventh Heaven

● **Quartal lines** The suggested fill over DΔ in bars 17–18 of the head is split between the hands, the left hand comprising an open triad (**R53**). In the right hand, play notes ascending in either fourths or fifths, keeping the sustain pedal down. Any note of the D major scale can be included, apart from the fourth (G).

Fig 9.43: (a) Up in fourths from 3 **(b) Up in fifths from 5**

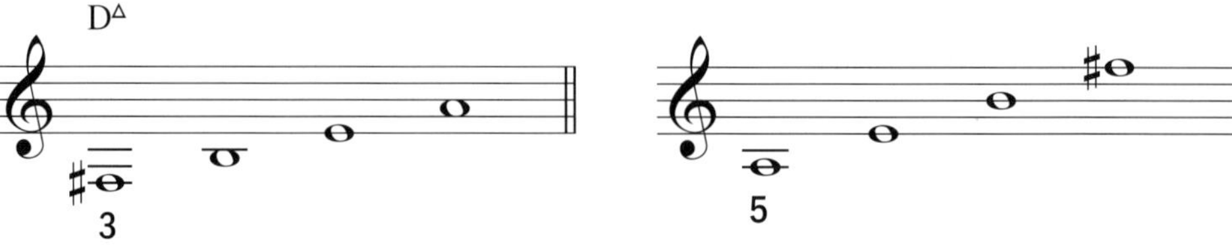

In bars 29–30 note the perfect fourths motif going up in fifths, like the ending fill given for *In a Sentimental Mood* (Vol. 1, p. 221 and Fig 5.73). To make this work, remember to start on **6** of the major chord:

Fig 9.44: Moving a three-note fourths motif up in fifths

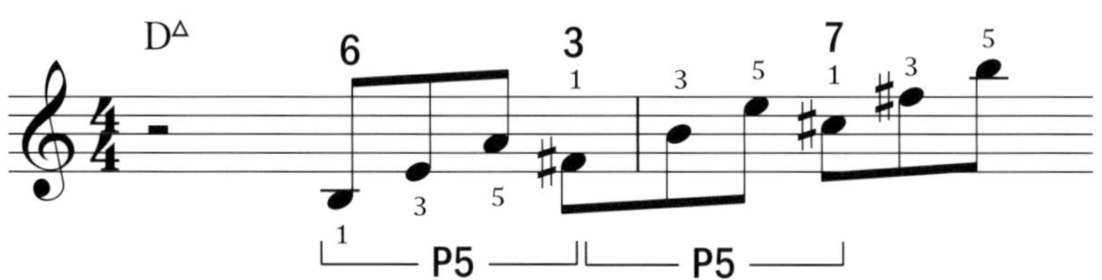

● **Phrygian mode on A** This contains three of the four possible altered notes for A7:

Fig 9.45

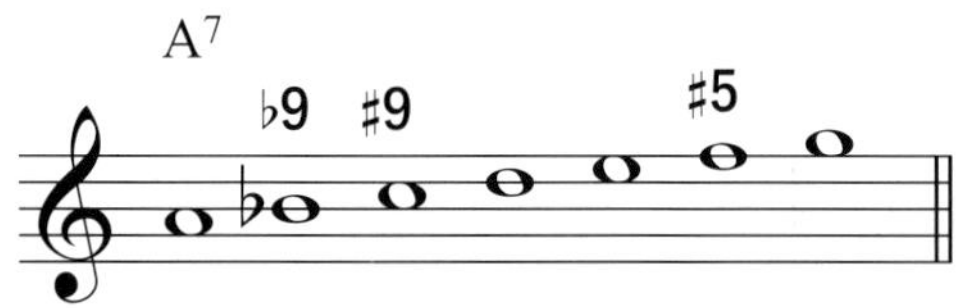

This scale has the same notes as the Lydian on B♭(they are both modes of F major), which is why it can be used horizontally over both B♭Δand A7 alt.

● **Altered scale** The Phrygian scale above does not include the third of the A7 chord (C♯), and the note E is a poor choice over A7alt. An alternative approach would be to use a different scale for each chord:

Fig 9.46: Scale choices for first eight bars of solo section

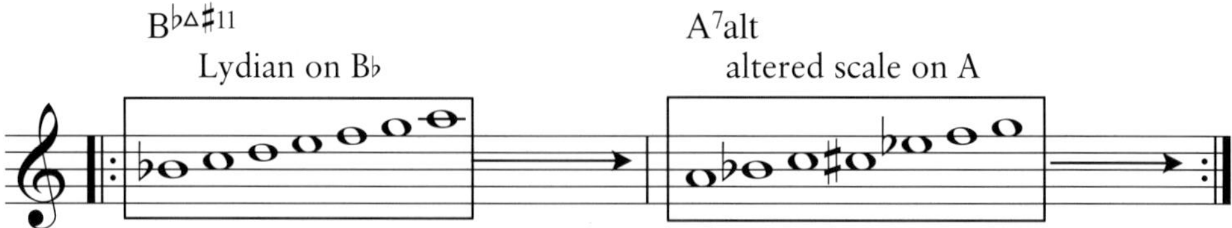

Assignments

❶ **Horizontal improvisation** Try out the Phrygian on A for both chords, playing along with track 37 (bass and drums only), chords in the left hand. When you get to the DΔ section, explore quartal patterns as suggested. Review 'Major scales and quartal harmony' (p. 34) and see also Fig 6.55.

❷ **Vertical improvisation** Repeat step 1, incorporating the altered scale for the A7 bars as shown in Fig 9.46. The last time through, jump to the intro instead of improvising over the DΔ section – this sets up the recap of the head.

❸ **Coda** Improvise horizontally over the alternating **I** and **IV** triads by choosing notes from the D major scale. Then try alternating the D and G pentatonics as suggested. Don't forget to include a blue third (♭**3**) in front of some of the major thirds. Top harmony would also be effective (see Vol. 1, Fig 1.47).

Oscar Peterson, one of the most popular mainstream pianists, shown here with Sam Jones (bass) and Louis Hayes (drums) in 1966. Oscar's ability to swing harder than anyone, even without drums, and the infectious enthusiasm generated by his impressive technique, compensate for the occasionally predictable content of his solos.

On Green Dolphin Street

Bronislau Kaper
arr. Tim Richards

This is the complete version of the tune whose first eight bars we looked at in Vol.1, p.42. The 32-bar ABAC sequence alternates a Latin feel for the 'A' sections, and swing for 'B' and 'C'.

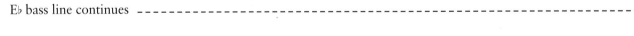

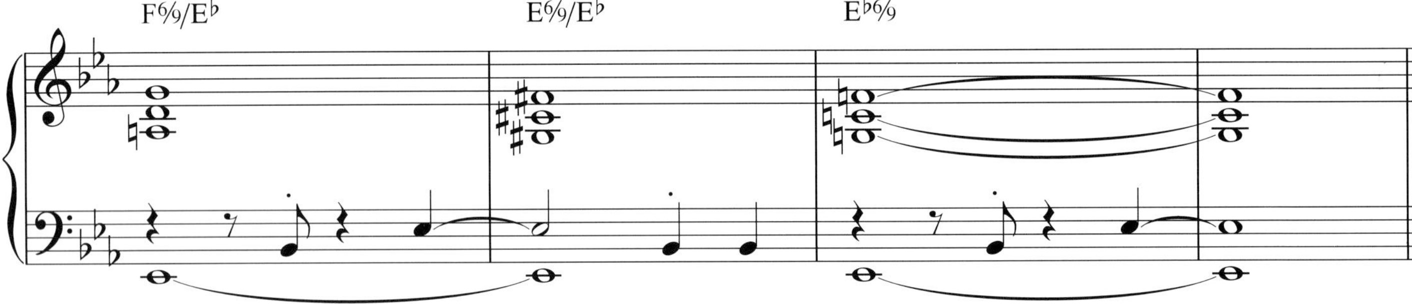

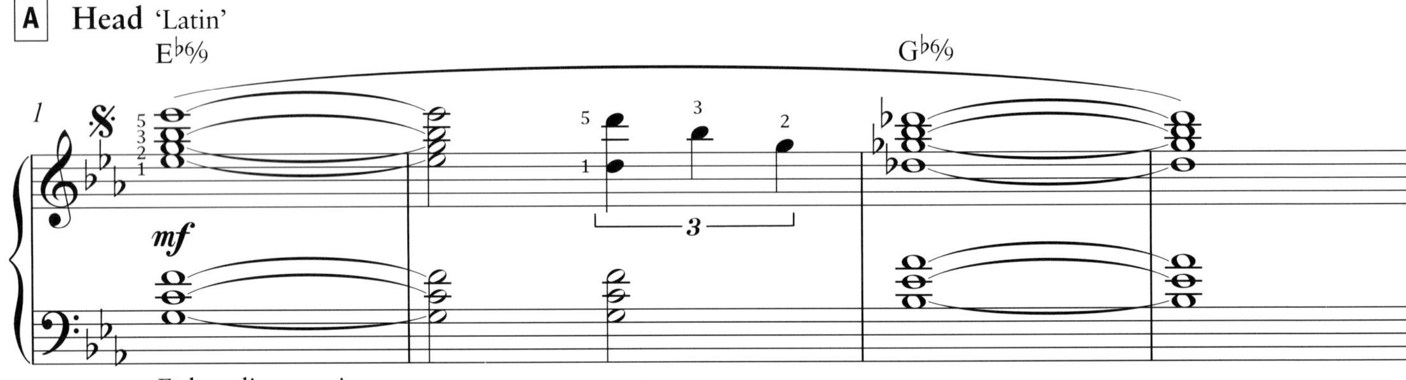

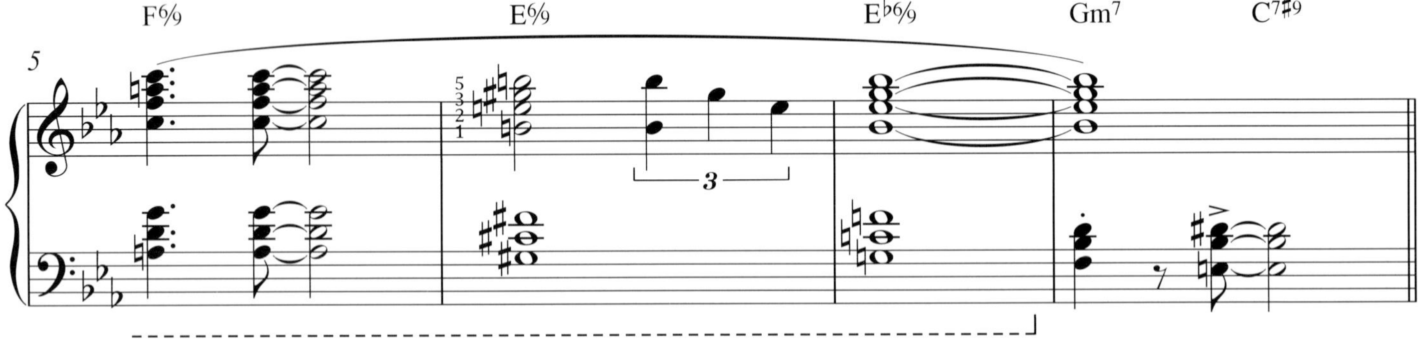

Music by Bronislau Kaper

D.S. for Solos
Coda 1st time on CD

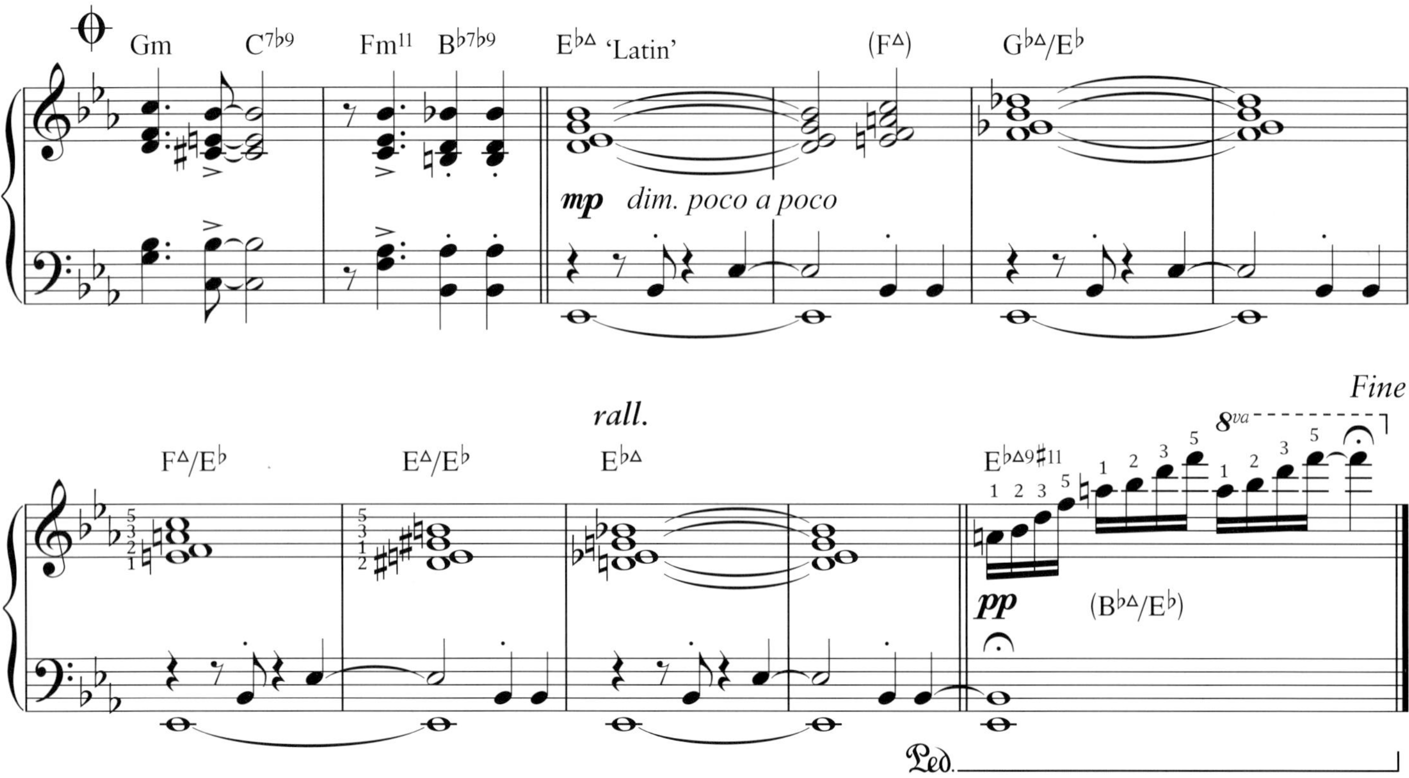

Checkpoint: On Green Dolphin Street

● **Intro** This has the same chords as the first eight bars of the melody and the last eight bars of the coda – parallel major chords over an unchanging E♭ pedal figure. Because there is no melody to the intro (or coda), you can play the chords any way you like, using any voicing or inversion that sounds good. So far we have used the following right-hand voicings:

- Second inversion major triads – **5R3** – Vol. 1, p. 42
- Three-note quartal 6/9 voicings – **369** – Intro, p. 206
- Third inversion major sevenths – **7R35** – Coda (this page)

Notice how the quartal 6/9 shapes give a contemporary slant to the harmony. They are formed by building perfect fourths on the third of each chord.

● **First 'A' section – block chords** The Latin sections of the head still have the E♭ bass line from the intro, but in this arrangement the melody is played in block chords, leaving the E♭ pedal to the bass player.

The quartal **369** voicings from the intro have been transferred to the left hand, with spread-position triads added in the right hand, melody note uppermost. The melody has been moved up an octave to make room for the full-sounding chords:

Fig 9.47: Block chords with quartal left hand

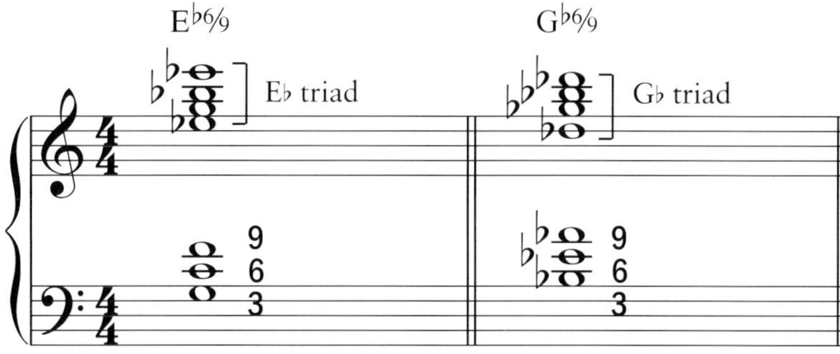

You can hear Oscar Peterson playing similar chords behind the bass solo in 'Oscar Peterson in Russia'. Compare this style of block chord to Red Garland's seven-note voicings on p. 189.

● **Second 'A' section** This features a 'smaller' version of the melody with only two notes in each hand. All notes are a perfect fourth apart, voiced as follows:

69/5R (bars 17–18) **36/95** (bars 19–23)

We have used these two-handed quartal voicings earlier in this chapter, in *Tune Up* (p. 183) and in *Rhythm Changes Comping #1* and #2 (pp. 192 and 196). See also Fig 9.16.

● **'B' section – altered chords** The first swing section is based around two **II** – **V** – **I**s in the keys of E♭ and G♭ major, the melody and chords moving up a minor third in bar 13. The notes of the melody in bars 10 and 14 imply altered dominant chords:

Fig 9.48: Bars 9–11 of melody

Don't play a B♭9 chord in bar 10, as this would clash with the **♭9** and **#9** melody notes. The same is true of the D♭7 chord on the next line – an ordinary D♭13 (**3679**) is not appropriate, so I have used D♭7alt (**3 #5 7 #9**).

● **'C' section** The key centres here go through F minor and C minor before returning to E♭ via a **III** – **VI** – **II** – **V** turnaround in bars 29–30 (see 'Chord substitution', p. 114).

The Dø in bar 26 can be thought of as Fm6 (both chords have the same notes), giving the sequence Fm – Fm7 – Fm6. Likewise the Aø two bars later could be Cm6. This type of minor sequence is very common and is usually played with a descending bottom note, often indicated by slash chords:

Fig 9.49: Descending bass lines

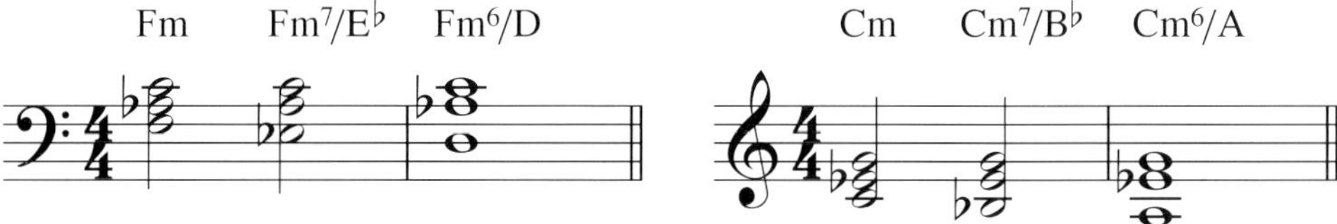

Because the Cm version above is too high for the melody, in bars 27–28 I have placed the moving note in the middle of the voicing instead. Remember that slash chords give information about the bass line which does not always need to be expressed by the pianist.

The Lydian dominant scale

We have already seen how an altered chord contains the same notes as a thirteenth chord whose root is a ♭**5** away (see 'Tritone substitution', pp. 178–9 and Fig 9.14). Applying this thinking to the **II** – **V** – **I** sequences in the 'B' section of *On Green Dolphin Street*:

Fm7 – B♭7alt – E♭Δ   A♭m7 – D♭7alt – G♭Δ
becomes
Fm7 – **E13** – E♭Δ   A♭m7 – **G13** – G♭Δ

The only thing that changes is the bass line under the dominant chord – the rootless left-hand shapes in bars 10 and 14 (p. 207) work for either chord. The advantage is that you're probably more familiar with thirteenth shapes than with altered shapes, so you're likely to find G13 quicker than D♭7alt!

This substitution has important implications when improvising. If playing over the original chords you would choose an altered scale for bar 10 as in (a) below:

Fig 9.50

(a) Altered scale on B♭

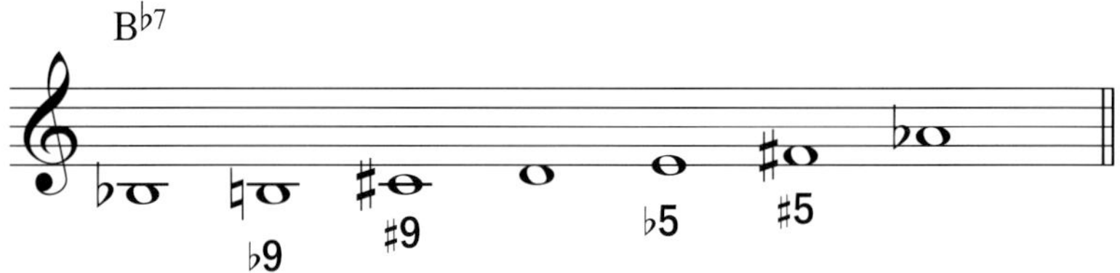

(b) The same notes starting on E (Lydian dominant)

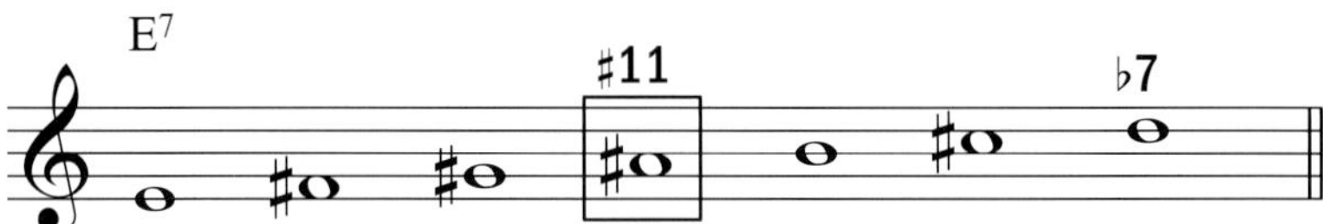

The second scale is a mode of the first and will fit over E13 – it is identical to a Mixolydian scale on E, apart from the A♮, which is a raised fourth (**#11**):

Altered scale on B♭ = Mixolydian on E with #11

As we saw in Fig 9.21, the usual name for this scale is 'Lydian dominant' (Lydian referring to the **♯11**, dominant to the ♭**7**). You can use it in place of any altered scale by thinking a ♭**5** away (tritone substitution). It can in fact be used with any dominant chord that resolves down a semitone. Note the following general rules:

- Use the altered scale if the dominant chord resolves up a fourth (**V** – **I**)
- Use the Lydian dominant if the dominant chord resolves down a semitone (♭**II – I**)

The second option is shown opposite over the other **II** – **V** – **I** from section 'B':

Fig 9.51: Scale choices for bars 13–15 of *On Green Dolphin Street*

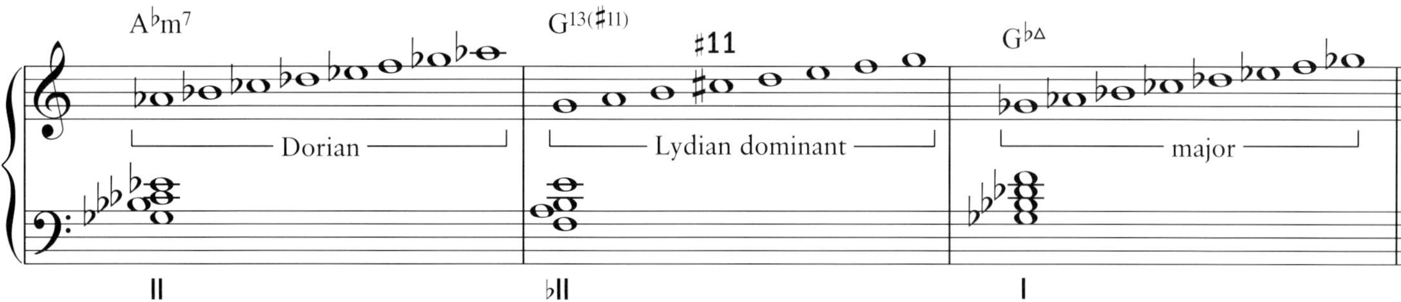

The G Lydian dominant scale shown above has the same notes as the altered scale on D♭, but is much easier to visualise. The bassist can interpret this bar as either G7♯11 or D♭7alt (see the walking bass line in *Tension & Release Blues ♯2*, p. 180).

Long II – Vs with altered dominants

The long **II – V** patterns we played on p. 105 can be used when improvising over the 'B' section of *On Green Dolphin Street*. If you're playing altered dominant shapes in the left hand, however, you'll need to adjust some of the notes to prevent any clashes. Here is the pattern from Fig 7.75(b) and its equivalent for an altered dominant:

Fig 9.52

(a) Ordinary long II – V pattern

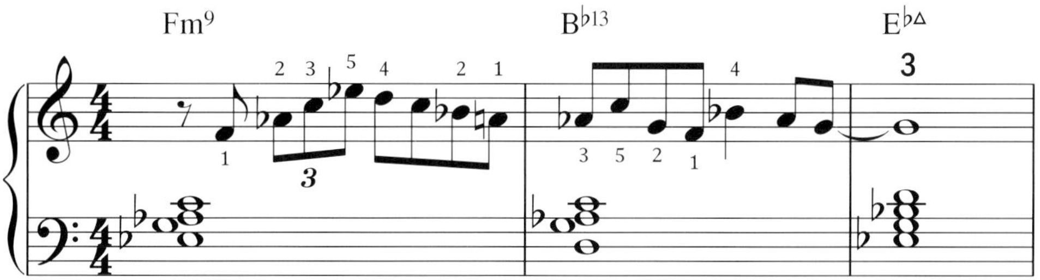

(b) Same pattern adapted for an altered dominant

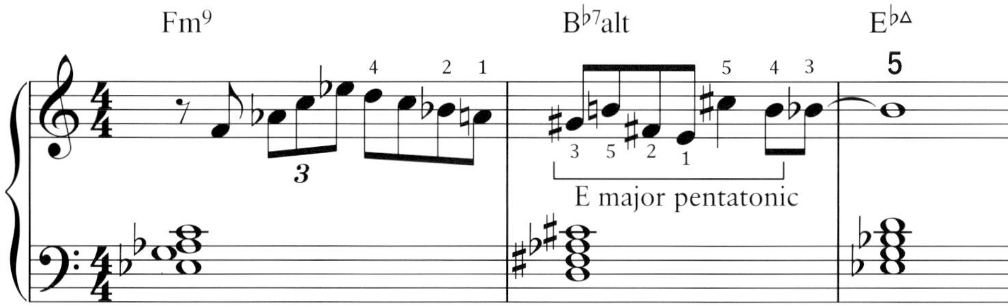

Notice the E major pentatonic scale in the B♭7 bar – this ties in with the E13 tritone substitute. Playing a major pentatonic on the ♭**5** is one easy way to approach improvising over altered chords. Try playing the notes in a different order, and vary the target note for E♭Δ:

Fig 9.53: Playing a major pentatonic based on ♭5 of the altered chord

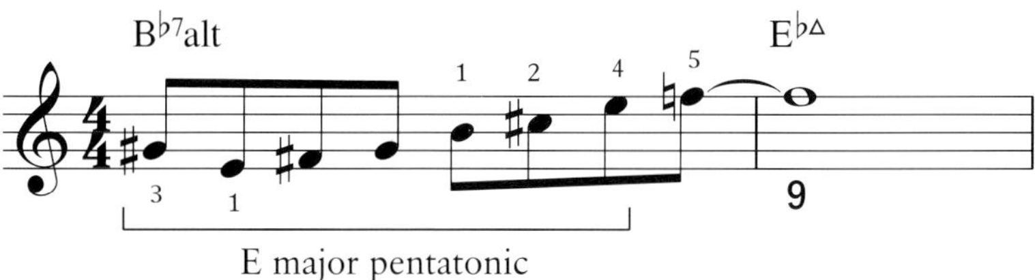

Some **II – V** patterns are specially designed to fit over altered dominants:

Fig 9.54: Altered II – V pattern

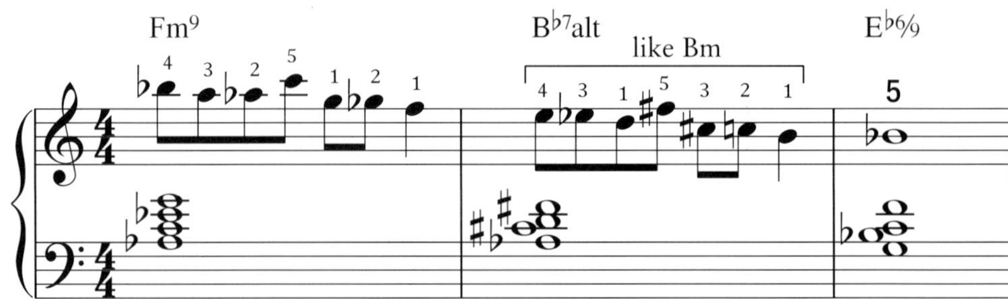

The first bar is transposed down a ♭**5** for the dominant chord. As the first bar is an Fm pattern, the second can be thought of as a Bm pattern, tying in with the derivation of the altered scale from a melodic minor scale a semitone up (see Fig 9.7).

The final example combines the long **II – V** pattern from Fig 7.75(a) with the classic altered lick shown in Fig 9.8 (which also implies Bm over the B♭7 alt chord):

Fig 9.55

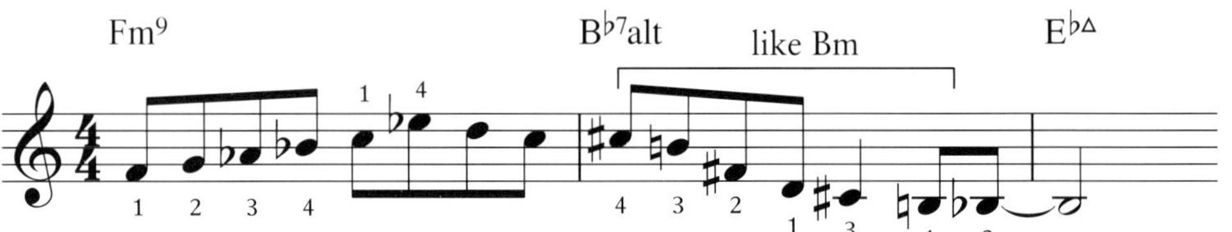

Assignments and Improvisation Tips: On Green Dolphin Street

❶ **'A' sections** Review the arpeggio exercises and improvisation suggestions given for the first eight bars of this tune in Vol. 1, pp. 44–47. Try your improvisation with the new left-hand chords from this chapter (bars 1–8, p. 206), playing along with the Vol. 1 CD, track 8, which repeats the 'A' section over and over.

❷ **'B' section** Practise improvising round these eight bars, over and over, using rootless left-hand chord shapes. In your solo you are free to treat the dominant chords in various ways. Here are some possibilities:

- Fm7 – B♭9 (or 13) – E♭Δ — E♭ major scale (Dorian on F) throughout
- Fm7 – B♭7#9 (or ♭9) – E♭Δ — Diminished scale over B♭7
- Fm7 – B♭7alt – E♭Δ — Altered scale over B♭7
- Fm7 – E13#11 – E♭Δ — Lydian dominant scale over E13

The last two options involve identical notes – the difference is in how you conceive of them. For these two options use the left-hand shapes given on p. 206. Don't play an altered left-hand chord if your right hand is playing either of the first two scale choices – your left and right hand must be compatible.

❸ **Long II – V patterns** Memorise some of the patterns given on pp. 211–12 and try to incorporate them into your solo over the 'B' section, instead of the scale approach from step 2.

❹ **'C' section** This is the hardest part of the tune to improvise over because of the rapidly changing chords. The best approach is often to simplify your thinking, improvising horizontally where possible. This is made easier once you realize that the following three chords all contain the same notes:

Dø = Fm6 = B♭9 (rootless)

The original chords for bars 25–28 were:

|| Fm Fm/E♭ | Dø G7 | Cm Cm/B♭ | Aø D7 ||

Replacing Dø with Fm6 and Aø with Cm6 gives:

Dorian on F ⟶ Dorian on C ⟶

|| Fm Fm7 | **Fm6** (G7) | Cm Cm7 | **Cm6** (D7) ||

You could now improvise using the two scales suggested without worrying about the G7 and D7 passing chords.

Another way to simplify the sequence might be to treat the Dø and Aø as B♭9 and F9 respectively, creating two long **II** – **V**s:

|| Fm7 | **B♭9** (G7) | Cm7 | **F9** (D7) ||

Don't feel obliged to play every left-hand chord, especially if playing with a bassist or the backing track. A different approach might be as follows:

|| Fm7 | G7 | Cm7 | D7 ||

For a more vertical result, review your arpeggio and short **II** – **V** patterns and use them over Dø – G7 and Aø - D7. Don't forget the **III** – **VI** – **II** – **V** in bars 29–30 too: Gm7 – C7 – Fm7 – B♭7 (see Fig 9.41).

❺ **Play along** Silence the piano on track 38 and use it to practise the head and left-hand chords until you have memorised them. Although the CD does not include a solo, use it also to practise the above ideas by omitting the head, launching into a chorus of improvisation (ABAC) straight after the intro.

Overleaf you'll find a transcription of Oscar Peterson's *On Green Dolphin Street* solo. Try to get hold of the recording so you can hear it in context.

♩ = 216 (swing 8s)

Oscar Peterson's solo in On Green Dolphin Street

This duo performance with bassist Neils-Henning Ørsted Pederson can be heard on one of the pianist's best albums, 'Oscar Peterson In Russia', recorded live in 1974.

Bronislau Kaper
transcr. Tim Richards

A1 2nd chorus (1:38)
E♭Δ
E♭m7
anticipates F chord
F
triad motif with ♭3
E
E♭
C7
triad motif with ♭3
chromatic
B
Fm7
B♭7
E♭Δ
E♭ blues scale
E♭ major pentatonic
A♭m7
D♭7
G♭Δ
Fm7
B♭7
repeated motif based on G♭ triad
arpeggio
A2
E♭Δ
lick encircling notes of E♭ triad
E♭m7
loco
extra note
F
scale pattern
E♭m bebop scale
broken triad motif
E
E♭
C7
loco
broken triad motif
bebop scale
C
Fm7
G7
Cm
AØ
D7
arpeggio
Gm7
C7
Fm7
B♭7
E♭
Break
E♭ triad

A1
3rd chorus (2:13)
E♭Δ
E♭m7
anticipates F chord
F
5
triad
E
R
5
triad
E♭
5
C7♭9
E♭ blues scale
B
Fm7
Dorian
B♭7
anticipates E♭ chord
E♭Δ
3
top harmony
E♭ blues scale
A♭m7
G♭ triad
D♭7alt
♯9
♯5
G♭Δ
Fm7
arpeggio
B♭7
anticipates E♭
A2
E♭Δ
E♭ blues scale
E♭m7
top harmony
anticipates F chord
F
lick based around F triad
(E)
implies F7 (not E!)
E♭
R
♭7
G⌀
C7♭9
triads
C
Fm∆
R
arpeggio
D⌀
diminished scale
G7♭9
B° arpeggio
Cm
R
(A⌀)
D7
chromatic
Gm7
C7
C9 arpeggio
Fm7
B♭7
anticipates E♭ chord
E♭
top harmony
E♭ blues scale
♭3 pentatonic on E♭

A1
4th chorus (2:49)
♭3 pentatonic on E♭
(C blues scale)
F triad
D° arpeggio
Dorian on E♭
B
top harmony
A♭m7
D♭7alt
B⌀ arpeggio
arpeggio
Dorian
A2
anticipates F chord
G triad
Fm triad
top harmony
C♯° arpeggio
C
arpeggio
diminished scale/arpeggio
anticipates E♭ chord
E♭ blues scale
to Bass Solo

Upper and lower neighbours

If you've studied Oscar Peterson's *On Green Dolphin Street* solo you'll have noticed how one of his most frequent devices is to encircle target notes (**R**, **3** or **5** of the chord), as indicated by the arrows above the transcription. So far in this book we have generally placed target notes on the first beat of the bar, but this solo demonstrates how an advanced improviser can place them on any downbeat:

Fig 9.56: Encircling target notes on the downbeats

(a) On the 1st beat (second chorus, bars 16–17)

Fm7 B♭7 E♭△ 3

(b) On the 2nd beat (third chorus, bar 27)

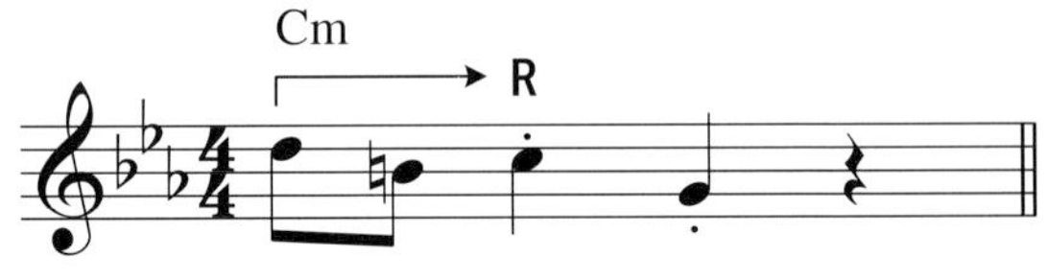

Cm R

(c) On the 3rd beat (third chorus, bar 5)

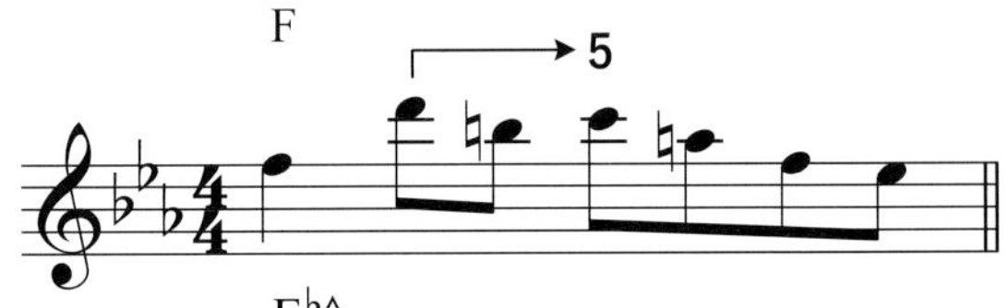

F 5

(d) On the 4th beat (fourth chorus, bar 7)

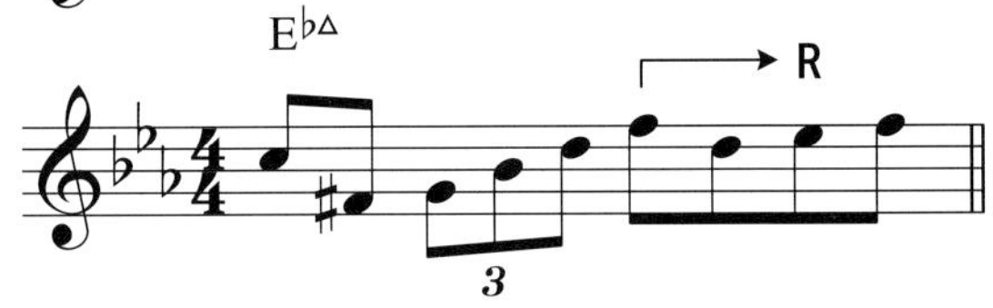

E♭△ R 3

● **Lower neighbour** This is the lower of the two encircling notes, generally a semitone below the target note. In the following useful licks, the **R**, **3** and **5** are not encircled, they are simply preceded by their lower neighbours:

Fig 9.57: Lower neighbours only

These phrases contain no sevenths, being based on major triads, so they'll work for both major and dominant chords. Similar phrases can be built on minor or diminished triads.

● **Upper neighbour** The upper note encircling a target note is most often the note above it in the prevailing scale. This may be a semitone or a tone above, depending on the position of the target note in the scale. Here are some licks using this concept:

Fig 9.58: Upper neighbours only

● **Combining upper and lower neighbours** Many classic jazz licks are based on this concept, in which each note of the triad is encircled in turn. Here's an easy way to practise it:

Fig 9.59: Using both neighbour notes

Oscar Peterson uses a similar idea in bar 21 of his third chorus, in sixteenth-notes:

Fig 9.60: Upper neighbours on the beat

All these phrases are capable of many variations. Here's another way of encircling:

Fig 9.61: Target notes on the beat

The following elegant version is a favourite of many saxophonists and trumpeters:

Fig 9.62: Alternating upper and lower neighbours

It is also possible to use two upper neighbours for each target note, a semitone and a tone above. This is demonstrated in bars 17–18 of Peterson's second chorus:

Fig 9.63: Two upper neighbours

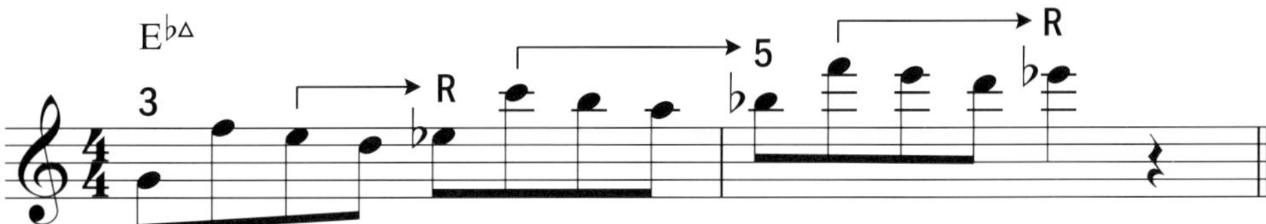

Assignments: Oscar Peterson's solo

❶ **Listen** Get hold of a copy of 'Oscar Peterson in Russia' and listen to *On Green Dolphin Street* with the transcription in front of you. It is essential to hear it – notation by itself can only give an approximate idea of the sound of jazz. If you've practised the solo already you may feel brave enough to try playing it along with the recording!

❷ **Left hand** Check out his left hand as well (not given in the transcription) and try to work out some of the chord voicings. You should be able to hear the top note of the chords. Experiment with different possibilities (rootless, shells, tritones, etc), bearing in mind the chord symbols, until you find ones which sound similar.

❸ **Encircling** Play the phrases on pp. 218–19 and spot how Peterson uses encircling and neighbour notes throughout his solo. Review 'Encircling notes with arpeggios' and 'Encircling the fifth of the dominant chord' (pp. 89 and 100).

❹ **Cycle of fifths** Choose one of the phrases on pp. 218–19 and work it out in all keys as preparation for playing over tracks such as *Dominant Seventh Workout #2, Bossa Nova Comping #2, Dominant Bebop Scale Workout* (pp. 94, 97 and 99) and *II – V – I Arpeggio Workout* (Vol. 1, p. 164), etc.
Then repeat with another pattern, and work out your own variations.

❺ **Improvise your own solos** Play along with track 38, including concepts such as neighbour notes, altered and diminished scales, **II – V** patterns, etc. Don't despair if you have difficulty at first – it takes time for new ideas to make the journey from brain to fingertips. Eliminating any technical problems (such as fingering) and constant practice will get you there in the end.

You'll get much more out of transcribed solos if you've actually worked them out for yourself, rather than reading transcriptions. See the next section for some tips.

Transcribing solos

Jazz is an aural art form. In the past, musicians learnt their craft by copying what they heard, either on records, or at live gigs. Jam sessions were an important part of this learning process, often taking place in the small hours of the morning. Nowadays it is possible to study jazz at school, university or music college, and of course from books such as this one. However, imitation remains the best way to achieve proficiency and is an important step in developing a style of your own.

Reading transcriptions like the ones in this book can be useful, but if you're serious about improving you should start working out solos for yourself. This develops your aural skills and with practice can help you achieve every jazz musician's goal – to be able to play instantly what you've just heard.

Transcription also has other benefits. If you write down the solos you are working on it can greatly improve your reading and writing skills, as you need to figure out how to notate the rhythms you are hearing. This will lead to a greater understanding of rhythm, and improve your sight-reading.

It also gives you insight into the thought processes of other musicians. Analysing the note choices of some of the great improvisers over a particular chord sequence can influence the way you tackle those changes yourself when you come to constructing your own solo, and is a great source of licks and patterns.

The sooner you embark on this process the quicker you'll make progress with the jazz idiom, no matter what style you're interested in playing. Choose easy solos to start with, not too fast, or in hard keys, or over complex chords. They don't have to be on piano – it is often easier to begin with solos on front-line instruments such as sax or trumpet, because they can only play single-note lines.

Assignments and Transcription Tips

❶ **Choose a tune** Select one that is familiar and which contains a solo that appeals to you. Use a recording on CD or cassette. (If you only have the tune on vinyl, make a cassette or burn a CD copy.) With cassettes, punch out the tabs on the edge to prevent erasing a section by mistake (easily done by pressing record in place of rewind).

❷ **Prepare your work space** Install your hi-fi system so that you can operate the controls whilst sitting at the piano – this is essential. Headphones are useful too – have a thought for your neighbours!

❸ **Work out the key** Listening to the melody is the best way to check this. If there are tuning problems, consider choosing something else – it is very hard to transcribe something that is a quarter-tone out! CDs are better in this respect as cassette machines often run fast or slow. If you have a digital piano you may be able to tune it to the recording.

❹ **Lay out the form** Using pencil and manuscript paper map out the form of the first chorus, allocating four bars to every line. Draw the bar-lines across two staves so that you can write any left-hand parts on the lower stave. If you do this correctly you'll be able to fit two choruses of a 12-bar blues on one page (for example). Use this format even if you're transcribing a single-note solo, as it is always clear to read. The lower stave will also be useful for corrections or alternative versions.

❺ **Work out the chords** Make sure you know the chords of the tune, in the right key. Write the chord symbols (in pencil) between the two staves. If you're unsure of the harmony try listening to the bassist – the notes played on the first beat of the bar are usually the roots of the chords.

❻ **Find the start of the solo** Locate the beginning of the first chorus, after the statement of the melody. Make a note of the time at which this occurs on the CD, or zero the counter of the cassette deck . Does the solo start in the first bar of the form or is there a pick-up into it? If you haven't left room for a pick-up when you laid out the form in step 4, don't worry – you can add it later, or write it on another scrap of paper.

❼ **Start transcribing** Always work in pencil so you can correct mistakes. You'll need patience and concentration, as it can be very repetitive and time-consuming. However, the more you do, the easier and quicker it will be. Here are some tips:

- Listen to the first bar of the solo and sing what you hear.
- Try to play what you've just sung on the piano. If transcribing a piano solo don't worry about the left-hand too much – concentrate on getting the right-hand lines down. You can go back and add left-hand chords later.
- Compare what you've played with the original, altering it if necessary until you're satisfied.
- Write down the notes that you think are correct, if possible in the correct timing.
- Check the timing by tapping your foot and counting as you listen back to the original. Find out which beat phrases begin and end on.
- If the phrase is fast or contains many notes break it down into smaller units – sometimes it is necessary to work on just a few notes at a time, building up the phrase bit by bit.
- Use the pause button to interrupt the recording while you sing what you've heard – don't press stop on the CD player as you'll lose your place.
- Alternate the pause and rewind buttons to listen repeatedly to difficult passages. Some tape recorders allow you to rewind automatically to where you've set the counter to zero. CD players can also have a looping facility that allows you to play passages over and over between certain points.
- Continually check notes with the harmony. If a phrase seems to contradict the chord symbols, become suspicious – you may be writing it in the wrong bar.
- Check the positioning of all phrases by counting bars and beats, and by listening to the bass player where necessary.
- Listen for target notes (usually notes of the chord, on the first beat of the bar). Once you have notated these in the correct place you can work backwards to find out the notes that precede them.
- If you come across a phrase that you can't sing, or that is too hard to write down, leave it for now and jump to the next part of the solo. Do what you can, going for the obvious parts first.
- When you've roughly transcribed the first chorus go over it again, filling in the details you missed first time. Then move on to successive choruses if you wish.
- If you get bogged down, leave it for a while, or come back another day. Don't get discouraged – the mind works best when it is fresh.

❽ **Use your memory** Many players memorise solos by singing along with the whole solo, without necessarily bothering to write anything down. This is great practice, but writing the solo down will help your reading and writing skills, and preserve your efforts for the years to come.

❾ **Play the solo** Whether you've transcribed just one chorus, or the entire solo, there'll come a time when you'll want to play it in unison with the recording. This can be great fun but you'll need to spend time practising it first, paying attention to such things as fingering, articulation and interpretation.

❿ **Analyse the solo** All your work is in vain if you neglect this important final step. The aim of transcribing is not just to play other musicians' solos note for note. As I've done throughout this book, ask yourself why the soloist has chosen these particular notes: What scales have they used? What are their favourite licks or patterns? Do they improvise vertically or horizontally?, etc...

Equally important, look at the soloist's phrasing, use of space, rhythm, repetition, motifs, dynamics, texture, and the overall construction of the solo. By studying the masters you can begin to apply these techniques to your own soloing. All great jazz musicians have been influenced by other players. When you find an idea you really like, make it your own! Learn it in other keys so you can use it in any tune.

Chapter Nine – Final Checkpoint

● **Dominant seventh scales** In this chapter we have greatly increased our options for voicing dominant seventh chords by including altered extensions such as **♯11**, **♭9**, **♯9**, **♭5** and **♯5**, in various combinations. Because many of these chords imply their own specific scales, there is a much wider range to choose from than for any other chord-type. Here is a summary of the possibilities, with typical rootless voicings shown in the left hand:

Fig 9.64: Scales choices for G7

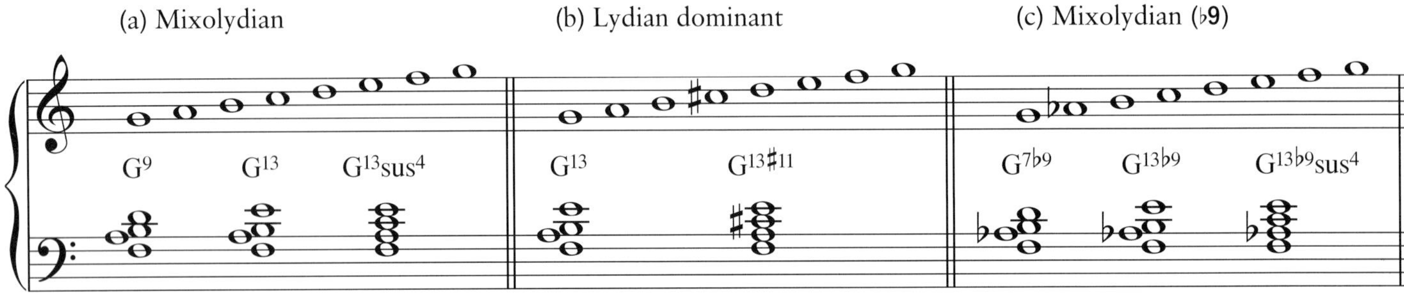

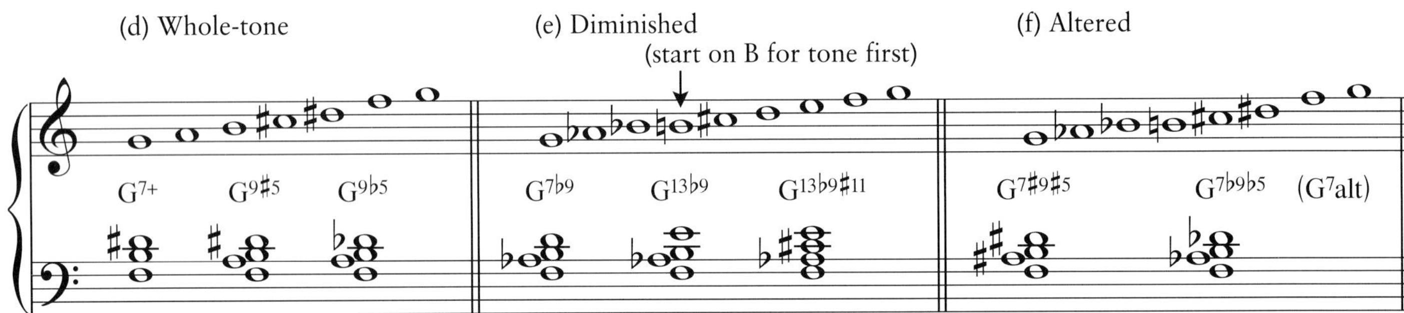

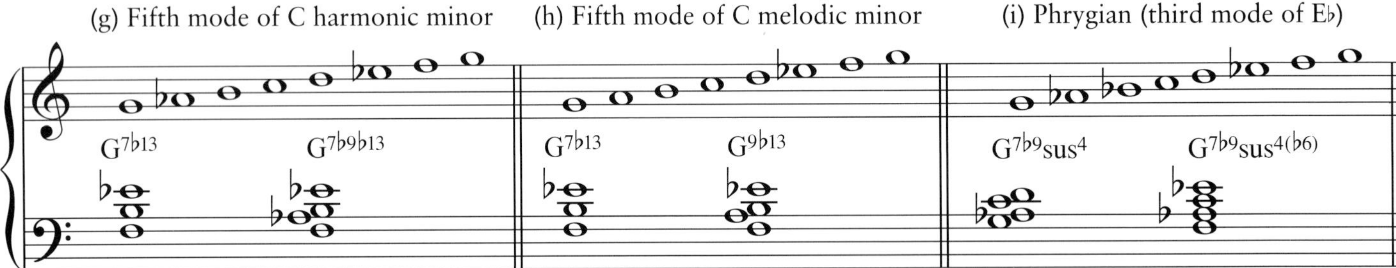

NB: In theory a chord or scale cannot contain a regular fifth together with **♭5** or **♯5**. If the ordinary fifth is present:

- The **♭5** should be called **♯4** or **♯11**
- The **♯5** should be called **♭6** or **♭13**

Similarly, a chord or scale cannot contain a regular ninth together with **♭9** or **♯9**, although both of the altered ninths can be present (as in the altered, diminished and Phrygian scales).

It is not always desirable to be totally specific. In order to give some choice to the performer, composers often use symbols such as G7alt or G7±5, which are easier to interpret than symbols with multiple extensions. Another technique common in contemporary jazz is to specify the scale required, rather than the extensions, eg: 'G7 (Phrygian)', or to indicate polychords such as Abm/G7, E♭/G7, etc.

Chapter Ten
Minor II-V-I

The minor version of the II – V – I sequence offers more choices for the improviser than any other set of chords. In this chapter we'll look at some of the options available, assimilating many of the techniques already discussed.

We dealt briefly with minor **II** – **V** – **I**s in *Fly Me to the Moon* (Vol. 1, p. 146), *Autumn Leaves* (Vol. 1, p. 150), and *Summertime* (p. 130 and Fig 8.19). To summarise what we already know about minor key harmony:

- The **II** chord is usually half-diminished
- The **V** chord often has an altered **5** and/or **9**
- The **I** chord can be m6, m7 or mΔ7
- Every minor key has a relative major key a minor third up
- The natural minor scale has the same notes as the relative major

● **The Locrian mode** This is the first choice scale for a half-diminished chord, whether it functions as **II** (Bø in A minor), or as **VII** (Bø in C major).

Fig 10.1: To find the Locrian scale, think up a semitone from the root of the half-diminished chord

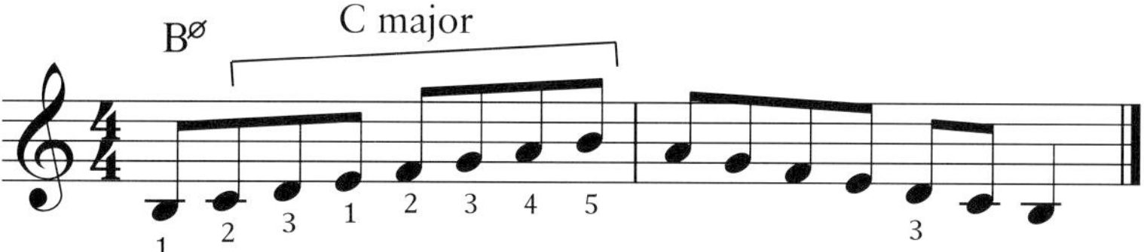

Although the Locrian scale on B has the same notes as C major, start with the thumb on B, rather than conserving the C major fingering (thumb on C).

● **The natural minor scale** An easy way to play over both major and minor **II** – **V** – **I**s is to play horizontally using the same scale over all three chords:

● C major scale	Dm7 – G7 – CΔ	(same notes as Dorian on D)
● A natural minor scale	Bø – E7 – Am	(same as Locrian on B)

The melody of *Blue Bossa* overleaf demonstrates this over a **II** – **V** – **I** in C minor, using the C natural minor scale. Although this doesn't give the third of the G7 chord (B♮), it is an effective way to begin improvising over minor **II** – **V** – **I**s:

Fig 10.2: Playing modes of E♭ major over a II – V – I in C minor

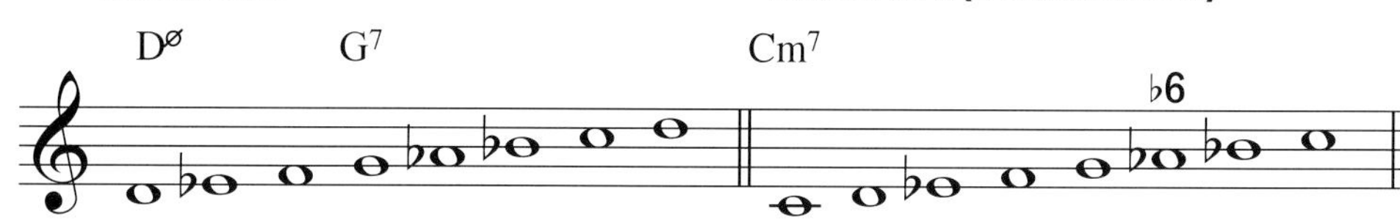

39

Blue Bossa

♩ = 160
(straight 8s)

Kenny Dorham
arr. Tim Richards

Trumpeter Dorham first recorded this tune on Joe Henderson's debut album 'Page One' (1963). It has since become a jazz classic, played at countless jam sessions the world over.

21
Dø
G7+
Cm9
25
E♭m9
A♭13
D♭Δ9
29
Dø
G7+
Cm9
Dø
G7+
33 Solo
Cm9
C natural minor
Fm9
(LH plays bass line only on CD)
37
Dø
G7+
Cm9
41
E♭m9
Dorian on E♭
A♭13
D♭6/9
D♭ major
same notes
45
Dø
Locrian on D
G7+
Cm9
C natural minor
G7+
same notes
D.C. al Fine

Checkpoint: Blue Bossa

● **Bass line** Like the one used in *Bossa Nova Comping #1* (Vol. 1, p. 145) and #2 (p. 97), this uses **R** and **5** of every chord. The fifth is played below the root for the G7 and A♭7 chords, preventing the bass line from rising too high. Note that the ♭**5** must be used for Dø, and is also present in the G7 bars, implying a G7♭5 chord.

● **Key centres** The first eight bars of the tune are in the key of Cm:

Cm7 – Fm7 – Dø – G7 – Cm7
I IV II V I

The second half modulates to the key of D♭ major:

E♭m7 – A♭7 – D♭Δ
II V I

before returning to Cm in the last four bars. The 16-bar form is repeated for the solos.

● **Four-note shapes** The chord symbols are given in the head as they would appear in most fakebooks, as ordinary sevenths. However, in the Partido Alto and solo sections, many of them have been interpreted as ninths, eg:

Cm9, Fm9, E♭m9, A♭13, D♭Δ9

These are played as one of two shapes: **3579** or its inversion, **7935**, alternating **3** and **7** on the bottom whenever the roots move up a fourth. The A♭7 shape has the sixth rather than the fifth as its top note, giving a thirteenth shape: **7936**.

● **The half-diminished chord** Notice that the ninth of the Dø chord (E) is not included, since it would clash with the E♭ in the melody. It also 'contradicts' the Cm tonality. In the Partido Alto section the Dø chord is played as a regular first inversion, with the root on top:

Fig 10.3: Ninths are not always appropriate with half-diminished chords

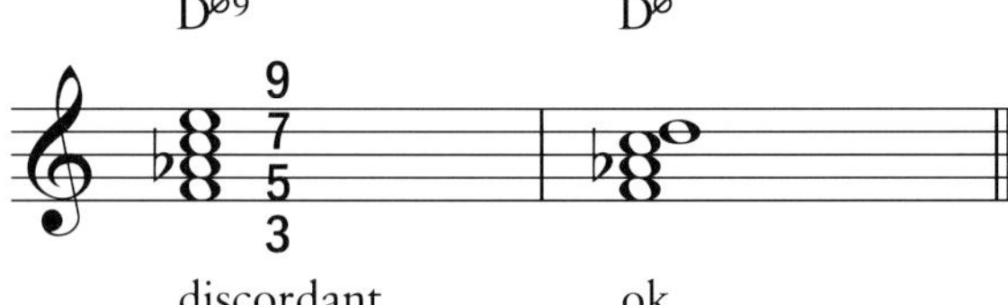

● **The V chord** E♭ is such an important note in the key of Cm that it is often included in the **V** chord (G7) as a **#5** or ♭**6**. Here G7+ is played throughout as a simple **73#5** three-note shape. We did the same thing in A minor for the **V** chord in bar 14 of *Summertime* (see Fig 8.19).

In minor keys, you should be prepared to alter dominant chords in this way even when not suggested by the chord symbol. G7♭5, G7#9, G7♭9 or G7alt are other possible options.

The Partido Alto

This is the Brazilian (Portuguese) name for the rhythm given in the right hand of the second section of *Blue Bossa*, which is a backing figure. Like the Bossa Nova 'clave' (p. 96), it is a two-bar pattern:

Fig 10.4

Clap the rhythm against the 4/4 foot-tap and check how the accents fall:

- The first two on the beat (bar 1, beats 1 and 2)
- The next three off the beat, the third one long (held)
- The last two on the beat again (bar 2, beats 3 and 4)

When there is a chord change in the middle of the pattern, the chord in the second bar should be played on the 'four and' of the previous bar, as in bars 21, 25, 29 and 31.

Playing the I chord as a minor sixth

As we saw in 'Major and minor tonic chord choices' (Vol. 1, p. 213), a minor seventh is not the only option for the **I** chord. To give an attractively 'dark' sound, try playing a Cm6/9 chord instead:

Fig 10.5: Three-note shapes for minor II – V – I

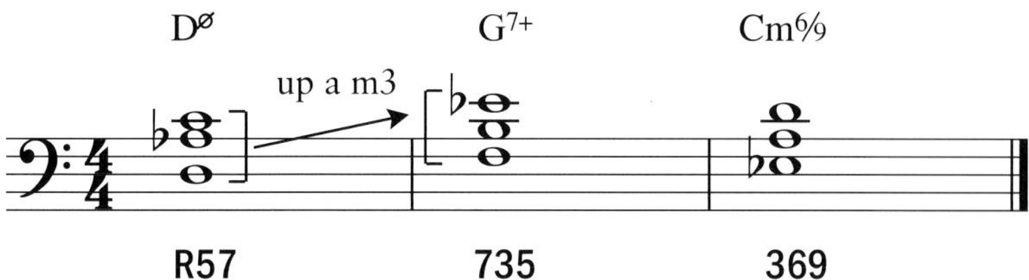

To improvise over Cm6/9 use the Dorian mode, or a ♭3 pentatonic on C. The C natural minor scale will not work since the ♭**6** clashes with the A in the chord.

See how moving the whole Dø shape up a minor third automatically gives you the G7+ shape. Remember this to help you play minor **II** – **V** – **I** chords in other keys.

Assignments: Blue Bossa

❶ **Memorise the bass line** Use the marked fingering to help you play without looking at the left hand – this will be essential later on.

❷ **Memorise the melody** Notice that the first two descending scales return to their starting notes in the third bar of each phrase, and that each phrase begins one note lower than the previous one. Play it with the bass line. The final melody on the CD is played in sixths, the right hand following the scales given in the solo section.

❸ **Partido Alto** Play the chords in the right hand only, using the bass line on the CD as a backing (solo section, track 39, from 0:51). Take care to play the correct rhythms and memorise the chord shapes.

Away from the CD, add the bass line in the left hand, working on the first two bars (Cm) over and over at a slow tempo, until you have mastered the co-ordination. Then gradually extend your practice, eg: alternate Cm9 and Fm9, or play Dø – G7+ – Cm9, over and over. When you have mastered each four-bar phrase, try to play the whole sequence with no hesitations.

❹ **Duos** Play the Partido Alto section as a backing whilst a friend plays the melody or improvises on top (on another instrument, or the top part of the piano). This type of accompaniment is useful when playing in a duo, without a bassist.

❺ **Simple improvisation** You can play over the whole piece using just the two scales – C natural minor and D♭ major, or modes of them. Accompany yourself with the bass line if playing alone, or with left-hand chords if playing with the CD.

❻ **Other scale choices** Now try using a wider variety of scales, eg:

Cm7	Dorian on C	Fm7	Dorian on F
Dø	Locrian on D	G7	altered scale

The Dorian on C is advisable if you wish to play Cm6 or Cm6/9 in the left hand. For the Dorian on F, only one note changes – A♮ becomes A♭, giving the same notes as C natural minor.

❼ **Partido Alto – left hand** Play the chord shapes from the solo section with the backing track on the CD, using the Partido Alto rhythm in the left hand. When you no longer need to read the rhythm, add the right-hand melody. This may be hard at first but will sound great when you've mastered it. Practise each two-and four-bar section over and over first, away from the CD. Also work on improvising in the right hand over the same left-hand pattern. You can miss out parts of the pattern, but avoid playing anything that contradicts it rhythmically.

❽ ***Bossa Nova Comping #1*** Use the Blue Bossa bass line and Partido Alto rhythm for the chords of this piece (Vol. 1, p. 145), and for *Fly Me to the Moon* (Vol. 1, p. 146).

❾ ***Bossa Nova Comping #2*** Play the right-hand chords of this piece (p. 97) in the Partido Alto rhythm, without altering the written bass line.

The under-rated Hampton Hawes, a West coast pianist with a uniquely swinging touch. Influenced by Charlie Parker and Bud Powell, he played with a percussive drive, mixing elements of the bebop idiom with blues and gospel licks to create his own unmistakable style. His 1950s trio albums were an influence on the young Oscar Peterson, and are essential purchases. He continued to record until his death in 1977.

Minor turnaround bass lines

Jerome Kern's *Yesterdays* overleaf begins with a turnaround in D minor, based on the **II** and **V** chords of the key. Here it is with a simple two-feel bass line:

Fig 10.6 **(a) Turnaround in Dm**

Dm7 Eø A7♭9

(b) With descending bass line

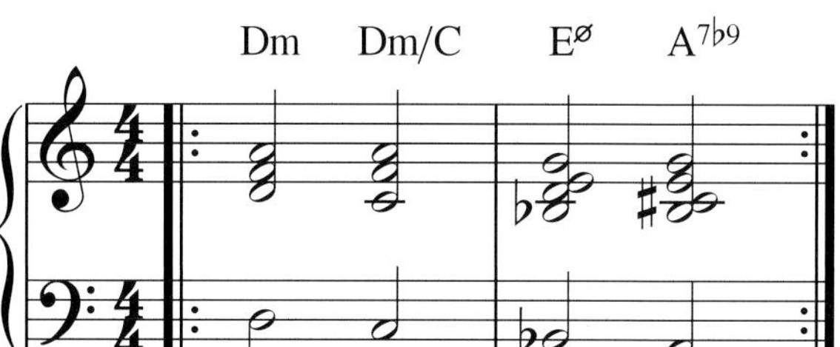

The descending bass line in example (b) is created by putting the fifth of the Eø chord (B♭) in the bass.

In the right hand of both examples the change from Eø to A7♭9 is made by moving one chord note only – D to C♯. Practise this with all four inversions of Eø, dropping the seventh to form rootless A7♭9 shapes, which are like G°, E°, C♯° and B♭°:

Fig 10.7: Each inversion of Eø is only one note different from A7♭9

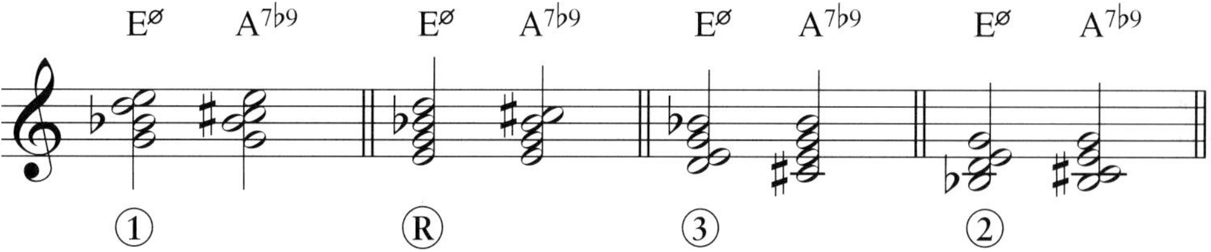

Instead of A7♭9, the **V** chord could also be played as A7♯9, A7+ or A7♭5, or any combination of these, ie: A7 alt.

The descending bass line can be harmonised in several different ways:

Fig 10.8 **(a) Replace Eø with B♭7**

Dm Dm/C B♭7 A7

(b) Replace Dm/C with C7

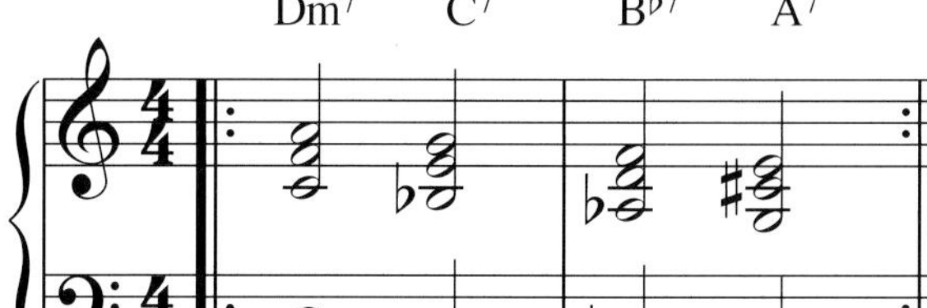

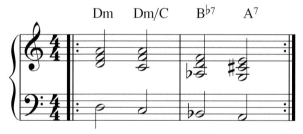

The second chord could also be Bø, setting up a **I – VI – II – V** sequence:

Fig 10.9: Minor I – VI – II – V turnaround

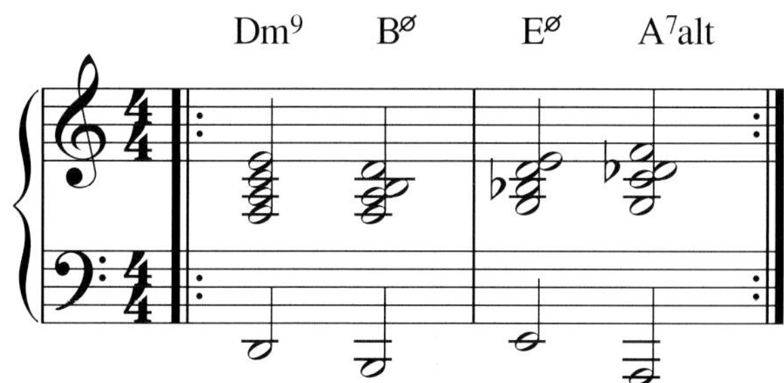

Although the first four bars of *Yesterdays* will work with any of the above, they are not all compatible with each other, so care must be taken if several musicians are present. The arrangement given overleaf sticks to the versions in Figs 10.6 and 10.7.

We'll be returning to Fig 10.9 in *Minor Turnaround Workout* on pp. 252–53.

40 with bass & drums

Yesterdays

♩ = 160
(swing 8s)

Jerome Kern
arr. Tim Richards

Like *Autumn Leaves*, this tune was written as a ballad, but is often played at a medium tempo. The left-hand accompaniment mixes up rootless voicings, shells and bass lines.

Checkpoint: Yesterdays

- **'A' section** The 16-bar melody is played twice, giving a 32-bar form. For the first sixteen bars, the left hand plays many of the chords as rootless voicings, apart from the shells in bars 13–16. This style is ideal with a bassist or with the CD.
- **'B' section** Although the second sixteen bars have the same melody and chords as the first, it would be very unimaginative to play them exactly the same way. On the whole, the 'B' section of this arrangement uses left-hand techniques more suitable for playing solo piano, such as the bass lines given for the first six bars. Note that the root is present at the bottom of every chord, except in bars 27–28.
- **Stretch voicings** The Em11 and E♭7♯11 chords in bars 15–16 have **R3** shells in the left hand. In the 'B' section and coda, they have **R5** in the left hand, stretch voicings in the right (see Fig 6.30). The final Dm11 chord is a quintal 'Kenny Barron' voicing (see Fig 6.32).
- **Dominant seventh cycle** In bars 9–12 the rootless voicings alternate **7** and **3** on the bottom. In bars 25–28 the right hand doubles the melody in octaves.

● **Bars 5–6** The biggest difference between 'A' and 'B' occurs in the left hand of these bars. The second time (bars 21–22), the walking bass line ends on **5** of Bø; it is basically another way of getting from Dm to Bø, with more movement. This bass line does not fit the original chords given in 'A' – it is sometimes harmonised thus:

Dm	A7/C♯	Dm7/C	G/B	B♭7	Dm/A	A♭°	C7/G

At 160 bpm it may not be feasible to play a chord on every beat as above – this type of approach is more suited to ballad tempos.

Overleaf is a transcription of Hampton Hawes' 1955 32-bar solo on *Yesterdays*.

♩ = 180
(swing 8s)

Hampton Hawes' solo on Yesterdays

transcr. Tim Richards

This improvisation can be heard on 'Vol. 2: The Trio – This is Hampton Hawes' (OJCCD 318-2). Only the right hand is given here, but a stave has been left free for you to pencil in a left hand if you wish.

A Dm E∅ A7♭9 Dm E∅ A7♭9
Dm△ (next chord)

5 Dm Dm△ Dm7 Dm6 B∅ E7
R ♮7 ♭7 Dm7 Dorian scale 3

9 A7 D7 G7 C7
♭5 ♯9 ♭9 ♭9 ♭9
Em A7alt 3 Dm7 3
(Am7 D7♭9 Dm7 G7♭9)

13 Cm7 F7 B♭△ E♭△ Em7 (△7) A7
♯9 ♭9 5 ♭9
Em△ C♯o

Checkpoint: Hampton Hawes' solo

● **Vertical style** This is a good example of an extremely vertical improvisation – every chord is clearly outlined, including the Dm – DmΔ – Dm7 – Dm6 sequence in bars 5–6 and 21–22. This is elegantly handled with arpeggio-type figures that stress the changing note every two beats: D – C♯ – C – B.

● **Encircling notes** This favourite Hawes' device occurs twelve times in the 32 bars. The arrows point to the target notes encircled on the first or third beat – in this solo they are either **3** or **5** of the chord.

Fig 10.10: In bars 10–11 a note is encircled every two beats

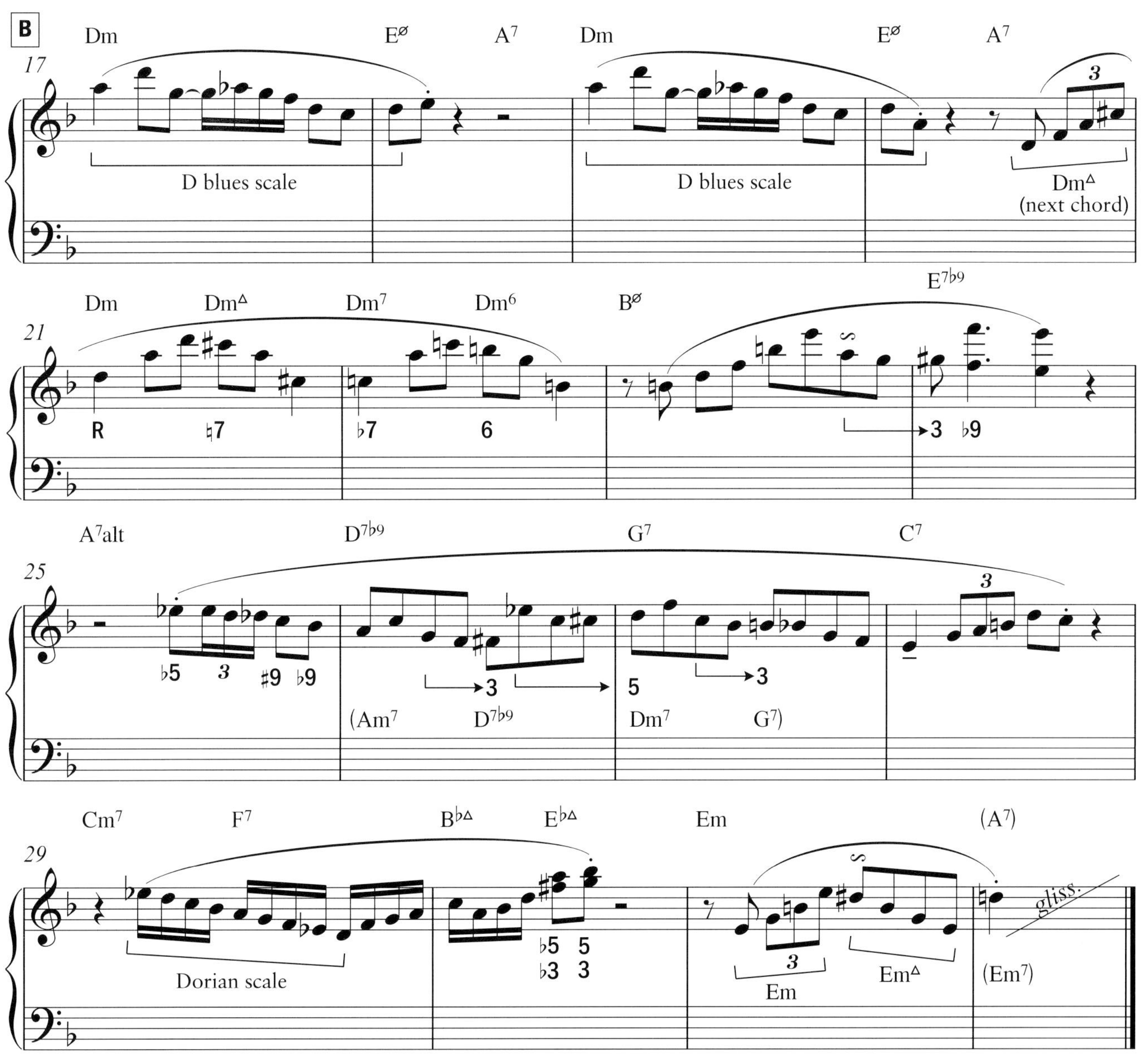

to Bass Solo

● **Turns** These ornaments, notated here by the symbol ~ , are another of Hawes' favourite mannerisms. For tips on their interpretation, see Vol. 1, Figs 4.49 and 5.53.

● **Encircling and turns combined** In bars 8, 14 and 23–24 a turn is played on the upper encircling note, creating a very elegant effect.

● **Adding II chords to the dominant seventh cycle** In true bebop style, Hawes often outlines a minor chord in front of a dominant seventh. This is clearest during the cycle in bars 9–11, A7 – D7 – G7. From the notes he plays it is obvious he is thinking like this:

| Em A^{7}alt | Am^{7} D$^{7\flat 9}$ | Dm^{7} G$^{7\flat 9}$ |

See also bars 26–27, in which the first four notes again imply Am7 and Dm7.

● **Fleshing out a long II – V** Another typical bebop device is to add passing chords to a long **II – V**, delaying the resolution to the **V** chord, so that:

| Em | A^{7} |

becomes

| Em Em$^{\triangle}$ | Em^{7} A^{7} |

These chords are clearly outlined in bars 15–16 and 31–32, even though the chord symbols only specify Em7 – A7.

Assignments and Improvisation Tips: Yesterdays

❶ **Memorise the melody** Work out your own arrangement using some of the devices suggested on pp. 232–3, but personalise it by adding some of your own voicings or rhythms. Play it with the CD (track 40, bass and drums only).

❷ **Listen to the solo** Get hold of the Hampton Hawes trio album and follow the transcription whilst listening to the track. Note the long *rubato* intro, leading to a flowery statement of the head; the solo starts at 2:34. Hawes re-enters after the bass solo, but instead of playing the head (section 'A') he improvises again for sixteen bars, coming in at 'B' for the final melody.

❸ **Left-hand chords** Notice how the pushy left-hand chords really help to drive the solo along. Listen to each bar in turn and work out which beat the chords are played on, marking them (in pencil) on the empty stave under the relevant right-hand notes.

When you have the rhythm of the chords try to hear which notes they contain. You might guess from the sound if it's a shell, a three-note or four-note voicing, etc. Try your own left-hand ideas too to see how they sound.

❹ **Play the solo** Once you've practised it, play the transcription at 160 bpm with track 40 (silencing the piano), without the left hand. Next you might add some left-hand chords. Then try playing the solo along with the record at 180 bpm!

❺ **Improvise your own solo** Using a left hand similar to that suggested for the head, try your own right-hand improvisation. First of all, try a vertical solo, using arpeggios, motifs, licks, **II** – **V** patterns, etc. For this style you need to be on top of the changes at all times. If you can't keep up, halve the tempo and try again.

❻ **Short II – V patterns** To help with the above, review *Short II – V Workout* and the associated patterns (pp. 68–71), adapting them to Eø – A7♭9. Remember also that any of the dominant chords in bars 9–12 can be played as a short **II** – **V**, as described in the Checkpoint.

❼ **Horizontal improvisation** You could try this over the first six bars, playing in the key of Dm (blues scale, natural minor or harmonic minor). Make sure not to play anything that clashes with your left-hand chords.

Minor II – V – I choices

The next piece, *Softly as in a Morning Sunrise,* features a **II** – **V** – **I** in C minor every two bars for the first sixteen bars:

| Cm | Dø G7 | Cm | Dø G7 |

When you see chord symbols like this in a fake book, you are being given quite a bit of choice. You could play them like this:

| Cm7 | Dø G7♭9 | Cm7 | Dø G7♯9 |

or like this: | Cm6 | Dø G7♯5 | Cm6 | Dø G7♯5 |

or like this: | Cm9 | Dø G7alt | Cm9 | Dø G7alt |

or any combination of the above. As we've seen, you could also add or substitute chords to give sequences like those on p. 229. In some situations it is also possible to simplify the sequence by omitting either the **II** or the **V** chord:

| Cm | G7 | Cm | G7 |

or: | Cm | Dø | Cm | Dø |

This last option corresponds to the chords we'll play in the left hand for the first eight bars of *Softly as in a Morning Sunrise* on p. 236.

In *Blue Bossa* I suggested improvising over Dø – G7 – Cm7 using the C natural minor scale, which has the same notes as E♭ major. By doing this you are really treating the key of Cm as if it were its relative major, E♭. The chords that fit C natural minor are the same as the chords from the scale of E♭ major, starting on Cm7:

Fig 10.11: C natural minor scale and the chords constructed from it

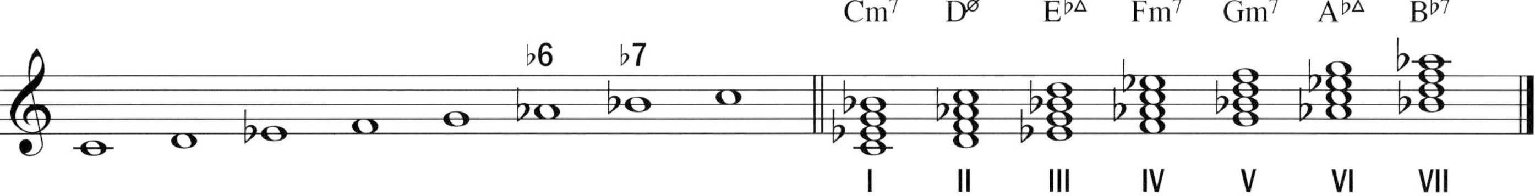

Although this is a convenient and simple solution, it is not completely satisfactory, mainly because of the lack of a dominant chord on **V**.

The harmonic minor scale

As its name suggests, this scale gives another set of chords which correspond better to the flavour of the minor key:

Fig 10.12: C harmonic minor scale and the chords constructed from it

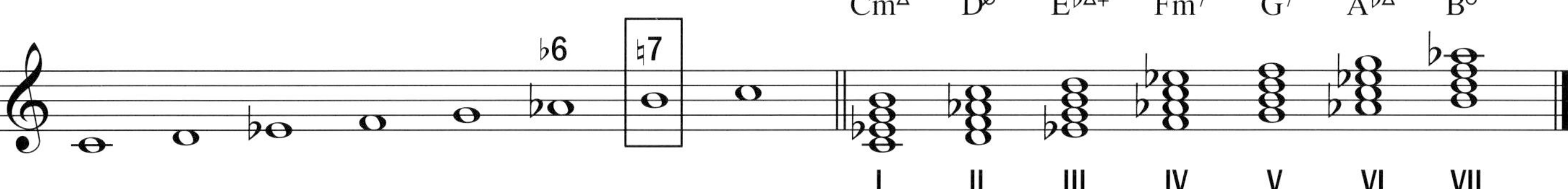

There's now a dominant seventh (G7) on **V**, but the **I** chord has changed to CmΔ because of the major seventh in the scale.

We've already come across the harmonic minor in the following contexts:

- *Montuno for Monty* (Vol. 1, p. 74)
  Key Dm: D harmonic minor over **V** – **I** triads: A – Dm
- *Fly Me to the Moon* (Vol. 1, Fig 4.18)
  Key Am: A harmonic minor over **II** – **V** – **I** chords: Bø – E7 – Am7
  Take care not to let the G♯ in the scale clash with the G in the Am7 chord
- *Summertime* (Fig 8.23)
  Key Am: A harmonic minor over alternating **I** – **V** chords: Am – E7
  There's no clash here, since an Am triad is used as the **I** chord.
- *White Russian* (Vol. 1, p. 215)
  Key Fm: F harmonic minor over ♭**VI** – **V** – **I** chords: D♭Δ – C7 – Fm
  As above, this works because **7** is absent from the **I** chord.

Try using a C harmonic minor scale to improvise over all three chords of a **II** – **V** – **I** in C minor, as in the solo sections of *Softly as in a Morning Sunrise* overleaf:

Fig 10.13: Horizontal improvisation using C harmonic minor scale

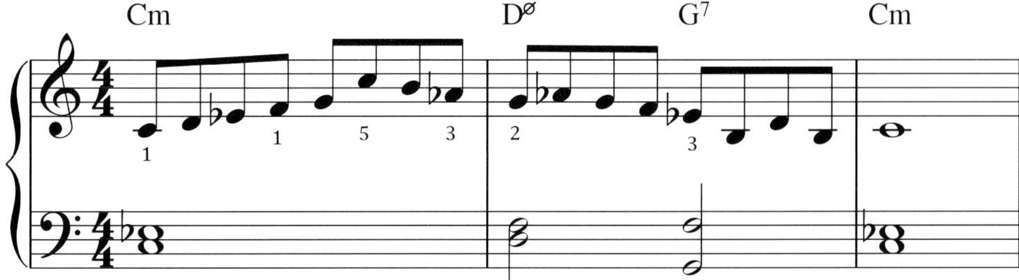

The Cm chord in Fig 10.13 is given as a **R3** shell to avoid the clash when Cm7 or Cm6 are played with the harmonic minor scale. See also 'Major and minor tonic chord choices', Vol. 1, p. 213.

41 with drums
Bass enters for solo

♩ = 144
(swing 8s)

Softly
as in a Morning Sunrise

Sigmund Romberg
arr. Tim Richards

A favourite tune with jazz musicians owing to the open nature of the 'A' sections, which contrast with the diminished harmonies in the bridge

D.S. (1st ending)

Minor II–V–I

Checkpoint: Softly as in a Morning Sunrise

● **'A' sections** Since there are three of these in the AABA form, you need some variety in the left-hand accompaniment. After a G pedal in bars 7–8 on the 'two' and 'four', the left hand abandons chords, switching to a two-feel bass line for 'A2'. The E♭ and A in the second half of the Cm bars could imply a **VI** chord, Aø, which has the same notes as Cm6.

● **Tritone substitution** In 'A3' an unexpected chord is added in the left hand, D♭7♯11. This is a tritone substitute for the G7 that appeared in bars 10 and 12.

Fig 10.14 **G7♭5 and D♭7♭5 have the same notes** **G7alt and D♭13 have the same notes**

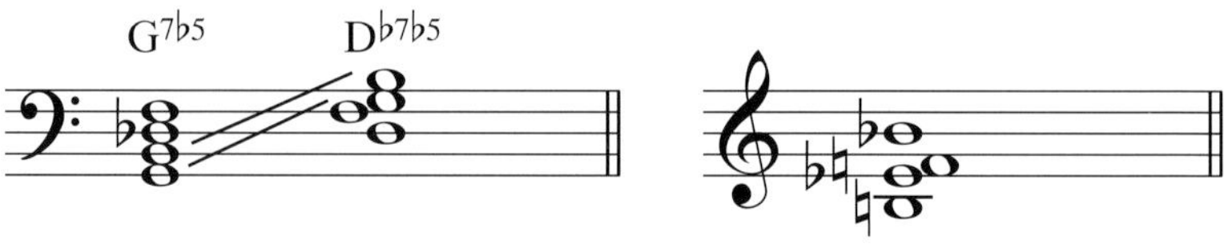

G7♭5 D♭7♭5

● **Quarter-note triplets in tenths** The **II** – **V** in bar 16 leads to the bridge – a modulation to the relative major. The left hand is a tenth below the right-hand melody, both following the notes of an E♭ major scale. Four bars later the left hand repeats this device below a similar right-hand phrase that leads to Fm7.

Practise playing scales with the hands a tenth apart, so that you can harmonise other melodies the same way, and eventually improvise using this technique.

● **Bridge** Various two-handed chordal techniques are used here, providing contrast with the single-note 'A' sections. These include three different quartal voicings:

Fig 10.15: Quartal voicings

Bar 17 **Fourths based on 3** **M3 on bottom** — E♭6/9 — P4, P4, P4, M3

Bar 18 **Fourths in both hands** **Hands also P4 apart** — E♭6/9 — P4, P4, P4

Bar 21 **'So What' voicing (see p. 36)** **M3 on top** — Fm7 — M3, P4, P4, P4

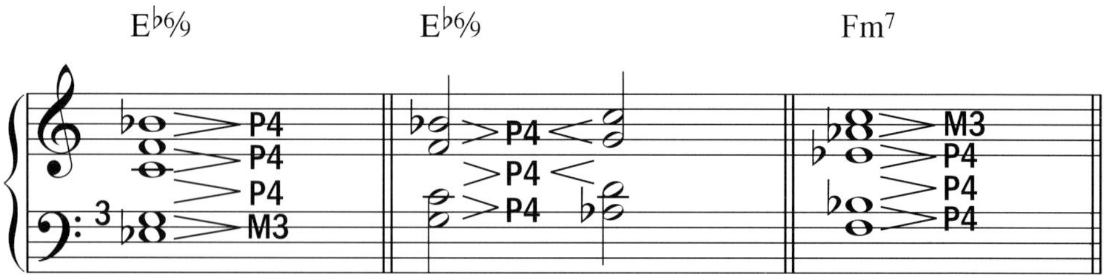

● **'Drop two' voicings** These are formed from a close voicing by dropping the second note from the top by an octave, where it is played by the left hand (see Vol. 1, p. 224):

Fig 10.16: 'Drop two' voicings in the bridge

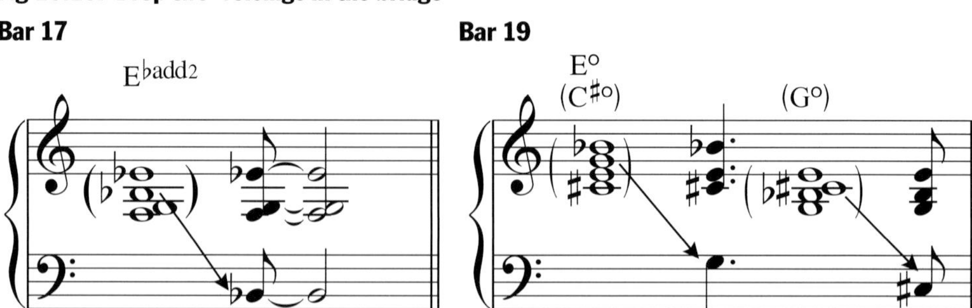

● **Solo** Left-hand shells are suggested to accompany your improvisation, but you could also use the bass line from 'A2'. When playing your solo, aim to put the left hand on 'autopilot' so that you can concentrate on your right-hand lines. In the bridge of the solo remember to vary the rhythm of the left-hand chords. If playing alone you could work out a bass line instead (two-feel, walking bass, or even 'Latin'), or perhaps a stride or 'pseudo-stride' accompaniment (see *Misty*, pp. 106–111). For Assignments, see p. 246.

Tritones for minor II – V – I

So far we've mainly used tritones as an easy way to play dominant seventh chords in the left hand – **37** or **73**. It is not possible to play a tritone for a major or minor seventh chord, because they contain no tritone intervals (unless you count **R – ♯11** in a major seventh, which may not be appropriate).

Half-diminished chords and minor sixth chords both include a tritone interval, however:

Fig 10.17

Providing a minor sixth is acceptable as the **I** chord, an easy way to play a minor **II – V – I** in the left hand is therefore:

Fig 10.18: Tritones for II – V – I in C minor

Fig 10.18 would also work for Dø – D♭7 – Cm6, since the tritones for G7 and D♭7 are the same. This would be an example of tritone substitution of the **V** chord, as in bars 25–28 of *Softly as in a Morning Sunrise* on p. 237.

The octave below middle C is the ideal register to play tritones – any higher and they sound rather thin. If playing in a different key you may need to invert them to keep them in the right place on the keyboard:

Fig 10.19: Tritones for II – V – I in G minor

The movement of the tritones is the same for both configurations of the minor **II – V – I** (Figs 10.18 and 10.19). Memorise the rules:

- For the **II** chord, play either a **R5** or a **5R** tritone
- Move it up a minor third for the **V** chord
- From **V**, move it down a tone for the **I** chord

In his solo on *Softly as in a Morning Sunrise* (given overleaf), Wynton Kelly uses tritone substitution on the **II** chord, giving A♭7 in place of the Dø in Fig 10.18:

Fig 10.20: Key C minor – tritone substitution on the II chord

♩ = 126
(swing 8s)

Wynton Kelly's solo on Softly

transcr. Tim Richards

This is the first chorus of the piano solo from the 1959 album 'Kelly Blue' (Riverside OJCCD-033-2), recorded the same year as 'Kind of Blue', with the same rhythm section – Paul Chambers (bass) and Jimmy Cobb (drums).

From THE NEW MOON
Music by Sigmund Romberg

Checkpoint: Wynton Kelly's solo

● **Horizontal style** This is a much more horizontal improvisation than Hampton Hawes' solo on *Yesterdays* (p. 232), at least during the 'A' sections. Note how Kelly uses the C blues scale not just over C minor, but over A♭7 and G7 too.

Actually both pianists would frequently mix both styles of improvising. I have selected these particular solos to demonstrate the difference.

● **Gospel IV – I** As well as some great blues scale phrases, there is also borrowing from the gospel idiom in bar 7, when the left hand inserts an F triad in front of the Cm chord, giving a **IV** – **I** 'Amen' cadence. This unexpected touch also crops up in the head on this track and was in fact a favourite device of Kelly's.

● **Diminished scale** Over the E° chord, Kelly plays an E diminished scale straight up in sixteenth-notes, starting on B♭, tone/semitone alternating. This is the same as a B♭ diminished scale. As you would expect, it is tone first.

● **Double-time passages** Playing lines in sixteenth-notes without 'fluffing' is a test of any pianist's technique, knowledge and time feel. Wynton Kelly and Hampton Hawes were both masters in this respect.

● **Swing eighth-note feel** Notation cannot adequately convey the nuances of swing, so without hearing the record you are unlikely to sound very convincing. Remember that eighth-note lines must be played with a triplet feel, thus:

● **Holding back** In places, such as the boxed phrase in bar 10, there is a delayed feel which is hard to transcribe accurately without making it impossible to read. I have given the first two notes in bar 11 as a triplet, with the quarter-note last – back to front from normal. Here's the whole phrase in triplet notation, showing that the notes are all the same length, with a quarter-note triplet straddling the bar-line!

Fig 10.21: Bars 10–11 notated in triplet feel

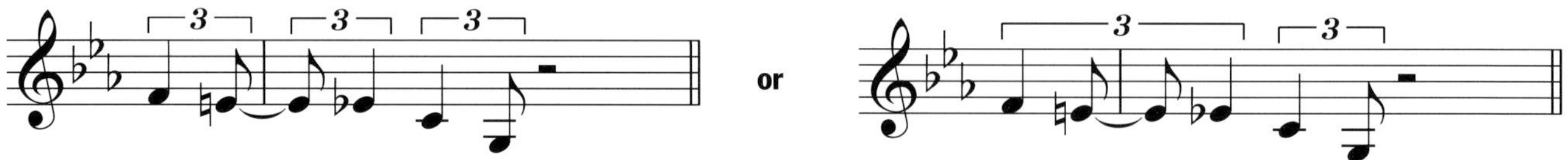

The diminished scale and minor II – V – I

We already know from Chapter 8 that a B diminished scale fits a G7♭9 chord. Because Dø and G7♭9 differ by only one note (see Fig 10.7) you can often use it for the half-diminished chord too. This is easy if you think of the diminished scale as beginning on D, the root of the **II** chord, instead of B:

Fig 10.22: For Dø – G7♭9 play a D diminished scale over both chords

Because the D diminished scale contains a C♯, care must be taken to avoid clashing with the C in the Dø chord, so this method is not perfect. One solution is to avoid playing the C♯ entirely:

Fig 10.23: Play the Dø phrase a minor third up for G7

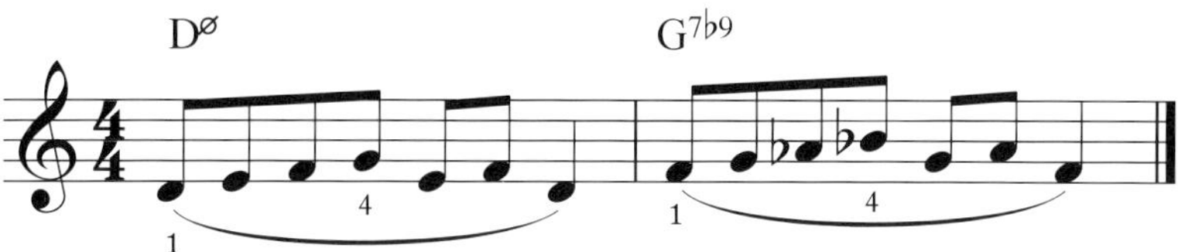

Fig 10.23 works even better with a little rhythmic displacement or forward motion:

Fig 10.24: The same phrase starting a beat earlier

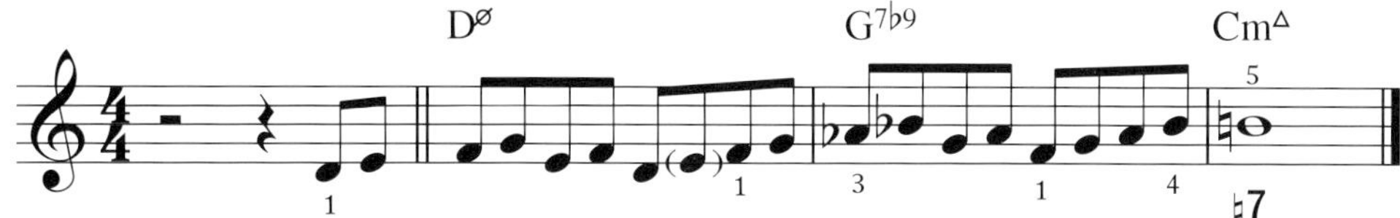

Another solution is to leave the area of the scale around C♯ until the G7 bar, where it becomes the **♯11**. In the short **II – V** examples below this occurs in (a) and (c):

Fig 10.25: Diminished patterns for short II – V

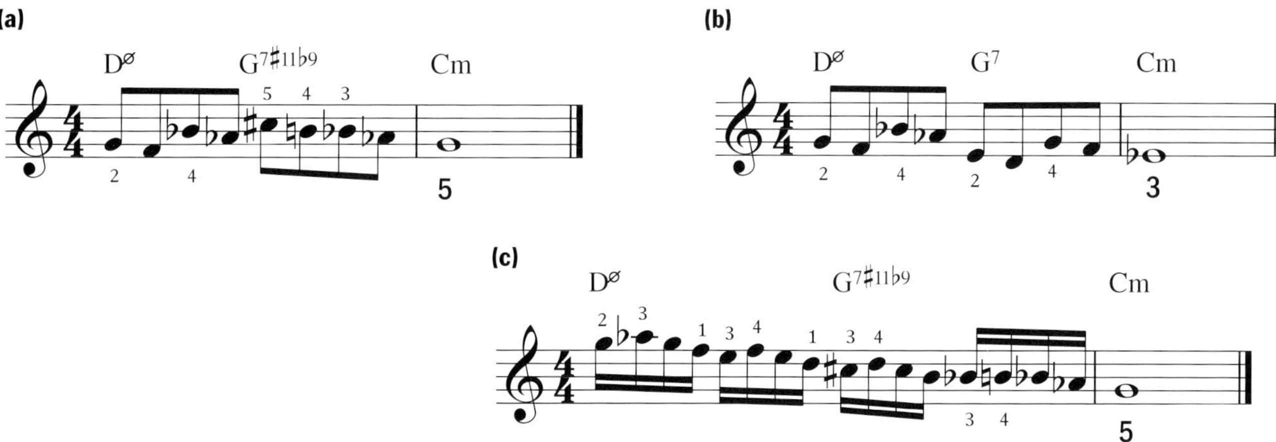

Any diminished phrase can be repeated at minor third intervals, giving four phrases 'for the price of one', which is part of its fascination for jazz musicians. When applying this over a minor **II – V – I** remember to avoid the aforementioned clash with the seventh of the half-diminished chord. I have given an example of this pitfall with the following pattern, which works fine if you start on D or F, but not on A♭ or B:

Fig 10.26: Diminished phrases can start in four different places

(a) Successful phrases

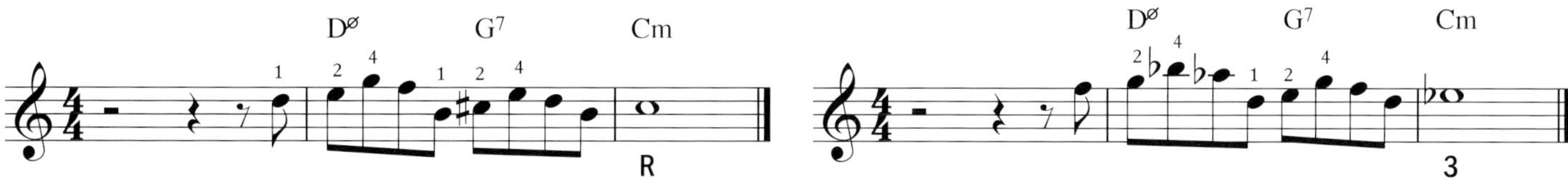

(b) Unsuccessful phrases

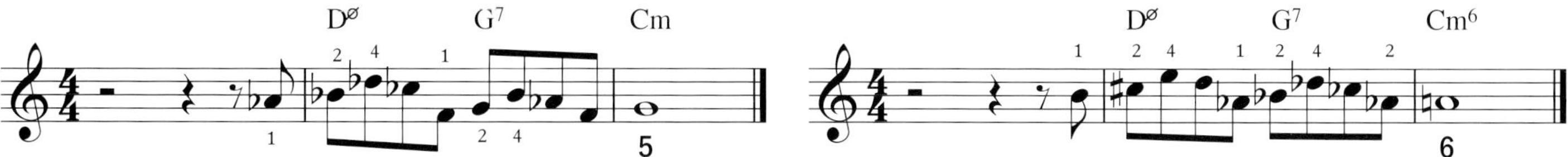

Notice that all the examples on this page resolve to a target note of the Cm chord – **R**, **3**, **5**, **6** or **7**. Don't leave your diminished lines hanging in the air!

The diminished scale in block chords

In addition to 'drop two' and quartal voicings, the bridge of *Softly as in a Morning Sunrise* on p. 236 contains the following voicing for a diminished chord, with the melody notes doubled in the left hand:

Fig 10.27: Bridge, bar 22

This is derived from the Shearing block chord technique described in Vol. 1, p. 223, adapted for a diminished scale. To visualise this on the keyboard, first of all play all four inversions of F♯° in the right hand, in close position, doubling the top note an octave lower in the left hand. For convenience we'll start on C°:

Fig 10.28: The F♯° family of inversions

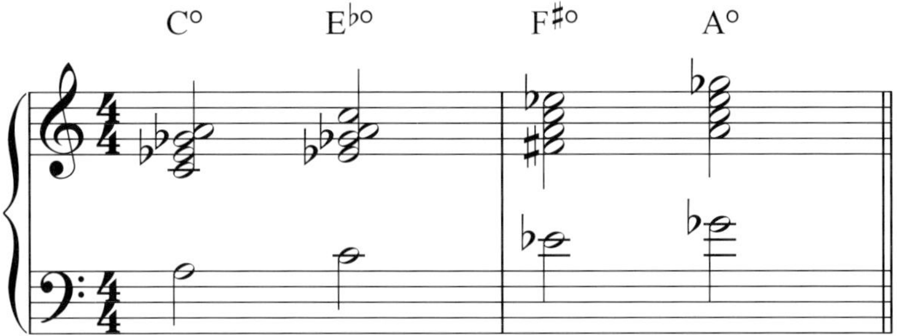

Without moving the inner voices, move the top note of each shape up a tone, following with the left hand too. This will give the notes of the diminished scale:

Fig 10.29: The diminished scale played in block chords

Play this over and over until memorised. To play it smoothly each diminished chord must be played with *1234* fingering, leaving the fifth finger for the single note that follows, which may feel awkward at first.

Now try the same thing coming down, this time playing the chords together with the fifth finger, the fourth finger following alone:

Fig 10.30: Descending block chord pattern

The ear-catching sound of Fig 10.30 is mainly due to the semitone clash between the left hand and the bottom note of each right-hand chord.

On the album 'Kelly Blue', Wynton Kelly plays a similar phrase over the E° in bars 19–20 of *Softly as in a Morning Sunrise* (at 1:12 on the recording):

Fig 10.31: Wynton Kelly's E° phrase

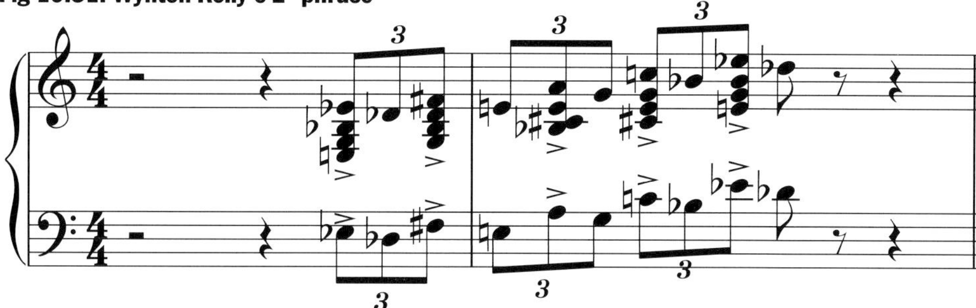

All the notes in Fig 10.31 are from the E diminished scale. The basic outline of the phrase is a two-note motif that moves up in minor thirds, as in (b) below.

Fig 10.32

(a) E diminished scale

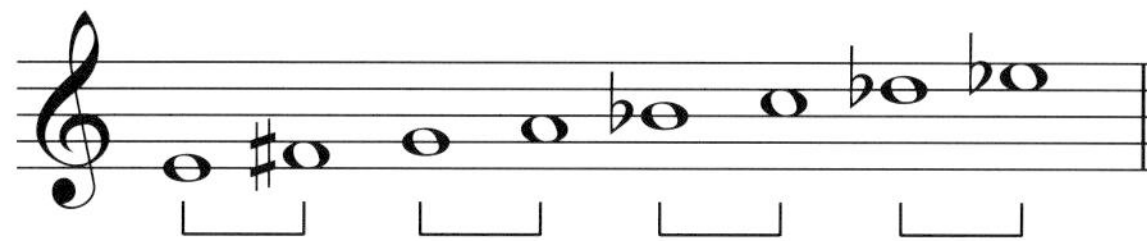

(b) E diminished scale pattern

Playing diminished chords as major triads

Phrases like Fig 10.31 are popular amongst contemporary pianists because of their distinctive sound. The right-hand chord shapes, like those in Fig 10.30, include a first inversion major triad as the top three notes:

Fig 10.33: Triad shapes in Wynton Kelly's E° phrase

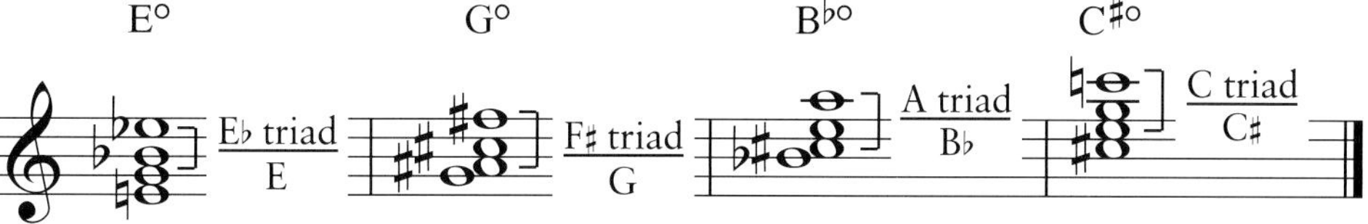

To imply a diminished chord, a major triad must be accompanied by the note a semitone up from the root. Although the triad shapes above are related to four diminished chords, all four can function as E° (as in Fig 10.31) or as any of the other three diminished chords in the same family – a minor third apart.

Since diminished chords are closely associated with dominant seventh flat nine chords (see p. 129), Figs 10.31 and 10.33 will also sound great over C7♭9 or C7♯9. Here are a couple of examples of this principle at work, this time using second inversion triads in the right hand:

Fig 10.34: V – I cadences with triads moving in minor thirds

(a) Going up (key of F minor)

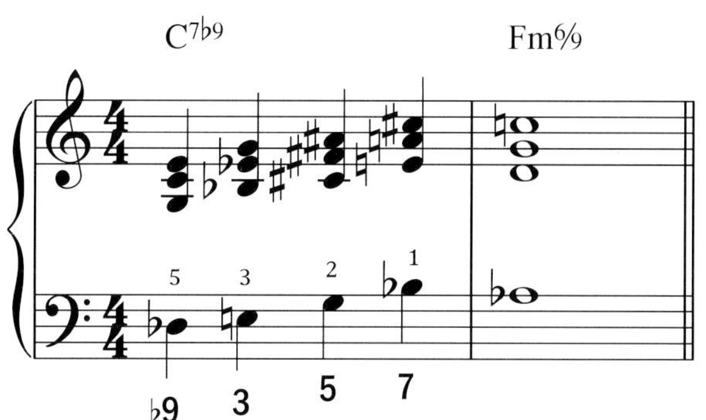

(b) Going down (blues in G, bars 10–11)

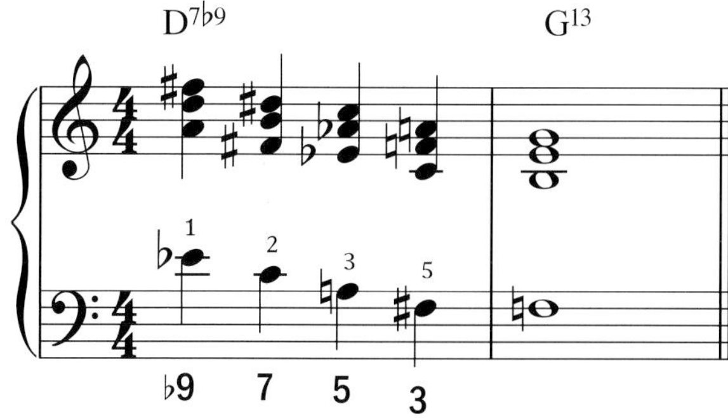

To memorise these voicings, think of the left hand outlining the notes of a diminished seventh, derived from **3**, **5**, **7** and **♭9** of the dominant chord.

Assignments: Softly as in a Morning Sunrise

❶ **Melody** Work on this with various left-hand accompaniments, as suggested on pp. 236–7 and the Checkpoint. Spend some time mastering the two-handed voicings in the bridge before attempting to play along with track 41, silencing the piano on the CD. Play bass lines in the first chorus only, which is just with drums. The remaining three choruses are with bass – play shells or chords in the left hand.

❷ **Listen to Wynton Kelly** Get hold of the 'Kelly Blue' album and listen to *Softly* while following the solo transcription. You might try to play the solo along with the recording (having practised it first), or you could have a shot at transcribing the second chorus (see p. 220 for some tips).

❸ **Minor II – V – I** Work on your right-hand improvisation for the 'A' sections, playing the Cm – Dø – G7 sequence over and over with some of the right-hand techniques suggested, eg:

- C harmonic minor scale over all three chords
- C blues scale over all three chords
- D diminished scale over Dø – G7 (see p. 242)
- Arpeggios of the chords (include ♭**9** or ♯**9** on G7)
- **II** – **V** licks, chord/scale licks, etc

The last few options are leading you into a more vertical style of improvising.

❹ **Left-hand accompaniment** Repeat step 3 with your choice of left hand, eg: bass lines, shells, the chords shown on pp. 236–7, tritones (Fig 10.18), or rootless voicings like those given for *Blue Bossa* in Fig 10.5. For more on rootless voicings for minor **II** – **V** – **I**, see Fig 10.52, and also the solo section of *Twelve by Three*, p. 271 (bar 2).

❺ **Bridge** Having memorised the melody and chords of the bridge, work on your improvisation, making sure you can join the chords together smoothly. It is not possible to improvise horizontally over these chords as you did in the 'A' sections. Practise your diminished scales and arpeggios for both E° and F♯° so that they are at your fingertips when the time comes.

❻ **Improvise round the AABA form** Putting steps 3, 4 and 5 together will result in a complete solo. Try this by yourself at first with a simple bass line or shells in the left hand, counting the bars carefully so you don't lose the form.

Then try it with the CD (track 41), with tritones or rootless voicings in the left hand. You can hear a chorus of improvisation at 0:56, followed by a chorus of comping at 1:47. When playing along, silence the piano, to give you three whole AABA choruses with bass to practise your solo.

❼ **Diminished sounds** Practise second inversion major triads in the right hand up and down in minor thirds. Then add the left-hand notes a semitone up as shown in Fig 10.34. Also practise the diminished scale in block chords as in Figs 10.29–10.31 until you are familiar with these hand positions for all three diminished scales.

Find places to use these sounds in the head and solo of *Softly*, and eventually in other tunes such as *Yesterdays*, *On Green Dolphin Street*, *In a Sentimental Mood*, *Misty*, *Summertime*, *Caravan*, *Tension & Release Blues*, etc. If necessary convert dominant sevenths to ♭**9** or ♯**9** chords so you can use the diminished sound. Here's an example for the first three notes of *Misty*:

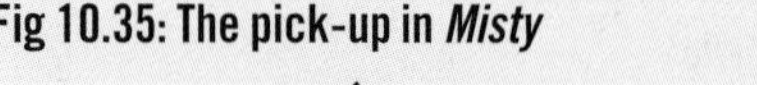

Fig 10.35: The pick-up in *Misty*

In the head you mustn't contradict the melody, but when improvising you have free rein!

❽ **Other versions** This tune has been recorded by many great jazzmen. Check out some other recordings, eg: John Coltrane 'Live at the Village Vanguard', Art Pepper 'Getting Together' (with Wynton Kelly on piano), Lee Konitz 'Windows' (duo album with pianist Hal Galper), Sonny Rollins 'A Night at the Village Vanguard' (no piano on this one), Bobby Timmons 'In Person', Sonny Clark Trio, etc.

❾ **Review *Yesterdays*** Apply some of the left- and right-hand techniques we've learnt in *Softly* to your solo in this tune (p. 230), playing along with track 40.

Wynton Kelly, one of the most swinging pianists of all time, shown here with Paul Chambers (bass) and Jimmy Cobb (drums), with whom he formed Miles Davis' rhythm section, *c.*1959–63. After acting as accompanist for singer Dinah Washington in the early 1950s, Kelly formed his own trio. He was one of the most popular sidemen of the 1960s, recording with John Coltrane, Cannonball Adderley, Hank Mobley, Sonny Rollins, Wes Montgomery and many others. His death in 1971 aged only 39 was a great loss to jazz.

BALDWIN

Tension and release with R235 patterns

In *Caravan* (p. 144) we moved a three-note rootless C7#9 shape up and down in minor thirds to give us variety in the left-hand accompaniment for C7 (Fig 8.58). This is a similar sound to the major triads moving in minor thirds shown in Fig 10.34(a):

C triad	E♭ triad	F# triad	A triad
C#	E	G	B♭

The bass note for each slash chord is a semitone up from the root of the triad. Play the voicings on the piano as in Fig 10.34 and see how each one implies a different type of C7 chord, all of which are derived from the E diminished scale. Apart from the first, all are rootless:

C7♭9	C7#9	C7♭9#11	C13♭9
(no **7**)		(no **3**)	

You played E♭, F# and A triads as the right-hand part of various C7 polychords in Chapter 8 (Fig 8.78). The above voicings are not strictly polychords, since the left hand is only playing a single note, not a chord. For that reason some of them are missing **3** or **7**, which wouldn't normally happen with a polychord. That's why these voicings work best when all four are played in combination, as in Fig 10.34.

When improvising, the right hand can extend this concept and play **R235** patterns instead of major triads:

Fig 10.36

(a) R235 going up in minor thirds

(b) R235 based on R and ♭5 of a dominant chord

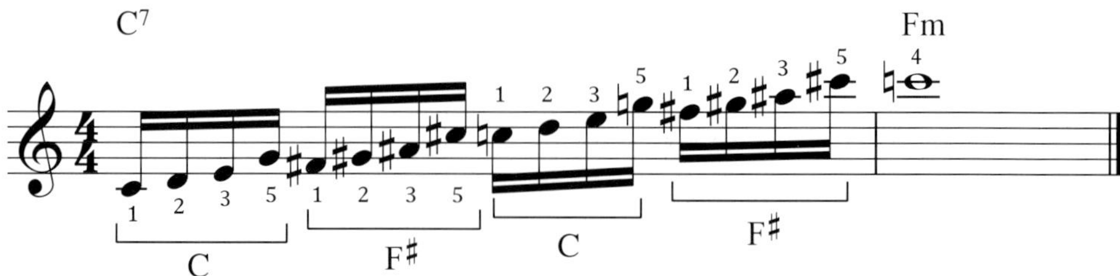

Adding the extra note to the triad (**2**) means that these right-hand lines no longer contain exclusively notes of the diminished scale – in fact the right hand is now playing some notes that contradict the C7 chord symbol, such as the second note (B♮) of the A major pattern in Fig 10.36(a). This is not a problem providing you resolve each line convincingly to finish – it's all about tension and release.

The **R235** patterns on C, E♭, F# and A each have a different amount of tension when played over C7. Try playing them in a different order from Fig 10.36 – you don't have to start on the C pattern. You could also move them up or down in tones or semitones instead of minor thirds. Use them to go 'in' and 'out' of the harmony, manipulating them to produce the effect you desire.

Using tension and release in this way is a typical postbop technique and may not sound appropriate in a more mainstream situation. On the following pages, we'll return to the minor **II – V – I** sequence, using a number of different scales to generate further **R235** patterns for use in your solos.

The melodic minor scale

In jazz this refers to the ascending form of this scale, which is like a major scale with a ♭**3**, and is played in both directions. The classical descending form is referred to as the natural minor, or the Aeolian mode.

Let's compare the chords generated by the melodic minor to those found in the harmonic and natural minors (Figs 10.11 and 10.12). Notice that the first five notes of these three scales are the same – the difference lies in **6** and **7**.

Fig 10.37(a): C melodic minor scale and the chords constructed from it

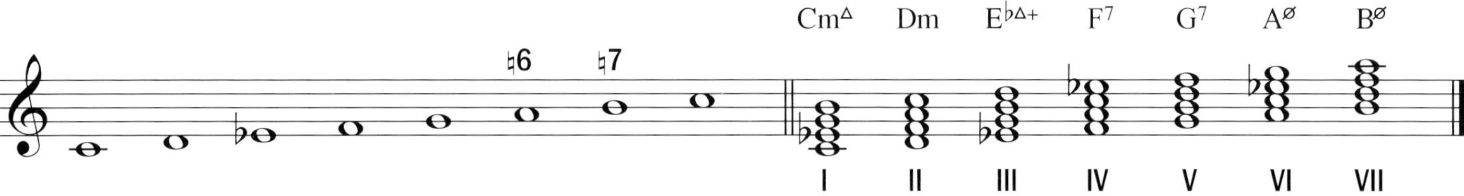

The melodic minor is very important because many of its modes are found disguised as other scales, one of which is the altered scale:

Fig 10.37(b): The seventh mode of C melodic minor

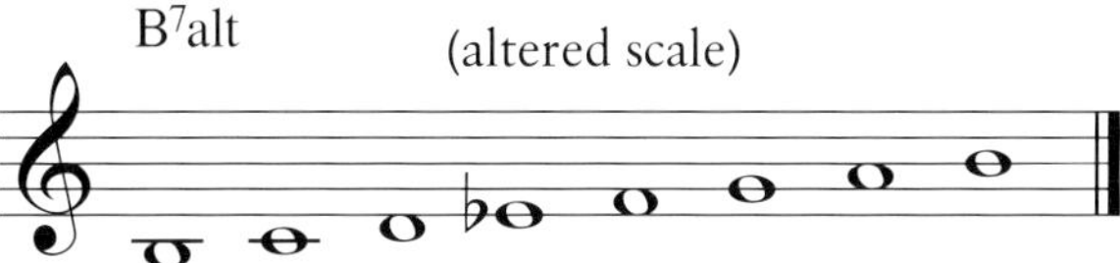

Although the **VII** chord in the melodic minor scale is Bø, this scale best fits an altered dominant chord (B7alt), since it contains the major third, D♯ (same as E♭).

One way to find the notes of an altered scale is to think up a semitone from the root of the dominant chord, giving the relevant melodic minor (eg: for G7alt, think A♭ melodic minor).

To generate **R235** patterns for the altered (or any other scale) it is not necessary to think in terms of four-note chords as in Fig 10.37(a) – triads are sufficient:

Fig 10.38: Triads belonging to G altered scale

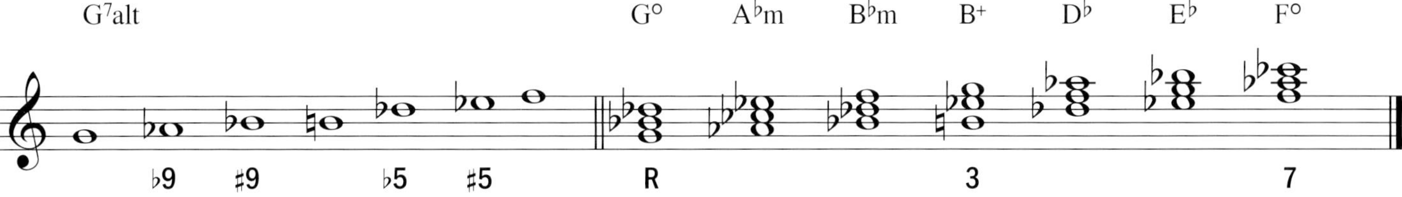

Memorise the result as follows:

For any altered scale, there are:

- Diminished triads on **R** and ♭**7** (tone apart)
- Augmented triad on **3**
- Minor triads on ♭**9** and ♯**9** (tone apart)
- Major triads on ♭**5** and ♯**5** (tone apart)

Notice that the two major triads a tone apart are the same ones we played in the right hand for altered dominant polychords (see Fig 9.3).

By adding a second to each of the triads in Fig 10.38 (using only notes from the altered scale), you'll generate a set of **R235** patterns that will work over G7alt. In the next section we'll apply this concept to all three chords in a minor **II – V – I**.

R235 patterns for minor II – V – I

In Chapter 8, p. 138, we played **R235** patterns over a major **II** – **V** – **I**, using patterns based on **3** or **5** of the chords as well as on the root. One thing you'll notice in minor harmony is that the **R235** pattern will sound good based on almost any note of the scale of each chord. That's because you don't have to worry about playing the fourth of the chord, whereas in major keys the fourth clashes with the major third in the **V** (dominant) and **I** (major) chords.

In minor keys, the fourth is fine with **II** (half-diminished) and **I** (minor) chords, and is not an option for the **V** chord if you use the altered or diminished scale (both of which contain **♯4** instead – same note as ♭**5**). The following examples include what I consider to be the four most useful patterns for each chord, but others are possible too, so experiment for yourself.

Fig 10.39: R235 choices following the scale of each chord

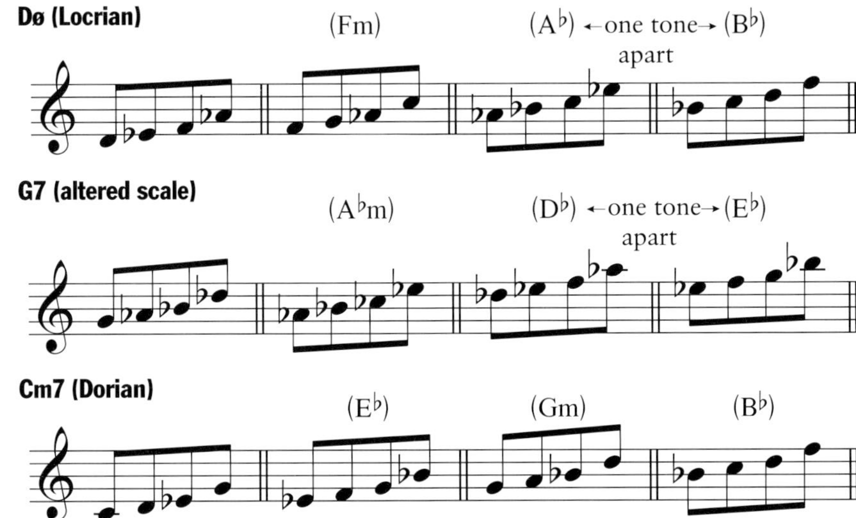

To help you remember the possibilities I have labelled each **R235** pattern above as a major or minor triad according to whether or not it has a ♭**3**. Try to memorise which notes of the chords the major and minor patterns occur on:

- Half-diminished chords minor on ♭**3** major on ♭**5** and ♭**6**
- Altered dominants minor on ♭**2** major on ♭**5** and **♯5**
- Minor seventh chords minor on **R** and **5** major on ♭**3** and ♭**7**

Other scale choices will yield slightly different **R235** patterns – for an example see p. 256, Fig 10.47. The fun begins when you try to combine patterns over a **II** – **V** – **I**, as shown on the next page. Since you have a choice of four or more positions for each chord, the number of combinations is infinite, especially when you permutate the notes within each **R235** pattern!

Fig 10.40: II – V – I in C minor (sample R235 patterns)

(a) Combining patterns

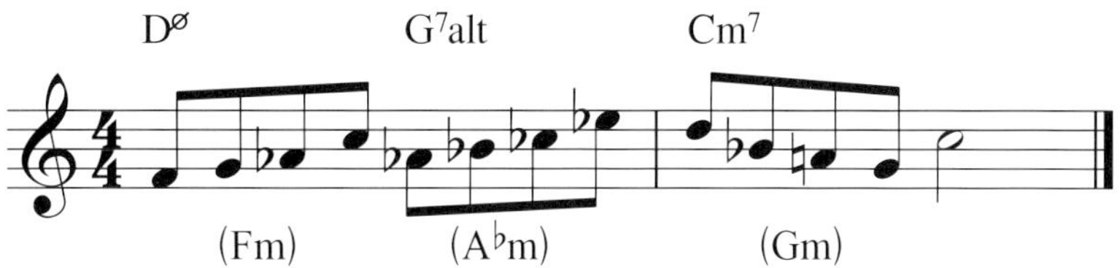

(b) Permutating the notes

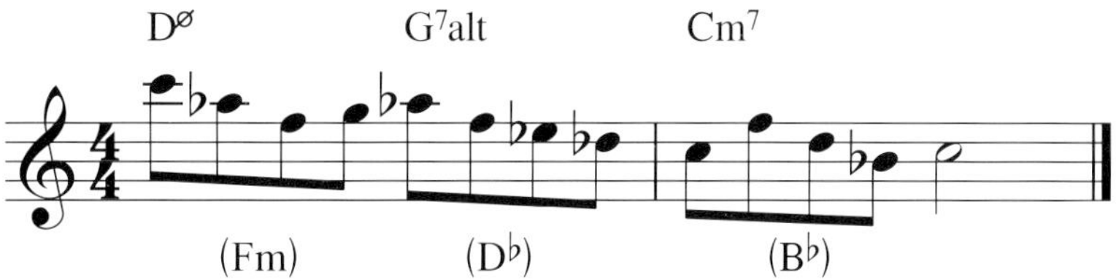

(c) Playing in double time

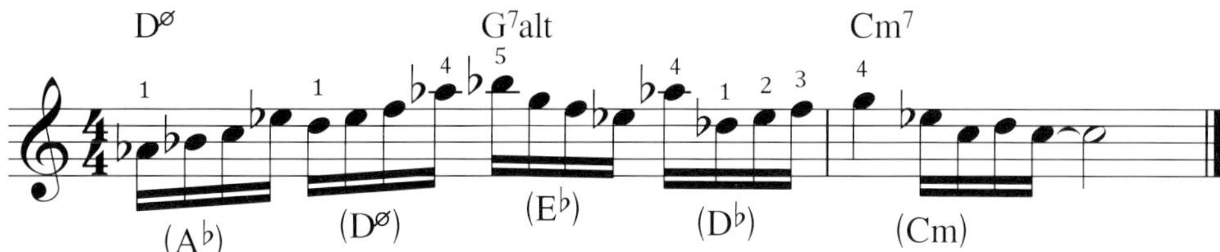

42

♩ = 108
(swing 8s)
stereo separation

Minor Turnaround Workout

Comping

Tim Richards

This features a selection of **I – VI – II – V** voicings in various rhythms over a walking bass line. Practise each key separately before playing the piece the whole way through.

Checkpoint: Minor Turnaround Workout #1

● **Bass line** This only uses notes of the chords (**R**, **3**, **5** or **7**), apart from the chromatic notes in the G minor section (boxed). The root usually falls on beats 'one' and 'three', but the last three keys sometimes have **3** or **5** instead. Practise the fingering to give a *legato* result.

● **Chords** All the rhythms are interchangeable between keys. Note the two kinds of 'on-off' rhythm in the A minor, D minor and F minor sections, 'pushed' chords in G minor (half a beat 'early'), and an 'off-on/on-off' pattern in C minor.

43 with bass & drums

♩ = 108 (swing 8s)

Minor Turnaround Workout

Improvisation

Tim Richards

This explores various ways of improvising over the same five keys as the first page, this time with chords in the left hand. Try out your own right-hand ideas during the repeat of each line.

Key: Am Horizontal improvisation – A blues scale over all chords

Key: Dm Horizontal improvisation – D harmonic minor scale over all chords

Key: Gm Bar 1: Dorian scale on G; bar 2: Locrian scale on A

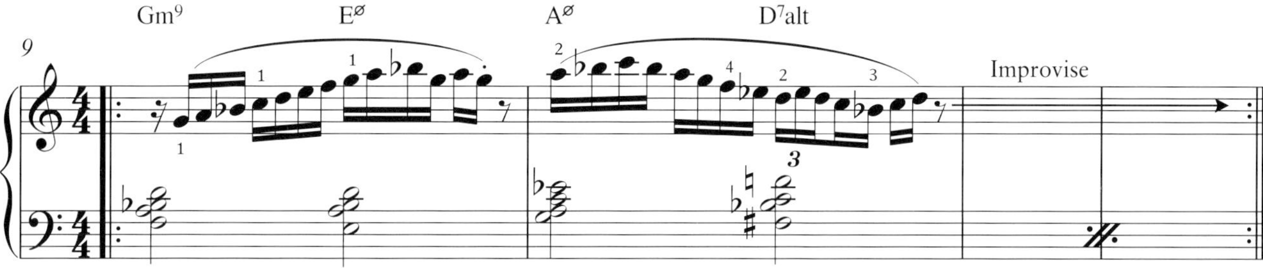

Key: Cm Vertical improvisation – bar 1: Arpeggios; bar 2: R235 patterns

Key: Fm Bar 1: Dorian scale on F; bar 2: G diminished scale

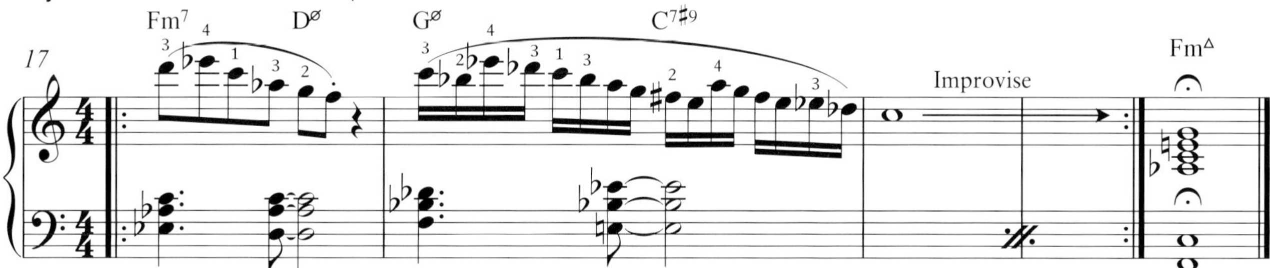

Assignments: Minor Turnaround Workout – Comping

❶ **Key of A minor** Play the bass line alone at first to get used to the fingering (first 4 bars only). Memorise the chord voicings and practise bass and chords together until you can keep a good groove. Don't go beyond the first line yet.

On a piece of paper, write out the right-hand rhythms used in each key, without worrying about the notes. Then comp in A minor as above, trying out each rhythm in turn over the same bass line.

❷ **Key of D minor** Repeat steps 1–2 for the second line. Stay with each rhythm for as long as you like, to give you a chance to settle into the groove.

❸ **Memorise the right-hand rhythms** Repeat steps 1–2 for the other keys. Aim to be able to play any rhythm with any bass line, in all five keys.

❹ **Mix up the bass lines** Study the construction of the walking bass lines. Transpose each one to all five keys so you don't always have to repeat the same patterns. A good walking bass can be as interesting as an improvised solo, even though you're only playing quarter-notes. It's also a useful accompaniment skill for duo dates.

❺ **Play along** If you've practised each key separately, you'll have no difficulty changing every eight bars, like the CD (track 42). Unlike other solo piano pieces in this book, this was recorded with stereo separation, so you can practise the right-hand chords with the bass line on the CD, by silencing the right-hand channel.

Assignments: Minor Turnaround Workout – Improvisation

❶ **Improvisation** Each key demonstrates a different approach to improvising over the **I – VI – II – V** sequence. Start by memorising the left-hand chord voicings. Apart from playing this workout as written, you should try the following:

- Practise the same right-hand concept (eg: blues scale) over all five keys
- Stay in one key and try out each of the five right-hand approaches in turn

❷ **Move away from reading the notes** Study the principles involved, so you can improvise your own phrases along similar lines. Don't worry if some of the techniques seem hard – every player gravitates naturally towards certain sounds, which is why no two jazz pianists sound the same. If you want to develop your style, practise the techniques that give you most trouble.

❸ **Double-time playing** I have included quite a lot of sixteenth-note lines because this is an area most people have difficulty with. At medium-slow tempos like this you can't afford to ignore them. One way of dealing with them is to double the tempo in your head and play in eighth-notes. Thus,

‖: Cm7 (1 2) Aø (3 4) | Dø (1 2) G7 (3 4) :‖ **becomes** ‖: Cm7 (1 2 3 4) | Aø (1 2 3 4) | Dø (1 2 3 4) | G7 (1 2 3 4) :‖

Either way, you're playing eight notes per chord. Remember that sixteenth-notes are not usually swung, however. Try the minor bebop scale in the first bar, as shown in Fig 10.43(b) – the Cm bebop scale works over Aø as well.

❹ **R235 patterns** Review Figs 10.38–10.40 to brush up on these. They'll give you a contemporary sound that is hard to achieve using scales alone. Over the G7alt chord in bar 14 I have included two patterns not suggested in Fig 10.39, one outlining an augmented triad, the other diminished:

Fig 10.41: R235 patterns based on 3 and 7 of the G altered scale

Also experiment with other scales such as those on pp. 256–7, giving you some alternative **R235** patterns.
Note that the C harmonic minor patterns in Fig 10.47 include the note D, so they'll work with a G7♭9 chord, but not with G7alt.

❺ **Improvise with the CD** When you're ready, try playing along with track 43 (or 42), silencing the right-hand speaker, so you can play with the walking bass alone. You'll need to move to a new key every eight bars. If you have difficulties, leave out the left-hand chords at first. Practising the left hand by itself is also time well spent.

Half-diminished eleventh voicings

In *Minor Turnaround Workout* you may have noticed that in all examples the seventh of the **I** chord drops a semitone to become the root of the **VI** chord:

Fig 10.42: In minor keys I and VI voicings differ by one note only

(a) C minor **(b) A minor** **(c) C minor** **(d) F minor**

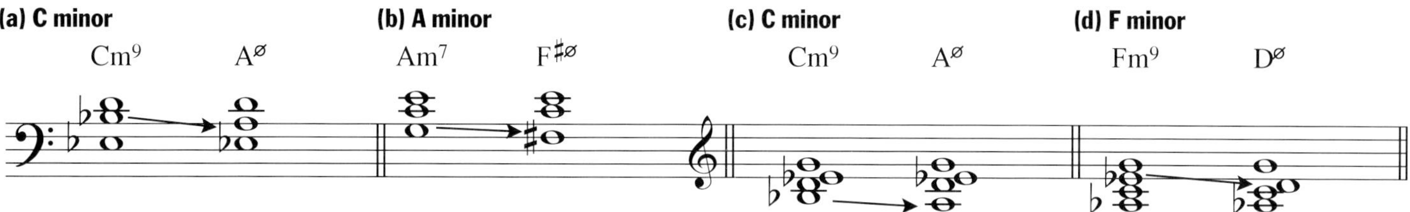

Note that this is similar to **I** and **VI** chords in major keys, eg: CΔ – Am7, where the seventh of CΔ drops a tone.

Although the half-diminished voicings above contain no thirds, they sound quite acceptable. Apart from F♯ø, they all contain a fourth instead. This could be indicated by including **11** in the chord symbol (as in Aø11), but this is rarely seen. Adding the fourth has become standard practice amongst jazz pianists, so don't wait to be told!

Although these shapes still contain roots, they blend in well with rootless voicings generally, and many musicians use them in preference to the ordinary half-diminished inversions we've used so far (see Fig 10.7).

Treating half-diminished chords as dominant chords

The **I** and **VI** chords in the examples above can both share the same scale:

Fig 10.43

(a) Dorian on C

(b) Minor bebop scale on C

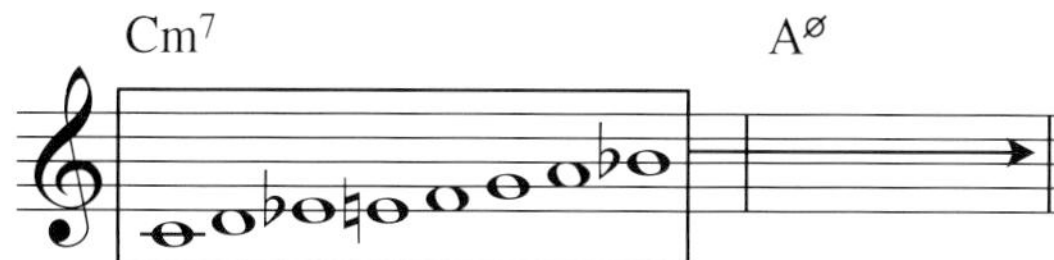

In example (a) the Dorian mode on C has the same notes as the Locrian on A (both are modes of B♭). In (b) the same bebop scale works with both chords (see Fig 7.67). These scale choices would also apply if the chords were Cm7 – F7, and indeed we find that the chord shape for Aø is the same as a rootless F9:

Fig 10.43

(c) Aø looks like F9

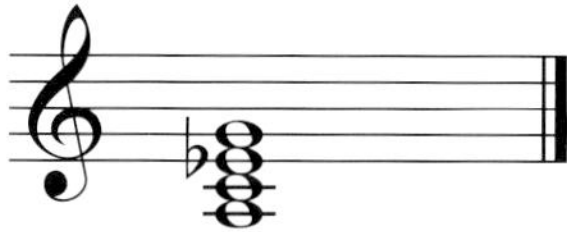

If the third of the half-diminished chord is replaced by the fourth, like the shapes in Fig 10.42, it looks like a rootless dominant thirteenth voicing. The shapes below all contain the same notes – they are inversions of each other:

Fig 10.44: Four-note shapes for Aø or F13

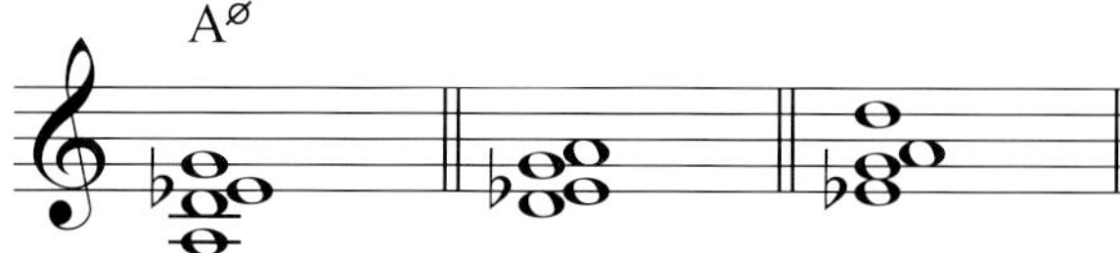

Here are three different ways of finding these half-diminished eleventh shapes easily:

- Replace **3** with **4** in any ordinary half-diminished inversion
- Think **R457** or **57R4**
- Play a dominant thirteenth shape whose root is a major third down

The bebop scale with half-diminished chords

Not only can you treat Aø as F13 (a dominant chord a major third down), you can also use an F dominant bebop scale to improvise over either chord, since it has the same notes as the C minor bebop scale in Fig 10.43(b).

Fig 10.45(a): Modes of F dominant bebop scale

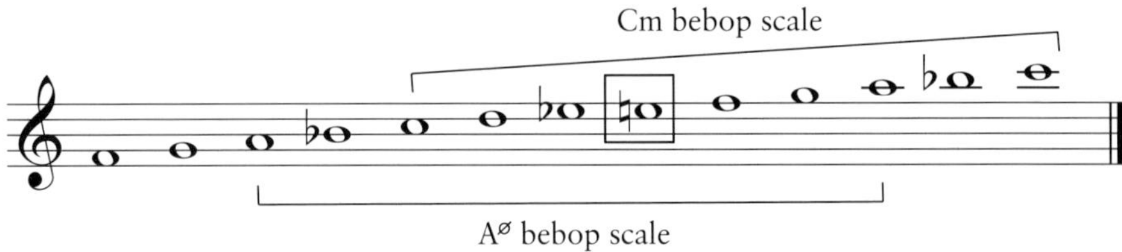

Thinking of this scale from the root of the half-diminished chord, it becomes clear that it is equivalent to the Locrian mode with an extra note between ♭**5** and ♭**6** (boxed above). Here's an example over the **II** chord in the key of C minor.

Fig 10.45(b): The B♭ dominant bebop scale over Dø

The fifth mode of the harmonic minor

We used a C harmonic minor scale to improvise over Dø – G7 – Cm in *Softly as in a Morning Sunrise* on p. 237 (see also Fig 10.13). Over the **V** chord, G7, think of the scale starting on the fifth note (G). Let's check what kind of G7 chord this implies:

Fig 10.46: The fifth mode of C harmonic minor

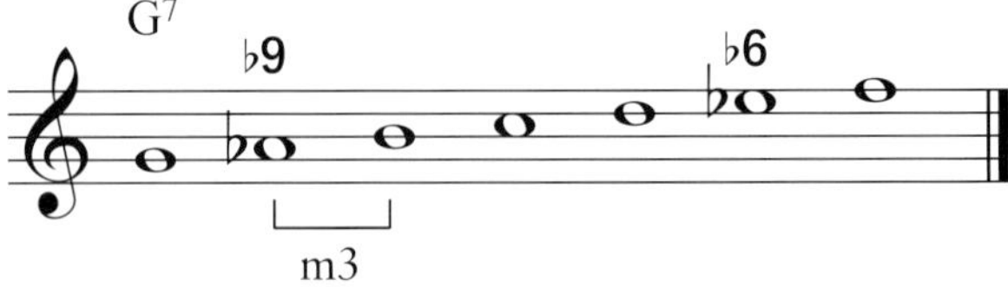

Technically, this chord should be given the symbol G7♭9♭13. The ♭**13** (E♭) is the same note as ♭**6**, and as ♯**5**, but the ♯**5** notation should be avoided in this case since the regular fifth (D) is present.

Although the scale doesn't have a proper name (other than given above), it is popular amongst improvisers because of its exotic sound, largely due to the minor third interval between ♭**9** and **3**. Cannonball Adderley and Charlie Parker used it extensively (check out the melody of Parker's *Donna Lee,* bar 2), and it can be identified in the piano improvisations of Bud Powell, Keith Jarrett and many others. Remember to use it over dominant seventh ♭**9** chords.

It can be used as an alternative to the altered scale to generate **R235** patterns over the **V** chord in a minor **II** – **V** – **I**, eg:

Fig 10.47: R235 patterns from C harmonic minor scale

Modes of the melodic minor

The fifth mode of the melodic minor could also be used over a dominant ♭**13** chord, but it lacks the ♭**9** and is not as effective as the harmonic minor version above. However, various other melodic minor modes are in common use, and have their own names, like the altered scale (which is the seventh mode, as we saw on p. 249). Here are two others:

● **The Lydian dominant scale** This has the same notes as an altered scale a ♭**5** away (see Fig 9.50). It follows that the Lydian dominant scale is also a mode of the melodic minor:

Fig 10.48: The fourth mode of C melodic minor

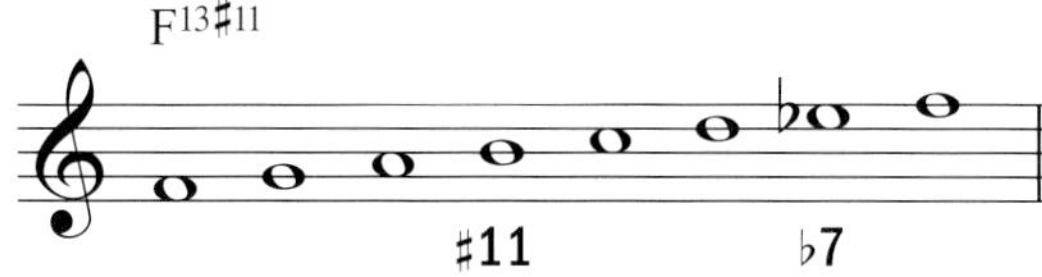

Starting this scale on B instead of F gives the altered scale for B7 (see Fig 10.37(b)). The two chords F13♯11 and B7alt are tritone substitutes of each other. In a minor **II** – **V** – **I**, you can use the Lydian dominant if you play the **V** chord as ♭**II**, eg:

F♯ø – B7alt – Em **becomes** F♯ø – **F13♯11** – Em

● **The Locrian #2 scale** The sixth mode of the melodic minor gives a scale we haven't seen before:

Fig 10.49: The sixth mode of C melodic minor

If you compare this scale to the ordinary Locrian scale used for Aø, you'll find the only difference is the second note, which is B instead of B♭. That's why it is sometimes called the 'Locrian #2' – a somewhat confusing term since **2** is only sharpened in comparison with the usual ♭**2** in the regular Locrian scale. A better description would be 'Locrian ♮2'.

Many contemporary pianists like to use this scale over half-diminished chords in preference to the ordinary Locrian mode. Try it to see how you like it – the **#2** can sound 'out' if you're not used to it...it all depends on the context.

Classification of R235 patterns

On the preceding pages we have discussed using Locrian, altered, Dorian, and modes of the harmonic and melodic minor scales as a basis for generating **R235** patterns to improvise over a minor **II** – **V** – **I**.

This results in a surprisingly large number of configurations, some of which are probably unfamiliar. In order to recognise and remember the different shapes it is useful to attempt to give them 'names', as we did in Fig 10.47:

Fig 10.50

(a) R235 patterns with major third

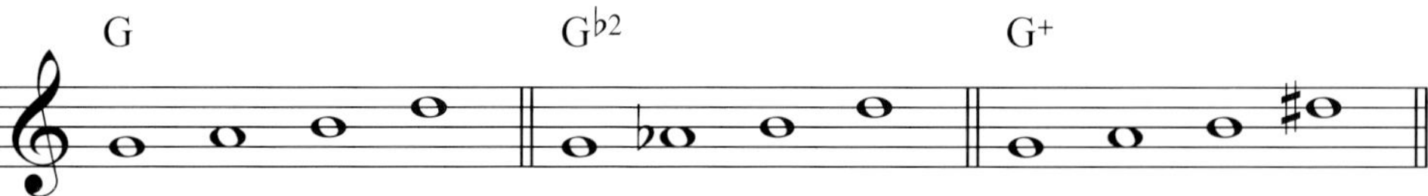

(b) R235 patterns with minor third

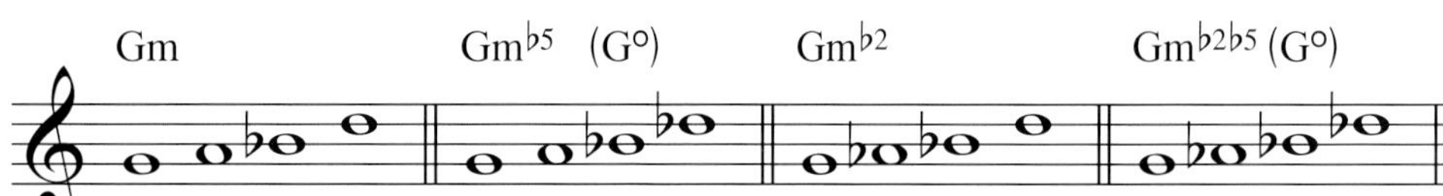

These should not be confused with chord symbols, although they serve much the same function.

Ambiguous voicings

The dominant thirteenth shapes suggested in Fig 10.44 for half-diminished chords are incredibly versatile voicings. To find out what other chords they could represent, play one in the right hand and try out various roots low down in the left hand.

Fig 10.51: Ambiguous four-note voicing

You already know that this chord could have the following roots:

- Play D in left hand — Dø — **5 7 R 4**
- Play B♭ in left hand — B♭13 — **7 9 3 6**

Other possibilities are:

- Play E in left hand — E7alt — **3 ♯5 7 ♯9**
- Play F in left hand — Fm6/9 — **3 5 6 9**
- Play G in left hand — Gsus4♭9 — **♭9 4 5 R**
- Play A♭ in left hand — A♭Δ♯11 — **R 3 ♯11 7**

It follows that you could play a minor **II – V – I** using only this shape, transposed as necessary. To avoid too much jumping around, the following examples include inversions of the shape (as in Fig 10.44):

Fig 10.52: Minor II – V – I using thirteenth voicings

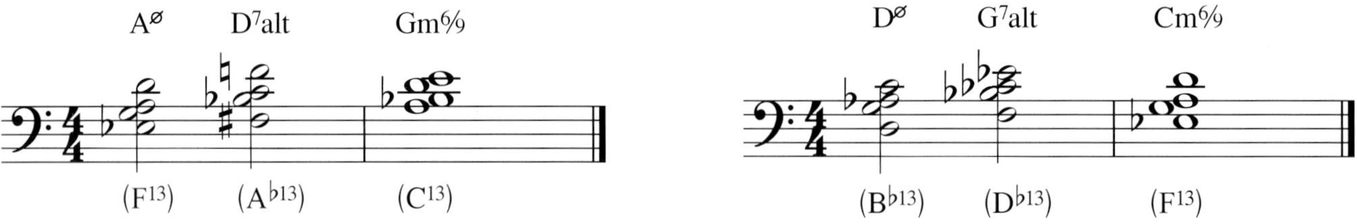

In both examples the half-diminished shape moves up a minor third to become the altered chord. We saw this intriguing relationship between half-diminished and altered chords before when playing three-note shapes in *Blue Bossa* (Fig 10.5). You also played it in bar 18 of *Minor Turnaround Workout – Comping* (p. 252): Gø to C7alt.

Here is an example of the 'minor third up' technique in the cycle of fifths sequence from the last eight bars of Victor Young's *Stella by Starlight*:

Fig 10.53: Moving half-diminished shapes up a minor third (see also Fig 10.61)

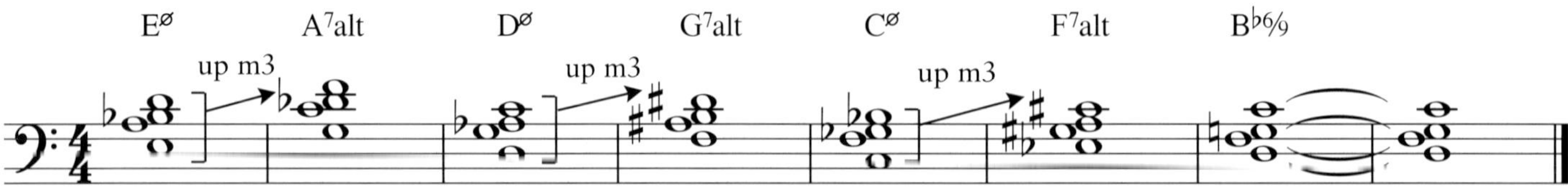

Similar four-note voicings are used overleaf in the left hand of the improvisation section of another Victor Young tune, *Beautiful Love*.

Joanne Brackeen's long career began in the late 1950s and includes a period with Art Blakey's 'Jazz Messengers' (1969–71). Touring and recording with major saxophonists such as Dexter Gordon, Charles Lloyd, Joe Henderson and Stan Getz, she established herself as an important and individual improviser. Since around 1980 she has concentrated on leading her own groups, performing original compositions which often feature quirky rhythms and melodies against a fascinatingly dark harmonic backdrop.

44 with bass & drums

♩ = 132 (swing 8s)

Beautiful Love

Victor Young
arr. Tim Richards

This medium-tempo ballad is played in a two-handed style for the head, switching (on the second page) to four-note left-hand voicings to accompany the improvisation

1 Solo
E⌀ (RH ad lib.) A7alt Dm (DmΔ9 Dm9 Dm6/9)
5
Gm9 C7alt FΔ A7alt
9
Dm9 Gm9 B♭13 A7alt
13 1.
Dm6/9 G7♯11 E⌀ A7♭9
29 2.
Dm6/9 B♭9 A7♯9 Dm9
D.S. al Coda
Coda
rall.
Dm7 B♭7 A7 Dm7 B♭7 A7 Dm6/9
Fine
Ped.

Checkpoint: Beautiful Love

● **Key centres** The key is established in the first four bars with a **II – V – I** in D minor. As in many minor tunes, there's a temporary modulation to the relative major, F (bars 5–7).

● **Form** The last four bars alternate first and second time, giving a 32-bar form for head and solos.

● **Five-part harmony** The head is played mainly with shells in the left hand and three notes in the right hand, giving five-note voicings with the melody uppermost. When playing in this style, try to avoid doubling notes.

● **'Drop two'** In bars 9–10, the melody is shadowed in the left hand a tenth below. These voicings are similar to those obtained with 'drop two' chords, where the left hand plays the second note from the top of a close voicing, an octave lower (see Fig 10.16 and Vol. 1, p. 224). For further examples of this principle, see Figs 10.58–10.59 opposite.

Assignments and Improvisation Tips

❶ **Memorise the melody and chords** Although you could improvise over the left-hand shells given on the first page, the four-note voicings on p. 261 flesh out the harmony much more, and are ideal for playing with the CD or a bassist.

❷ **Horizontal improvisation** With the exception of the C# in bars 8 and 14, the melody contains only notes from the F major scale – the same scale as D natural minor. If you're looking for an easy way to improvise over these changes, this is it! You'll need to use your ears at all times to avoid stressing notes that clash, like the following combinations: A over B♭7, E over A7alt, B♭ over Dm7, etc.

❸ **Arpeggios** I have not suggested any particular note choices for the right hand of your solo, because there are so many options. The first step towards a more vertical approach is to learn and play arpeggios and broken chord patterns over all the chords in the tune. Then base your whole solo on notes of the chords, linking them together as suggested for *Tune Up* (Fig 9.22). See also *II – V – I Arpeggio Workout*, Vol. 1, p. 164.

❹ **Scale choices** Use this tune to explore some of the scales covered so far, eg:

● Eø	Locrian mode, diminished scale, C7 bebop scale
● A7alt, C7alt	altered scale
● Dm	Dorian mode, blues scale, ♭3 pentatonic, harmonic/melodic minors
● G7#11	Lydian dominant

The different types of Dm chord in bar 4 are optional – you are free to treat these two bars (and the other Dm bars) as you wish, as long as the left and right hands play compatible chords and scales (see Vol. 1, Figs 5.50–5.51).

You could also play the A7alt and C7alt chords as A7♭9 and C7♭9, allowing you further opportunities to use the diminished scale (see pp. 242–3).

❺ **R235 patterns** Apart from bar 30, each chord lasts a whole bar, so you can play two **R235** patterns for each one. Work on doing this in as many different ways as possible, especially over the two **II – V – I**s:

Eø – A7 – Dm (see p. 250 and Fig. 10.40)
Gm7 – C7 – FΔ (see pp. 138–41)

Although a whole solo comprising nothing but **R235** patterns is not recommended, practising this type of idea can move your improvising in another direction. You need as many strings to your bow as possible, especially in a long solo, so that you don't end up repeating the same ideas over and over.

❻ **Play along** Practise all the ideas above with the CD (track 44). There is one 32-bar solo on the recording, during which I comp with the rootless voicings shown. Silencing the piano and omitting the head will give you three 32-bar choruses over which to play your solo.

The melodic minor bebop scale

You'll recall that a major bebop scale is an eight-note scale formed by adding an extra note between **5** and **6** of the major scale (see p. 91). The same note (♭**6**) can be successfully added to the melodic minor scale:

Fig 10.54

(a) C major bebop scale

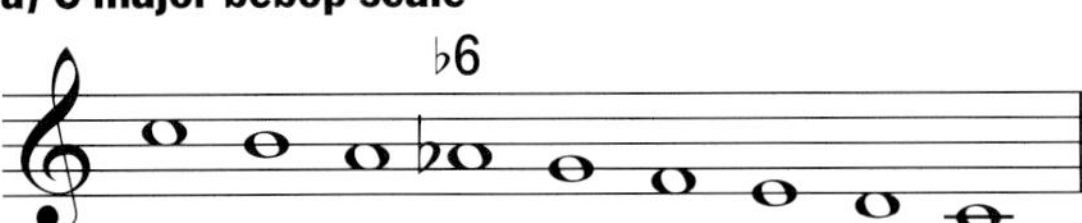

(b) C melodic minor bebop scale

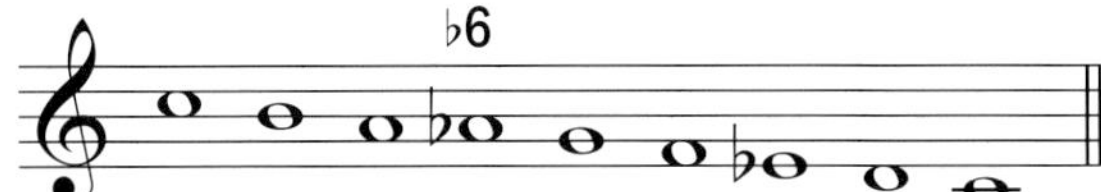

This scale works well when improvising over tonic minor chords (ie: CmΔ or Cm6) as long as the ♭**6** falls on an upbeat. It really comes into its own when played in block chords. The following example contains no notes outside the scale:

Fig 10.55: C melodic minor bebop scale in block chords

There's a satisfying symmetry here, as the Cm6 inversions alternate with diminished chords belonging to the G7♭9 family. You're really playing Cm6 – G7♭9 – Cm6 – G7♭9, and so on. We did something similar with minor seventh chords in *Summertime* (Fig 8.27).

Here's a common lick, beloved by saxophone players, which uses one of the diminished arpeggios from Fig 10.55 to create tension and release in C minor:

Fig 10.56: Cm lick incorporating diminished arpeggios

Getting back to block chords, play Fig 10.55 in both directions, with the top note doubled in the left hand, as we did for various scales in Vol. 1, pp. 223–224:

Fig 10.57: Shearing block chords for C melodic minor

To use this effect in a tune, look for melodies that move stepwise over minor chords:

Fig 10.58: *Beautiful Love* pick-up

Now try moving the note below the melody note an octave down, playing it with the left hand instead of the doubled melody note, giving a harmony line:

Fig 10.59: 'Drop two' voicings

Minor blues

Like major blues, minor blues has many variations. The most basic twelve-bar sequence goes something like this:

	Gm	%	%	%
Cm	%	Gm	%
Aø	D^{7}	Gm	%	

The **IV** chord (Cm) is often present in bar 2, and E♭7 can replace Aø by tritone substitution in bar 9:

	Gm	**Cm**	Gm	G^{7}
Cm	%	Gm	%
E♭7	D^{7}alt	Gm	D^{7}alt	

See *Blues in Three* (IBP, p. 220) for a blues in G minor similar to the above. Another version might be as follows, with a **II – V** in place of the **IV** chord in bar 2:

	Gm	**Aø D7**	Gm	G^{7}alt
Cm	%	Gm	**Eø**
Aø	D^{7}alt	Gm	E$^{♭7}$ D^{7}alt	

This example also includes a **VI** chord (Eø), creating a **I – VI – II – V** in bars 7–10 (see *Minor Turnaround Workout*, pp. 252–3). This turnaround can also be used in the last two bars instead of the given one, by playing only two beats on each chord:

| Gm Eø | Aø D^{7}alt ||

Here are some important minor twelve-bar heads you should check out:

Equinox (John Coltrane) – from 'Coltrane's Sound'
Footprints (Wayne Shorter) – a 24-bar blues in 3/4, from 'Adam's Apple'
Interplay (Bill Evans) – from 'Interplay'
Israel (Johnny Carisi) – from Bill Evans' 'Explorations' and 'Trio 65'
The Jody Grind (Horace Silver) – from 'The Jody Grind'
Mr PC (John Coltrane) – from 'Giant Steps'
One for Daddy-O (Nat Adderley) – from Cannonball Adderley's 'Something Else'
Señor Blues (Horace Silver) – from 'Six Pieces of Silver'
Solar (Miles Davis) – with altered changes, from Bill Evans' 'At the Village Vanguard'
Steps (Chick Corea) – from 'Now He Sings, Now He Sobs'
Witchhunt (Wayne Shorter) – from 'Speak No Evil'

Witchhunt, like *Dustbiter* (p. 52) and *Orinoco* (Vol. 1, p. 210), is a 24-bar blues with completely unexpected chords for the last eight bars. Variations in a minor blues can take many forms – sometimes the **IV** chord is major (as in *Solar*) or dominant, as in *The Jody Grind*. The latter also has unusual changes in bars 9–10:

	B$^{♭}$m^{7}	%	%	%
E♭7	%	B$^{♭}$m^{7}	%
A7	**B7**	B$^{♭}$m^{7}	%	

Other tunes have an unexpected change in place of the **IV** chord in bars 5–6, as with *Witchhunt* and *Orinoco*, which go to ♭**III** instead. *Señor Blues* goes to ♭**VI**:

	E$^{♭}$m6/9	%	%	%
B7♯11	%	E$^{♭}$m6/9	%
B$^{♭7}$	A$^{♭7}$	E$^{♭}$m6/9	%	

Two-handed comping for minor II – V – I

In preparation for *Blues in Fourths* next, here are some essential voicings following the 'two notes in each hand' technique that we explored in Chapter 9, p. 182. Whilst these were rootless voicings, for half-diminished chords the root is included in preference to the ninth.

Fig 10.60: Comping voicings with left-hand tritones

(a) starting with 5R in left hand

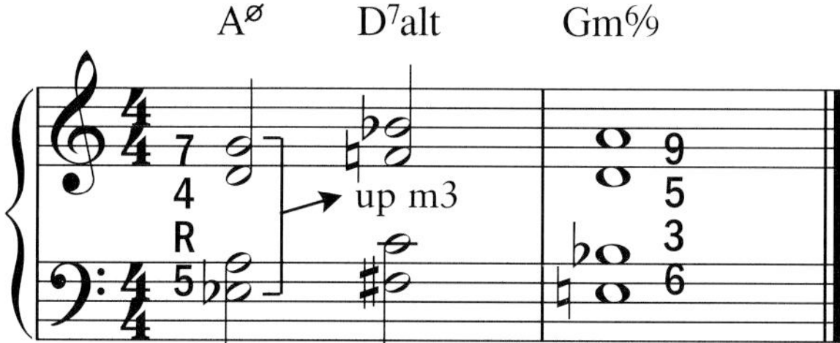

(b) starting with R5 in left hand

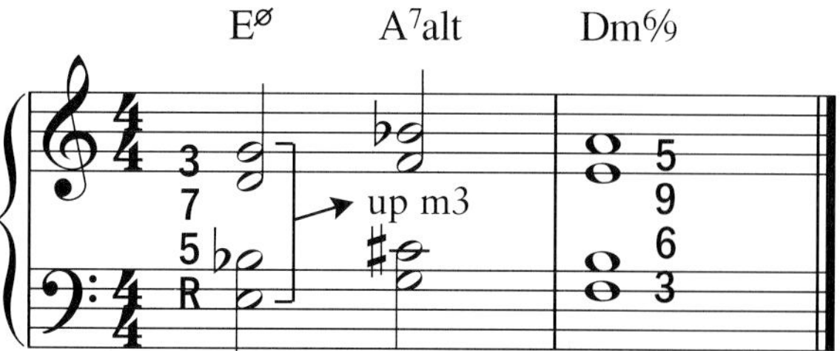

Notice the perfect fourths in the right hand above. It is also possible to play similar voicings with perfect fifths in the right hand instead:

Fig 10.61: Comping for last eight bars of *Stella by Starlight* (see also Fig 10.53)

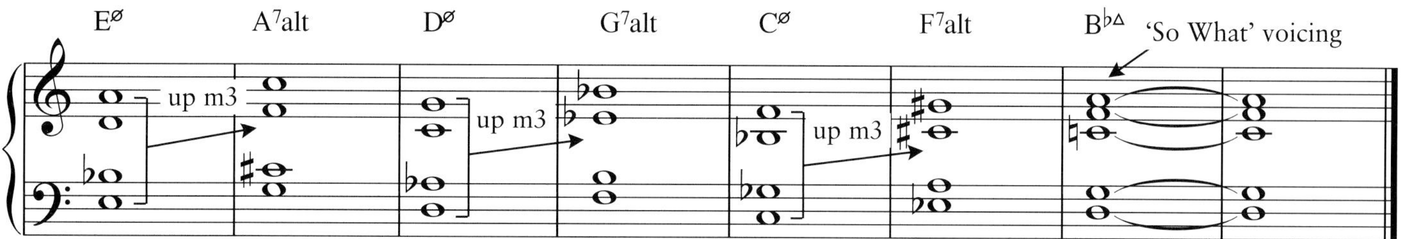

The following five-note voicings are also useful, as played in the melody of *Beautiful Love*. Practise both sets (and the voicings above) round the cycle of fifths:

Fig 10.62: Comping voicings with left-hand shells

(a) starting with a R3 shell

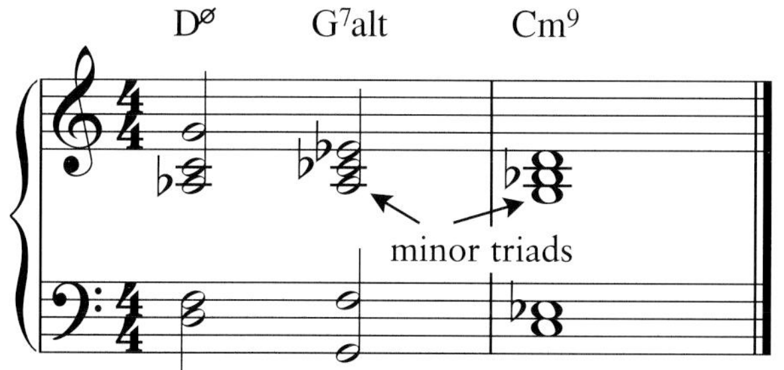

(b) starting with a R7 shell

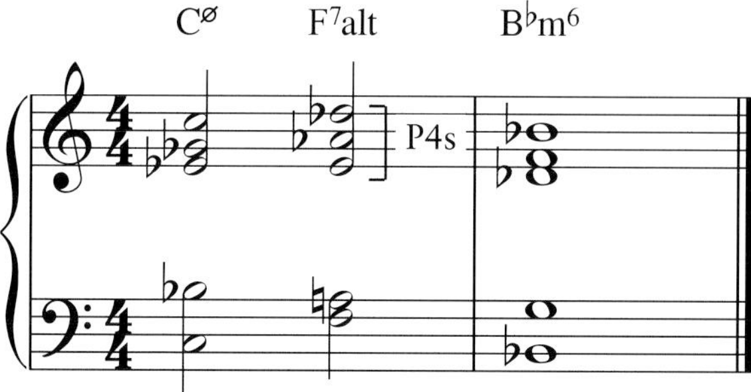

● **Polychords** Note the minor triads in the right hand of Fig 10.62(a) – the first time we have used them as the right-hand part of a polychord. The altered voicing is easy to remember as the triad is based a semitone up from the root of the chord. The triad also drops a semitone when resolving to Cm, so you could memorise these voicings by thinking:

G7alt = A♭m triad / G7 Cm9 = Gm triad / Cm

Polychords are used alongside 'So What' voicings and the other quartal shapes above in the next piece, *Blues in Fourths.*

45 **with bass & drums**

♩ = 184
(swing 8s)

Blues in Fourths

Tim Richards

The first twelve bars feature typical minor blues quartal comping with two notes in each hand. Chunkier voicings are used for the second chorus ('B') with five or six notes spread between the hands.

Checkpoint: Blues in Fourths

● **First chorus (section 'A')** The formation of these voicings is shown in Fig 10.60 – they are similar to those in *Dustbiter* (p. 52) and *Tune Up* (p. 183). Playing two notes in each hand is an ideal style of comping for up-tempo tunes, but you must make sure that all four notes are different. Work on the fingering so you can alternate adjacent voicings:

Fig 10.63: Rapid alternation between two voicings for the same chord

Moving voicings up or down a tone or semitone and back is another useful effect that creates interest. As above this is easily done if you use the right fingering:

Fig 10.64: Moving a voicing up a semitone and back

● **Second chorus (section 'B')** These five- or six-note voicings can be used in a band situation when you really want your comping to cut through, or for the climax of a solo after previously using the 'smaller' voicings above. Three styles of voicing are present:

- Three-note rootless shapes (left hand) with perfect fourths in right hand
- Three-note rootless shapes (left hand) with triads in right hand (polychords)
- Perfect fourths in left hand with two notes in right hand ('So What' voicings)

The 'So What' voicings (bars 5–8) follow the Dorian modes on C or G (see Figs 6.48 & 6.60).

Assignments and Improvisation Tips

❶ **Blues in G minor** Memorise the chord sequence and practise the written voicings at a slow tempo, gradually increasing it over a period of time until you're ready to play along with the CD (track 45, bass and drums only). Once you've tried the rhythms suggested, experiment with your own chordal rhythms. Try out other voicings too, as you see fit.

❷ **Rootless left-hand chords** Work out a set of three-note voicings for the minor blues sequence, memorise them, and practise them with the backing track, without any right hand. Here are some guidelines:

- Minor chords — play **379** or **369**, **735** or **635**
- Half-diminished chords — play **R57** or **5R4**
- Dominant chords — play **379**, **735** or **736** (sharpen **9** and **5** for altered chords)

Choose your shapes so that they flow from one to the next without any big jumps. Also try some four-note shapes like those on pp. 258 and 261 and others in this chapter.

❸ **Improvisation** Play along with track 45 (bass and drums only) with chords in the left hand. The easiest approach for the right hand is to play a G blues scale throughout. You could also use Dorian scales on G and C for Gm and Cm respectively. Then try other techniques such as diminished scales (Aø), altered scales (G7 and D7alt) and **R235** patterns (as described on p. 250).

❹ **♭3 pentatonics** Don't neglect these scales which will sound great on G and C for Gm and Cm. See overleaf for tips on using them over the other chords too:

- ♭3 pentatonic on C for Aø
- ♭3 pentatonic on E♭ for D7alt
- ♭3 pentatonic on A♭ for G7alt
- ♭3 pentatonic on B♭ for E♭13

The ♭3 pentatonic scale revisited

You will recall that the ♭3 pentatonic scale is like a major pentatonic whose third has been flattened (Vol. 1, p. 190), giving the notes **R – 2 – ♭3 – 5 – 6**. It is also known as the 'minor sixth' pentatonic, since it contains all the notes of a minor sixth chord.

If you're unfamiliar with it, the ♭3 pentatonic can take time to integrate into your playing, as it contains a major third interval between two of its notes – **♭3** and **5** (no other scale has this). As with any other scale, practising patterns is an important part of getting to know it. To start with, familiarise yourself with the basic four-note hand positions:

Fig 10.65: Four-note groups derived from the ♭3 pentatonic on G

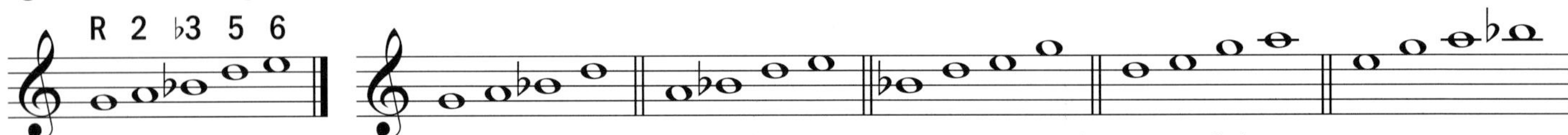

Only the first and last of these correspond to one of the **R235** patterns we used earlier in this chapter (see Fig 10.45). Try playing a four-note phrase in each of these hand positions, using the same contour and fingering for each phrase:

Fig 10.66: Playing the same motif in each four-note group

In order to best assimilate the patterns that follow, you must know these notes so well that you can play as if there were no other notes on the keyboard.

Fig 10.67: Joining alternate four-note groups, with rhythmic displacement

Now try playing alternate notes up and down the scale, the equivalent of **R3**, **24**, **35** for an ordinary scale – pentatonic 'thirds' (see Vol. 1, Fig 5.10):

Fig 10.68

(a) Alternate notes

(b) Same pattern in triplets

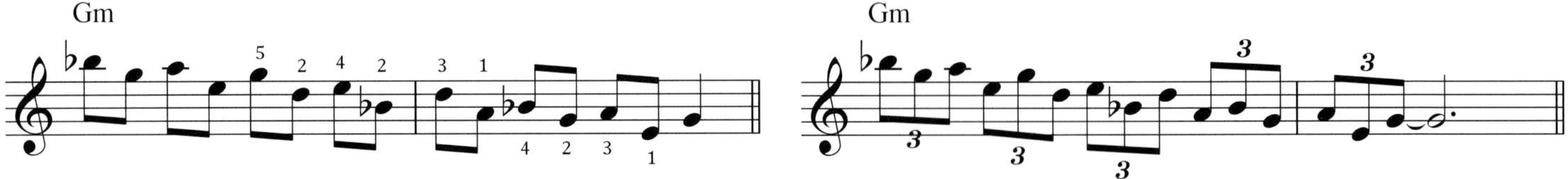

As well as 'thirds' it's also possible to think in terms of pentatonic 'triads', as in **R35**, **246** with an ordinary scale. Five interesting hand positions are created:

Fig 10.69: ♭3 pentatonic 'triads'

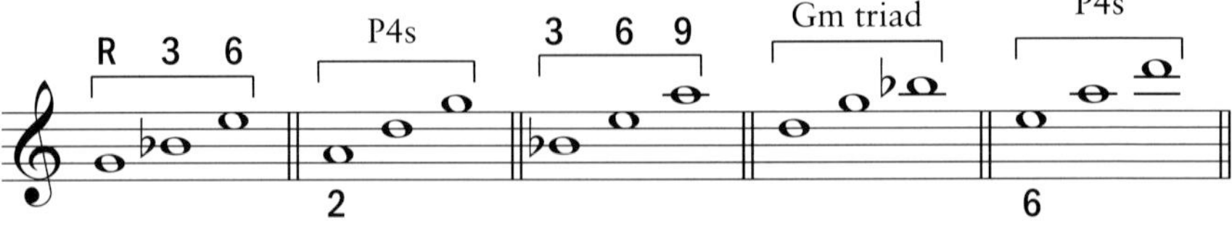

Only the fourth one of these is a conventional triad. Note the perfect fourths shapes based on **2** and **6** of the scale – memorising this will help you find these shapes for ♭3 pentatonics in other keys. Here's an idea using 'triad' shapes:

Fig 10.70: ♭3 pentatonic 'triad' motif

All the ♭3 pentatonic patterns opposite can be played over Gm6, GmΔ7, or Gm7 – but that's not all. They'll actually fit over many other chord types too, giving a distinctive sound over each, as long as you start the scale on the right note of the chord.

The following examples show the ♭3 pentatonic on C in the context of five different chords:

● **Half-diminished chords** Base the scale on **♭3** (minor third up):

Fig 10.71: Aø with ♭3 pentatonic on C

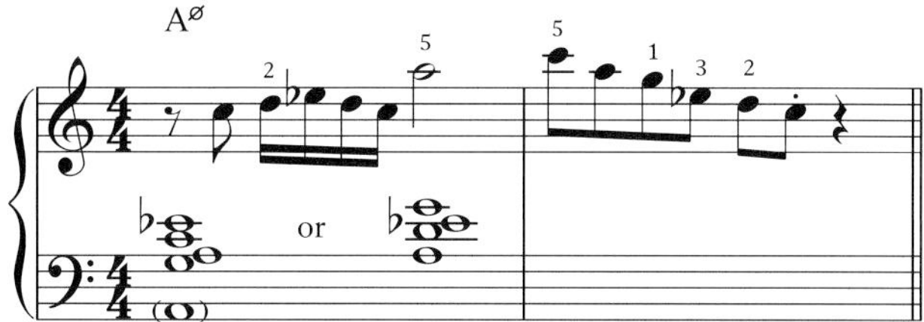

● **Dominant sevenths or thirteenths** Base the scale on **5**:

Fig 10.72: F13 with ♭3 pentatonic on C

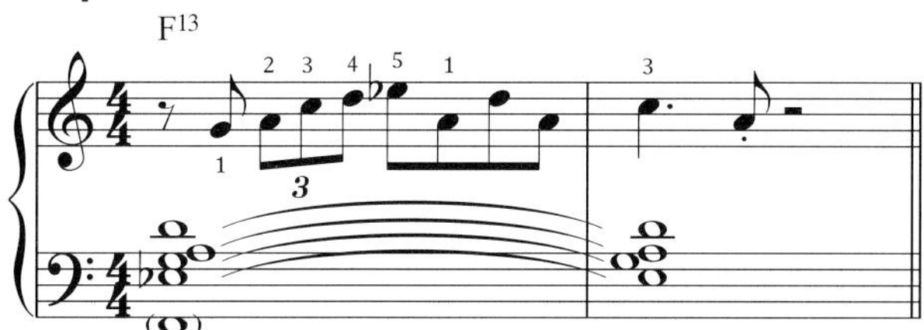

● **Dominant chords with ♭9 or ♯9** Base the scale on **♭7** (tone down):

Fig 10.73: D7♭9 or D7♯9 with ♭3 pentatonic on C

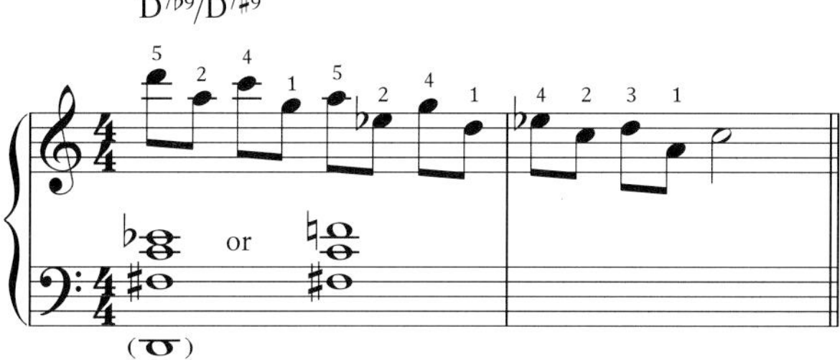

● **Altered dominant chords** Base the scale on **♭9** (semitone up):

Fig 10.74: B7alt with ♭3 pentatonic on C

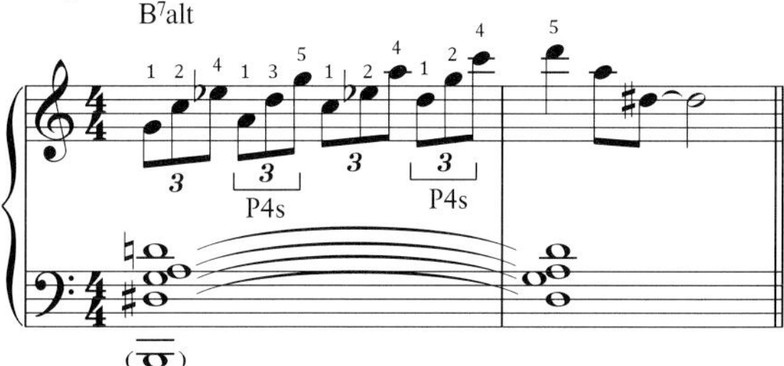

● **Major ♯11 chords** Base the scale on **6** (minor third down):

Fig 10.75: E♭Δ♯11 with ♭3 pentatonic on C

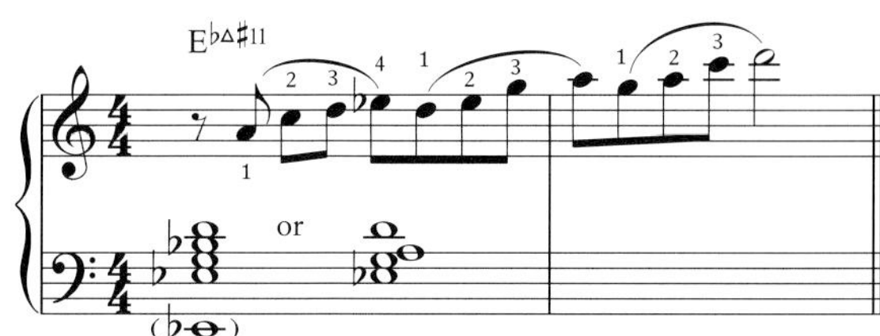

Mastering this concept will give your improvising a uniquely contemporary edge – try it over the chords of *Beautiful Love* and *Blues in Fourths*. It is demonstrated in more detail in the next and final tune, *Twelve by Three*, a blues in F minor.

46 with bass & drums

Twelve by Three

Tim Richards

♩ = 120 (swing 8s)

This minor blues can be heard on my trio CD 'Twelve by Three' (33Jazz072). The heavy shuffle groove in the intro gives way to a lighter swing feel in the head, only to return in bar 11.

Fm6
Db7
C7#9
Fm6
Db7
C7alt
sf
Solo
Fm9
Gø
C7#9
Fm9
C9
R 2 3 5
B9
b3 pentatonics
Bbm6/9
Fm9
Eb13
R 2 3 5
D13
Db13
C7alt
Fm9
minor pentatonic
1.
Gø
C7#9
2.
Db7
D.S. al Coda
Coda (Shuffle)
Fm6
mf
Db7
C7#9
Gø
C7#9
Db7
C7#9
Fm6
cresc.
Db7
C7#9
f
Gø
C7#9
Db7
C7
rall.
ff
F
Fine

Checkpoint: Twelve by Three

● **Opening phrase** This is a typical blues lick, based on the F blues scale with an F top harmony note added by the little finger. Play the B♭ grace note at the same time as the top F, using the third finger for both B♭ and C♭. To achieve an authentic effect slide rapidly off the black note with an incisive hand and arm movement towards your body, like a glancing blow to the B♭ in front of the C♭.

● **Shuffle groove** This refers to the blues drum pattern heard on the CD, typified by exaggeratedly swung eighth-notes on the snare and a heavy backbeat on 'two' and 'four'. Lock in with this feel by accenting the chords on 'two' and 'four' in the Fm bars as marked.

● **Intro** The Fm6 bars feature parallel movement of the inner voices in both hands, the top and bottom notes remaining on F, in a manner similar to *Smooth Blues* (IBP, p. 93). See also *Song for Sally* (Vol. 1, Fig 2.46). The intro reappears as an eight-bar interlude after bar 10 of the head, and again (with variations) in the coda.

● **Twelve-bar sequence** The chords in the head and solo follow an ordinary minor blues sequence similar to those given for G minor on p. 242, with some chromatic passing chords added in bars 4 and 8. The last two bars of the head (11–12) double as the first two of the interlude in a surprise return to the 'shuffle' intro.

● **Polychords** The C7alt and G7alt voicings in the last bar of the intro and bar 8 of the head both feature a major triad in the right hand based on ♭**6** of the chord:

C7 alt = A♭ triad / C7#9 G7 alt = E♭ triad / G7

● **Shearing block chords** Bars 1, 3, 5 and 7 of the head feature the melody played in block chord style, as described in Vol. 1, p. 223 – a four-note chord in the right hand, single notes in the left hand doubling the top note an octave below.

● **Solo sequence** The chords are simplified a little for the solo, but the distinctive chromatically descending dominant chords are still retained in bars 4 and 8 (C9 – B9 and E♭13 – D13). If you wish, you may improvise over a more standard twelve-bar by omitting these chords and remaining on Fm9 in these bars instead.

● **'Tierce de Picardie'** This is the classical name for a major ending to a minor tune, as played here in the final bar – an F major triad. You could embellish this chord if you wish, by adding a ♭**7** (making it F7) or by playing a right-hand blues fill based on the F blues scale. To do this hold the given chord with the sustain pedal and play the fill at the top end of the keyboard, as on the CD.

Assignments and Improvisation Tips

❶ **Intro and head** Practise these separately, paying special attention to the fingering in each. The left-hand octaves in bar 4 of the intro require a quick 'dive' down to the lowest D on the keyboard where they rise up in semitones back to F.

❷ **Solo** Practise the left-hand chords given, playing them along with the CD (track 46, bass and drums only), without the right hand, until you have them memorised. Vary the rhythms as desired.

❸ **Blues scale** Before attempting the right-hand solo suggestions, try the F blues scale over all the chords, playing along with the left-hand chords as above. Over the D♭13 in bar 9 be careful to play the ♭**5** of the scale (B) rather than a C, which will clash.

The blues scale will not work so well over the C9 – B9 and E♭13 – D13 bars, so you might play Fm chords instead here as suggested in the Checkpoint. That will bring the number of Fm bars up to six – 50% of the twelve-bar sequence.

❹ **Vertical improvisation** If you decide to play the C9 – B9 and E♭13 – D13 chords, vertical improvisation will be necessary in the right hand for these bars. Try playing arpeggio patterns or motifs based on the chords, half a bar on each, practising bars 4–5 and 8–9 over and over to develop a range of possibilities.

❺ **R235 patterns** The patterns suggested in the boxes for the C9 – B9 and E♭13 – D13 bars are an alternative way of achieving a similar result. As we saw on p. 140, **R235** patterns can be based on **3** and **5** of the chord as well as **R**, and each one can be permutated to give many different results. Here are a few ideas following the Mixolydian scale of each dominant chord:

Fig 10.76: Bars 4–5, sample improvisations using R235 patterns

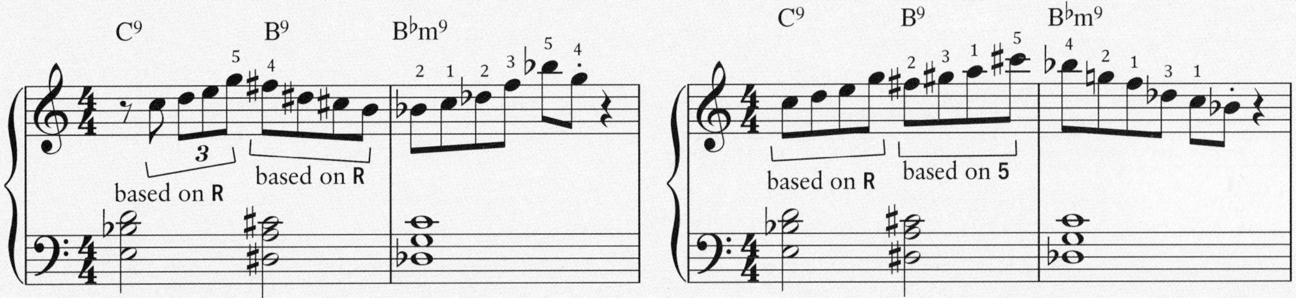

Fig 10.77: Bars 8–9, sample improvisations using R235 patterns

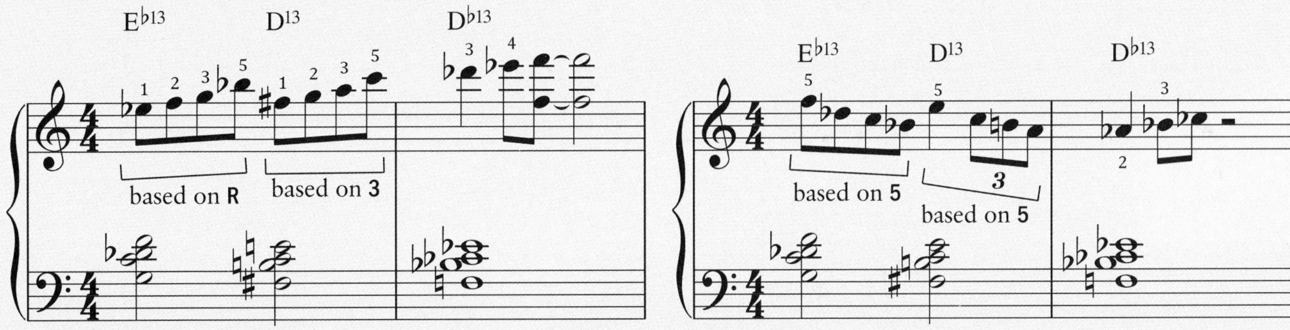

R235 patterns can of course be used over the other chords as well, in the manner described on p. 250.

❻ ♭**3 pentatonics** Practise these as shown, transposing the patterns given on pp. 268–9 to fit each chord. Improvise round two- or four-bar chunks of the sequence over and over, working out on the various pentatonics until the correct notes fall under your fingers without too much thought. Visualising four-note groups and hand positions for each chord will help. Here's an example over the last four bars:

Fig 10.78: Bars 9–12, sample improvisation using ♭3 pentatonics

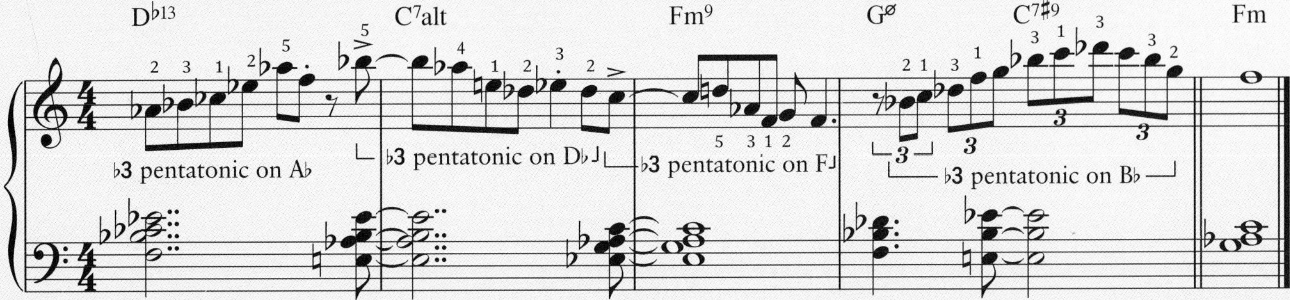

❼ **Consolidate** Playing nothing but ♭3 pentatonics all the time would lead to a very stilted solo! Once you've assimilated them into your style, use them alongside other techniques such as ordinary scale patterns (eg: Dorian), F blues scale, F harmonic minor scale, diminished and altered scales, **II – V** licks, **R235** patterns, quartal lines, etc. Practise all these over the backing track with chords in the left hand.

Chapter Ten – Final Checkpoint

● **Minor II – V – I** In this chapter we've explored several ways of improvising over these chords, so many that you're unlikely to assimilate them all at once into your playing. Concentrate on one or two approaches that appeal to you, applying them to different tunes and situations, and make sure you are familiar with them in different keys.

Later you can go back and explore some of the other techniques, expanding your vocabulary as necessary to give you a wider range of options in your solos. Like any creative artist, the jazz pianist is always searching for new possibilities.

● **Ambiguous chords** As you've progressed through this book, you've seen that many of the three- and four-note voicings used in modern jazz can have several different roots (see p. 258). Although this concept is easy enough to understand, finding the various shapes when confronted with a chord symbol takes practice. To help you visualise and identify these shapes, here's a 'Chord Quiz'.

Chord Quiz

All these chords have multiple identities – to find out what they are, play them in the right hand with a selection of bass notes in the left hand. Three solutions are given for the first chord; some of the others may have even more. Answers on p. 285.

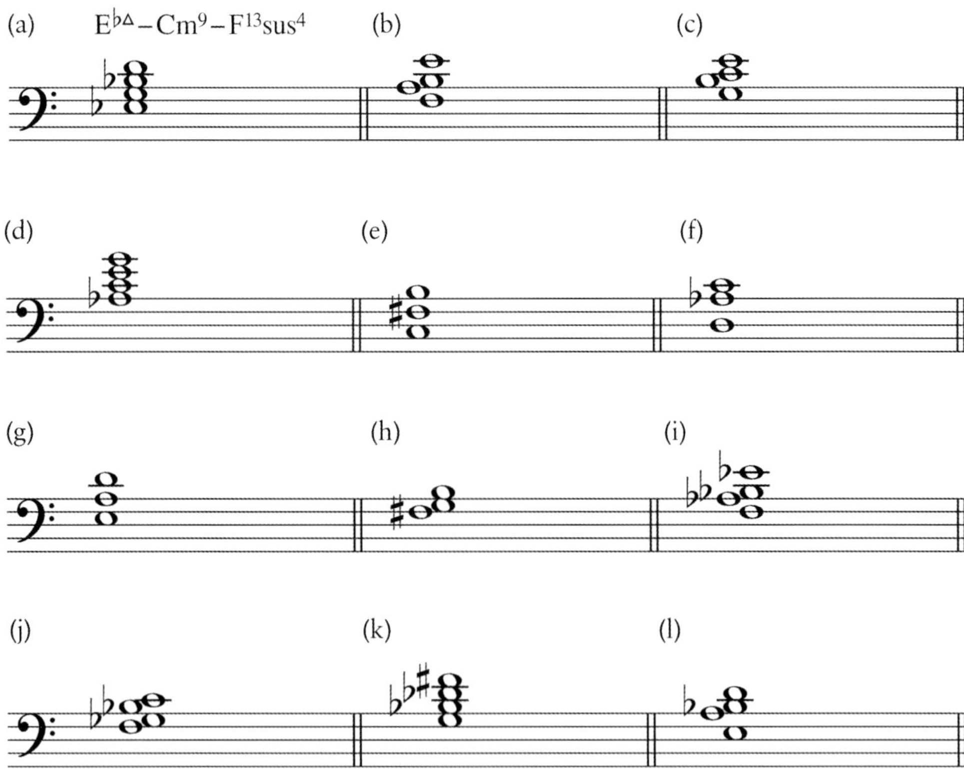

Final Assignments: Minor II – V – I cycle

● **Practice routine** Many musicians practise the minor **II** – **V** – **I** round the cycle of fifths, just as we did in major keys:

‖: F♯ø	B7alt	Em	⁒ :‖	‖: Eø	A7alt	Dm	⁒ :‖
‖: Dø	G7alt	Cm	⁒ :‖	‖: Cø	F7alt	B♭m	⁒ :‖
‖: B♭ø	E♭7alt	A♭m	⁒ :‖	‖: A♭ø	D♭7alt	G♭m	⁒ :‖

You can play the dominant chords as flat nine instead of altered chords. The minor chords can be m7, m9, m6, m6/9, mΔ7, or mΔ9. Cycles like this can be used to practise most of the concepts in this chapter:

Left hand	**Right hand**
bass line	chords (three or four notes)
shells	arpeggios and broken chords
tritones	horizontal improvisation (in the key)
three-note voicings	pentatonic scales
four-note voicings	scales or patterns (vertical)

All the topics in this list are interchangeable between the hands. Stay in each key for as long as it takes to master your chosen task, spending longer in the harder keys to sort out any note or fingering problems. Eventually you should be able to play through all six keys, keeping time without a break. You can then turn your attention to the other cycle, starting on Bø to cover the remaining six keys.

● **Two-handed voicings** Don't forget to practise these round the cycle too, using the following configurations:

- Two notes in each hand (Fig 10.60)
- Shells in left hand, three notes in right (Fig 10.62)
- Three notes in each hand (Fig 10.79 below)

Strive to keep the chords in the centre of the piano to avoid them sounding too high (thin) or too low (muddy). Make sure you learn both versions of each configuration, so that you can switch to the other one when the chords get too low.

The third configuration was played in bars 2–3 of the second chorus of *Blues in Fourths* (p. 266). Here it is, transposed to E minor for the start of the cycle:

Fig 10.79: Quartal voicings (perfect fourths in right hand)

(a)

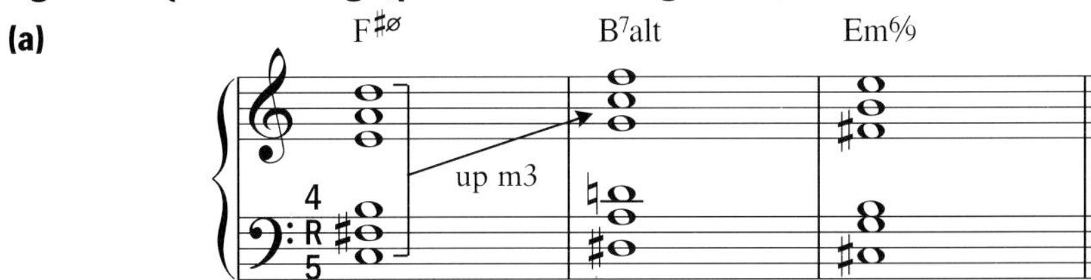

By the time you reach C minor, you'll need to switch to the opposite voicing:

(b)

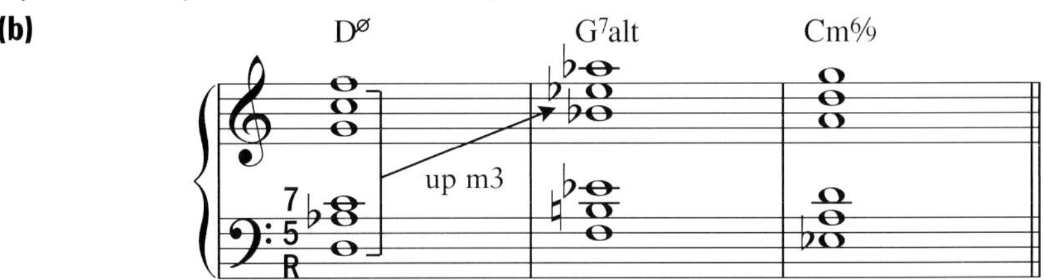

To help find the correct notes for the half-diminished voicings in Fig 10.79, check that they resemble dominant thirteenth chords a major third down (see p. 255), eg:

F#ø = D13 Dø = B♭13

Coda

We've covered a lot of ground since we started on major triads in Vol. 1. You'll probably need a period of consolidation, revisiting some of the earlier pieces with the hindsight of your new knowledge and ability. Apply the left- and right-hand techniques and improvisation suggestions in the later chapters to everything that comes before, in both volumes.

In truth, the jazz pianist's journey is never complete – however much you know, there'll always be new tunes to learn, topics to explore or a fresh slant to throw on old ideas. Should you wish to continue beyond this volume, some options for further study are suggested below.

Part of the joy of jazz piano, and indeed all music, is that it's a wide enough field to keep you busy for several lifetimes! The day you wake up realising there's nothing more to learn will be a sad day indeed...

No book by itself can turn you into a jazz pianist – you'll learn more quickly if you can get some playing experience with other musicians. Listening to jazz is also an essential source of inspiration, both live and on record. One of the questions I sometimes ask students is 'Who is your favourite jazz pianist?' or 'Who have you been listening to?' Too often a typical answer is: 'Well, no one in particular ... I don't have many jazz records actually ... '

In Appendix I, Vol. 1 (p. 228), I listed some of the great jazz pianists and their best recordings. Don't confine your listening to pianists, however – front-line instruments such as saxophone and trumpet (collectively known as 'horns') have been incredibly influential in the history of jazz, with great innovators like Louis Armstrong, Charlie Parker, John Coltrane and Miles Davis irrevocably changing the course of the music.

Appendix V (p. 278 in this volume) focuses briefly on some of the most important names, other than pianists. As with learning a language, immersing yourself in the sound of jazz is a vital part of the process of becoming a jazz musician.

Further study

Advanced subjects such as modal interchange, reharmonisation and 'Coltrane' changes are the pre-occupation of many contemporary jazz musicians. In order to further your development, I recommend the following books:

- *Jazz Piano from Scratch* Charles Beale (ABRSM, London): A useful starter and guide to the Associated Board's jazz piano exam syllabus, Grades 1–5.
- *Practical Jazz* Lionel Grigson (Stainer & Bell, London): An excellent and concise introduction for all instruments.
- *Jazz Keyboard Harmony* Phil DeGreg (Jamey Aebersold Publications, USA): Like many jazz piano books, this focuses on the harmonic aspect of the craft, rather than on improvisation. Includes a play-along CD.
- *Jazz Piano Voicing Skills* Dan Haerle (Jamey Aebersold Publications, USA): A very methodical approach using the cycle of fifths to help learn voicings in all keys. Suitable for individual or class study.
- *The Jazz Piano Book* Mark Levine (Chuck Sher Publications, USA): The bible for many professional pianists and jazz students, a lovingly compiled collection of advanced techniques, with copious examples from the standards repertoire, and references to recorded solos by many bebop, hard bop and contemporary masters.

● *Stride and Swing Piano* John Valerio (Hal Leonard, USA): A good tutor for those interested in older styles, such as Jelly Roll Morton, Fats Waller, Teddy Wilson and Art Tatum. Includes a CD.
● *How to Play Bebop* David Baker (Alfred Publishing Co, USA): Vol. 1 covers the bebop scale in depth, plus a section on whole-tone and diminished patterns.
● *Coltrane – A Players Guide to his Harmony* Weiskopf & Ricker (Jamey Aebersold Publications, USA): A good grounding in some of the postbop techniques that are beyond the scope of this book. Useful tips for pianists, such as the voicings for Coltrane's ground-breaking composition *Giant Steps.*
● *The Harmony of Bill Evans* Jack Reilly (Unichrom/Hal Leonard, USA): Rigorous analysis of several Bill Evans compositions, and his reharmonisations of the standards *I Should Care* and *How Deep is the Ocean.*
● *Handbook of Chord Substitutions* Andy Laverne (Warner Bros, USA): A useful collection of 30 arrangements demonstrating reharmonisation principles for many well-known standards, by a pianist who studied with Bill Evans.
● *The Best Chord Changes for the World's Greatest Standards* Frank Mantooth (Hal Leonard, USA).
● *Professional Chord Changes and Substitutions for100 Tunes Every Musician Should Know* Dick Hyman (Ekay Publishing, USA).
● *The Standards Real Book* (Sher Music Co, USA): Along with their 3-volume *New Real Book* series, the best and most accurate legal fake books published.
● *Play-Along Series* (Jamey Aebersold Publications, USA): An encyclopedic series of over 100 play-along CDs accompanied by books with parts in C, B♭, E♭ and bass clef. Vols. 24, 1, 3 and 16 (in order of difficulty) are useful for practical theory; most other volumes are collections of tunes themed by composer. Rhythm sections vary, often with famous names, eg: Kenny Barron is pianist on Vols. 6 (Charlie Parker), 11 (Herbie Hancock), 12 (Duke Ellington), 17 (Horace Silver) and 33 (Wayne Shorter). Other volumes feature great players such as Dave Brubeck, Hal Galper, Cedar Walton, Mulgrew Miller, Mark Levine, Dan Haerle, Richie Bierach, Andy Laverne, George Cables, etc. Vol. 54 (*Maiden Voyage*) contains a selection of easy tunes at medium tempos, including *Autumn Leaves*, *Impressions*, *Summertime*, *Song for my Father*, *Footprints*, *Watermelon Man* and *Blues in F.*

Most of these should be available worldwide through mail-order outlets such as **www.jazzwise.com** or **www.jazzbooks.com**

Appendix V: Suggested listening – other instruments

I've dealt exhaustively with the piano in Appendix I (Vol. 1). Don't confine your listening to pianists, however – some of the best piano playing can be heard in small group sessions led by horn players.

The following are some of the most important names (arranged in approximately chronological order) and their best albums. Once again, there isn't room for everybody, so please don't get upset if I've left out any of your own personal favourites!

You probably won't find a representative selection of jazz albums in your local high street record store. Try the jazz sections of the large chains or even better, the specialist shops such as:
Ray's Jazz Shop, Foyles: 113-119 Charing Cross Road, London WC2H 0EB. Tel: 020 7440 3205
or the following mail order specialist:
Crazy Jazz: 1 Hearn Road, Romford RM1 2DP, United Kingdom. Tel: 08707 469 210.
www.crazyjazz.co.uk

Alto saxophone

Johnny Hodges *Jeep's Blues*, see also Ellington *Back to Back, Far East Suite*
Benny Carter *The Complete Recordings 1930–40, The King, Jazz Giant*
Charlie Parker *Bird Symbols, Jazz at Massey Hall, On Savoy, Complete Dial Sessions*
Lee Konitz *Subconscious-Lee, Live at the Half-Note, Motion*
Art Pepper *Gettin' Together, Art Pepper meets the Rhythm Section, Intensity*
Cannonball Adderley *Mercy Mercy Mercy, At the Lighthouse, Somethin' Else*, see also Miles Davis *Milestones, Kind of Blue*
Jackie McLean *Bluesnik, New Soil, Let Freedom Ring, The Jackie Mac Attack Live, Dynasty*
Paul Desmond *Paul Desmond Quartet Live*, see also Dave Brubeck *Time Out, Time Further Out*
Ornette Coleman *The Shape of Jazz to Come, Ornette!, Free Jazz*, see also Pat Metheny *Song X*
Eric Dolphy *Out to Lunch*, see also Oliver Nelson *Blues & the Abstract Truth*, Charles Mingus *Mingus at Antibes, Mingus Presents Mingus*
David Sanborn *Upfront, Inside*, see also Gil Evans *Princess*
Kenny Garrett *Introducing Kenny Garrett, Standard of Language, Black Hope, Songbook*, see also Miles Davis *Amandla*, Mulgrew Miller *Hand in Hand*, Woody Shaw *Solid*
Steve Coleman *The Tao of Mad Phat*, see also Dave Holland *Extensions*

Tenor saxophone

Lester Young *The President Plays, With the Oscar Peterson Trio*, see also Count Basie *1938–39*
Coleman Hawkins *Body and Soul, Coleman Hawkins and Bud Powell in Germany*, see also Thelonious Monk *With John Coltrane*
Ben Webster *Soulville, The Soul of Ben Webster, Meets Oscar Peterson*, see also Duke Ellington *Masterpieces 1926–49, The Indispensable Vols. 5–6 (1940)*
Sonny Rollins *Saxophone Colossus, Tenor Madness, Sonny Side Up, Newks' Time, The Bridge*
Dexter Gordon *Go!, Our Man in Paris*, see also Herbie Hancock *Takin' Off*
Stan Getz *Getz & Gilberto, Sweet Rain, The Dolphin*
Hank Mobley *Soul Station*, see also Miles Davis *Someday my Prince Will Come*, Horace Silver *And The Jazz Messengers*
John Coltrane *Traneing In, Giant Steps, Plays the Blues, A Love Supreme, Live at the Village Vanguard, Coltrane's Sound, Africa Brass*
Joe Henderson *Inner Urge, So Near So Far*, see also McCoy Tyner *The Real McCoy*, Horace Silver *Song for my Father*, Lee Morgan *The Sidewinder*
Roland Kirk *Rip Rig and Panic, The Inflated Tear, Volunteered Slavery, Bright Moments*
Pharoah Sanders *Karma, Journey to the One, Africa*, see also John Coltrane *Ascension, Meditations*
Stanley Turrentine *Gene Harris Trio Plus One*
Wayne Shorter *Night Dreamer, Juju, Speak No Evil*, see also any Miles Davis 1963–68, any Weather Report
Bob Berg *Short Stories, Another Standard*, see also Cedar Walton *Eastern Rebellion II, First Set*, Miles Davis *You're Under Arrest*
Mike Brecker *Michael Brecker, Don't Try This at Home, Now You See It*, see also John Abercrombie *Getting There*
Jan Garbarek see Kenny Wheeler *Deer Wan*, Keith Jarrett *Belonging, My Song*
Joshua Redman *Wish, Mood Swing*
Branford Marsalis *Crazy People Music, Bloomington, The Dark Keys*
Joe Lovano *From the Soul, Live At the Village Vanguard*, see also John Scofield *What We Do, Time on my Hands*

Baritone saxophone

Harry Carney any Duke Ellington orchestra 1927–73, eg: *At Newport, Far East Suite*
Serge Chaloff *Blue Serge*, see also Woody Herman *Keeper of the Flame*
Gerry Mulligan *The Original Quartet, Meets Ben Webster*, see also Miles Davis *Birth of The Cool*
Pepper Adams *Encounter!, Conjuration*, see also Thad Jones *Mean What You Say*
John Surman *Morning Glory, The Brass Project, Stranger Than Fiction*, see also John Taylor *Ambleside Days*

Trumpet

Bix Beiderbecke *Bix Beiderbecke and the Wolverines, Bix Lives*
Louis Armstrong *The Hot Fives & Sevens (1925–30), Louis Armstrong & Duke Ellington*
Roy Eldridge *Little Jazz: The Best of the Verve Years, Roy and Diz*, see also Gene Krupa *Drummer Man*
Dizzy Gillespie *Groovin' High, Sonny Side Up*, see also Charlie Parker *Jazz at Massey Hall, On Savoy*
Clifford Brown *Clifford Brown & Max Roach*, see also Art Blakey *A Night at Birdland*
Miles Davis *Milestones, Cookin'/Relaxin', Kind of Blue, My Funny Valentine/Four and More, ESP, In a Silent Way, Bitches Brew, Tutu, Jack Johnson*
Freddie Hubbard *Hub Tones, Backlash*, see also Herbie Hancock *Takin' Off*, Art Blakey *Caravan*
Lee Morgan *The Sidewinder, Cornbread, Delightful-Lee*, see also John Coltrane *Blue Train*
Woody Shaw *The Moontrane, Solid*, see also Horace Silver *The Jody Grind, Cape Verdean Blues*
Wynton Marsalis *Think of One, J Mood, Live at Blues Alley, Black Codes, Standard Time*
Tom Harrell *Moon Alley, Visions, Passages, Labyrinth*
Roy Hargrove *Diamond in the Rough, With the Tenors of our Time*
Kenny Wheeler *Deer Wan, Double Double You, Music for Large and Small Ensembles, Flutter By Butterfly*
Dave Douglas *Magic Triangle*

Trombone

Jack Teagarden *I Gotta a Right to Sing the Blues, The Indispensable, That's a Serious Thing*
Tommy Dorsey *The Complete Tommy Dorsey and his Orchestra 1928–35, Well Git It!*
JJ Johnson *The Eminent Jay Jay Johnson Vol. 1, Trombone Master, J.J. Inc*
Slide Hampton *Roots, Dedicated to Diz*
Curtis Fuller *Blues-ette, With Red Garland*, see also John Coltrane *Blue Train*
Steve Turré *Right There, Steve Turré, Lotus Flower*, see also Woody Shaw *The Moontrane*

Clarinet

Johnny Dodds *Wild Man Blues*, see also Louis Armstrong *Hot Fives and Sevens Vol. 1*
Sidney Bechet *Really the Blues, King Jazz Vol. 1 (soprano saxophone)*
Barney Bigard see any Duke Ellington1927–42, Louis Armstrong *Plays WC Handy*
Benny Goodman *After You've Gone, Avalon, Carnegie Hall Concert (1938)*
Artie Shaw *Beguine the Beguine, Blues in the Night*
Buddy de Franco *You Must Believe in Swing*
Jimmy Giuffre *The Jimmy Giuffre 3, 1961*
Tony Scott *A Day in New York, Sung Heroes*
Eddie Daniels *Benny Rides Again*
Tony Coe *Some Other Autumn, Tournée du Chat, Nutty on Willisau, Ruby*

Guitar

Django Reinhardt *Swing from Paris*
Charlie Christian *Solo Flight, Genius of the Electric Guitar*
Barney Kessel *The Pollwinners, Red Hot and Blues*, see also Hampton Hawes *Four*
Wes Montgomery *The Incredible Jazz Guitar, Smokin' at the Half Note, Full House*, see also Jimmy Smith *The Dynamic Duo*
Kenny Burrell *Bluesy Burrell, Midnight Blue*, see also Jimmy Smith *Home Cookin', The Master*
Grant Green *Idle Moments, Matador, Complete Quartets with Sonny Clark, Street of Dreams*
Pat Martino *Strings!, El Hombre*
Jim Hall *Dialogues, Panorama*, see also Bill Evans *Undercurrent, Interplay*, Sonny Rollins *The Bridge*, Hampton Hawes *All Night Session*
John McLaughlin *Extrapolation, Inner Mounting Flame, After the Rain*, see also Miles Davis *Bitches Brew*
Pat Metheny *Bright Size Life, Pat Metheny Group, 80-81, Song X*, see also Gary Burton *Passengers*

Mike Stern see Mike Brecker *Don't Try This at Home,* Miles Davis *We Want Miles*
John Abercrombie *Timeless, November,* see also Kenny Wheeler *Music for Large and Small Ensembles*
John Scofield *Hand Jive, A Go Go, What We Do, Time on my Hands,* see also Miles Davis *You're Under Arrest*
Sonny Sharrock *Guitar,* see also Herbie Mann *Memphis Underground,* Wayne Shorter *Supernova*

Bass

Jimmy Blanton see Duke Ellington *The Blanton Era, The IndispensableVols. 5–6 (1940)*
Oscar Pettiford *Memorial Album,* see also Sonny Rollins *Freedom Jazz Suite,* Thelonious Monk *Plays Duke Ellington, Brilliant Corners*
Ray Brown *Bassface, Live at Sculler's,* see also Oscar Peterson *Night Train, We Get Requests,* Gene Harris *Trio Plus One,* Sonny Rollins *Way Out West*
Charles Mingus *Oh Yeah!, Mingus Ah Um, Mingus Mingus Mingus, Mingus Presents Mingus,* see also Duke Ellington *Money Jungle*
Paul Chambers *Bass on Top, Whims of Chambers* see also John Coltrane *Giant Steps, Blue Train,* Miles Davis *Milestones, Kind of Blue,* Art Pepper *Meets the Rhythm Section*
Scott LaFaro see Bill Evans *Portrait in Jazz, At the Village Vanguard,* Hampton Hawes *Four,* Victor Feldman *Arrival,* Ornette Coleman *Free Jazz*
Charlie Haden *Quartet West,* see also Ornette Coleman *The Shape of Jazz to Come,* Keith Jarrett *Expectations, Survivor's Suite,* Hampton Hawes *As Long as There's Music*
Ron Carter see Herbie Hancock *Maiden Voyage,* Miles Davis *My Funny Valentine/Four and More, Live at the Plugged Nickel, Miles Smiles,* Wayne Shorter *Speak No Evil,* McCoy Tyner *The Real McCoy*
Dave Holland *Extensions,* see also Joe Henderson *So Near So Far,* Miles Davis *In a Silent Way, Bitches Brew,* Kenny Wheeler *Deer Wan, Double Double You*
Jaco Pastorius (elec.) *Jaco Pastorius, Word of Mouth,* see also Weather Report *Black Market, Heavy Weather, 8.30,* Pat Metheny *Bright Size Life*
Marcus Miller (elec.) see David Sanborn *Upfront, Inside,* Miles Davis *Tutu, We Want Miles*
Christian McBride *Gettin' To It, Number Two Express,* see also Benny Green *Testifyin',* Brad Meldhau *Introducing Brad Mehldau*
Robert Hurst *One for Namesake, Presents Robert Hurst,* see also Wynton Marsalis *Standard Time, Live at Blues Alley*

Drums

Sid Catlett *1944–46,* see also Benny Goodman *Roll 'Em*
Gene Krupa *Drummer Man,* see also Benny Goodman *Solo Flight, At The Carnegie Hall*
Jo Jones *Jo Jones Trio,* see also Count Basie *1933–39*
Kenny Clarke see Dexter Gordon *Our Man in Paris,* Kenny Burrell *Introducing Kenny Burrell*
Buddy Rich *Illusion, Swinging' New Big Band*
Max Roach *Jazz in 3/4 Time, Clifford Brown & Max Roach,* see also Duke Ellington *Money Jungle,* Bud Powell *The Amazing Bud Powell*
Roy Haynes see Chick Corea *Now He Sings Now He Sobs,* Thelonious Monk *Live at the Five Spot*
Philly Joe Jones see Bill Evans *Everybody Digs Bill Evans,* John Coltrane *Blue Train,* Miles Davis *Milestones*
Art Blakey *Jazz Messengers at Birdland, Caravan, Moanin',* see also Horace Silver *Trio,* Thelonious Monk *Genius of Modern Music,* Cannonball Adderley *Somethin' Else*
Billy Higgins see Herbie Hancock *Takin' Off,* Cedar Walton *Eastern Rebellion,* Dexter Gordon *Go!,* Hank Mobley *Turnaround, Dippin'*
Elvin Jones *Dear John C,* see also any Coltrane album *1960–65,* McCoy Tyner *The Real McCoy*
Tony Williams see Jackie McLean *Vertigo,* Eric Dolphy *Out to Lunch,* Herbie Hancock *Maiden Voyage,* Miles Davis *My Funny Valentine/Four And More, Miles Smiles, In a Silent Way*
Paul Motian *Misterioso,* see also Bill Evans *Portrait in Jazz, At the Village Vanguard,* Keith Jarrett *Expectations, The Survivor's Suite, Bop-Be*
Jack DeJohnette see Miles Davis *Bitches Brew,* Keith Jarrett *Standards,* Kenny Wheeler *Deer Wan*
Peter Erskine *Sweet Soul, You Never Know,* see also John Taylor *Time Being, As It Is,* Weather Report *8.30*
Steve Gadd see Chick Corea *Three Quartets,* Steps Ahead *Smokin' In The Pit*
Jeff Watts *Megawatts,* see also Branford Marsalis *Crazy People Music, Dark Keys, Bloomington,* Wynton Marsalis *Live at Blues Alley*
Brian Blade see Brad Mehldau *Introducing Brad Mehldau,* Kenny Garrett *Triology, Black Hope*

Organ

Jimmy Smith *Groovin' At Small's Paradise, Back at The Chicken Shack, The Cat, The Master*
Jimmy McGriff *Pulling Out the Stops*
Jack McDuff *Live!,* see also Roland Kirk *Kirk's Work*
Larry Young *Unity,* see also Grant Green *Street of Dreams*
Joey de Francesco *Live at the Five Spot, Goodfellas,* John McLaughlin *After the Rain*
Larry Goldings *Whatever it Takes, Moonbird, Sweet Science*

Vibes

Lionel Hampton *The Complete Quartets and Quintets with Oscar Peterson,* see also Benny Goodman *After You've Gone, Avalon*
Milt Jackson *The Milt Jackson Quartet, Opus De Jazz, Soul Brothers (with Ray Charles),* see also Benny Carter *The King,* any Modern Jazz Quartet
Gary Burton *Hotel Hello, Gary Burton & Keith Jarrett, Crystal Silence (with Chick Corea), Like Minds*
Bobby Hutcherson *Happenings, Total Eclipse, Stick-Ups!,* see also McCoy Tyner *Sama Layuca,* Grant Green *Idle Moments,* Eric Dolphy *Out to Lunch*
Steve Nelson *Communications,* see also Mulgrew Miller *Hand in Hand,* George Shearing *That Shearing Sound,* Dave Holland *Points of View.*

Appendix VI: Chord voicings chart

* Although most of the voicings in the third column are rootless, the root has been included in some of the major ♯11 and half-diminished shapes.

* Although most of the voicings in the third column are rootless, the root has been included in the sus4♭9 shapes.

Appendix VII: Practice routines

It is a common misconception that jazz musicians do not need to practise, they just 'make it up as they go along'. In fact, most good improvisers put in hours of work honing their techniques, brushing up their aural and rhythmic skills, and making sure they can play their ideas in all keys.

Many people who claim to practise several hours a day are in fact mostly playing what they already know. Practising involves learning something new or developing your technique, both of which require concentration. It's advisable to make a clear distinction between practising and playing for your enjoyment, perhaps allocating a certain amount of time daily for each.

The following suggestions for structuring your practice can be expanded to suit the amount of time you have available. Generally it's best to practise little and often, so half an hour every day is better than three hours once a week. Here are two possible formats:

- **One hour a day** Select what you consider to be the three most important units from the seven listed below, and spend 20 minutes on each of them.
- **Half an hour a day** Spend your allotted time on one unit only, moving to another unit for your next practice session. This format rotates the topics from day to day.

Use the cycle of fifths to practise everything. Several cycles are possible:

- **Diatonic cycle**: Stays in one key (Vol. 1, p. 144 and Figs 4.23, 4.30).
- **Cycles that use only one chord-type**:

Major triads (Vol. 1, pp. 22–24 and 32).
Minor triads (Vol. 1, Fig 2.8 and p. 78).
Open triads (Vol. 1, Fig 2.45 and p. 84).
Major sevenths (Vol. 1, p. 96).
Dominant sevenths (Vol. 1, pp. 117–118; Vol. 2, pp. 94–99 and Fig 8.79).

- **II – V cycle**: Minor to dominant (Vol. 1, p. 172 and Fig 5.29; Vol. 2, p. 120.
- **Major II – V – I cycle**: Resolves to a major **I** chord (Vol. 1, pp. 162–164 and Fig 5.28; Vol. 2, pp. 76–7).
- **Minor II – V – I cycle**: Resolves to a minor **I** chord; **II** chord is half-diminished (Vol. 2, p. 275).

The play-along tracks in this book enable you to practise with rhythm section backing in your own home. There's also a useful multi-volume series of play-along CDs marketed by US jazz educator Jamey Aebersold – Vols. 1, 3 and 16 contain some good cycle tracks.

Each of the following units can last as long as you want it to:

Unit 1: Chord voicings

Choose a cycle and play some of the following options round all chords:

- **Left-hand shells** Alternate **R7** and **R3** round the cycle, then vice versa.
- **Two-handed voicings** Add the missing right-hand notes to make **R7/35** or **R3/79** (p. 76, Figs 7.23–24).
- **Five-note voicings** Add an extra right-hand note to make **R7/359** or **R3/795** (p. 76, Figs 7.25–26).

NB: In dominant sevenths, **6** replaces **5**. In 6/9 chords, **6** replaces **7**. Apply these rules to the voicings below too.

- **Three-note rootless voicings** Play in right hand first – **379** or **735** (p. 84, Figs 7.34 and 7.36). Add a left-hand bass line when ready. Then learn the voicings in the left hand.
- **Four-note rootless voicings** Play in right hand first – **3579** or **7935** (p. 84, Figs 7.35 and 7.37). Add a left-hand bass line when ready. Then learn the voicings in the left hand.
- **Two-handed rootless voicings** Play two notes in each hand – **37/95** or **73/59** (p. 182, Fig 9.16).
- **Altered dominants** In a **II** – **V** – **I** cycle repeat the above with altered **V** chords (pp. 160, 182, 187 and 211).
- **Other voicings** Polychords (Figs 8.74 and 8.79), block chords (Figs 5.56–5.58 and 10.28–10.34), quartal voicings (Figs 6.79 and 10.15), 'drop two' voicings (Figs 5.60 and 10.16) and stride piano (Figs 7.79–7.84) can all be systematically practised round the cycle.

All voicings should be played in time, with a foot-tap, in a variety of rhythms, feels and tempos. Try 'on-off', 'off-on' and other comping rhythms, as shown in Figs 7.30–7.33.

Unit 2: Scales and arpeggios

The standard classical way of practising scales and arpeggios hands together is great for developing technique and co-ordination. Playing them like this will also help you improvise lines with both hands in unison, a speciality of pianists such as Phineas Newborn Jr, Oscar Peterson, Chick Corea, Benny Green, and others. See the 'Daily practice routine' given on p. 119.

An equally important skill for the jazz pianist is to play scales in the right hand, while the left hand keeps time with chords or bass lines. This not only develops your time feel (the left hand must keep track of the first beat of the bar), but also teaches you chord/scale relationships (Vol. 1, p. 134).

Playing scales and arpeggios to a beat and over a chord is fun, and is only one step away from improvisation. Here are some possible routines:

- **Choose a chord-type** Play it in the left hand in root position around the centre of the piano. Play the scale that fits the chord in the right hand, up and down one or two octaves, as in Vol. 1, Figs 3.72 or 3.65.
- **Play round the cycle** Repeat the chord and scale up a fourth (or down a fifth) in both hands, gradually moving round the cycle until you have played in all twelve keys. Using inversions or rootless voicings in the left hand will keep the chords from going too high. See *Dominant Bebop Scale Workout*, p. 99.
- **Repeat with a different chord-type** You may wish to leave this until your next practice session. At first, spend as much time in each key as you wish, until you're secure with the notes and fingering. Eventually you should be able to change from one chord/scale to the next without losing the beat.
- **Arpeggios, broken chords and pentatonic scales** Play these in the right hand, keeping time with left-hand chords as above.
- **II** – **V** – **I** Play scales, arpeggios or pentatonics over the chords of this cycle, changing to fit each chord type where necessary (the same scale fits all three chords, but see Vol. 1, Figs 4.40–4.42).

Working on scales, arpeggios and patterns is very like learning a language – they are the grammar and vocabulary with which we express our ideas.

Unit 3: Licks and patterns

This is the logical extension to Unit 2 and should not be attempted until the basic scales, arpeggios and pentatonics are well known.

- **Choose a pattern** Start with three- or four-note groups or thirds (Vol. 1, p. 98). Apply the pattern to a scale or mode and play it up and down over the relevant left-hand chord. Consider playing a rootless left-hand voicing for a more jazzy effect.
- **Move round the cycle** Play the same pattern and chord up a fourth (or down a fifth) in both hands, continuing this process until you have played it in all twelve keys.
- **Pentatonic patterns** Apply the same pattern to a suitable pentatonic scale for the chord your left hand is playing, practising it up and down and exploring the variations suggested in Vol. 1, pp. 182–183. Move this chord/pattern round the cycle as above, keeping good time as much as possible.
- **II – V licks** Practise long and short **II** – **V** patterns (see Figs 7.15 and 7.73–7.75) round the cycle with left-hand accompaniment, starting with shells and moving on to rootless voicings or bass lines. If playing over a **II** – **V** – **I** cycle you could go back to ordinary scale patterns over the **I** chord.
- **Other techniques** Systematically practise right-hand ideas like ninth arpeggios, encircling notes, upper and lower neighbours, quartal lines, bebop scales, chord/scale licks, **R235** patterns, etc, over left-hand chords and cycles. Also practise these techniques over the chord sequences of tunes that you like.

Unit 4: Ear-training

Perhaps the most important thing of all...

- **Major intervals** Play a note and sing it. Select a note of the major scale above that note and sing it (without playing it first). Then check you are correct. Start with obvious notes like **3** and **5**, then move on to **2**, **4**, **6**, **7** and **8**.
- **Minor intervals** Repeat the previous exercise with ♭**2**, ♭**3**, ♭**5**, ♭**6** and ♭**7**.
- **Descending intervals** Repeat the above with notes below the starting note.
- **Sing triads** Choose a note and sing major or minor triads (**R**, **3**, **5**) starting on that note. When you're confident with this, try augmented and diminished triads too.
- **Sing four-note chords** Learn to sing **R**, **3**, **5**, **7** for all five chord types (see Fig 8.1), starting on any note. Also try sixth chords (major and minor) and m∆.
- **Sing major scales** Practise singing major scales starting on any note. Then try Mixolydian (♭**7**) and Dorian (♭**3** and ♭**7**) modes, eventually extending this to all the other modes as well (see Fig 4.51).
- **Other scales** Sing harmonic and melodic minors, pentatonic, whole-tone, diminished and altered scales, etc, starting on any note. Don't try these all at once, start with the easy ones and move on when you're confident. Always play the notes after singing to check if you were correct.
- **Interval, chord and scale recognition** All the above should be done in reverse if possible. Get your teacher or friend to play while you sing and identify.
- **Play along with records** Try to develop an instinctive sense for improvising along with records by ear (on piano), even if you don't know the tune or chords. Working out the key of the piece will help – then alternate short bursts of playing and listening. Experienced jazz musicians are skilled at doing both at the same time.
- **Play what you sing** Improvise phrases vocally and find the notes on the piano (copy the phrasing as well). At first, try singing lines that only use the five notes of a major, ♭3, or minor pentatonic scale. This also accustoms your ear to the sound of these scales. Eventually extend this method to ordinary scales and modes. Your aim is to be able to play what you sing, finding the correct notes straight away with no mistakes.

Unit 5: Transcribing

Keep a manuscript book specially for transcribing and use it to jot down phrases you hear on records. Also make a note of solos that grab your attention, so you can spend time transcribing them at your next practice session – otherwise it's easy to forget. Sight-reading and ear-training practice will both make transcribing easier. For guidance see p. 220.

Unit 6: Reading

- **Conventional music** There are many graded books available for developing the sight-reading skills necessary to read sheet music in bass and treble clefs. The ability to read both hands simultaneously can be improved with regular practice. The important thing is to keep going – choose a slow tempo the first time round and never go back to correct mistakes. Good sight-readers look one or two bars ahead all the time so that nothing catches them by surprise.
- **Fake books** Purchase a fake book (see Vol. 1, p. 170) as a source of jazz tunes for reading practice. Classical sight-reading skills do not prepare you for interpreting tunes from lead sheets. You'll need to develop an awareness of jazz phrasing and swing feel, and to cultivate rhythmic accuracy with anticipated and off-beat notes.

You'll also need to interpret the given chord symbols, creating a left-hand accompaniment as you see fit – this is the essence of the jazz pianist's skill and the result will be a reflection of your taste, knowledge and experience. Practise continuously over a variety of tunes, following the steps given in Unit 7.

Unit 7: Repertoire

Learning new tunes on a regular basis is important for any musician. As a pianist it is important to memorise the harmony as well as the melody of a tune. Here are some steps for learning and interpreting a tune from a fake book or lead sheet:

- **Play roots of chords only** Accompany the right-hand melody with single notes in the left hand, low down on the keyboard, playing one note in every bar, unless the chords change more often. As soon as possible, remove the music and memorise melody and root movement. To achieve this, work on 4- or 8-bar passages at a time.
- **Two-feel bass line** When a chord lasts a bar or more, play the fifth halfway through the bar, low down as before, alternating with **R**. If the chords change twice a bar, play roots only, playing half-notes throughout (see *Take the 'A' Train*, Vol. 1, p. 64).
- **Walking bass line** Repeat the melody with quarter-notes in the left hand following either the notes or the scale of the chord. For guidelines see Figs 2.24–2.27.
- **Thicken the melody** Over any of the above bass lines, add some right-hand chords together with the main melody notes, making sure these are at the top of the chords (see the bridge of *Caravan*, p. 145, and Fig 8.52). Alternatively, use some top harmony (see Figs 5.21, 5.23 and 8.53).
- **Shells in left hand** Going back to the single-note melody, accompany it with **R3** or **R7** in the left-hand, as in *Ornithology* (Vol. 1, p. 156).
- **Two-handed voicings** Retaining the same left-hand shells, add notes below the main melody notes in the right hand to fill out the chords, trying to ensure both **3** and **7** are present. See *Ladybird* and *Misty* for examples (pp. 78 and 106).
- **Rootless voicings** Work out some rootless left-hand voicings with which to accompany the single-note melody. This is the standard way to play when a bassist is present. Fill out the voicings if you wish with some extra right-hand notes, as in Fig 8.60.
- **Solo piano** In the absence of a bassist you may wish to work out a stride or pseudo-stride left-hand accompaniment as an alternative to the bass lines suggested earlier. Some guidelines are given in pp. 109–110.

This not an exhaustive list – feel free to create your own topics. Keep a record of your practice in a special notebook. Always play with a strong sense of pulse, tap your foot, and play with the metronome as often as possible (see p. 200).

Practising can free you from having to think of notes and fingering, enabling the brain to concentrate on the musical and expressive aspects of your playing. It's no good hearing the most fantastic ideas in your head if you lack the technique to play them!

Appendix VIII: Symbols used in this book

● **Notes of the scale** Throughout this book, bold numbers refer to the notes of the scale, from **R** (the root) to **7**. The major scale is used as reference point, eg: a harmonic minor scale is described as having ♭**3** and ♭**6**, the minor third and flattened sixth.

The basic formulae for the construction of triads and seventh chords are **R35** and **R357**. Notes above the seventh (**9**, **11** or **13**) are called extensions:

9	same as **2**	eg: D added to a C chord
11	same as **4**	eg: F added to a C chord
13	same as **6**	eg: A added to a C chord

NB: The use of **9**, **11** or **13** in a chord symbol implies the inclusion of a seventh in the chord as well – otherwise the added notes would appear as **2**, **4** or **6** instead. Remember also that **R**, ♭**3** or ♭**7** are never used as part of a chord symbol (see below).

● **Intervals** Here are the symbols for all the intervals up to the fifth note of the scale:

st	Semitone (half step). Same as a minor second	C to C♯
t	Tone (step). Same as a major second. One **t** = two **st**	C to D
m3	Minor third (one and a half tones)	C to E♭
M3	Major third (two tones)	C to E
P4	Perfect fourth (two and a half tones)	C to F
#4	Augmented fourth (three tones)	C to F♯
♭**5**	Diminished fifth (same as augmented fourth)	C to G♭
3t	Tritone (three tones)—same as ♯**4** or ♭**5**	as above
P5	Perfect fifth (three and a half tones)	C to G

Although I've used two kinds of 'm' above, to denote major and minor intervals, this is not recommended when writing chord symbols, as one's handwriting can so easily be misread.

● **Chord symbols** Unfortunately these have still not been completely standardised, with different writers and publishers using quite a wide range of symbols to mean the same thing (see Fig 8.1). However, the following basic rules are universally accepted:

m	Always indicates a minor third (♭**3**). Some people use a minus sign (**–**) instead.
7	By itself always indicates a flattened seventh (♭**7** – B♭ in a C chord).
	The major seventh (B in a C chord) is indicated by Δ, Δ7, maj7 or ♮7.

The three commonest chord-types are:

major	eg: CΔ, CΔ9, C6, C6/9, CΔ6/9, CΔ♯11
dominant	eg: C7, C9, Csus4, C13
minor	eg: Cm7, Cm9, Cm11, Cm6, Cm6/9, CmΔ7, CmΔ9

Any note in a dominant chord (apart from **R**, **3** and **7**) can be raised or lowered, giving chords such as C7♯5 (or C7+), C7♭5, C7♯11, C7♭13, C7♭9 and C7♯9. Combining raised or lowered fifths and ninths gives altered dominants, eg: C7♭9♭5 or C7♯9♯5, often conveniently described by the symbol C7alt. See Fig 8.1 for other commonly used chord symbols.

● **Inversions** In this book a chord's inversion status is often indicated by the following symbols:

Ⓡ	Root position	**R** on bottom
①	First inversion	**3** on bottom
②	Second inversion	**5** on bottom
③	Third inversion	**7** on bottom

● **Roman numerals** To avoid confusion with ordinary numbers (which refer to individual notes), chords are denoted by the numerals **I** to **VII**, according to their position in the key:

I	a chord based on the root of the scale – often called the **tonic**
II	a chord whose root is the second note of the scale or key
III	a chord whose root is the third note of the scale or key
IV	a chord whose root is the fourth note of the scale – the **sub-dominant**
V	a chord whose root is the fifth note of the scale – the **dominant**

Flats and sharps can appear in front of roman numerals, eg:

♯**V**	a G♯ chord in the key of C (same as ♭**VI**, an A♭ chord)
♭**VII**	a B♭ chord in the key of C

Qualifying indicators can be added to indicate the type of chord, eg:

VIx	Dominant – an A7 chord in the key of C
♯**IVm**	Minor – an F♯m7 chord in the key of C
IIIø	Half-diminished – an Em7b5 chord in the key of C
♭**II°**	Diminished – a D♭° chord in the key of C

Without these indicators the roman numerals are assumed to indicate the chord-type naturally occurring in the key: **I** and **IV** are Δ7, **II**, **III** and **VI** are m7, **V** is dominant and **VII** is half-diminished (ø).

Quiz Answers

(a) $E^{\flat\Delta}$ – Cm^{9} – $F^{13}sus^{4}$

(b) $F^{\Delta\sharp 11}$ – G^{13} – $D^{\flat 7}alt$ – $B^{ø}$ – $Dm^{6/9}$ – $E^{7}sus^{4\flat 9}$

(c) C^{Δ} – Am^{9} – $D^{13}sus^{4}$

(d) $A^{\flat\Delta\sharp 5}$ – $Fm^{\Delta 9}$ – $B^{\flat 13\sharp 11}$

(e) $C^{\Delta\sharp 11}$ – D^{13} – $A^{\flat 7\sharp 9}$ – $F^{\sharp ø}$ – $Am^{6/9}$ – C°

(f) $D^{ø}$ – $B^{\flat 9}$ – $E^{7\sharp 5}$ – $Fm^{6/9}$ – $A^{\flat\flat 5}$

(g) $E^{7}sus^{4}$ – Em^{11} – Bm^{11} – Am^{11} – $A^{7}sus^{4}$ – $C^{\Delta 6/9}$ – F^{Δ} – $B^{\flat\Delta\sharp 11}$

(h) Em^{9} – A^{13} – $C^{\Delta\sharp 11}$ – $C^{\sharp ø}$ – G^{Δ}

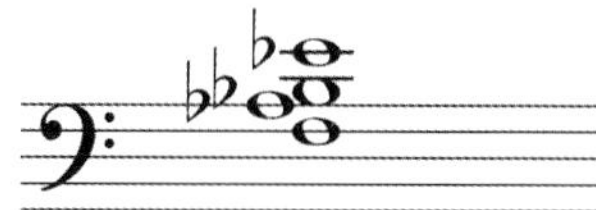

(i) Fm^{11} – $D^{\flat\Delta 6/9}$ – $B^{\flat 7}sus^{4}$ – $E^{\flat}sus^{4}$

(j) $G^{\flat\Delta\sharp 11}$ – $A^{\flat 13}$ – $D^{7}alt$ – $C^{ø}$ – $E^{\flat}m^{6/9}$ – $Fsus^{4\flat 9}$

(k) G° – $B^{\flat\circ}$ – $D^{\flat}$ – E°
$E^{\flat 7\sharp 9}$ – $G^{\flat\flat 9}$ – $A^{13\flat 9}$ – $C^{7\flat 9\sharp 11}$

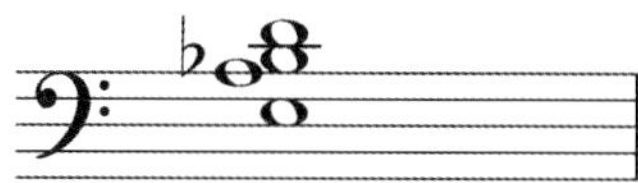

(l) $B^{\flat\Delta\sharp 11}$ – C^{13} – $G^{\flat 7}alt$ – $E^{ø}$ – $Gm^{6/9}$ – $Asus^{4\flat 9}$

NB:

- (a) and (c) are inversions of the same shape (in two different keys).
  That's why both have the same three solutions: Δ, m9, sus4
- (b), (j) and (l) are all inversions of the shape shown in Fig 10.51 (in various keys).
  Each one has the same six solutions: Δ♯11, 13, alt, ø, m6/9, sus4♭9

Index

All tunes are in italic type.
Page numbers may refer to music as well as text.
Page references in bold type indicate a photograph of the artist or the main appearance of the tune.

A

B

C

D

E

G

H

Herbie Hancock: Arguably the most influential jazz pianist of them all. A teenage prodigy, his first album as a leader was made when he was only 21 and included the bluesy *Watermelon Man*, an instant hit. He then took over Wynton Kelly's piano chair in Miles Davis' band (*c.*1963–68) where he was given the freedom to play long abstract solos and to show his admiration for the harmonies of modern classical music. Not content to have been part of the premier improvising group of the C20th, in the 1970s he went on to pioneer electric jazz and jazz funk with his band 'Headhunters'. He also ushered in the era of hiphop and drum 'n' bass with his 1983 hit single *Rockit* from the album 'Future Shock'. Not withstanding his commercial success, he still finds time to play modern jazz and to tour and record on acoustic piano.

S

T

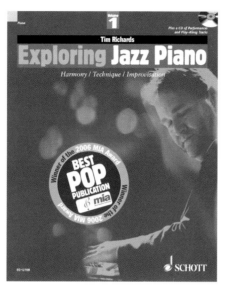

CD track listing: volume 2

This is not an ordinary audio CD. For educational purposes the piano has been panned to the right speaker on all tracks, apart from those marked piano only. The panned tracks can be used as play-along tracks by silencing the piano on the recording, using the balance knob on your amplifier. For more details, see p. 9.

Chapter 6: Elevenths, fourths and quartal harmony

1	**Reflections**	(with drums)
2	**Eleventh Hour**	(with bass & drums)
3	**Hot and Cold**	(piano only)
4	**Hot and Cold – Montuno**	(with drums)
5	**Impressions** *John Coltrane*	(with bass & drums)
6	**Quartal Comping**	(with bass & drums)
7	**First Impression**	(with bass & drums)
8	**Dustbiter**	(with bass & drums)

Chapter 7: Thirteenth chords

9	**The Message**	(with bass & drums)
10	**Thirteenth Groove**	(with bass & drums)
11	**Short II – V Workout**	(with bass & drums)
12	**II – V Comping**	(with bass & drums)
13	**Ladybird** *Tadd Dameron*	(with bass & drums)
14	**Swinging Comping #1**	(with drums)
15	**Swinging Comping #2**	(with drums)
16	**Dominant Seventh Workout #2**	(with drums)
17	**Bossa Nova Comping #2**	(piano only)
18	**Dominant Bebop Scale Workout**	(with bass & drums)
19	**Bebop Bridge**	(with bass & drums)
20	**Misty** *Erroll Garner*	(piano only)
21	**Turnaround Workout #1** (E♭)	(with drums)

Chapter 8: Diminished chords and scales

22	**Crossing the Tracks**	(piano only)
23	**Don't Stop the Carnival** *Traditional*	(with drums)
24	**Summertime** *George Gershwin*	(with drums)
25	**Dominant Seventh Flat Nine Workout**	(with bass & drums)
26	**Turnaround Workout #2** (C)	(with bass & drums)
27	**Caravan** *Duke Ellington & Juan Tizol*	(with drums)
28	**Diminished Scale Workout**	(with bass & drums)
29	**Tension & Release Blues #1** (F)	(with bass & drums)
30	**Bird Blues Comping**	(with bass & drums)
31	**Blues Turnaround Workout**	(with bass & drums)

Chapter 9: Altered chords and scales

32	**Blue In Green** *Bill Evans & Miles Davis*	(with bass & drums)
33	**Tension & Release Blues #2** (B♭)	(with bass & drums)
34	**Tune Up** *Miles Davis*	(with bass & drums)
35	**Rhythm Changes Comping #1**	(with bass & drums)
36	**Rhythm Changes Comping #2**	(with bass & drums)
37	**Seventh Heaven**	(with bass & drums)
38	**On Green Dolphin Street** *Bronislau Kaper*	(with bass & drums)

Chapter 10: Minor II – V – I

39	**Blue Bossa** *Kenny Dorham*	(piano only)
40	**Yesterdays** *Jerome Kern*	(with bass & drums)
41	**Softly as in a Morning Sunrise** *Sigmund Romberg*	(with bass & drums)
42	**Minor Turnaround Workout – Comping**	(piano only)
43	**Minor Turnaround Workout – Improvisation**	(with bass & drums)
44	**Beautiful Love** *Victor Young*	(with bass & drums)
45	**Blues in Fourths**	(with bass & drums)
46	**Twelve by Three**	(with bass & drums)

Tim Richards (piano), Dominic Howles (bass), Matt Home (drums). Recorded and mixed at Red Gables Studios, London (engineer: Dick Hammett), except tracks 1, 3 and 4, recorded at Premises Studios, London (engineer: Justin Underhill).